ALBERT BALLIN

BUSINESS AND POLITICS
IN IMPERIAL GERMANY,
1888-1918

Christening of the Hamburg-American Line's
Imperator (1912). At the foot of the stairs,
Ballin (left) and Kaiser Wilhelm II (right).

Albert Ballin

BUSINESS AND POLITICS

IN IMPERIAL GERMANY,

1888-1918

BY LAMAR CECIL

PRINCETON, NEW JERSEY

PRINCETON UNIVERSITY PRESS

1967

Publication of this book has been aided by the Whitney Darrow
Publication Reserve Fund of Princeton University Press and
the Department of History, Princeton University.

Printed in the United States of America by Princeton
University Press, Princeton, New Jersey

FOR

Mary Reed Cecil

Preface

The efforts of historians to reconstruct the German empire from its birth in 1871 to its extinction in 1918 have been burdened by a diplomatic development as well as an internal paradox, neither of which has been adequately investigated. The first concerns the unfortunate deterioration of relations between Germany and Great Britain, nations which were ethnically and culturally kindred and closely tied economically. This book offers new data on two important aspects of Anglo-German relations: the economic rivalry in international shipping between the two nations and their race in naval construction. The internal paradox is the fact that while the German empire was one of the most intensively industrialized nations in the world it retained a reactionary political and social order based on feudal, agricultural relationships. Why in Germany, unlike England, did liberalism fail to accompany industrialism? Here I have attempted to explore only one of many avenues of explanation by concentrating on the position taken by one member of the German *haute bourgeoisie* on the question of political reform.

In the first instance, the life of Albert Ballin, from 1899 to 1918 the managing director (*Generaldirektor*) of the Hamburg-American Line (HAPAG), then the world's greatest steamship company, is very revealing, for he was in many ways deeply involved in Germany's relations with England. On the question of political reform, Ballin's position is more difficult to determine since he made no systematic exposition of his views. The evidence available supports the argument advanced in this study that Ballin was opposed to reform because for many years he was reasonably satisfied with the way in which Germany was governed; because he preferred working within the existing political structure to altering it, fearing that reform might uncontrollably degenerate into socialism; and because he was convinced that there were unofficial means whereby he could influence the economic and political policies of the German government along lines which he favored.

The German upper middle class was, like Ballin, adverse to reform. There seems to be reason to suspect that the failure of this group of important men, especially those in commerce and banking, to endorse reform arose from the same considerations which motivated Ballin to reject it. I am, of course, not justified in attributing to the entire German *haute bourgeoisie* attitudes on this question that the material consulted for this biography allows me to apply only to Ballin. Hopefully, this study of Ballin may encourage more extensive probing of this segment of society under William II, so that eventually it will be possible for the arguments made here for one man to be advanced, or altered—or refuted—for the class to which he belonged. In that sense, I can claim for the investigation which follows only a preliminary significance. Very little scholarship has been devoted to the German plutocracy, and one reason doubtless is that very few personal papers of such men have survived the confiscations of the Nazi era or the war which concluded it. Obtaining access to those materials which do still exist is almost always arduous and frequently impossible. Studies recently written on both sides of the Atlantic have done much to illuminate the role of the military and parliamentary leadership of Germany prior to 1918, but the political and social structure of the aristocracy and of the upper middle class has remained virtually unexamined. Until we know very much more about the Kaiser and his court and the bureaucracy, about Emil and Walther Rathenau, the Warburgs, Karl Helfferich, the Krupps, and others like them, our understanding of imperial Germany will remain unbalanced.

I would like to anticipate one legitimate objection that may be raised against the approach I have adopted in this book. That would be that I have paid inadequate attention to Ballin's remarkably successful management of the HAPAG, an achievement which has assured his place in the economic history of modern Germany. It is true that an ideal biography of the man might perhaps be one which would be a study of the line revolving around the accomplishments of its long-time chief, with Ballin's political activities being relegated to the secondary role which they in fact played in his life. I might have been inclined to follow such a pattern had all the HAPAG's archives for the period of Ballin's association with the line been preserved and had I been able to secure unrestricted access to them. Many files have disappeared or have been destroyed, however, and there were others which could not be opened for my inspection. As a result, I turned to Ballin's involvement in affairs of state, a hitherto neglected aspect of his life on which copious documentation was available, and which, if investigated, might advance our understanding of Wilhelmine Germany. The result is an examination of the interaction of business and politics, of businessmen and politicians.

My gratitude for assistance and for many sorts of kindness in the course of my research is very great and I am happy now to be able to thank in print those who made my pursuit of Ballin not only possible, but stimulating and agreeable as well. At the Johns Hopkins University, where this book originated as a doctoral dissertation, I am indebted to Professors Frederic C. Lane and David Spring not only for reading the manuscript in dissertation form, but for their remarkable talents as teachers of European history as well. All who have done graduate work in history at the Hopkins will share my appreciation for the friendship and unfailing good humor of the department's secretary, Lilly E. Lavarello, who lightened my work in countless ways. Garnette Northcott Pitts, good friend and press agent extraordinary, together with Louis F. Schnemann, set in motion a series of events which began in Texas and from there led to my introduction to officials of the Hamburg-American Line. The directors of the line graciously allowed me to examine and to quote from many documents dealing with Ballin. Professor Fritz Fischer of the University of Hamburg provided a valuable introduction which greatly facilitated my research.

Several men who knew Ballin were generous with their time and retraced with me the events and personalities of a long-vanished era. In this respect, I am particularly happy to acknowledge my obligation to Dr. Eduard Rosenbaum of London; to Magnus Baron von Braun of Oberaudorf am Inn (Oberbayern); to General Hans Henning von Holtzendorff of Hanover; to Gustav Hillard of Lübeck; and to the late Senator Peter Franz Stubmann of Hamburg, an earlier biographer of Ballin. A number of libraries and archives—particularly the Hauptarchiv in Berlin-Dahlem, the Hamburg Staatsbibliothek and Staatsarchiv, the Public Record Office and the Wiener Library in London—welcomed me cordially and were most helpful. I owe a large measure of thanks to Dr. Wolfgang Mommsen and Fräulein E. Kinder of the Bundesarchiv in Koblenz for their very knowledgeable assistance in the manuscript sources. A timely grant from the West German government enabled me to spend a year in Germany. The Department of History of Princeton University, together with the Whitney Darrow Publication Reserve Fund of the Princeton University Press, liberally underwrote the costs of publication.

There are, finally, four persons to whom I should like to record a special indebtedness, one which I cannot sufficiently discharge by entering their names here. Without the help of Dr. Ursula Huffmann, archivist and statistician of the Hamburg-American Line, this book could not have been written. It was she who searched with me along the dusty shelves in the basement of the HAPAG building in Hamburg, who gave freely of her own extensive knowledge of Ballin, and who did much to make the many months I spent at the HAPAG pleasant as well as productive. To Ballin's godson, Eric M. Warburg of Hamburg and New York, I am grateful for permission to consult his father's papers, for many introductions to or inquiries of heirs of men who figure in these pages. Out of a busy life, he has frequently taken time to recall his association with Ballin and to assist me in my research. Professor Hans W. Gatzke, formerly of Johns Hopkins and now at Yale University, directed the dissertation and closely examined the final draft. His astute criticism and unrivalled command of German history made it possible for many of my errors to be excised, and he suggested many lines of investigation which had not occurred to me. The blemishes which have persisted are due to my own perversity or ignorance. My greatest debt is to the person to whom this book is dedicated.

Lamar Cecil

Princeton
May 5, 1966

Key to Abbreviations

Sources which have been assigned abbreviations in the footnotes of the text are listed below in alphabetical order. The more important of these collections are fully described in the Bibliographical Essay under the archives in which they are deposited. See the note below for *AA* references.

*AA, Eng. Nr. 71b	"Englische Marine"
AA, Eng. Nr. 78 no. 3, secr.	"Frage einer Verständigung Deutschlands mit England über Flottenbauten"
AA, Eng. Nr. 83, secr.	"Beziehungen Englands zu Russland"
AA, Hamburg Nr. 1	"Innere Verhältnisse Hamburgs"
AA, Hamburg Nr. 1, secr.	"Innere Verhältnisse Hamburgs"
AA, Hamburg Nr. 2, secr.	"Streik der Hafenarbeiter in Hamburg"

* Microfilm copies of German Foreign Ministry documents are cited in the text in the following order: name of author, name of addressee, date of document, *AA* (Auswärtiges Amt) archive designation and volume number, the microfilm reel number, followed by a virgule and the frame number. In some cases, the microfilm does not bear frame numbers. Whenever the microfilm document has been printed in *Die grosse Politik der europäischen Kabinette* the number assigned therein to the printed document is given in parentheses at the end of the citation. So, for example: Kühlmann to Bethmann, May 30, 1913, *AA*, Türkei Nr. 152, vol. 61, 418/00442-43 (*GP* 14,742). Where writer, addressee and date are not significant, they have been omitted. To determine in which archives or libraries these microfilms are available, consult American Historical Association, Committee for the Study of War Documents, *A Catalog of Files and Microfilms of the German Foreign Ministry Archives 1867-1920*, n.p., 1952, except for *AA*, Marine-Kabinets, which is on file in the Public Record Office, London. The originals of all these documents are in the Politisches Archiv des Auswärtigen Amtes, Bonn.

AA, Marine-Kabinets	"Akten des kaiserlichen Marine-Kabinets betreffend Flottenpolitik"
AA, Persien Nr. 1	"Allgemeine Angelegenheiten Persiens"
AA, Preussen 1 Nr. 1 no. 4m	"Besuch der Hansestädte durch Seine Majestät"
AA, Türkei Nr. 152	"Eisenbahnen in der asiatischen Türkei"
AA, Türkei Nr. 165	"Arabien"
AA, Weltkrieg	"Krieg 1914: der Weltkrieg"
AA, Weltkrieg, geh.	"Krieg 1914: der Weltkrieg"
AA, WK Nr. 2	"Krieg 1914: Vermittlungsaktionen"
AA, WK Nr. 2, geh.	"Krieg 1914: Vermittlungsaktionen"
AA, WK Nr. 15	"Material zu den Friedensverhandlungen"
AA, WK Nr. 18, geh.	"Krieg 1914: Unterseebootkrieg gegen England und andere feindliche Staaten"
BAB	Folder marked "Berichte an Albert Ballin," HAPAG archive, Hamburg.
Ballin-Heineken	Folder marked "Briefwechsel mit Generaldirektor Heineken, vom 1. Mai 1915 bis 1. Nov. 1916, A23," 3 vols., HAPAG archive.
Ballin-Holtzendorff, Private	Folder marked "Briefkopien Ballin an von Holtzen-

xiv

dorff, 1915-1918, Paket XV," HAPAG archive.

Ballin, Misc. Corr.   Folder marked "Corr[espondenz] Ballin, Boden #7, Kiste #2, Politik: 1915/1918," HAPAG archive.

Ballin-Schinckel   Folder marked "Briefwechsel mit Max Schinckel vom 1. Aug. 1914 bis 28. Aug. 1918, Kiste 3, A23," HAPAG archive.

BD   G. P. Gooch and H. W. V. Temperley, eds., *British Documents on the Origins of the War, 1898-1914*, 11 vols., London, 1925-38.

Berg "Nachlass"   Typescript entitled "Aufzeichnungen von Friedrich von Berg aus der Zeit seiner Tätigkeit als Chef des Zivilcabinettes über den Zeitraum 14.1.-1918-1.11.1918. 1920 Fol. 1-73, Nr. 331-2," Bundesarchiv, Koblenz.

Brockdorff-Rantzau "Nachlass"   Microfilm copy in the National Archives, Washington, of three files from the papers of Ulrich Count von Brockdorff-Rantzau: "Mission Andersen Privat"; "Briefe aus Kopenhagen, XI-

1918-V 18"; and "Brock-dorff-Rantzau Privat-briefe 1916/17, Nr. 6,7: Kopenhagen I u. II." This "Nachlass" is so dis-organized that I have re-ferred to documents in it by their microfilm refer-ence, which is relatively simple to trace, rather than by their archival designation.

Bülow "Nachlass" — Papers of Bernhard Fürst von Bülow. Where no other identification is given, documents cited are from "Albert Ballin 1903-1918, Nr. 60." Other folders cited are: "Schriftwechsel betr. Rö-mische Mission, Heft II, Nr. 39"; "Prozess Graf Kuno Moltke/Maximil-ian Harden 1907-1909, Nr. 32"; "Eugen Zim-mermann, Nr. 131"; *No-tizen* (diary) and *Merk-blätter* (a miscellany), Bundesarchiv, Koblenz.

DDF — France, Ministère des Af-faires Etrangères, *Docu-ments Diplomatiques Français (1871-1914)* . . . , 40 vols., Paris, 1929-36.

Freyer "Nachlass"	"Familiengeschichte des Fregattenkapitäns d. Res. a.D. Walter Paul Christian Freyer (1872-1959) für den Zeitraum 1892-1944," 3 vols., Bundesarchiv, Koblenz.
GP	Johannes Lepsius *et al.*, eds., *Die grosse Politik der europäischen Kabinette 1871-1914 . . .* , 40 vols., Berlin, 1923-27.
Haller "Nachlass"	Typescript by Johannes Haller entitled "30 Jahre im Dienste der Hamburg-Amerika Linie," HAPAG archive.
Hansard	*Parliamentary Debates*
HAPAG, "Privat-Post"	Folder marked "Privat-Post für Herrn General Direktor Ballin: Combinations (Morgan) Contracte, Entwürfe und Notizen, 1901," HAPAG archive.
HAPAG-V	Folder marked "Hamburg-Amerika Linie, V, von Holtzendorff A23," HAPAG archive.
Harden "Nachlass"	Letters by Ballin to Maximilian Harden, folders 4-7, Bundesarchiv, Koblenz.
Holtzendorff-A	16 vols. marked "Berichte Holtzendorff, Repertorium 300, Reichsinstitut

	für Geschichte des neuen Deutschlands," consisting of correspondence between Ballin and Arndt von Holtzendorff, Hauptarchiv, Berlin-Dahlem.
Holtzendorff-B	22 vols. consisting primarily of extracts of the originals in *Holtzendorff-A*, HAPAG archive.
Huldermann	Bernhard Huldermann, *Albert Ballin*, Oldenburg i.O. and Berlin, 1922.
Kriegs-Zeitschrift	*Kriegs-Zeitschrift der Hamburg-Amerika Linie* (1915-18), HAPAG archive.
Landau "Nachlass"	Copies of 18 letters dating from 1894 to 1918 by Ballin to Dr. J. Landau, editor of the *Berliner Börsen-Zeitung*, HAPAG archive.
Merck "Nachlass"	Typescript by Johannes Merck entitled "Meine Erinnerungen an die Hamburg-Amerika Linie und an Albert Ballin . . . 1896-1918," in addition to a number of appendices, all filed in II 8 Konv[olut] 2b and 4; and also a number of folders containing correspondence between Merck and

HAPAG officials, filed in II 8 Konv. 5, all in Familienarchiv Merck, Staatsarchiv, Hamburg.

Reichstag   *Stenographische Berichte der Verhandlungen des deutschen Reichstages,* Berlin, 1871 *et seq.*

Solf "Nachlass"   Papers of Wilhelm Solf, "Schriftwechsel mit Albert Ballin 1913-1918 (1919) Nr. 96," Bundesarchiv, Koblenz.

Stresemann "Nachlass"   Papers of Gustav Stresemann, microfilm copy in the National Archives, Washington, of the originals in the Politisches Archiv des Auswärtigen Amtes, Bonn. When citing this "Nachlass," I have given first the archival designation of the document consulted, followed by the microfilm reference consisting of reel number followed by a virgule and the frame number.

Stubmann   Peter Franz Stubmann, *Mein Feld ist die Welt: Albert Ballin, sein Leben,* Hamburg, 1960.

Warburg "Nachlass"   Correspondence between

	Ballin and Max Warburg, Warburg Institute, London. The letters are cited by author, receiver, date, followed by the Warburg archive designation of Laufende Nr., Fach Nr., Archiv Nr.; so, for example, Ballin to Warburg, Dec. 8, 1908, 1014/9/801.
Widenmann "Nachlass"	Typescript by Wilhelm Widenmann entitled "Erinnerungen und Erlebnisse mit geschichtlichen Personen, Nr. 1," Bundesarchiv, Koblenz.
Wönckhaus "Nachlass"	A small and miscellaneous collection in the possession of Frau Alice Wönckhaus, Hamburg.
Zeitschrift	*Zeitschrift der Hamburg-Amerika Linie* (1901-1914), HAPAG archive.

Contents

ALBERT BALLIN

BUSINESS AND POLITICS
IN IMPERIAL GERMANY,
1888-1918

CHAPTER I

Hamburg and the HAPAG, 1880-1900

𝕿HE ELBE, broad, quiet, almost limpid, is not a spectacular river. Like the Danube or the Mississippi, it is a methodical stream, determined but not angry, with an even-tempered concentration on the work at hand on its languid surface. Upstream from Cuxhaven, rising from the salt marshes near the river's mouth, the restfully verdant landscape drifts on mile after mile with little variation. It is only sixty miles inland as Hamburg is approached that the Elbe gradually becomes congested with ships and its banks begin to acquire an urban character.

At the end of the century, Hamburg's harbor was tight with vessels of manifold variety and nationality: ancient sailing ships, embryonic transatlantic steamers, and still others of a temporizing, hybrid sort, from whose decks sprouted both sailing masts and funnels. Squat brick warehouses lined the slips, forests of scaffolding concealed the noisy shipyards and drydocks. A steady traffic of stevedores and horse-drawn carts laden with drums and crates passed back and forth from ship to shore. Passengers moved along the piers to seek out the ships that would take them to destinations around the world. Half a million busy people attended to the work of the city, most of them dependent on the water and its traffic for their livelihood. Hamburg was prosperous, its trade expanding and its future seemingly unlimited. And so its citizens were an optimistic people, enjoying—quietly, never exuberantly—their good fortune, a satisfaction translated in the consumption of stupendous quantities of good food, usually in mellow silence. It was a merchant city, sustained by the work of hands and backs and by a shrewd calculation of the possibilities of profit. Things intellectual were not in vogue; Hamburg boasted no university and there was little feeling that one was needed. Young men destined for the world of trade received their education in the offices along the wharves and on ships at sea. Success produced a measure of rest and much solid comfort, but wealth seldom bred effeteness or watered the commercial blood of Hamburg's merchants. Capable fathers as a rule sired capable sons, and thus the chronicle of Hamburg's greatness is often family history. Houses such as Woermann, Laeisz, and Godeffroy, the so-called *königliche Kaufleute* of Hamburg, and the shipping companies which bore their names, were for generations the backbone of the city's economic life.[1]

[1] The literature dealing with the economic aspects of Hamburg's history in the Wilhelmine era is rich and varied. The most convenient survey of the material is Kurt Detlev Möller and Annelise Tecke, *Bücherkunde zur hamburgischen Geschichte*, 2 parts, Hamburg, 1939-56, which covers the items printed between 1900 and 1954. The official statistical collections published by the city's *Statistisches Amt* are particularly valuable: *Statistik des hamburgischen Staats*, Hamburg, 1871 *et seq.* (hereafter cited as Hamburg, *Statistik*); *Hamburg's Handel*, Hamburg, 1868 *et seq.*; *Statistisches Handbuch für den hamburgischen Staat*, published irregularly in the late 19th century but discontinued from 1891 to 1920; and the *Tabellarische Uebersichten des hamburgischen Handels*, Hamburg, 1851-1911, continued as *Hamburgs Handel und Schiffahrt*, Hamburg, 1912 *et seq.* There are a number of valuable memoirs, especially Max Warburg, *Aus meinen Aufzeichnungen*, n.p., 1952; Carl August Schröder, *Aus Hamburgs Blütezeit*, Hamburg, 1921; Max von Schinckel, *Lebenserinnerungen*, Hamburg, n.d.; as well as the second volume of Percy E. Schramm's family history, *Neun Generationen: dreihundert Jahre deutscher 'Kulturgeschichte' im Lichte der Schicksale einer hamburger Bürgerfamilie*, 2 vols., Göttingen, 1963-64. The following secondary sources are the most helpful: Ernst Baasch, *Geschichte Hamburgs 1814-1918*, 2 vols., Stuttgart and Gotha, 1924-25, and

4

The proud face Hamburg turned to the world belied a certain internal anxiety, however, for the prosperity which it had achieved was dependent on external forces over which the city could often exercise only partial control. An economy such as Hamburg's, based so singly on the earnings of international trade, was constantly affected by fluctuations in the world's markets. Hamburg followed the pulse of the British economy with particular concern, for most of its goods and passengers were destined for ports across the North Sea, and from these English harbors and from Britain's colonial domains came the bulk of the city's imports. Britain's trade with Hamburg proved so profitable that the Elbe port became a bailiwick of British shipping, and throughout the nineteenth century the number of Union Jacks found along the river outnumbered the ensigns of other foreign nations and even those of Hamburg itself.[2] As the century progressed, Hamburg increased its fleet as well as the number of points around the world which it served, and by the 1880's its merchant marine outweighed that of any other port in Germany. The mainstay of the city's trade remained unchanged until 1914: England was always the great customer, with the United States following at a distance in second place. Consequently, a depression in England or in America found its doleful reflection on the Elbe. Ship loadings were sluggish, while passengers, forewarned of hard times in the land of promise, preferred to face adversity on familiar soil. Trade dried up and ships gathered barnacles and rust at their moorings.

Die Handelskammer zu Hamburg 1665-1915, 3 vols., Hamburg, 1915; Otto Mathies, *Hamburgs Reederei 1814-1914*, Hamburg, 1924; and Adolf Goetz, *25 Jahre hamburgische Seeschiffahrtspolitik*, Hamburg, 1911.

[2] *Statistisches Handbuch* (1891), table 143, p. 128; *ibid.* (1920), table 3, p. 179; table 3, p. 184. See also *Hamburgs Handel und Schiffahrt* (1913), part I, table 10, pp. 64-65; table 12, p. 68.

There were also problems closer at hand. Berlin, like foreign markets, contributed to the frailty of Hamburg's prosperity. In the early years of the Bismarckian Reich, an uneasy peace prevailed between the two cities, for ideological as well as commercial differences separated the Elbe and the Spree. Hamburg was proud of its history as a free Hanseatic city, of its international connections and world renown. To Hamburg, Prussia was a mighty but a parochial state, administered from a presumptuous city, a people whose military traditions and agrarian economy were the antithesis of Hamburg's own relatively democratic and mercantile heritage. Nor did the city have much in common with the other states of the empire. It was a port, a cosmopolitan waterway to the world, indulgent of national peculiarities and religious diversity. A thoroughly bourgeois city, 90 per cent Lutheran but happily embracing some fifty-odd sects in the remaining tenth of its population, Hamburg could not be expected to have much sympathy for the dynastic and confessional quarrels rife elsewhere in Germany. Similarly, Hamburg in vain opposed the protectionist tariff which Bismarck forced through the Reichstag in 1879.[3] The city's merchants argued that a tariff designed to protect German agriculture and industry from Russian, American, and British competition would reduce imports into Germany and cause a corresponding attenuation in Hamburg's overseas trade. These fears proved unwarranted, however, and the volume of the city's maritime traffic mounted steadily from 1879 to 1914.

More dangerous to Hamburg's economic welfare than erratic world markets or imperial tariff policy was the

[3] Reich-Hamburg relations during the tariff crisis are treated in Ivo J. Lambi, *Free Trade and Protection in Germany 1868-1879*, Wiesbaden, 1963, and in Ernst Hiecke, *Hamburgs Stellung zum deutschen Zollverein 1879-1882: ein Beitrag zur Wirtschaftspolitik Bismarcks*, Quackenbrück, 1935.

6

intense competition which the city faced in making its claim to trade routes and profitable shipping services. Its rivals were numerous and powerful—Antwerp, Le Havre, and Rotterdam were its principal continental competitors—but the most irritating was nestled only sixty miles away on the Weser.

Like Hamburg, Bremen could look back on a long and distinguished history as a free Hansa city with wide shipping connections.[4] Bremen had pioneered the transatlantic trade with the New World, and America had become the axis of its commerce much as Great Britain constituted that of Hamburg. The city's traffic was one which was strong in people as well as in freight, for Bremen was the first German port to become an emigration point for those Germans moved by dissatisfaction or compelled by adversity to leave the fatherland.

The factors giving rise to German emigration in the nineteenth century were varied.[5] Political unrest, a feeling

[4] An excellent introduction to Bremen is Ludwig Beutin, *Bremen und Amerika: zur Geschichte der Weltwirtschaft und der Beziehungen Deutschlands zu den Vereinigten Staaten*, Bremen, 1953; see also his "Handel und Schiffahrt Bremens bis zum Weltkriege," in H. Knittenmeyer and D. Steilen, eds., *Bremen: Lebenskreis einer Hansastadt*, Bremen, 1942, pp. 292-317. The standard general history by Wilhelm von Bippen, *Geschichte der Stadt Bremen*, 3 vols., Bremen, 1892-1904, is summarized in Georg Bessell, *Bremen: Geschichte einer deutschen Stadt*, Bremen, 1955. Richard Duckwitz, *Aufstieg und Blüte einer Hansestadt: von bremischer Leistung in der Welt. Bürgermeister Barkhausen und seine Zeit*, Bremen, n.d., is also of considerable interest.

[5] For the history of German emigration, see in particular Mack Walker, *Germany and the Emigration 1816-1885*, Cambridge, Mass., 1964; Eugen von Philippovich, ed., *Auswanderung und Auswanderungspolitik in Deutschland . . .* , Leipzig, 1892; Marcus Lee Hansen, *The Atlantic Migration 1607-1860: A History of the Continuing Settlement of the United States*, Cambridge, Mass., 1945; Alfred Vagts, *Deutschland und die Vereinigten Staaten in der Weltpolitik*, 2 vols., London, 1935, esp. I, chap. viii. Vagts has also dealt with eastward emigration in his *Deutsch-amerikanische*

7

of alienation in a rapidly changing world, a desire to preserve old ways in a new environment were important
considerations, but economic distress seems to have been
the paramount cause. The Revolutionary-Napoleonic
wars, climatic disasters, and the rapid industrialization of
Europe had forced vast economic hardship on all Germans, but particularly on artisans and merchants in the
villages and towns and on agricultural workers and small
farmers in the countryside. It was from these depressed
groups that the great waves of German emigration
proceeded.

The first of these German emigrants—those who left in
the 1830's—had moved northward to Le Havre and Antwerp, where they boarded ships for America. Bremen was
the logical port for these travelers, but it was blocked
from the south by a multiplicity of tolls on the Weser and
Rhine. By 1840, however, the newly established *Zollverein*
had eliminated most of these transit barriers and Bremen
had emerged as a successful competitor for the German
emigrants. The emigrant, like any other customer, relied
on hearsay and rumor in making his choice of an embarkation point. Though Bremen's increasing volume of
passengers was due chiefly to its propinquity to the emigrant areas of western Germany, part of the city's early
success as a carrier was doubtless attributable to its solicitude for the well-being of the emigrants themselves, a
concern seldom encountered elsewhere in Europe at this
time. As early as 1832, Bremen's magistrates had passed
laws designed to protect the travelers from unscrupulous
townspeople.[6] The emigrants were not blind to such good
treatment and they recommended the Weser port to those

---

*Rückwanderung: Probleme—Phänomene—Statistik—Politik—Sozi-
ologie—Biographie*, Heidelberg, 1960.
    [6] For these reforms, see Beutin, *Bremen und Amerika*, pp. 41-44.

at home who were on the verge of following their friends and relatives to America.

Hamburg at first showed litle inclination to follow Bremen's lead in entering the emigration business, a reluctance due no doubt to the hostility of the city government to such enterprise. The Senate and *Bürgerschaft* of Hamburg at first often overlooked the profits which many of the city's citizens derived from the emigration business. Instead they pointed insistently to the disorder and disease which the travelers brought in their wake and enacted a number of regulations which encumbered the shipping companies engaged in emigration. The disparity of outlook between the two Hanseatic ports was reflected in traffic statistics. In the decade between 1836 and 1846, for every emigrant who embarked at Hamburg almost nine took ship from Bremen.[7]

Nothing was able to goad the jealous merchants of Hamburg so much as the prosperity to be noted on the Weser, and it was quite obvious that much of Bremen's increasing wealth was due to its profitable emigration trade. Bremen shipowners, confronted by more emigrants than their ships could hold, frequently chartered vessels from their relatively idle competitors in Hamburg. Other emigrants, unable to find ships in Hamburg, were sometimes forced to take their business to Bremen.[8] In the late 1830's and 1840's, the Hamburg Senate relaxed much of its emigration legislation and almost at once a number of new shipping lines were incorporated in the city.

Once the *königliche Kaufleute* had resolved to enter the emigration business in earnest, they wasted no time in making Hamburg notorious to all competitors for ruth-

[7] Hamburg, *Statistik* (1872), table 1, p. 110.

[8] Ernst Baasch, "Gesetzgebung und Einrichtungen im Interesse des Auswanderungswesens in Hamburg," in Philippovich, ed., *Auswanderung und Auswanderungspolitik*, pp. 389-90; Hansen, *Atlantic Migration*, p. 193.

9

lessness and to the luckless emigrants for knavery and deceit. At the center of the scandal were the emigration agents (*Auswanderungsagenten*), who were responsible for procuring emigrants to fill the ships sailing from the port. In spite of the growing number of Europeans longing to emigrate to the New World, the agents' task was often not an easy one. Most German states placed difficulties in the way of would-be emigrants who were still liable for military service, in debt, or merely anxious to abandon a burdensome wife and family to public charity. The agents had to work hard to find their customers, and therefore they often signed contracts with men whose emigration was forbidden by law. They enticed ignorant peasants with fanciful tales of Hamburg's fine ships and cheap fares and seduced travelers from agents representing other lines. Once in Hamburg, the emigrants often found that they had been duped and that their ships would not sail for days after the contracted date.

The victims of this guile were forced to mark time in Hamburg until their agents finally booked passage for them. Here they were subjected to further sharp practice from the innkeepers, trollops, and counterfeiters who lay in wait in the narrow streets of the St. Pauli district. At the same time, in more luxurious surroundings across town, the emigration agents could be observed enjoying the rich cuisine of Hamburg's foremost hostelries, their cravats ornamented by diamond stick pins.[9] In the face of such deprivation by both agents and urban underworld, the emigrant and his meager savings were soon parted and he often became a penniless ward of the city's welfare agencies. So notorious was Hamburg's crass handling of emigrants that in 1837 the Bavarian government publicly warned travelers against taking ships from Hamburg,

[9] Bernhard Guttmann, *Schattenriss einer Generation 1888-1919*, Stuttgart, 1950, p. 242.

"where," the caveat ran, "they will not be treated much better than Negro slaves." Munich subsequently refused to allow Hamburg agents to sign contracts with Bavarian subjects and recommended Bremen as a more desirable point of embarkation.[10] By mid-century, the various German states required all shipping lines to obtain concessions. These provided that agents must post bond and could be jailed or fined if they failed to fulfill the contracts arrived at with the emigrants.[11]

The government of Hamburg eventually became no less alarmed than its sister states at the emigrants' condition, particularly after it became apparent that the manner in which the city's emigration business was being conducted on both ship and shore was poisoning its reputation and hurting its economy. The Senate, already burdened with the obvious problems of maintaining order in a sailor's paradise, was in no mood to tolerate additional abuses of civic decency. So in 1855, some twenty years after the enactment of similar legislation in Bremen, the Senate drew up a detailed emigration law modeled on those al-

[10] Baasch, in Philippovich, ed., *Auswanderung und Auswanderungspolitik*, pp. 393-94. The Bavarian restriction against Hamburg agents was raised in 1847. It is doubtful that Bremen's ships represented any improvement, although emigration conditions in Bremen itself were much better. A city official declared in 1836 that they were virtual "slave ships." See Beutin, *Bremen und Amerika*, p. 42.

[11] The relationship of the agents to the various governments is fairly clear, but not that to the shipping lines which they served. Some material is assembled in Philippovich, ed., *Auswanderung und Auswanderungspolitik*, esp. pp. 23, 47-55, 142-46, 151-53, 187-204, 338-39, 342-45, 380-83, 468-72. The legal position of the agents after 1897 is clarified in Walter Eidam, *Die staatsrechtliche Stellung des Auswanderungsunternehmers auf Grund des Reichsgesetzes über das Auswanderungswesen vom 9. Juni 1897*, Ansbach, 1905. See also Hermann Wätjen, *Aus der Frühzeit des Nordatlantikverkehrs: Studien zur Geschichte der deutschen Auswanderung nach den Vereinigten Staaten bis zum Ende des amerikanischen Bürgerkrieges*, Leipzig, 1932, pp. 116-21.

11

ready passed by the other German states.[12] Under the terms of this statute, a Committee for Emigrants' Affairs was established to mediate differences arising between the emigrants on one hand and the agents, ship lines, and innkeepers on the other.[13]

The certified agents of concessioned shipping lines, in spite of their energy and salesmanship, did not catch all the impoverished and frustrated Germans setting out for America. Competing with these certified agents was another group, the independent emigration agents. The independents contracted with would-be emigrants in the hinterland and then, once they knew how many billets were needed, presented themselves to Hamburg's ship lines to purchase the space required. The activity of these independent agents was bothersome to the Hamburg lines because there could never be any certainty as to which line or lines the independents would apply. The shipping companies decided therefore to run the independent agents out of business. About 1850, these lines simply began to refuse to assign berths on their ships to the independent agents, and the emigrant, if he wished to begin his voyage from Hamburg, was faced with the choice of dealing with the lines' regular agents or staying at home. The shipping companies could not run the independents out of business, however, for so great had the flood of emigration become by now that Hamburg's passenger fleet could not possibly handle all the traffic. The independent agents, with thousands of emigrants under contract for transatlantic passage but denied space by the Hamburg lines, were in pressing need of ships. In their desperation these agents turned to England.

[12] For the provisions of this law, see Hamburg, *Statistik* (1872), pp. 98-99.

[13] The annual reports of this committee were printed as *Jahresbericht der Behörde für das Auswanderungswesen*, Hamburg, 1856 *et seq.*

The cooperation between the independent German agents and British shipping lines was natural enough, for if the agents could supply emigrants, England, with the world's greatest merchant marine, could certainly furnish ships. A bargain along such lines was struck about 1850 between the two interested parties. The independent brokers brought emigrants to Hamburg, where they were picked up by small British craft and transferred to ports on the east coast of England. Once on land, the passengers were hastened by rail to Liverpool and put aboard ships bound for America.

In this manner, a second form of emigration, the so-called indirect traffic, came into existence.[14] This indirect service had the advantage of being both quicker and less expensive than sailing direct from Hamburg, nor was it subject to the city's emigration legislation, an omission against which the direct carriers protested.[15] But there were also drawbacks. The many changes and linguistic complications involved, plus the fact that the emigrants were often forced out on deck during the trip to England made the indirect route somewhat more arduous. The indirect service never claimed the popularity which direct emigration enjoyed, but it nevertheless constituted a vital lifeline for the dozen or so independent agents in Hamburg after the ship lines of the city refused to sell them space.[16]

In the second half of the nineteenth century, emigration from Hamburg was thus clearly and antagonistically divided into two channels. The rivalry between the direct

[14] See Stubmann, p. 19, for a different explanation of the origins of the indirect service.

[15] This hostility is well treated by Baasch, in Philippovich, ed., *Auswanderung und Auswanderungspolitik*, pp. 383-86.

[16] See Hamburg, *Statistik* (1872), table 1, p. 110, for figures of direct and indirect emigration from Hamburg, 1852-70. For the period 1870-79, see *Statistisches Handbuch* (1891), table 74, p. 71; for 1893-1914, *ibid.* (1920), table 2, p. 74. The figures for 1890-92

and indirect carriers was acrimonious, and frequently police protection had to be invoked to prevent one agent from filching another's passengers. The established companies were constantly being challenged by new competitors, for each decade saw the incorporation of lines eager to be cut in on the traffic. In bad years when emigration declined, the struggle for business became especially tempestuous.

In the mid-1880's, the Carr Line, a recently incorporated German firm active in the direct emigration business, began to disturb the older lines by its success in claiming an increasingly large share of the city's passenger traffic. Particularly troubled by this new competitor was the *Hamburg-Amerikanische-Paketfahrt-Aktien-Gesellschaft* (HAPAG), one of Hamburg's first transatlantic shipping companies, which by the 1880's had emerged in the weltering, overcrowded maritime market as the largest passenger line on the Elbe. The Hamburg-American Line or Hamburg-Amerika Linie, the official name of the company after 1893, which had digested a string of worrisome competitors during the course of its ascent, determined now to acquire the Carr Line as well. Protracted negotiations between the two companies followed, and in June 1886 an agreement was reached whereby the HAPAG not only purchased the fleet of the Carr Line but also hired the chief of its passenger division, an ambitious young man, Albert Ballin, then not quite twenty-nine years old.

---

must be extracted from the appropriate volumes of the *Statistik*. The relevant percentages are:

	Direct	*Indirect*
1852-59	83.1	16.9
1860-69	88.4	11.6
1870-79	75.3	24.7
1880-89	70.1	29.9
1890-99	86.5	13.5
1900-09	97.1	2.9
1910-14	95.2	4.8

The narrow house in the Stubbenhuk in which Albert Ballin was born on August 15, 1857, lay not more than a hundred feet from a corner of Hamburg's busy harbor. A few years later, the boy and his family moved to the Baumwall and thereafter resided directly on the waterfront. Here, surrounded by ships and sailors, Albert grew up. The Baumwall was more a commercial than a residential district, where hardworking people earning a modest living from the sea and its commerce lived above their stores and offices. The playful life of childhood was short in such struggling families and the introduction to man's work necessarily came early. An undistinguished attendance at Professor Goldmann's academy, during which Albert took a passing interest in the cello, was the extent of the boy's formal education. When probably not more than fifteen, he left the schoolroom to enter the family business, a not very successful independent emigration agency.[17]

Albert's father, Samuel Joel Ballin, a sober, elephantine Jew, had emigrated from Denmark to Hamburg about 1830. Here he set himself up as a dyer and glazer of fabrics and before long had established a prosperous business. Following the death of his first wife, Samuel Ballin took as his bride in 1841 Amalia Meyer, the sixteen-year-old daughter of a moderately wealthy Hamburg merchant, who bore her husband nine children, of whom Albert was the last. By the time Albert had arrived in the world, however, his father's once successful concern had gone bankrupt. Saved only by a timely inheritance from his

[17] The details of Ballin's early years are taken primarily from the biographies by Huldermann and Stubmann. The treatment of this period in Ballin's life in these works is slight, for he declined to provide particulars of his boyhood. A small amount of additional information can be derived from obituary notices in Hamburg papers. For the genealogy of the family, see Oscar Ballin, *Die Familie Ballin, mit besonderer Berücksichtigung ihres hannoverisch-braunschweigischen Zweiges*, Gandersheim, 1931.

15

father-in-law, the elder Ballin and an associate, Samuel Hirsch, opened an office as independent emigrant agents in 1852, for undiscovered reasons under the name Morris & Company. This new firm never enjoyed the success which, for a while at least, had greeted Ballin's textile venture. Morris & Co. had to share the indirect brokerage business with a dozen similar Hamburg firms, and in bad years there was not enough traffic for any of the agents to show a profit. Under Samuel Ballin's leadership, Morris & Co. barely managed to cover the needs of his large family, and when he died in 1874 there was little patrimony to pass on to his numerous offspring other than the partial ownership of a struggling and unpromising emigration agency.

It was a hard year for a death in the family. The worsening depression in America drastically reduced the number of indirect emigrants in 1875 to barely one-half of the total for the year before. The figures for the next few years continued to sag. It was therefore no wonder that an older son, Joseph, who had been designated by his father to take charge of Morris & Co., soon abandoned to Albert what gave every indication of continuing to be a profitless enterprise. Shoring up a moribund concern did not much appeal to Albert either, and at one time he seriously considered closing the firm and joining Joseph in the machine tool business. For some reason, however, he changed his mind and decided to stick with his inheritance. In 1877, Albert bought out Wilhelm Wolffsohn, who had succeeded Hirsch as the elder Ballin's partner, and became sole owner of Morris & Co., Emigration Agents.

Ballin's outright acquisition of the firm coincided with a conspicuous improvement in its fortunes, an amelioration due initially to the lifting of the depression in America in 1879. Once there was a certainty of finding jobs across the Atlantic, legions of emigrants once again began to troop

16

to Hamburg. Morris & Co. could naturally expect to share in the rejuvenated market, but the ascendancy which it soon achieved over the other independent emigration agencies of Hamburg—by the mid-1880's Ballin's firm was handling one out of every three indirect passengers—was due to the ability of its young proprietor. Since Morris & Co.'s customers were forwarded solely on British ships, Ballin was quick to appreciate the value of cordial relations with shipping firms in England. Like his father, he had made several extended business trips to England, where he acquired a masterful fluency in the language.

Even though Morris & Co. had become the largest independent emigrant agency in Hamburg, its future as such was limited, for indirect emigration was doomed to a secondary place since direct service remained the emigrants' favored means of reaching America. The gains to be made from the indirect traffic were as circumscribed as the number of people choosing this route. The profit per passenger accruing to the independent agents was small, for every commission had to be shared with English agents who shepherded the emigrants from their ports of arrival to Liverpool. The future and its profits clearly belonged to the great shipping lines which could offer the emigrants what they wanted: cheap, rapid, unbroken connections between European and North American ports. There was, however, no place for firms such as Morris & Co. on this horizon, for the direct carriers had their own accredited agents and had long refused to deal with the independents. For an independent agent anxious to advance beyond the narrow possibilities offered in servicing the indirect emigration, the only access to the direct traffic was to establish a passenger line himself. Ballin, whose ambition had already involved him in an unsuccessful project to produce emigrants for a new colony in the un-

17

charted Brazilian jungle, soon discovered in the firm of Edward Carr & Company a means of doing just that.

Edward Carr was a nephew of the Hamburg shipping magnate, Robert M. Sloman, Jr., and had joined his uncle's firm in 1867.[18] After a dozen years with the Sloman Line, Carr set himself up in business as a ship broker and proprietor of a miniature fleet consisting of two freighters. In 1881, Ballin approached Carr with an adventurous suggestion: why not convert the upper decks of two new freighters Carr was building for the accommodation of passengers? Ballin felt sure that Morris & Co. could supply the emigrants provided Carr would make over space for them on his ships. A minimal renovation would be required, for—according to Ballin's plan—the passenger area would not be divided into cabins but rather into large multiple-purpose rooms. What by day served as lounge and dining area became a dormitory at nightfall. To compensate for the primitiveness of such quarters, the emigrants would be given free run of the open decks, a preserve of first and second class passengers on traditionally outfitted transatlantic vessels. The absence of housing refinements meant that more room could be reserved for cargo, which, in turn, would enable the Carr Line to confront more luxurious steamships with dangerously competitive rates.

Carr agreed to Ballin's overtures and the two young men signed a contract in 1881. Carr was to provide two ships, each capable of transporting 640 passengers for 82 marks per head, Hamburg to New York, a price which contrasted favorably with the 120 marks charged by the leading Hamburg and Bremen steamship companies for steerage accommodations. The first shipload of emigrants departing for America under the Carr-Ballin association

[18] On Carr and his line, see Mathies, *Hamburgs Reederei*, p. 93; Huldermann, pp. 12-23; and Stubmann, pp. 24-26.

left Hamburg in June of the same year. The new undertaking proved an instantaneous success, for emigration from Hamburg rose markedly in the early 1880's. Carr, encouraged by the 4,000 passengers which Ballin was able to deliver in the first year of their partnership, lost no time in enlarging his fleet. By the next year, Carr had tripled his ship holdings to six vessels, and Ballin did almost as well, presenting his associate with 11,000 emigrants.

The success of the Carr Line in drawing off an increasingly large share of Hamburg's emigration traffic though lower fares and more spacious, if less private, quarters was not without effect on the Hamburg-American Line. Though the Carr Line's business was trifling compared to that of the mighty HAPAG, any competitor spelled danger, for the only means of eliminating troublemakers was either to purchase them outright or to destroy them by undercutting fares. Both courses could be financially disastrous in a business in which capital had to be husbanded for construction and expansion. The HAPAG, however, rejected any attempt to purchase its competitor and in May 1882 entered into a rate war with Carr and Ballin, reducing its steerage fare first to 90 and subsequently to 80 marks. Carr and Ballin answered by paring down their passage prices more and more. As the rate war increased in intensity, the competing lines were compelled to forego their customary dividends, and the deteriorating situation caused the entire *Vorstand* of the HAPAG to resign so that the company could be radically reorganized. For months and months, in spite of their mounting difficulties, neither the HAPAG nor the Carr Line were willing to compromise, and it was not until the summer of 1886 that a settlement was reached. Under the terms of the agreement, the Union Line (the title adopted by the Carr Line in 1885 following a merger with another Hamburg company) remained corporately independent and was allowed to

19

charge lower prices than the HAPAG. The Hamburg-American Line, however, assumed the mangement of the passenger services of both lines, guaranteeing to send at least one-fourth of the total number of passengers on the Union Line. At the same time, the HAPAG signed a separate contract it considered to be of "particular importance" with Ballin which provided that he would be appointed chief of the HAPAG's passenger division and thus supervise the emigration business of both lines.[19] On the first day of June 1886, Ballin took up his new position with the HAPAG.

The Hamburg-American Line had been founded in 1847 by a group of Hamburg shipowners for the purpose, stated in its original by-laws, of providing a "regular connection between Hamburg and North America by means of sailing ships under the Hamburg flag."[20] Its vessels would be plain but dependable and offer cheap, punctual transportation to America. In the first decades of its existence, the company plowed back much of its profits into expansion and improvement programs for its fleet and soon

[19] For the agreement between the HAPAG, Carr, and Ballin, see Huldermann, pp. 20-26.

[20] The history of the Hamburg-American Line was once a perennial exercise for German journalists, and there is consequently a wealth of literature on the subject. The most useful studies, in addition to the biographies of Ballin by Stubmann and Huldermann, are: Kurt Himer, *75 Jahre Hamburg-Amerika Linie: I. Teil, Adolph Godeffroy und seine Nachfolger bis 1886*, Hamburg, n.d., and his *Geschichte der Hamburg-Amerika Linie: 2. Teil, Albert Ballin*, Hamburg, n.d.; Frank Herschel, *HAPAG: Entwicklung und Bedeutung der Hamburg-Amerika Linie*, Berlin, 1912; and Karl Thiess, *Die Hamburg-Amerika Linie: eine Stütze der deutschen Volkswirtschaft*, Berlin, n.d. None of the above are as informative as the company's Annual Reports and the confidential house organ, *Zeitschrift der Hamburg-Amerika Linie*, which contains a complete listing of literature on the company from 1901 to 1914. Indispensable for the background against which the HAPAG operated are Baasch, *Geschichte Hamburgs*; Beutin, *Bremen und Amerika*; and Mathies, *Hamburgs Reederei*.

20

established itself as the leading shipping firm in Hamburg.[21] Staying on top was hard work, however, and a year—such as 1853—in which a dividend equal to 28 per cent of capital was paid, might be followed by one in which the stockholders received nothing but a dismaying annual report. When world trade was slack, there were stretches of as many as five years in which no dividends could be paid.

In Hamburg itself, the HAPAG had no real competitors in the North Atlantic trade, for its commanding position on the Elbe was never again effectively challenged after its acquisition of Carr's Union Line, and Ballin, in 1886. In terms of tonnage, the great British colossi—the Peninsula & Orient and British-India Lines, J. A. Allan, and other firms—France's Messageries Maritimes and Compagnie Générale Transatlantique, and the Navigazione Generale Italiana were the world's greatest carriers against which the Hamburg-American Line had to compete. At the time Ballin joined the HAPAG, the line ranked twenty-second in size, falling well behind all these foreign firms.[22] The HAPAG's most serious rivalry, however, was with Bremen's North German Lloyd (*Norddeutscher Lloyd*), which stood between the mighty British lines and the relatively inconsequential HAPAG.[23]

[21] For detailed figures showing the increasing volume of passengers and freight forwarded by the HAPAG, see Wilhelm Böhmert, *Die Hamburg-Amerika-Linie und der Norddeutsche Lloyd: ein Beitrag zur Geschichte der grossen Unternehmungen in Deutschland*, Berlin, 1909, pp. 15-16; and in Thiess, *Hamburg-Amerika Linie*, pp. 57-58.

[22] *Lloyd's Register of British and Foreign Shipping* (1883), appendix, pp. 3-94.

[23] On the Lloyd, see Paul Neubaur, *Der Norddeutsche Lloyd: 50 Jahre der Entwicklung 1857-1907*, 3 vols., Leipzig, 1907; F. C. Brinkmann, "Die Entstehung der bremer Schiffahrt in den letzten 100 Jahren unter besonderer Berücksichtigung des Auswandererverkehrs," diss., Marburg, 1924; and A. Petzet, *Heinrich Wiegand: ein Lebensbild*, Bremen, 1932.

21

Ballin was determined that the Hamburg-American Line measure up to the old Hanseatic device—*Mein Feld ist die Welt* (My Field is the World)—which it had adopted on its incorporation in 1847. His energy and competence soon attracted the attention of Carl Laeisz, one of the titans of Hamburg's maritime empire and a director of the HAPAG. Impressed by Ballin's performance, Laeisz saw to it that in 1888 the passenger chief was promoted to a directorship.[24] Although continuing as head of the passenger division, which throughout his life retained his first interest, Ballin quickly extended his influence into every aspect of the line's operation. After 1888, the HAPAG may fairly be said to be his creation and the product of his genius. Under Ballin's direction, the line in the following decade added eleven new routes and increased the number of ships serving other connections already in existence.[25] At the same time, Ballin effected a number of reforms in the design and employment of his ships.

In 1881, the North German Lloyd introduced a type of ship which remains today, with enormous modernization, the standard oceanic liner. These vessels were the so-called *Schnelldampfer*, craft designed to serve cabin passengers in speed and elegance unlike the stolid, profitable, older ships with their plain accommodations and leisurely pace. The Hamburg-American Line, reluctant to sink the large sums required to construct such luxury liners, at first declined to follow the Lloyd's lead. But in 1887, due to Ballin's enthusiastic recommendations, the HAPAG let contracts for two such ships, the *Auguste Victoria* and the *Columbia*, which were first put into service during the summer season of 1889 and which quickly

[24] Schinckel, *Lebenserinnerungen*, p. 266.
[25] The most satisfactory manner in which to trace the growth of the HAPAG is to read the company's Annual Reports. See Huldermann, pp. 166-68, for a summary.

22

captured the coveted Blue Ribbon of the Atlantic from the older Lloyd *Schnelldampfer*.

The Hamburg-American Line's two new ships were noted for interior arrangements calculated to pamper passengers. The HAPAG proudly declared the liners to be "unsurpassed in regard to their appointments and to the comfort of their accommodations."[26] The *Auguste Victoria* went to sea complete with a rococo stairhall, illuminated by a milky way of pear-shaped prisms and naked light bulbs clutched by gilded cherubs, a reception court choked with palm trees and a dark and gothic smoking room. If Ballin's taste was faulty, it was unquestionably in tune with the times, and from the moment the *Auguste Victoria* docked in New York on its maiden voyage greeted by 30,000 curious onlookers the ship was an immediate success with the oceangoing carriage trade, even though it shook and rattled alarmingly in heavy seas.[27]

Ballin's swift luxury liners, although winning the acclaim of those who could afford to travel on them, did not prove economical. In order to maintain high speeds, the ships had to devour gigantic quantities of coal, and therefore there was little room left over for freight. Moreover, the ships carried relatively fewer steerage passengers and therefore produced income only in the six-month period between April and October during which affluent Americans and Europeans were on the move. In winter, such luxury vessels, unlike the slower ships on which emigrant traffic predominated, crossed the ocean half empty. And in exceptionally bad weather, the HAPAG could not risk sending the costly ships down the ice-packed Elbe to be-

[26] Annual Report, 1887.

[27] For the *Schnelldampfer*, see R. Landerer, *Geschichte der Hamburg-Amerikanischen Paketfahrt Actien Gesellschaft zur Feier des fünfzigjährigen Bestehens der Gesellschaft*, Hamburg, 1897; Himer, *Geschichte der Hamburg-Amerika Linie*, pp. 17-18; Huldermann, pp. 32-37.

gin the voyage across the Atlantic. To offset these disadvantages, at the turn of the century Ballin instituted long
Mediterranean and Far Eastern cruises for his *Schnelldampfer* during the winter months. Defects they had, but
the prestige value of these elegant liners for the HAPAG
was incalculable.

The Hamburg-American Line's business was profits,
however, and though Ballin continued to be keenly aware
that glamor, together with the more prosaic factors of
dependability, punctuality, convenience, and economy,
played a not unimportant role in attracting customers,
after 1896 most HAPAG liners were less romantic and more
remunerative. The first such ship was the cyclopean
Pennsylvania (1896), the largest ship then afloat, a plain
but comfortable liner of only moderate speed but one
which proved very economical because of its extensive
freight capacity. This and other subsequent *P*-ships, all
bearing names beginning with the same letter, reflected the
company's growing conviction that freight, and not emigration, would in the future constitute the base of the
HAPAG's Atlantic service. Owing to a severe depression in
America, emigration from Hamburg fell off disturbingly
in the mid-1890's. A cholera epidemic which swept
through the city in 1892-93 was also largely responsible
for the decline, for the city government placed restrictions
on the steerage service from Hamburg until the pestilence
had disappeared. There were also factors on the other side
of the Atlantic which threatened to have an equally disastrous effect on the emigration traffic. Ballin and his fellow
directors were becoming increasingly concerned by American nativism, and there was uncertainty at the HAPAG as to
how extensively American lawmakers might someday move
to thwart the entry of those Europeans they considered
ethnically undesirable.[28]

[28] See the company's Annual Report for 1896, in which the fu-

If the future of emigration was therefore somewhat open to doubt, there were fewer clouds obscuring the prospects for trade with the United States. It was true that freight rates were low, but the HAPAG expected that the economy of the *P*-ships would compensate for this disadvantage. The volume of the HAPAG's trade with America fluctuated; in some years it was necessary for its ships to carry extra coal as ballast, while at other times the line had to charter ships to keep up with its business. The HAPAG was concerned that the Congress might raise the tariff, a move that seemed likely in the mid-1890's should the Republicans triumph in the 1896 elections. Even if this happened, however, Ballin was optimistic that trade between Germany and the United States would continue to increase, though perhaps at a reduced rate.[29] The real work of the Hamburg-American Line after 1896, if the less dramatic aspect of its history, was the expansion of freight services to almost every corner of the world. Ship after ship slid down the launching rails and steamed away under the blue and white HAPAG ensign, and by the end of the century the line had become the largest steamship company in the world, claiming to possess more tonnage than the entire merchant marine of any nation in continental Europe except Germany.[30]

The HAPAG's judgment that the future lay with freight did not prove erroneous, and almost every succeeding year brought a pronounced increase in the quantity of goods forwarded on its ships. Each year, a new connection, a modernized service, or an improved agency was opened. Unlike the changes prior to 1896, these alterations dealt with the business of moving freight from one part of the

---

ture of emigration and freight services to America is considered in detail.

[29] Annual Reports, 1895-96.   [30] *ibid.*, 1899.

world to another. But the line's passenger ships were not forgotten, and their *renomée* for speed and service in some classes, and for economy in others, often overshadowed the stalwart accomplishments of its more pedestrian freighters. The fact that it was Albert Ballin who had been primarily responsible for the company's success found recognition in his appointment in October 1899 as managing director of the Hamburg-American Line.

CHAPTER II

The World Is My Field: The West

AT FORTY-TWO, the new managing director was, as a German diplomat frankly observed, "something less than handsome."[1] A good, if somewhat spiteful, friend enlarged on the subject with graphic candor. The Berlin banker Carl Fürstenberg, who was himself frequently mistaken for King Edward VII, noted that Ballin's face appeared as though "formed of rubber, so that on first appearance it had an almost comic effect."[2] It was indeed a rather bizarre profile. The large head, framed by tight black curls which eventually grayed at the temples and retreated toward the crown, was perpetually inclined to one side. A calabash nose hung over a carefully trimmed moustache, which in turn obscured a pair of puffy lips. Ballin's dark and welcoming eyes, however, beckoning behind a pince-nez, seldom failed to elicit a wondering comment from those who knew him. Those "piercing, passionate, wise, truly 'speaking' eyes"—so Theodor Wolff recalled them—coupled with a resonant, melodious voice, made up for whatever was lacking in the composition or arrangement of his other features.[3] He made much of limited endowments.

Like Ballin's arresting exterior, curious if not really ugly and yet somehow admittedly attractive, there were contradictions in the man's personality and behavior. A figure

[1] Richard von Kühlmann, *Erinnerungen*, Heidelberg, 1948, 214.
[2] Hans Fürstenberg, *Carl Fürstenberg: die Lebensgeschichte eines deutschen Bankiers*, Wiesbaden, n.d., p. 436; see also A. Petzet, *Heinrich Wiegand: ein Lebensbild*, Bremen, 1932, p. 33.
[3] Wolff, *Der Marsch durch zwei Jahrzehnte*, Amsterdam, 1936, p. 238.

27

of considerable sartorial fashion, from formal attire to yachting dress Ballin wore his clothes with a knowing grace and mixed easily with men of high station. He wrote and spoke in a facile style; his letters which have survived are short and persuasive, sometimes witty, almost never contrived. Ballin's manners were faultless, and he possessed an intuitive sense of the appropriateness of this gesture or that remark. Here was a man of elegance and refinement, at home in society though of humble lineage.[4] "The genial Jew," his best friend hailed him—warm, considerate, generous to extravagance, yet endowed with a temper whose inflammability was notorious. "Ballin raged," recalled a junior associate who had once unavoidably kept the great man waiting for an hour, "and by God Ballin could rage."[5] He was, however, quick to regret his frequent loss of self-control, and he seldom failed to try to mend feelings he had hurt. A man of immense industry and ambition who had risen to the top of a strenuously competitive business, Ballin was straightforward and unquestionably honorable but also capable of a ruthlessness and hard-heartedness which others, particularly his rivals, bitterly condemned. He was, at the same time, a person of exceedingly delicate feelings, easily piqued, and swift to sense insult where often none was

[4] Such knowing judges of deportment as Prince Bülow and Count Bernstorff remarked on Ballin's assurance in society. See Bernhard Fürst von Bülow, *Denkwürdigkeiten*, 4 vols., Berlin, 1930-31, III, 285; Johann Heinrich Graf Bernstorff, *Memoirs of Count Bernstorff*, trans. Eric Sutton, New York, 1936, pp. 101-02. Theodor Wolff, who prided himself on being a judge of such matters, contrasted Ballin's poise with that of the lead-footed *Bankdirektoren*, and Bernhard Guttmann observed that he was more self-assured in the presence of the *haut monde* than was, for all his efforts, Walther Rathenau. Wolff, *Marsch*, pp. 239-42; Guttmann, *Schattenriss einer Generation 1888-1919*, Stuttgart, 1950, p. 243.

[5] Haller "Nachlass," p. 2.

intended; he also possessed an almost feminine sensitivity, became enthralled by questions of taste and design, and involved himself with gusto in the most miniscule matters of etiquette and propriety. Ballin was, certainly, a man who had much to offer those who knew him best: an open friendliness, modesty, and a desire to please which—so at least his critics held—bordered on servility. He was intelligent and well-informed, a marvelous host, an imaginative raconteur, and a knowledgeable *Feinschmecker*. But Ballin could also be overly impulsive, given to instantaneous decisions on business and political affairs and to equally quick assessments of personalities. The rapidity with which Ballin acted often proved an asset, but there were also many situations in which he had, on reflection, to revise or reverse what he had done or thought. Because he himself moved at such an accelerated pace, Ballin was impatient of others whose minds functioned in a more leisurely fashion. He was also prejudiced, imperious, and volatile, and—perhaps this was the aspect of his personality which most frequently puzzled his friends—unpredictable, forever oscillating between an optimistic exuberance and a neurotic, despairing, and cynical fatalism.

Ballin's day began in the imposing sandstone pile near the outer Alster lake—"a palazzo" declared a jealous millionaire—where he lived in punctilious opulence with his wife and daughter. Marianne Rauert, whom Ballin married in January 1883, was descended from a middle-class Gentile family in Hamburg. A handsome woman, a few years older and several inches taller than her husband, Frau Ballin, according to a Hamburg socialite who knew her, was a "napkin folder" rather than an inspired hostess. Retiring by nature, she did not enjoy the role which Ballin's prominence thrust upon her. But she was pleasant, kindly, and devoted to her husband, and she performed her social obligations, if not with éclat, as-

suredly with dignity. Their marriage, a happy and con-
genial one, proved childless, and in 1894 the Ballins
adopted a two-year old orphan, a survivor of the cholera
epidemic which had just ravaged Hamburg and claimed
her parents among its victims. Little Irmgard, or "Peter,"
became a great favorite of her father, and Ballin's family
provided him a quiet haven where he could find release
from his increasingly complicated business and political
activity.

From his house, Ballin could walk along the Alster
promenade to the ornate building which the Hamburg-
American Line had erected along the water front. The
managing director's office was furnished in discreet luxury,
fragrant with his favorite cut flowers and lined with por-
traits and photographs of friends and associates. Ballin
was very much lord in his own domain. Although the size
of the HAPAG forced the managing director to delegate
responsibility within the various departments of the line,
Ballin's passion for detail and his lust for perfection involved him in every aspect of his company's business,
from the selection of cigars for his passenger liners to the
design of engines for these mammoth vessels. On board
a HAPAG ship, Ballin was somewhat imperial, moving
from passenger to passenger with a word of greeting for
each, while an anxious crew stood nervously at attention.
Or he could be a capricious autocrat, commanding changes
of course or speed in order to suit his convenience.[6]

The conduct of business in the HAPAG's main office in
Hamburg was turbulent, and Ballin was always at the
center. The managing director did not seclude himself behind a battery of vice-presidents or flunkeys; his door stood
open to all who had suggestions or complaints to make
about the operation of the line.[7] The Hamburg-American

[6] *ibid.*, p. 29.
[7] Eduard Rosenbaum, "Albert Ballin: A Note on the Style of His

Line became in time the personal creation of its master, with Ballin impulsively hiring men whom he had never known before, but who appealed to him, for responsible posts in the line. Sometimes his precipitousness backfired; more often these sudden choices proved remarkably astute. Ballin had a curious and highly developed distrust of marine engineers, and no technical expert ever sat on the HAPAG board as long as he was in charge. The decline of the North German Lloyd, he often said, had been due to bad advice the line had received from its mechanical department. What was needed at the HAPAG were boldly imaginative men, willing to run risks and contemptuous of the dry world of statistics, figures, and measurements: men, in a word, very like Ballin himself.[8] Feuds and vendettas among the directors and officials of the line were endemic, and there was an anti- as well as a pro-Ballin faction within the HAPAG. A long-time member and chairman of the board, and one who often found himself at odds with the managing director, wearily observed that "*in der* HAPAG *was immer etwas los.*"[9]

Ballin's sympathy for the economic and political aspirations of German labor was limited and his relations with

Economic and Political Activities," in Leo Baeck Institute of Jews from Germany, *Year Book*, III (1958), 269, and "Albert Ballin," *Die neue Merkur*, VI, no. 2 (May 1922), 112; Bjarne Aagaard, "The Life of Albert Ballin," *Fairplay* (Jan. 26, 1922), 396; Huldermann, pp. 394-95.

[8] Ballin, "Seeschiffahrt," in *Soziale Kultur und Volkswohlfahrt während der ersten 25 Regierungsjahre Kaiser Wilhelms II.: ein Gedenkwerk in ausgewählten Einzelabschnitten*, Berlin, 1913, 627-28; *Zeitschrift*, VI (March 5, 1907), 55. See also Stubmann, pp. 116-17, and Huldermann, pp. 176-77.

[9] Max von Schinckel, *Lebenserinnerungen*, Hamburg, n.d., p. 267. For Ballin's sometimes unpleasant relations with Schinckel, see Ballin to Warburg, Oct. 28, 1909, Warburg "Nachlass," 1014/9/801. The deplorable friction between the managing director and his associates is vividly pictured in the "Nachlass" of a director, Johannes Merck.

the rank and file of the Hamburg-American Line's employees were ragged.[10] He did not, in the first place, enjoy dealing with laboring men, for he preferred sophisticated and elegant company and was uncomfortable when compelled to cope with problems accompanied by violence. Ballin once wrote to a friend that labor disputes were "the most hateful duty which is connected with my work and one which leaves me weary and enervated."[11] He took a conspiratorial view of organized labor and believed that the peril it represented could be met only if management presented a united and obdurate front. Unfortunately, he noted, German employers did not seem disposed to act in unison, nor did they receive much support from Berlin in dealing with this menacing problem.[12]

Hamburg, with its huge proletarian population and the exposure of its seafarers to working class political activity in other countries, was a socialist stronghold and the scene of much labor unrest. Ballin's thirty years with the HAPAG were punctuated by two labor crises of considerable magnitude and by an unending series of relatively minor disputes. Ballin, like the other great Hamburg shipping magnates of his day, was inclined to paternalism when labor was quiet and to a firm but not entirely unreasonable stand whenever trouble broke out. In the great harbor strike of 1896-97, the line attempted to head off trouble by offering its laborers limited wage in-

[10] Siegfried Heckscher, "Albert Ballin," *Roter Tag* (Jan. 3, 1922); Merck "Nachlass," "Erinnerungen," pp. 25-26, and II Konv. 4, vol. 2, Anlage 1. Even Ballin's admirers admitted his inability to put himself on a satisfactory footing with his workers. See Huldermann, pp. 389-92; Stubmann, p. 118; and cf. Stubmann's *Ballin: Leben und Werk eines deutschen Reeders*, Berlin-Grunewald, 1926, p. 159.

[11] Letter to Ernst Francke, April 12, 1907, Stubmann, p. 119. See also Ballin to Harden, April 24, 1913, Harden "Nachlass."

[12] Ballin to Harden, April 24, 1913, Harden "Nachlass"; Warburg to Ballin, Oct. 18, 1910, Warburg "Nachlass," 2302/9/802.

creases and other benefits, but when these offers were refused it hired scabs—most of them imported from England—and quartered them on ships standing in the Elbe so that they would be safe from reprisal by those on strike. The strikers proved no match for the HAPAG and after many long weeks without work they agreed to settle for circumscribed gains.[13]

Ten years later, the dockworkers struck again, and this time Ballin confronted them not only as managing director of the HAPAG but also as president of the *Verein Hamburger Reeder*, a body established to protect Hamburg shipping against attacks by labor and by foreign competitors. At the beginning of the strike, Ballin stipulated that no negotiations could be entered into with the seamen's union, which had called its men off their jobs, until such time as its representatives at the bargaining table were bona fide sailors and not professional "agitators." Ballin was enraged because of attacks which had been made on him in *Der Seemann*, the union's newspaper. The sheet had described the managing director as a "capitalist beast" and Ballin had replied in kind, charging the union with practicing terrorism over those workers who refused to support its policy and blaming the outside "agitators" for the paper's scandalous editorial policy.[14] Although Ballin was worried that the municipal police would not be sufficiently strong to maintain order in the city and that the shipping lines therefore might have to give in, he moved resolutely against the strikers.[15] Scabs,

[13] On the strike, see *AA*, Hamburg Nr. 2, secr., vol. 1; Ernst Baasch, *Geschichte Hamburgs 1814-1918*, 2 vols., Stuttgart and Gotha, 1924-25, II, 245-48; Huldermann, pp. 389-90.

[14] *Zeitschrift*, v, no. 8 (April 20, 1906), 70-72; VI, no. 8 (April 5, 1907), 74-76.

[15] Heyking (Prussian minister to the Hanseatic cities and the Mecklenburgs) to chancellor Bülow, April 28, 1906, *AA*, Hamburg Nr. 1, vol. 3, reel 166/00354-57.

33

again Englishmen, were brought to Hamburg, and there was no interruption in the HAPAG's business. In order to undermine labor associations, the line drew up a system of job categories, some of which were to be closed to union members in the future. The Social Democratic representatives in the Reichstag—including August Bebel, who held a seat for Hamburg—protested violently and maintained that the line's action was not only illegal but insulting to the workers' dignity as well.[16] As in 1896-97, the strikers eventually capitulated and agreed to a settlement which met only part of their demands.

At the same time, Ballin was engaged in a quarrel with the HAPAG's captains and engineers, almost all of whom belonged to the *Verein der Kapitäne und Offiziere der Handelsmarine in Hamburg*. Immediately after becoming managing director, Ballin announced that he wanted the line's officers to avoid any association with the union, but his interdict went unheeded and well over half of the HAPAG's officers retained their memberships. Personal accusations by union officials and Ballin excoriating one another followed.[17] The antagonism between Ballin and his officers grew acute when, in 1906, the *Verein* became involved in a controversy with the Woermann Line. The Woermanns charged that its officers were fraternizing with the Social Democrats and declared that such traffic was incompatible with the dignity of a merchant marine officer. The *Verein* denied the accusation and brought an injury suit against the Woermann Line for having falsely labeled it as socialist. A particular butt of Ballin's wrath was Walter Freyer, a former North German Lloyd employee

[16] *Reichstag*, XL. Legislaturperiode, II. Session, vol. 40, 111. Sitzung, May 23, 1906, remarks by Herzfeld, cols. 3504-06, and Bebel, cols. 3451-52.
[17] *ibid.*, X. Legislaturperiode, I. Session, vol. 6, 176. Sitzung, March 26, 1900, remarks by deputies Metzger, col. 4966; Raab, col. 4981; and Hahn, col. 4988.

who was now the union's chairman.[18] Ballin despised Freyer and tried in vain to have him ejected from his position. The officers' union, like its counterpart among the ordinary sailors, published a paper, *Die Seefahrt*, which was predictably hostile to Ballin. In December 1906, the HAPAG-led *Verein Hamburger Reeder* announced publicly that any officer of a member line known to belong to the union would be dismissed. This threat had the desired result, and 305 of the Hamburg-American Line's 309 captains quickly renounced all connection with the union. In return, the shipping companies agreed to grant some of the officers' demands, such as the establishment of a pension fund.[19] Freyer eventually relinquished his post and the union ceased to give Ballin any more trouble.

Paralleling the HAPAG's strife with its employees was the development of a social welfare program which had been instituted in 1873, well before Bismarck's imperial *Sozialpolitik* was introduced. On becoming managing director, Ballin greatly expanded the coverage and increased the benefits of the plan. Ballin's associates were divided as to whether he was motivated by a genuine concern for the line's workers or by a cynical conviction that such a program would keep labor quiet.[20] Like the Iron Chancellor, Ballin seems to have been led to welfare measures by political rather than charitable considerations. We know, for example, that he arranged free performances for HAPAG employees at Hamburg's distinguished *Schauspielhaus* not to broaden his workers' intellectual horizons

[18] See Freyer "Nachlass" for details.

[19] *Zeitschrift*, v, no. 24 (Dec. 20, 1906), 232; vi, no. 2 (Jan. 14, 1907), 14.

[20] Merck "Nachlass," "Erinnerungen," pp. 25-26; Huldermann, p. 389; Stubmann, pp. 159-60. One of Ballin's good friends was Ernst Francke, from 1897 to 1921 the editor of *Soziale Praxis*, a journal advocating extensive private and public welfare measures. A mutual admiration for Prince Bülow seems, however, to have been what brought the two men together.

35

but because he felt that a cultural as well as a material offensive was necessary to wean them away from Social Democracy.[21] In spite of such benevolence from above, Ballin never succeeded in winning the personal allegiance of the HAPAG's laborers, while his relations with his captains and fellow executives were always characterized by a degree of tension. For all his success in combatting the line's competitors, Ballin was never able to live entirely comfortably with the men with whom he worked.

Every afternoon, Ballin—often accompanied by his friend Max Warburg, their top hats tilted toward one another—walked to the stock exchange. Here, seated on a wicker couch in the HAPAG's *Kontor*, he conversed with his fellow buisnessmen, collecting and dispensing useful information. Ballin's appearance at the exchange as the head of the greatest steamship company, not only in Hamburg but in the world, must have aroused feelings of irritation as well as admiration among the mercantile patricians of the city. Seldom if ever in Hamburg's history had an ascent been so rapid yet launched from circumstances of such meager promise. Ballin had sprung to prominence from surroundings which had little in common with those of the men whose peer, as managing director of the Hamburg-American Line, he now became. He was, first of all, a Jew in a city whose ruling class had not always hastened to welcome non-Gentiles. In Ballin's time there was little open animosity toward Jews in Hamburg. As Max Warburg wrote to his brother Aby in 1913: "Here, in Hamburg, there is no open anti-Semitism, but much latent anti-Semitic feeling."[22] Business

[21] Heyking to Bülow, April 20, 1907, *AA*, Hamburg Nr. 1, vol. 4, reel 339/00617-19.

[22] George L. Mosse, *The Crisis of the German Ideology: Intellectual Origins of the Third Reich*, New York, 1964, p. 145. Mosse is confused as to which Warburg was the writer; it seems more likely to me that it was Max. See note 52, p. 335. For the vicissi-

relations were generally very cordial, but in the realm of society Hanseatic custom sometimes prescribed a rigid segregation of the races. Thus Jews and Gentiles, who had negotiated with each other at the exchange, took separate tables at the Alster Pavillon during the coffee hour at the close of the day's trading.[23]

Ballin's religious life was quite nominal, limited to a rare appearance in the synagogue, an occasional donation to a Jewish cause, and a qualified interest in Zionism. Unlike his friend Walther Rathenau, he never turned his back on his heritage and was critical of those who did so.[24] Some Jews, certainly, had become distinguished leaders in Hamburg's affairs. The Warburg dynasty, prominent in the city's financial circles since the end of the eighteenth century, presided over one of Europe's great private banking houses, and by Ballin's day the family was one of immense wealth, distinction, and prestige. No Jews, however, had achieved notable success in Hamburg's shipping trade. In view of his undistinguished origins, Ballin could not be reckoned among the *königliche Kaufleute*. But in Hamburg, where commerce ruled, a striking advance such as Ballin's at the HAPAG did much to counteract mediocrity of birth. Ballin's business success, combined as it was with modesty, tact, and a rare charm of manner, made his inclusion in the city's business elite easier than it might ordinarily have been.

Ballin became a friend of all the great men of the city, the Laeiszes, Burchards, Woermanns, and other Elbe magnates, men from whose ranks the *Bürgermeister* and

tudes of Hamburg's Jewry, see Percy E. Schramm, *Hamburg, Deutschland, und die Welt . . .* , Munich, 1943, pp. 411-24; Baasch, *Geschichte Hamburgs*, II, 106-08.

[23] Gustav Mayer, *Vom Journalisten zum Historiker der deutschen Arbeiterbewegung: Erinnerungen*, Vienna, 1949, pp. 154-55.

[24] Merck "Nachlass," "Erinnerungen," p. 185; Huldermann, pp. 388-89.

other civic dignitaries were chosen, and men who were either his competitors or his associates on the board of the Hamburg-American Line. As the years went by, Ballin spent less and less time in Hamburg, travelling instead over his far-flung empire and becoming increasingly concerned with political affairs in Berlin as the HAPAG expanded and his acquaintance with leading figures in Germany and in other nations deepened. Externally, the managing director lost none of the marks of his origin. His accent was immediately identified, and he ate, drank, and smoked in the Hamburg manner. But Ballin gradually became more than a citizen of Hamburg, more really than a German: he was a *Weltbürger*, embroiled in the taxing complexities of international commerce and an occasional participant in the practice of European politics. Unlike his fellow merchants, he did not involve himself in the various municipal bodies charged with the administration of the city. He was never *Bürgermeister* nor even a member of the *Bürgerschaft*, and no Ballin escutcheon today adorns the Rathaus façade as do those of many less famous men of Hamburg. He held no membership in the *Handelskammer*, though it once awarded him its highest decoration. Ballin's rare appearances to present his views before that body were a matter of great interest, and he was treated, a friend recalled, rather like the "representative of a foreign power."[25] Fellow citizens were anxious to win his support for municipal projects, and often Ballin gave advice, or money, or used his influence in Berlin to Hamburg's advantage. But he viewed local patriotism as a stultifying *Kirchturmspolitik*, and he sometimes refused to serve as spokesman for the city's interests.[26] Ballin

[25] Letter of Eduard Rosenbaum, secretary of the *Handelskammer* 1918-34, to author, Jan. 13, 1963.
[26] Ballin to Warburg, Dec. 16, 1909, Warburg "Nachlass," 1014/9/801; same to same, Feb. 10 and April 19, 1911, *ibid.*,

once even went so far as to suggest that Hamburg's economic future would be more promising if the city were
annexed to Prussia, a proposition regarded on the Elbe as
the most incredible heresy.[27]

Managing Hamburg's greatest maritime concern was a
very complicated task. The Hamburg-American Line's
business was divided into two separate but closely related
departments: passenger and freight. The movement of
people on the Atlantic always proved more difficult and
unpredictable than that of goods, and it was primarily to
the problems connected with this passenger traffic with the
west that Ballin addressed himself.

The bulk of the HAPAG's passengers continued to be
emigrants making their way to the Americas, but the
ethnic composition of the horde pouring into Hamburg
to board ships changed radically in the second half of the
nineteenth century. By 1850, the industrial revolution in
Germany began to create enough jobs to provide for those
unable to find farm lands, and native German emigration
slowly decreased. Twenty years later, it had fallen off decidedly in favor of floods of emigrants from the Austro-
Hungarian empire and Russia.[28] With the addition of

2302/9/802, for Ballin's efforts to have the federal court for colonial affairs transferred to Hamburg. On his refusal to assist
in the founding of a university in Hamburg, see Werner von Melle,
*Dreissig Jahre hamburger Wissenschaft 1891-1921: Rückblicke und
persönliche Erinnerungen*, 2 vols., Hamburg, 1923-24, II, 448. See
also Wolff, *Marsch*, p. 241.

[27] Bülow (Prussian minister to the Hanseatic cities and the
Mecklenburgs) to under state secretary Zimmerman, May 25, 1911,
AA, Hamburg Nr. 1, secr., vol. 1, reel 166/00462-63. See also
Huldermann, p. 387.

[28] In the 1850's, German emigration from Hamburg made up
81% of the total, in the 1860's, 77%, and by the 1870's, only
58%. In the same period the average Austro-Hungarian-Russian

large numbers of Slavic emigrants the management of emigration services became extremely complicated. Not only did the two east European governments impose measures which attempted to restrict the mobility of their citizens, but the emigrants themselves, for the most part people of scant education and barbaric notions of hygiene, posed severe problems for the lines engaged in removing them to a more advanced civilization across the Atlantic.

There were, moreover, difficulties in Hamburg itself. In the 1870's and 1880's, the Senate, whose determination to regulate the emigration business had not abated, enacted a series of statutes prescribing with increasing exactitude the manner in which emigration could legally be conducted through Hamburg. Some of this legislation was justified by prevailing abuses and did much to remedy the miserable conditions in which the emigrants were forced to live both on shore and on ship. Some ordinances, however, appeared to the ship owners to be perverse and capricious interferences in a legitimate and profitable business. The friction between the city and the passenger lines reached a peak during the calamitous cholera epidemic in the summer of 1892. The municipal authorities, certain that the HAPAG's Slavic passengers were the carriers of the pestilence, refused to admit any travelers from Russia or Austria-Hungary within the city walls. The abrupt sealing of the port to east Europeans greatly reduced the HAPAG's emigration traffic. Even after Hamburg had proved itself infection-free, the Senate declined to relax some of its restrictive edicts, and much of the city's emigration business shifted to ports which did not discriminate against

---

emigration increased from an annual average of 5% to 22½%. See *Statistik des hamburgischen Staats*, Hamburg, 1871 *et seq.*, IV (1872), 111-13, which gives the percentages for 1851-70. Thereafter, the figures must be extracted from each successive volume of the *Statistik*.

the Russian and Habsburg emigrants.[29] In the annual report for 1893, the HAPAG announced that it had made an arrangement with the North German Lloyd to move the company's headquarters to Bremen and the passenger and freight depots to Nordenham on the Weser should such a course prove necessary. The Hamburg Senate, faced with the prospect of losing a corporation which annually expended over sixty million marks in Hamburg in the form of wages, purchases, or taxes, retracted the emigration statutes against which the HAPAG had protested.[30] The line stayed in Hamburg and its relations with the Senate improved, though Ballin periodically complained at the high rent it was forced to pay for dock space.

The cholera epidemic had repercussions far beyond the Elbe. The United States, anxious to avoid an extension of the European plague, refused to admit any emigrants manifesting symptoms of cholera or other diseases. The unfortunate emigrants who were rejected by American quarantine officials usually had no funds with which to pay for the return trip to Europe and as a result they became the responsibility of the ship lines. Once back in Germany, however, parish, state, and imperial relief agencies had to provide for their wants and see that they were returned to their native villages. It was therefore in the interest of the various German governments and the carriers to insure that no emigrants were rejected by the United States on grounds of poor health. To weed out the sick from the well, the Prussian government, following a suggestion by the North German Lloyd, erected a chain of "control stations" (*Kontrollstationen*) along the Russian and Austrian frontiers, a plan soon followed by the kingdoms of Saxony and Bavaria. In the future, emigrants were

---

[29] *Jahresbericht der Handelskammer zu Hamburg über das Jahr 1893*, Hamburg, 1893, pp. 5-6.

[30] *Zeitschrift*, I, no. 3 (Sept. 20, 1901), 21.

allowed to pass over into Prussia only via these points. The stations themselves were erected in 1894 by the Prussian government and then turned over to the Lloyd and HAPAG for joint administration.[31]

Foreign lines—particularly British competitors—often complained that the two German companies abused their semi-official position at these stations, forcing passengers holding tickets on non-German lines to choose between buying HAPAG or Lloyd space or being sent back to their native lands. In one acerbic newspaper skirmish, Lord Inverclyde, president of the Cunard, accused Ballin of intimidating emigrants into redeeming their Cunard passage in favor of billets on HAPAG ships before allowing them to leave the control stations with clean bills of health. Ballin did not categorically deny Inverclyde's charges, and it appears that there may indeed have been illicit cooperation between HAPAG agents and frontier police to the disadvantage of non-German carriers.[32]

Assuming no undue harassment from HAPAG or Lloyd agents, the emigrant, on arrival at the control station, was medically examined and required to show a validated passport and a railroad ticket to the port of embarkation he had chosen. If the emigrant's papers were in order and he could exhibit the necessary evidence of solvency and good health, he could then proceed. In the case of the HAPAG's

[31] On the Kontrollstationen, see Petzet, *Wiegand*, pp. 36-40, and Kurt Himer, *Geschichte der Hamburg-Amerika Linie: 2. Teil, Albert Ballin*, Hamburg, n.d., pp. 37-38.

[32] Inverclyde to editor, London *Times* (May 11, 1904); Ballin to same (May 16). A Board of Trade committee in 1918 found that one of the handicaps under which British lines had operated in the prewar period was the privileged position which the Central Powers awarded their lines at the control stations. Great Britain, Board of Trade, *Reports of the departmental committee appointed by the Board of Trade to consider the position of the shipping & shipbuilding industries after the war*, London, 1918. See also Alfred Vagts, *Deutschland und die Vereinigten Staaten in der Weltpolitik*, 2 vols., New York, 1935, I, 534.

passengers, they were sent by rail to Hamburg and on arrival were taken to the *Auswandererhallen* which the line began erecting in 1891 for the accommodation of its passengers until their ships were ready for departure.[33] This passenger depot, completed in 1904, was equipped with its own railroad terminal and was adjacent to the quays at which the ships were boarded. After the completion of this system, the emigrants never ventured into Hamburg itself to spread disease or to be taken advantage of by the urban demimonde. On arrival at the *Auswandererhallen*, the emigrants were relieved of their clothing and the contents of their baggage, all of which was then hung on revolving racks and passed through an elaborate steam disinfection process. While their belongings were being deterged, the new arrivals were bathed and examined by HAPAG doctors. In spite of the physical inspection at the control stations, many emigrants passing through the *Auswandererhallen* were found medically defective, with a particularly high incidence of disqualifying trachoma.[34] Maintaining high standards of cleanliness in the emigration center was rendered very difficult because of the resistance of many emigrants, whose hygienic obscurantism made them suspicious of the rite of purification.[35]

[33] The HAPAG's emigrant quarters are fully described in an anonymous brochure, "Die Auswandererhallen in Hamburg," Hamburg, 1904, HAPAG archive.

[34] Ludwig Beutin, *Bremen und Amerika: zur Geschichte der Weltwirtschaft und der Beziehungen Deutschlands zu den Vereinigten Staaten*, Bremen, 1953, p. 161.

[35] The Hamburg Senate reported to the Prussian Interior Ministry in 1905 that many "measures, particularly bathing and disinfecting, were taken very badly by the emigrants and so despised by not a small number that they sought to avoid passing through the *Kontrollstationen*." See *ibid*. In order to accommodate the primitiveness of the emigrants' customs, at the Hamburg center the HAPAG had to substitute *sièges à la turque* for ordinary toilets, which many emigrants had never seen and did not know how to use. See "Auswandererhallen in Hamburg," pp. 17-18.

At the HAPAG depot, those who were able paid a mark a day for room, board, baths, disinfection, and any medication required. The indigent paid nothing. More affluent emigrants could, on payment of a surcharge, put up in two more refined structures, the Hôtels Sud et Nord, where each room boasted a maximum of four beds. These establishments, like the ordinary barracks, differentiated absolutely between the sexes, and special matrons were employed to tend to the virtue of unaccompanied females. Sects and nationalities likely to quarrel with one another were separated. The line maintained churches and synagogues on the grounds, and a kosher kitchen provided for the special diet of the orthodox. Immediately before boarding ship for America, the United States consul or his deputy examined, at the HAPAG's expense, both the emigrants and the quarters they would occupy aboard.[36] As a farewell gesture, a brass band marched beside the emigrants as they walked along the piers to the gangplank.

The problems which Ballin had to resolve with unclean emigrants, hostile European governments, and the Senate of Hamburg were minor compared to those which he constantly encountered at the hands of the Hamburg-American Line's numerous competitors. The transatlantic passenger business had to cope with almost annual crises arising from the fact that although the tide of westward-bound emigration was mounting decade after decade, the increase was by no means constant. Some years were booms, while in others the HAPAG's traffic fell off noticeably because of economic depression

[36] There was much haggling about the fee involved. See Hugh Pitcairn, United States consul, to ass't. sec'y. of state William R. Day, Jan. 27, Feb. 24, March 15, April 13, and May 2, 1898, United States, Department of State, Consular Reports, Hamburg, microfilm copy in the National Archives, Washington, series T-211, reel 32, vol. 32.

on either side of the Atlantic, because of new anti-emigration legislation in Russia or in the Habsburg domains, or because new competitors entered the trade and made inroads upon its passenger revenues. Because of the unpredictable nature of the business, an attempt was made by the long-established lines near the end of the century to assign each carrier a fair percentage of the traffic and thus create a solid front against newly incorporated competitors. In this manner a system of pools and treaties came into existence regulating the Atlantic passenger business of each member line.[37] Ballin proved to be a master at negotiating the complicated arrangements. Because of his intelligence and tact, as well as his fluency in both English and German, he usually played the leading role in the meetings of representatives of the various lines.

The first such agreement, one entered into in 1886 by a number of British and German steamship companies, affected only ships sailing from Hamburg. Ballin was responsible for the inspiration and execution of this initial combination, and his efforts, if somewhat roundabout, were highly successful. Shortly after joining the HAPAG, Ballin established a Stettin-Göteborg-New York passenger service, thereby breaking what had been a dominating hold on the Scandinavian emigration traffic by British lines. At the same time, he announced the HAPAG's intention of establishing a steerage service which would call at British ports, an aggressive move inasmuch as the British had heretofore enjoyed a monopoly in

[37] The standard work dealing with the Atlantic agreements, and one on which all other accounts are based, is Erich Murken, *Die grossen transatlantischen Linienreederei-Verbände* . . . , Jena, 1922. Murken was a special assistant to Ballin for many years and later served as secretary of the central pool committee. The Merck "Nachlass" adds many details on the subject.

native emigration. As Ballin had foreseen, the British lines were sufficiently worried by the prospect of a German invasion of their preserve to agree to negotiate. So in September 1886, he went to London and quickly arrived at an understanding with his English competitors. The HAPAG agreed to stop calling at Göteborg and dropped its plans to inaugurate a service to England. In return, the British lines adjusted their fares and limited their Hamburg passengers to a specific percentage of the port's traffic. Once a settlement had been reached with the British carriers, the German lines operating out of Hamburg then drew up a common price schedule and thereby avoided the danger of a ruinous rate war.[38]

In the early 1890's, Ballin and Heinrich Wiegand, the head of the North German Lloyd, began to discuss means of creating a great transatlantic pool which would include all continental and British lines and which would have jurisdiction over all European ports offering passenger connections to the New World. The two men sent out feelers to other shipping companies, and British as well as French, Belgian, and Dutch lines entered into the negotiations. The powerful Compagnie Générale Transatlantique (CGT) soon retreated from the conference table, and just as a final agreement was within sight the English also withdrew. Eventually the pact had only four signatories: the HAPAG, the Lloyd, the Belgian Red Star Line, and the Holland-American Line. These four companies joined together in 1892 to form the first of the great transatlantic shipping pools, the North Atlantic Steamship Association (*Nordatlantischer-Dampfer-Linien-Verband*).

The North Atlantic Association was essentially a combination in which the four member lines set common prices and arrived at a mutually satisfactory division of the

---

[38] See Huldermann, pp. 27-29, for the settlement.

steerage traffic. Fares varied according to the quality of the member line's vessels, while the share of business allotted to the pool members was based on the traffic carried by each line in the ten-year period from 1882 to 1891. Provisions were made for altering this ratio in the event that one or more lines increased or decreased either their tonnage or the number of passengers carried. Each member was assigned specific European ports, which thereafter were not to be used by ships belonging to other signatories. The HAPAG, for example, was given exclusive rights in Hamburg and all other Elbe ports, Stettin, and Le Havre. Finally, the pool set maximum commissions for its agents, forbid unfair advertising directed against another member's services, and provided for a permanent secretary resident at Cologne to arbitrate disputes and administer a central headquarters.

With its clearly defined fares, percentages, and ports, the North Atlantic Association ironed out many of the difficulties facing its members. But it did not represent a comprehensive settlement, for the four lines accounted for only some 35 per cent of the total transatlantic traffic, and there was, of course, nothing to prevent the great British and French lines which refused to join the pool from setting lower fares or from maintaining their own connections at Hamburg, Bremen, and elsewhere in the pool area. In addition, the association's fare and percentage agreement concerned steerage passengers only and had no effect on first and second class business. Ballin realized that he must somehow persuade the English and French to join the pool and then extend its operations to all classes of passengers. In spite of vigorous efforts, however, neither the Cunard nor the CGT would agree to join the North Atlantic Association, and though Ballin offered a 100,000 mark prize to anyone who could devise a viable first and second class pool, no solution was forthcoming. It was not until he received some troublesome help from America that any progress was made.

The shipping industry of the United States, beset by high construction and operating costs, fell into decay in the second half of the nineteenth century. American investment in European lines, however, was extensive, and many foreign shipping lines were controlled by investors in the United States. The desirability of greater American participation in world shipping had been repeatedly expressed by business leaders and by members of Congress, but without much effect. In 1901, however, one of the captains of Wall Street decided to make himself the master of the Atlantic. In April of that year, J. Pierpont Morgan, who had just arranged the purchase of Andrew Carnegie's steel empire for almost a half billion dollars, bought a majority interest in the sizeable Leyland Line of Liverpool for a relatively paltry ten and one-half million dollars.[39] After pocketing the Leyland holdings, Morgan turned his acquisitive eye on a still greater prize, Great Britain's famous and solidly financed White Star Line, largely owned by Thomas H. Ismay, his son J. Bruce Ismay, and William James Pirrie, head of Harland and Wolff of Belfast, one of the largest shipbuilding firms in the world. Rumors immediately began to spread that Morgan was bent on establishing a gigantic shipping combine—the

[39] Morgan's biographers have paid slight attention to the financier's oceanic ambitions, which proved to be one of the few failures in an otherwise fabulous career. The more satisfactory treatments are in Lewis Corey, *The House of Morgan: A Social Biography of the Masters of Money*, New York, 1930, and Carl Hovey, *The Life Story of Pierpont Morgan: A Biography*, New York, 1911. Vagts had discussed the matter in his *Deutschland und die Vereinigten Staaten*, I, 398-406. There is, peculiarly, no personal correspondence concerning the Morgan Trust in Morgan's papers in the Morgan Library in New York City, and the archives of the United States Lines Co., which later acquired Morgan's steamship venture, are equally barren.

48

"Morgan Trust," as it was popularly hailed—to rule the sea lanes between Europe and North America.

Ballin had heard these reports as he passed through New York in May 1901 on his return from a trip to China and Japan. After reaching Hamburg, he communicated his concern at Morgan's alleged maneuvers to the German government and also drew up a memorandum on the matter for his friend, the aristocratic industrialist Guido Prince Henckel-Donnersmarck.[40] Ballin was convinced that Morgan was attempting to set up a combine in anticipation of shipping subsidies which the American financier hoped the new Republican-dominated Congress would pass. The existence of a mammoth competitor did not in itself alarm Ballin, for, as he pointed out, it was easier to negotiate with a single giant than with a collection of Lilliputians.[41] But he did envision two threats. The first was that Morgan might establish a preferential connection between his new shipping trust and the Atlantic seaboard railroads under his control, to the detriment of foreign lines remaining outside the trust. Secondly, Morgan might attempt to buy up a controlling interest in the Hamburg-American Line.[42]

Ballin consulted his friend Pirrie to determine how the HAPAG and the White Star could best cope with the Ameri-

[40] The memorandum, undated but apparently written in Aug. or Sept. 1901, is printed in Huldermann, pp. 69-74.

[41] See Ballin's article in the *Hamburger Correspondent* (Nov. 11, 1901), reprinted in *Zeitschrift*, I, no. 7 (Nov. 20, 1901), 50-51, and also the report of an interview with Ballin in the *Hamburger Nachrichten* (June 6, 1901).

[42] Vagts, *Deutschland und die Vereinigten Staaten*, I, 398. HAPAG stock, unlike that of the English lines for which Morgan was negotiating, was largely parcelled out in small holdings, making it unlikely that Morgan could have bought up a majority interest. See *ibid.*, I, 399 n3, 401, and Paul Overzier, *Der amerikanisch-englische Schiffahrtstrust, mit besonderer Berücksichtigung seiner Beziehungen zu den deutschen Dampfschiffahrtsgesellschaften*, Berlin, 1912, pp. 68-69.

can danger. Both men agreed that it would be desirable, if not quite imperative, for the two lines to come to an understanding with Morgan. To Pirrie, this meant the physical incorporation of the White Star in the trust under as generous terms as he could secure from Morgan. To Ballin, however, an understanding could only mean arriving at a modus vivendi whereby the HAPAG would retain its corporate identity and independence but establish a community of interest with Morgan. Pirrie went to New York and saw Morgan, who confirmed that he wanted to acquire the White Star. The two men thereupon worked out an agreement whereby the line, while not passing into Morgan's ownership, was to be subordinated to his envisioned trust. At the same time, Morgan declared to Pirrie that he had no intention of attempting to buy a controlling interest in the HAPAG. One of Pirrie's associates warned Ballin, however, that the trust had already begun to establish preferential arrangements with railroads in the United States under Morgan's control. Morgan was reported to be willing to negotiate some sort of agreement with the HAPAG, provided, of course, that it did not jeopardize the interests of the trust.[43]

Discussions between the HAPAG and Morgan's group were begun in London in the fall of 1901, and the first draft of an agreement was composed on September 10.[44] Though personally convinced of the necessity of reaching an accommodation with Morgan, Ballin encountered

[43] Huldermann, p. 75. Morgan's relations with American railroads on this point is unclear. George W. Perkins, a Morgan associate, later admitted that the trust would "practically result in stretching our railroad terminals across the Atlantic." Perkins declared, however, that no American railroad would receive an interest in the trust. New York *Times* (April 20, 1902). The president of the Pennsylvania Railroad informed Wiegand in July 1901 that he had no intention of joining in any deal with Morgan. Petzet, *Wiegand*, p. 88.

[44] HAPAG, "Privat-Post."

50

considerable difficulty in persuading the HAPAG board to follow his lead. Some directors feared the economic consequences and others the political ramifications of such a move.[45] Finally, however, he succeeded in obtaining unanimous, if grudging, approval for the terms which he had worked out in London. But this was not enough. Ballin declared that he was unwilling to carry out the agreement unless both the Kaiser and the chancellor consented to its provisions.

Count Bülow's reaction to rumors of Morgan's activity is unknown. The Kaiser, characteristically, pictured the trust as a sinister plot by the American plutocracy to prostrate Germany, if not Europe itself.[46] On October 16, 1901, Ballin was summoned to Berlin to explain to William II what was afoot. Ballin was able to satisfy his sovereign that under the terms of the proposed arrangement the HAPAG would retain complete independence. The Kaiser and Ballin then thoroughly examined the text of the document, and William made a number of corrections.[47] After several hours of close scrutiny, the Kaiser announced his unqualified approval of the plan but also charged Ballin with seeing that the Lloyd as well was brought into affiliation with the trust.[48]

On the following day, Ballin and Wiegand attended a conference with several members of various government

[45] Undated letter of Johannes Merck to Walter Freyer, Freyer "Nachlass," I, 13, 47-48. See also Schinckel, *Lebenserinnerungen*, p. 271.

[46] Gaston de Ségur, "Impressions de Norvège," *La Revue de Paris*, XVI (Nov.-Dec. 1901), 76-94. See also W. T. Stead, *The Americanization of the World: Or the Trend of the 20th Century*, New York and London, 1901, pp. 171-72. Cf. Vagts, *Deutschland und die Vereinigten Staaten*, I, 404 n2.

[47] HAPAG, "Privat-Post," second draft, dated Nov. 6, 1901, which bears marks of the Kaiser's suggestions.

[48] For Ballin's meeting with the Kaiser see Huldermann, pp. 77-79.

51

departments, including the Foreign Office (*Auswärtiges Amt*) and the Imperial Naval Office (*Reichsmarineamt*). The purpose of the meeting, according to a memorandum drawn up later, was to discuss "measures to protect German steamship lines from falling into American hands."[49] Ballin argued that Morgan's trust represented a grave peril for both German lines and that the HAPAG and the Lloyd must therefore affiliate with Morgan under as favorable conditions as could be obtained. Wiegand was strongly opposed to Ballin's intention to cooperate with the trust, and he said so frankly. The Lloyd chief admitted that there was some possibility of danger arising from Morgan's maritime schemes, but he did not consider the peril to be imminent enough to compel the German lines immediately to join forces with the American group. William II, anxious to resolve Ballin and Wiegand's differences, invited both men to dinner. The jealous rivals flanked their ruler left and right, with William pointedly sympathizing with Ballin and berating Wiegand as an "obstinate Frisian" (*eigensinniger Friese*). It proved that Wiegand's principal objection to the combine was a stock participation plan provided for in the draft, and Ballin therefore proposed that his provision be altered in favor of some more satisfactory formula. Thanks to the ingenuity of Adolf von Hansemann of the *Disconto-Gesellschaft* a compromise was worked out whereby the two German lines agreed to pay the trust a share of whatever dividends they might declare in the future in return for a fixed annual payment to each line from the trust.[50]

Once the German lines had formed a common front, a treaty with Morgan could be signed. On February 20,

[49] HAPAG, "Privat-Post," photostatic copy of an unsigned report concerning a meeting in Berlin on Oct. 17, 1901.

[50] Petzet, *Wiegand*, p. 84; Vagts, *Deutschland und die Vereinigten Staaten*, I, 399-402.

1902, Ballin, Wiegand, and Morgan's representatives signed the final instrument, which was to be formally ratified by the participants before January 1st of the following year.[51] The agreement provided for the annual payment plan and declared that no trust ship would inaugurate services to Germany, while all three parties agreed not to acquire stock in each other's enterprises. The trust furthermore granted exclusive rights for routes to and from East Asia and the West Indies and New York to the HAPAG, provided that the German line did not increase its tonnage on these routes. A first and second class passenger pool was to be established, with steerage quotas being arrived at by the North Atlantic Association agreement of 1892. The HAPAG and the Lloyd promised in return not to send any steamers to Great Britain or Belgium, though this provision did not affect the maintenance of the lines' existing services. Any extension of established routes, or the inauguration of new ones, was to be discussed by the signatories, and arrangements were made for noncompulsory arbitration of disputes.[52].

The treaty with Morgan signed by the HAPAG and the

[51] The HAPAG archive possesses the original treaty, filed in Miscellany, vol. 58, "Internat. Mercantile Marine Co.," and the ratification, delayed until Feb. 5, 1903, in "Contract Buch, geh[eim]," pp. 43-44.

[52] In a simultaneous maneuver, Morgan purchased 51% of the shares of the Holland-American Line, a quarter of which he in turn sold to each of the two German lines, thereby enlarging their newly established community of interest. See HAPAG archive, "Contract Buch, geh.," agreement of April 7, 1902, between J. P. Morgan & Co. and the Holland-American Line, pp. 20-23; Miscellany, vol. 21, "Beteiligung 1899/1902," correspondence between Pirrie and HAPAG officials. Pirrie's share of the spoils was the so-called "Builder's Contract," whereby Harland and Wolff would be awarded construction orders for a percentage of the ships which the trust might build in the future. See Murken, *Linienreederei-Verbände*, pp. 168, 174; London *Times* (May 13, 1902). On Pirrie, see Herbert Jefferson, *Viscount Pirrie of Belfast*, Belfast, n.d., an insipid work of little value.

53

Lloyd was kept absolutely secret, for Ballin was worried about the reaction its publication would cause at home and abroad. Long before an agreement had been reached, he had warned that "under all circumstances we must avoid letting the Hamburg-American Line be represented in American and English reports as having been bought up or fused" into the trust.[53] The HAPAG's stockholders and the public were informed of the deal with Morgan at the annual meeting late in May 1902, three months after its conclusion, with great emphasis being put on the fact that the line had in no way surrendered its autonomy. Voices were raised at the meeting questioning the wisdom of the agreement. Most prominent of Ballin's critics was Dr. Diederich Hahn, a Conservative Reichstag deputy and head of the influential *Bund der Landwirte*, the mouthpiece of Prussian agrarianism. Hahn inquired if the treaty would not inevitably result in the dumping of American farm products on the German market because of Morgan's tie with railroads leading into the American Midwest. Ballin briskly replied that the American railroads were much more interested in increasing their west-bound traffic to equalize the already well developed business in the opposite direction. The agrarians, he concluded, therefore had no cause for alarm. Ballin's defense of the agreement was greeted by applause, and the stockholders —presumably including a reassured Dr. Hahn—approved

[53] HAPAG, "Privat-Post," undated note in Ballin's hand, presumably about Nov. 1, 1901; *ibid.*, photostatic copy of an unsigned report concerning a meeting in Berlin on Oct. 17, 1901. To head off any criticism, the line drafted changes in its bylaws to require that members of both *Aufsichtsrat* and *Vorstand* be German citizens resident in Germany. Corporate legislation was also adopted which provided that any shift of the company's headquarters or any merger with another corporation had to be approved at two consecutive annual meetings by an overwhelming percentage of the stockholders. See Overzier, *Morgan-Trust*, p. 70.

the measure by acclamation.[54] There were other conservatives in Germany who were less satisfied, however, and the Morgan deal produced a number of demands in the Reichstag and in the press that the HAPAG be nationalized in order to insure its remaining in German hands. The appeals for such a step attracted no following and eventually died out.[55]

The signing of the treaty was hailed as a personal triumph for Ballin, and it was even rumored that Morgan had offered him a million dollar a year salary to head the new trust.[56] The Kaiser, who was thoroughly delighted with the whole affair, invested Ballin with the order of the Red Eagle, second class with crown. Morgan himself steamed across the ocean in his magnificent *Corsair* early in June and was received by William II with unusual attention. The response of the German press to the agreement was more than favorable: it was smug. Not only had Morgan taken outright possession of the Leyland Line, but the White Star and a number of smaller British lines had been reduced to little more than creatures of the American banker's oceanic ambitions. Even before the report of the trust's negotiations with the German lines had been officially announced, Berlin's *National Zeitung* remarked with gratuitous sympathy that "the blow to England is all the greater since the German companies have

[54] *Berliner Tageblatt und Handels-Zeitung* (May 28, 1902); London *Times* (May 29).

[55] Adolf Goetz, *25 Jahre hamburgische Seeschiffahrtspolitik*, Hamburg, 1911, pp. 193-201; Plutus (pseud.), "Morgan-Ballin," *Die Zukunft*, x, no. 10 (Dec. 7, 1901), 402-04; Friedrich Kleinwaechter, "Der Morgan Trust," *ibid.*, no. 48 (Aug. 30, 1902), 344-53. See also the remarks of deputy Roesicke in *Reichstag*, x. Legislaturperiode, II. Session, vol. 4, 127. Sitzung, Jan. 25, 1902, cols. 3658-63.

[56] Fürstenberg, *Lebensgeschichte*, p. 434; London *Times* (May 26, 1902); Bjarne Aagaard, "The Life of Albert Ballin," *Fairplay* (Jan. 5, 1922), 147.

55

been able to keep out of the trust and maintain their independence."[57] The British did not need the *National Zeitung* to remind them of the threat to their shipping supremacy on the Atlantic. The news of the HAPAG-Lloyd-Morgan bargain aroused much uneasiness in England, and the House of Commons felt called upon to appoint a committee "to devise means for heading off some of the ruinous effects" of the trust.[58] The agreement gave new impetus to the movement already under way in Great Britain advocating the payment of construction subsidies to merchant marine lines. Among the members of the Balfour cabinet, Joseph Chamberlain, the colonial secretary, took a particularly outspoken position against the American menace and was determined that those British shipping companies which had eluded Morgan, and especially the Cunard, preserve their independence.[59] There were many in parliament who agreed with Chamberlain, and late in 1902 the Cunard was granted an annual subsidy of 150,000 pounds, to be paid as long as the line remained entirely in British hands.

The Cunard accepted the subsidy and its conditions and gave Morgan and his German associates notice that it had no intention of giving in to its confederated rivals. In spite of Morgan's threats and cajolery, the British company declined to collaborate with the trust, a stand

[57] Edition of May 13, 1902, quoted in London *Times* (May 14). Similar commiseration is expressed in the *Berliner Tageblatt und Handels-Zeitung* (May 24). See also the report of the *Times'* Vienna correspondent (May 22), and the notice of the meeting of the General Ship Owners Society (May 16), as well as the following letters to the editor of the *Times*: C. H. Cramp (April 22), Lord Brassey (May 15), and Joseph Lawrence, M.P. (May 16).

[58] *Commercial and Financial Chronicle* (July 16, 1902), quoted in Corey, *House of Morgan*, p. 305.

[59] Chamberlain to the duke of Devonshire, Sept. 22, 1902, in James L. Garvin and Julian Amery, *The Life of Joseph Chamberlain*, 4 vols., London, 1929-51, IV, 410. See also Chamberlain to Lord Lansdowne, June 10, 1902, *ibid.*, 411.

also taken by the smaller, shakily financed and heavily subsidized CGT. The Cunard's refusal to cooperate meant that no cabin passenger pool could be created, and neither Morgan nor the German lines felt strong enough to attempt to browbeat the Cunard into adopting a more conciliatory attitude by engaging in a rate war.[60]

The Morgan combine and its collateral treaties, in the end, was not an offensive measure which clarified the status quo and enabled the members to expand under the protection of the trust, but a sterile arrangement, conceived in greed and entered into in fear by the German lines to guard themselves from what appeared at the time to be a grave danger. Signing the deal with Morgan cost the HAPAG money, for the annual dividend payments it was required to make to the trust always exceeded the fixed annual sum Morgan paid in return.[61] And its great competitor, the Cunard, received a handsome subsidy as a result of the trust threat. Ballin was satisfied, however, for the compromise with Morgan at least eliminated the danger of the American's establishing a service to German ports and thereby avoided the rate war which Ballin feared surely would have resulted.[62]

The subsequent history of the trust was a doleful record of increasing difficulty, repeated crisis, and finally failure. The New York Stock Exchange refused to list the watered stock on its board, the lively freight market resulting from the Boer War began to decline the moment the trust went into operation, investors shied away from a company so obviously overcapitalized, and Morgan was left with the bonds he had hoped to dispose of at a profit. "The ocean,"

[60] HAPAG, "Privat-Post," minutes of conclusion reached at a meeting attended by Pirrie, Ballin, and Wiegand in London, June 9-10, 1902.
[61] Overzier, *Morgan-Trust*, p. 78.
[62] Huldermann, p. 88.

commented the *Wall Street Journal,* "was too big for the old man."[63]

In the relatively uncomplicated days before J. P. Morgan ventured into the ocean trade, pooling arrangements had been a matter of business and were accomplished without much political interference from the governments under whose flags the participating ships sailed. The Morgan trust was more involved, however, for it was a matter of concern to statesmen and ordinary citizens as well as to the great shipping tycoons. The association of nationalistic sentiment with the merchant marine, paralleling the similar development of navalism at the turn of the century, was reflected during the Morgan affair in the personal intervention of the German emperor, the attitude of the German press, and in the parliamentary movement for additional shipping subsidies in Great Britain. This maritime nationalism also began to manifest itself in Italy, Austria, Hungary, Russia, and Canada at precisely the same time, with the result that the problems and tensions between the transatlantic steamship lines were substantially increased. The emergence of this new factor made the formation of the post-Morgan pools almost as much a matter of politics as of business.

The Hamburg-American Line's tangled relations with the governments of these nations has been exhaustively treated by Erich Murken in his exemplary history of the Atlantic shipping pools, and it is therefore necessary only to summarize his findings.[64]

[63] Quoted in Murken, *Linienreederei-Verbände,* p. 240.

[64] For the HAPAG's difficulties in Italy, see *ibid.,* 69, 247, 362-407, 460-66, and the HAPAG Annual Report for 1909. The Hungarian complications are treated in Murken on pp. 243-56, 270-85, 303-10, 430-35. There is additional interesting material in the "Nachlass" of Count Brockdorff-Rantzau, who served as German

Shortly after the turn of the century, Canada, Russia, Italy, Austria, and Hungary passed legislation designed to aid native shipowners by extending the state's regulatory powers over emigration and by awarding subsidies for ship construction and operation. The result was a scramble to incorporate new steamship companies, lines which were more articles of national pride than the products of sound business calculation. These new companies had poor routes—Ballin characterized Hungary's Fiume-New York connection as a "geographical rape" (*geographische Notzucht*)—and therefore did only a meager business. But they survived because of the artificial sustenance provided by the state and they became annoying quantities with which the older European lines had to reckon. To circumvent legislation favoring domestic lines, foreign carriers—including the HAPAG—were forced to incorporate subsidiary companies whose ships sailed under native registry.[65]

Under Ballin's leadership, the newly established national carriers as well as the subsidiaries of the older lines were frequently included in the North Atlantic pool system. But the Cunard, fortified by its handsome subsidy, operated as a counter power, seeking to persuade Austria, Hungary, and the other nations involved not to found native lines and enter the pools but to grant the Cunard

consul general in Budapest in the early 1900's. See reel 3434, frames 229176-84, 229070-83, 229546-47, 229577-83, 229585-91, 229754-56, 229757-65, 229897-98. Murken, pp. 256-64, 495-520, 560-65, deals with the Austrian situation. On the HAPAG and Russia, see Murken, pp. 297-303, 415-27; Warburg to Ballin, Feb. 15 and April 19, 1912, Warburg "Nachlass," 2302/9/802. For a curious but questionably accurate portrayal of some of the line's activities in Russia, see the *Sigilla Veri* (*Ph. Stauff's Semi-Kürschner*) . . . , 5 vols., Erfurt, 1929-32, I, 371.

[65] *Nauticus: Jahrbuch für Deutschlands Seeinteressen*, II (1900), 367n.

emigration monopolies. The British line did not succeed in this plan and shifted instead to a policy of attempting to secure privileges in St. Petersburg, Vienna, and elsewhere which would protect it from competition from other lines. Particularly in the Habsburg domains, the Cunard waged a continuous battle to wrest business from the HAPAG and the Lloyd. At every turn, Inverclyde's Cunard stepped forward to challenge Ballin and his associates. No peaceful solution appeared possible, even though emigration was booming after 1900 and there was ample business for everyone.

It was only in 1907, as rumors arose that a transatlantic rate war was imminent, that the Cunard agreed to negotiate. The line was desperately short of cash, for it had just sunk immense sums into three new passenger liners, one of which was the subsequently ill-fated *Lusitania*. In February 1908, Ballin went to England and presided over a series of talks which resulted in the establishment of the North Atlantic Conference, a body closely resembling, but much more comprehensive than, the old North Atlantic Association of 1892. The Cunard and ten other member lines, representing the major north Atlantic steamship companies with the exception of the CGT, agreed on price schedules for first and second class passengers and established minimum rates and a percentage pool for the steerage traffic.[66] Ballin was delighted with the agreement, as was the Kaiser, who awarded him another order to mark the occasion. Ballin hoped that the amicable settlement of the shipping question would soon be followed by an improvement in diplomatic relations between Great Britain and Germany.[67]

[66] The agreement is printed in Murken, *Linienreederei-Verbände*, pp. 659-79.

[67] Lucius (Prussian chargé in Hamburg) to Bülow, Feb. 18, 1908, *AA*, Türkei Nr. 165, vol. 28, reel 455/00871-72.

After 1908, the Cunard's dealings with the continental lines were for the most part entirely satisfactory, and the Conference did much to relax one tension which had complicated Anglo-German relations for many decades. The Hamburg-American Line and the North German Lloyd could never successfully compose their differences, however, and the discord between the two German lines grew worse after the establishment of the North Atlantic Conference. The fault lay in Hamburg rather than in Bremen. The cause of the quarrel was the HAPAG's construction of three superliners, the *Imperator* (1912), *Vaterland* (1913), and *Bismarck* (1914), and Ballin's insistence that the addition of these three leviathans entitled his line to a correspondingly larger share of the Conference steerage pool. The Lloyd, backed by the other Conference members, summarily rejected Ballin's demand, since pool percentages were traditionally based on passenger figures for past years rather than on projected increases because of recently constructed tonnage. Moreover, the HAPAG's claim seemed particularly unwarranted since, at the time Ballin made his proposal, the *Bismarck* had not even been launched, much less outfitted for sea. Ballin declared that the unfavorable reaction to his demand obliged the HAPAG to sever its relations with the Conference, and on January 31, 1914, it formally withdrew.

Owing, once again, to the intervention of the Kaiser, Ballin agreed to reconsider his move and accepted an interim pooling arrangement until the dispute between the lines could be resolved. Talks between representatives of the various companies to work out a definitive settlement were begun in Berlin in April. William II, thinking to create a mood conducive to reconciliation, commanded a gala performance of "Aïda" at the royal opera to which he invited all the negotiators. Subsequent conversations went smoothly and good progress was made by the German,

British, and American lines toward finding a compromise. A conference to iron out the last difficulties was set for Wednesday, August 5, 1914. By then, of course, all the laboriously contrived and carefully balanced agreements which Ballin had brought about were only meaningless scraps of paper.

CHAPTER III

The World Is My Field: The East

O N THE next to last day of the nineteenth century, Adolph Woermann, head of one of Hamburg's leading private shipping lines and the man for whom Bismarck many years earlier had coined the expression "*königlicher Kaufmann*," delivered the annual presidential address to the municipal *Handelskammer*. Woermann's message to his fellow merchants was that it was time for a change, that the opening of a new century must occasion an intensification of the old Hanseatic spirit of commercial discovery and expansion. Hamburg, the ageing seafarer declared, "must turn its gaze to distant lands and manifest its individuality and its power in these places if it intends to retain its position among the powers. . . ."[1] Woermann's exhortation could only in 1899 have referred to the East, and his audience responded a few months later by joining with a number of Bremen business leaders in forming an *Ostasiatischer Verband* to stimulate interest in trade with the Orient.

Ballin, however, had anticipated Woermann. In the mid-1890's, he had begun to argue that the Hamburg-American Line could not depend solely on the Atlantic for its livelihood. The transatlantic trade, in both goods and passengers, was one whose size fluctuated greatly, in which competition was intense, and in which outbreaks of disease, the vagaries of lawmakers, the tastes of travelers

---

[1] Günther Jantzen, *Hamburgs Ausfuhrhandel im XX. Jahrhundert: ein Beitrag zur Geschichte eines deutschen Kaufmannsständen und des "Verein Hamburger Exporteure" 1903-1953*, Hamburg, 1953, p. 8.

and climatic or economic reverses might suddenly result in a disastrous decline in business. The early years of the decade had provided the HAPAG with an instructive lesson in how quickly good times could turn to bad in the Atlantic. First bad harvests and cattle disease undermined the freight market; next cholera all but ruined the passenger trade. No sooner were these problems overcome than depression in America did further damage to both branches of the HAPAG's business. Ballin had therefore come to the conclusion that the line must widen its field of operations in order to diminish its dependence on America. With shipping connections to many points, the risks involved in any one market could be spread, and a bad year in one area would hopefully be offset by a good one in another part of the world.[2]

It was natural that Ballin's thought, like Woermann's, had turned to the Orient when he considered to what parts of the world the HAPAG's services might be extended. The Atlantic from Labrador to Capetown was thoroughly covered by German freighters and passenger ships, and it had been Woermann himself who in the late 1860's had opened the West African coast to German shipping. Beyond the Atlantic, however, the seas and their commerce in the late nineteenth century belonged for the most part to Great Britain, and the number of German merchantmen spotted beyond Good Hope or the Straits of Magellan was not great.

In 1900, China constituted the principal locale for German shipping outside the Atlantic. The number of German ships in China and the quantity of goods shipped between China and Europe in German bottoms was very modest, however, although there was considerable activity

[2] Huldermann, pp. 109-10; HAPAG Annual Reports, 1890-96. See also pp. 24-26.

by German ship lines in the Chinese coastal trade.[3] Several thousand German merchants were resident in the great harbors and inland trade centers of the Celestial Empire. But everywhere in the country and in every occupation, it was the British who predominated and who were the most numerous among the Europeans. The Chinese littoral by the end of the century had assumed a distinctively English character. The British, under the energetic command of Sir Robert Hart, played a predominant role in the Chinese customs service, English served as the lingua franca, Englishmen were in charge of many of the local constabularies, and English modes and manners were *de rigeur* in the European colonies.

Relations between German and Englishman in China were for the most part quite good. Lord Charles Beresford, who traveled extensively through the land in 1898-99 in

[3] On German shipping in China, see Hermann Wätjen, "Die deutsche Handelsschiffahrt in chinesischen Gewässern um die Mitte des 19. Jahrhunderts," *Hansische Geschichtsblätter*, 67/68 (1942-43), 222-50; Maj. Max Schlagintweit, "Deutsche Seeschiffahrt nach Ostasien," *Asien*, II, no. 4 (Jan. 1903), 55-58; Adalbert Korff, "Der direkte deutsch-chinesische Schiffahrtsverkehr von seiner Entstehung bis zum Ausbruch des Weltkrieges," diss., Kiel (1922); Heinz Beutler, "Hundert Jahre Carlowitz & Co.: Hamburg und China," diss., Hamburg (1948).
The extent of Germany's trade with the Far East is best followed in the *Statistik des deutschen Reichs*, Berlin, 1873 *et seq.*, and in the official statistical surveys of Hamburg and Bremen, especially the *Statistik des hamburgischen Staats*, Hamburg, 1871 *et seq.* Much of this material is summarized in Helmuth Stöcker, *Deutschland und China im 19. Jahrhundert: das Eindringen des deutschen Kapitalismus*, Berlin, 1958; Otto Franke, *Die Grossmächte in Ostasien von 1884 bis 1914: ein Beitrag zur Vorgeschichte des Krieges*, Braunschweig and Hamburg, 1923; Bernhard Harms, *Deutschlands Anteil an Welthandel und Weltschiffahrt*, Stuttgart etc., 1916; Fend-chen Chang (Peng Djen Djan), *The Diplomatic Relations between China and Germany since 1898*, Shanghai, 1936; and in anon., "Die wirthschaftlichen Interessen Deutschlands in China," *Nauticus: Jahrbuch für Deutschlands Seeinteressen*, II (1900), 249-73.

behalf of the Association of British Chambers of Commerce, described Anglo-German relations at Tientsin as being on a "most sympathetic and satisfying footing," with German merchants eager to express their appreciation to the British for having pioneered the opening of so valuable an area to the traders of other nations. Similarly, Sir Eric Teichman, a long-time consular official in China, found relations between the two competitors "relatively cordial and their policies usually in line," a fact which he attributed to their mutual concern at Russian ambitions in northern China. He also noted that the German merchants in China went about hungrily drumming up business, while their British counterparts were more indolent and spent an inordinate amount of time in sports and society.[4] Germans transplanted to China found British customs officials fair and their maintenance of law and order very welcome, though they sometimes sensed a smugness about the English that was irritating.[5]

In the late 1890's, only three German firms maintained regular sailings between Germany and the East. Two, the Rickmers Line and the North German Lloyd, were located in Bremen, while the third, the *Deutsche Dampfschiffs-Rhederei zu Hamburg*, or Kingsin Line, had its headquarters in Hamburg. The Lloyd's revenues from its oriental operations were bolstered by a mail subsidy, paid to the line by the German government after 1885. The Rickmers and Kingsin lines, however, needed both more ships and more capital to render their business profitable, and

[4] Beresford, *The Breakup of China* . . . , New York and London, 1900, pp. 21-22; Teichman, *Affairs of China: A Survey of Recent History and Present Circumstances of the Republic of China*, London, 1938, pp. 73-75.

[5] On this point, see the interesting reminiscences of Otto Franke, *Erinnerungen aus zwei Welten: Randglossen zur eigenen Lebensgeschichte*, Berlin, 1954, and Elisabeth von Heyking, *Tagebücher aus vier Weltteilen 1886/1904*, Leipzig, 1926.

in 1897 the two lines turned to the HAPAG for help. On January 3, 1898, the Rickmers Line and the HAPAG together established a freight service from Hamburg to the Orient. Two months later, Ballin bought out the King-sin Line and took over its operations. The North German Lloyd, alarmed by Ballin's entry into the eastern market, decided to strike a bargain with its competitor. In February 1898, the Lloyd therefore signed an agreement with the HAPAG which provided for a joint mail and freight service to the East.[6] Anxious to encourage the China trade, the German government promised to grant both partners a subsidy. These payments were to begin in 1900, and the HAPAG's contract called for an annual grant of approximately 375,000 marks.[7] The line continued to receive this payment until 1904, when it withdrew from its contract with the government. On February 25, 1898, the first HAPAG ship left Hamburg for the East, and by the end of the year the line was sending four or five ships a month to call at Penang, Singapore, Hong Kong, Shanghai, Foochow, Tsingtao, Tientsin, Yokohama, and other ports in China and Japan. Ballin was pleased to note in the Annual Report for 1898 that freight loadings both to and from the Orient had proved quite satisfactory.

Political events as well as economic progress heightened Ballin's interest in China at the turn of the century. In November 1897, Germany occupied Tsingtao and in the following year forced the Chinese government to grant a lease for the port as well as extensive economic concessions in adjacent territory on the Shantung peninsula. The German appetite for Chinese holdings was rapidly imitated

[6] For details, see Kurt Himer, *Geschichte der Hamburg-Amerika Linie: 2. Teil, Albert Ballin*, Hamburg, n.d., pp. 44-46. There appears to be no basis in fact for the opinion advanced in Himer's account that the HAPAG's interest in the East was due to the "clear-sighted intentions" of the Kaiser.

[7] Ballin to editor, London *Times* (Aug. 28, 1901); see also *ibid.* (Nov. 13, 1901).

by Russia, France, and Great Britain, each of which extorted leases on strategic ports. The resentment of many Chinese at this expropriation culminated in the Boxer Rebellion of May 1900, which endangered the lives and property of the European community. An international relief expedition was organized, and the HAPAG was awarded the contract of transporting the German contingent, under the command of Ballin's friend, Field Marshal Count Waldersee, to the theater of operations. The task of moving this force to China proved an unprofitable one for the line, since it was required to withdraw ships both from the heavy freight trade with South Africa occasioned by the Boer War as well as from the North Atlantic passenger traffic, which was especially busy in 1900 as Americans flocked to Paris to behold the Exposition at the Trocadero.[8]

Once order had been restored in China, Ballin decided to make a trip to the Orient to investigate the possibilities of extending the HAPAG's interests there. Accompanied by Frau Ballin and a large party, Ballin departed from Hamburg by ship and proceeded east at a leisurely pace, arriving in China on February 13, 1901.[9] For six weeks, he visited the major ports and trading centers, noting the good relations which seemed to prevail between German and British merchants. He also observed the work of German firms and calculated the volume of freight and passenger business the HAPAG might develop not only between Germany and China but along the China coast and on the broad rivers of the empire. Ballin's findings confirmed his belief that European trade with China would continue to increase. While German commerce was in-

---

[8] Annual Report, 1900; Stubmann, p. 86.

[9] During the course of his trip, Ballin sent a series of long and informative letters to his aged mother and to his associates at the HAPAG. Huldermann (pp. 123-39) and Stubmann (pp. 153-71) have each printed a sampling of these *Chinabriefe*.

deed trailing behind that of Great Britain, he felt that its position was solid and that the German merchant was gradually overtaking his British competitor.[10] That being the case, there was certainly no reason why the HAPAG should not try to increase its participation in the China market. An extension of services to the Orient, Ballin warned, might not immediately result in increased profits, but the prompt establishment of a strong foothold was necessary in order to ensure that the line would share fully in the future exploitation of China.[11] Ballin laid the groundwork while still in the Far East. A headquarters for HAPAG operations was established in Hong Kong, a German line engaged in the Yangtse traffic was purchased, and docks and warehouses were acquired at Shanghai. Negotiations were begun for the absorption of other shipping lines and plans were drawn up for a Hong Kong-Vladivostok service. On his return to Germany in May 1901, Ballin was received by the Kaiser, who, on hearing Ballin's account of his trip, presented an autographed photograph to his "clairvoyant and indefatigable pioneer."[12]

Ballin realized that the British government would view with hostility any extension of the HAPAG's services to or in China. Though the traders of the two nations resident in China got on well, the interests of their governments in the area sometimes conflicted. In 1900, Great Britain and Germany were trying to effect a *détente*, if not an alliance, and part of the preliminary work toward that end was the formulation of an agreement, signed on October 16, 1900, concerning the position of the two powers in China. The wording of this document was so flatulent, however,

[10] Metternich to Bülow, June 1, 1900, *GP*, XVII, no. 5,018, p. 81; Huldermann, p. 137.

[11] Huldermann, p. 137.

[12] Noailles, ambassador in Berlin, to Delcassé, June 22, 1901, *DDF*, 2. Série, I, no. 295, pp. 342-43.

that it enabled the Germans to hold that it guaranteed the signatories equal status in the Yangtse area, while the British interpreted the text as being more favorable to themselves.[13] Relations were further disturbed by Berlin's insistence, over British protests, on maintaining a garrison in Shanghai to protect Germany's commercial interests there. German economic advances were regarded with equal suspicion, and Ballin's journey increased British fears that Germany had designs beyond the sphere of influence it had created on the Shantung peninsula. In 1916, the Austrian statesman, Josef Redlich, recorded in his diary a conversation with Alexander Count Hoyos, who as a young man had served in the Austrian consular service in China. Hoyos, Redlich noted,

> remembered how when he lived in China British diplomats expressed their grave concern at Ballin's appearance and at the forwardness (*Vordringen*) of the Germans. The most decisive point was that the German government put all its powers at the service of the very ambitious Germans in finance and industry in the Far East as well as in Asia Minor. The English said then: we don't do this; we leave our finance and our trade to their own devices in international competition. But as the Germans behave, so, too, must we—it's no longer fair competition.[14]

[13] See William L. Langer, *The Diplomacy of Imperialism 1890-1902*, 2d edn., New York, 1956, pp. 700-05.

[14] Redlich, *Schicksalsjahre Österreichs 1900-1919: das politische Tagebuch Josef Redlichs*, 2 vols., Graz and Cologne, 1953-54, II, 153. I have altered Hoyos' faulty English idiom in the last sentence. For a similar British observation on the HAPAG's activity on the Yangtse, see Schlagintweit, "Deutsche Seeschiffahrt," 56. See also *DDF*, 2. Série, I, 342-43, and the remarks of Joseph Walton, M.P., in Feb. 1904, noting that British shipping to China was falling off while Germany's was increasing, a fact which Walton attributed to Britain's failure to support its merchants abroad as energetically as other powers did. *Hansard*, 4th ser., CXXIX, col. 607.

On Ballin's return to Hamburg, reports were issued by the HAPAG concerning its plans for developing the Far East market. These statements were carried in the British press at the end of May 1901. A week later, the London *Times* printed a portion of the remarks made by Ballin in an interview in the Berlin *Lokal-Anzeiger*. Ballin, the *Times* noted, had declared that the Hamburg-American Line intended to extend its coastal and river service in China, a market in which German firms had previously lagged far behind the British. "But Herr Ballin," the article concluded, "had no reason to doubt that the English companies, without engaging in a rate war, would recognize the necessity of allowing the German flag to take a fair share of the trade."[15] A few days later, a question was addressed in the House of Commons to Viscount Cranborne, the president of the Board of Trade and prime minister Salisbury's heir, as to whether the Board was familiar with Ballin's China plans. Cranborne replied that the Board knew nothing about them and added that it would rely on British merchants to maintain England's position in China, with His Majesty's Government prepared to back them up.[16]

Ballin was undeterred by British criticism of his ambitions, and in the next few years he proceeded to expand the HAPAG's Chinese operations.[17] In 1901, a service was established from Hamburg to Shanghai, Tsingtao, and Tienstin, and a joint shipping service on the Yangtse between Hankow and Shanghai was arranged with the

[15] *Times* (June 7, 1901); see also Huldermann, p. 135.

[16] *Hansard*, 4th ser., xciv, Roberts, June 10, 1901, cols. 1462-63. See also Lord Lansdowne's remarks in the House of Lords, *ibid.*, xcviii, Aug. 6, 1901, cols. 1361-62.

[17] For particulars of the HAPAG's Chinese services, see Schlagintweit, "Deutsche Seeschiffahrt," and Oberlt. Kolshorn, "Die Entwicklung des Kiautschou-Gebietes in der Zeit vom Oktober 1906 bis Oktober 1907," *Asien*, vii, no. 10 (July 1908), 141-43.

71

North German Lloyd. In the following year the Hong Kong-Vladivostok connection was inaugurated, and in 1905 the HAPAG's world network was completed by the introduction of a service between the Orient and the west coast of North America. Ballin's optimism about the prospect of profits to be made in the Orient proved quite correct, for trade between China and Germany increased greatly after 1900. The services established in the Far East under Ballin's leadership proved remunerative additions to the line's oceanic empire, although they never approached in importance those which the HAPAG maintained in the Atlantic.

Once the Hamburg-American Line became involved in the Far East, it was necessary for it to establish way stations and agencies along the major routes between Europe and the Orient at which its freighters could take on coal and cargo and receive sailing information. HAPAG offices were therefore opened along the African coast, in Madagascar, India, Cochin China, and in the Dutch East Indies, and this far-flung structure functioned with smoothness and dispatch. The value of being able to offer a service which was worldwide rather than one restricted to the Atlantic became clear very shortly after Ballin's trip to Asia.

Wars are usually rich harvests for ship lines, especially those which fly neutral flags and which therefore are not legally subject to attack, for huge quantities of strategic matériel and whole armies must be delivered to the war zone. The mounting demand for tonnage sharply increases freight rates, and belligerent governments often purchase freighters or passenger liners for use as transports or for rapid conversion into auxiliary cruisers. Though the services rendered by the Hamburg-American Line during the Boxer Rebellion had not been profitable, during the Spanish-American war of 1898 the line made an advantageous sale of two of its outmoded *Schnelldampfer* to the Spanish government, which refitted them as ships-of-the-line.[18] During the Boer War, the freight market between northern Europe, North America, and South Africa had been brisk and very profitable. At the conclusion of the conflict, however, the shipping business fell into one of its periodic doldrums. The outbreak of the Russo-Japanese War in February 1904 was, to the world's shipowners, a welcome sign that business would soon pick up.

In December 1903, Ballin, sensing that the troubled situation in the Far East would result in war, sent representatives to St. Petersburg who succeeded in selling sixteen liners and freighters to the Russian government for conversion into warships or for use as auxiliaries. In June of the following year, the HAPAG, without prior consultation with the German government, signed a contract with a Russian firm representing the tsar's government which obligated the line to furnish 338,200 tons of coal, almost all of it to be from anthracite mines in Wales, to the fleet of Admiral Zinovi Rozhdestvenski.[19] In October 1904, Rozhdestvenski set out from Kronshtadt to sail to Vladivostok, from which point he intended to carry out an attack on Port Arthur, which had been besieged by the Japanese since the previous May. From October 1904 until May 1905, HAPAG ships coaled Rozhdestvenski in neutral ports from Denmark to Cochin China. The coaling of the Russian fleet exhibited the expertise with which the HAPAG's newly established eastern agents did their work. The line's representatives from Madagascar to Saigon forwarded information to Hamburg

[18] Huldermann, pp. 112-13.
[19] Ballin's involvement with Russia in the coaling affair is treated in detail in my article, "Coal for the Fleet That Had to Die," *American Historical Review*, LXIX, no. 4 (July 1964), 990-1005.

on movements of both Rozhdestvenski's armada as well as scouting Japanese warships, and they insured that HAPAG colliers were present in neutral harbors to coal the Russians on arrival. Rozhdestvenski was favorably impressed by the service he received.

Once the HAPAG's dealings with the Russians were made public in September 1904, the coaling contract became the subject of controversy between London, Berlin, and St. Petersburg. The line's involvement constituted an embarrassment to the German government, for the British were opposed to any activity—such as the unhindered transport of domestic coal—which appeared to impugn their neutrality, especially if it proved a comfort to the Russians. The Japanese entered protests in Berlin against the HAPAG's coaling operations, declaring them to be breaches of neutrality. At the same time, both Ballin and the German government had good cause to persevere with the coaling even though it was accompanied by such danger. For the HAPAG, the Russian contract was a profitable undertaking, especially welcome because of the prevailing lethargy of the shipping market. To William II, the fact that the German government allowed Ballin to coal Rozhdestvenski in spite of the risk involved gave Germany a claim on tsar Nicholas II's gratitude, a claim which the German emperor hoped might someday be transformed into an alliance.

As the war progressed, however, the dangers of continuing the coaling contract seemed to increase. In December 1904, the British, who were allied with Japan, intervened to limit, though not to curtail, the cargoes of British coal which HAPAG ships were taking on for eventual delivery to Rozhdestvenski. The German government thereupon became alarmed that London might terminate the coaling altogether, a step which would be regarded in Berlin as an unwarranted interference with international

74

trade and which therefore might lead to grave consequences. At the same time, as Rozhdestvenski's fleet moved closer to Japan, the danger increased that Admiral Togo's enemy warships would surprise it and seize or sink Ballin's colliers. The result of such an encounter could lead to war between Germany and Japan, one in which England would have difficulty in avoiding becoming involved.

Consequently, in February 1905, William II, greatly to the consternation of the tsar, ordered the HAPAG to terminate its contract. Nicholas at once appealed to the Kaiser to allow Ballin to continue his operations. He was supported by chancellor Bülow, who correctly pointed out to William that if Rozhdestvenski, then impatiently awaiting coal at Nossi-bé in Madagascar, was not allowed to take on coal the fleet could not proceed to the theater of war. Russia would have to sue for peace, and the tsar would blame the German emperor for having caused Russia ignominiously to conclude the war with Japan. William therefore reversed himself, and Ballin was permitted to continue his coaling operations as far as Saigon. Fortunately, the British, who were not anxious to complicate the situation, did not further interfere with the HAPAG's coal loadings in England, and Ballin's colliers never came within range of Togo's cruisers. The matter closed with a handsome profit on the HAPAG's books.

In the summer of 1900, at the same time that Ballin began to plan his forthcoming voyage to China, he was also considering a second area in which the Hamburg-American Line might expand. This was the Persian Gulf.[20]

[20] The most useful secondary accounts of German interests in the Persian Gulf prior to 1914 are Bradford G. Martin, *German-Persian Diplomatic Relations 1873-1912*, The Hague, 1959; Wilhelm Litten, *Persien von der "Pénétration pacifique" zum "Protek-*

The Middle East, like the Orient, was an area over which the British had exercised an economic predominance for years, leaving German merchants and shipping lines to occupy a secondary position. As was the case in China, the administrative incapacity of Persia's rulers and their inability to preserve order in the southern portion of their kingdom enabled the British to win control over political functions, and Englishmen from the Indian Civil Service were in charge of postal and quarantine services and also supervised dredging and piloting operations along the Persian Gulf.[21] In matters of commerce, the Gulf, as well as the rivers flowing into its northern neck, were British preserves. In the Gulf, Frank Strick & Co. of Liverpool was the leading navigation company, and a smaller firm, Bucknall Brothers, maintained a poorly run service from Hamburg to the Gulf after 1900. According to the testimony of German merchants in the area, the British lines took advantage of their commanding position, setting high freight rates and altering sailing schedules at will.[22] The completeness of England's control on the Persian, as well as the Ottoman, rivers was indicated by the fact that the stretch of the Tigris and Shatt-al-Arab between Bagdad and Basra as well as the Karun between Ahwaz and Isfahan were both known popularly as the "Lynch road," after Stephen Lynch. Lynch headed the Euphrates Steam

---

torat:" *Urkunden und Tatsachen zur Geschichte des europäischen "pénétration pacifique" in Persien 1860-1919*, Berlin and Leipzig, 1920; Malek Esmaïli, *Le Golfe persique et les îles de Bahrein*, Paris, 1936; M. Vadala, *Le Golfe persique*, Paris, 1920; and Ulrich Gehrke, *Persien in der deutschen Orientpolitik während des ersten Weltkrieges*, 2 vols., Stuttgart, n.d., which contains a brief account of the prewar period.

[21] Litten, *Persien*, pp. 98-103.

[22] For German indignation at the quality of British steamship service in the Gulf, see *AA*, Türkei Nr. 165, vol. 10, reel 453/-00776-79, and vol. 26, reel 455/00666-71, 00734-35.

Navigation Company, which since 1861 had held from the Ottoman sultan the only foreign concession for river steamers.[23] The British firm worked closely with the Ottoman government, which itself controlled a shipping company on the Tigris. Lynch assiduously exploited his privileged status, and the Euphrates Co. erected a maze of wholesale trading centers at which goods were handled on its own account, thus enabling Lynch to compete directly with older mercantile concerns which traditionally had used his firm as a carrier.[24] There was for that reason considerable hostility toward Lynch on the part of these merchants, some of whom were Germans.

German merchants and shipowners became active in the Persian Gulf only as the nineteenth century neared its close. In 1895, three German shipping firms were incorporated for trade with the Persian Gulf, but within a year all were driven out of business by British competitors. In 1897, a young Hamburger, Robert Wönckhaus, appeared at Lingeh on the Persian coast and joined forces with a Scotsman to form the firm of Robert Wönckhaus & Co., a mercantile and shipping business, which, interestingly, was referred to by the natives simply as "Germany," and which soon won over a number of clients from British firms long established in the area.[25] Commerce in the Gulf

[23] Sir Valentine Chirol, *Fifty Years in a Changing World*, London, 1927, p. 162; Sir Arnold T. Wilson, *SW. Persia: A Political Officer's Diary, 1907-1914*, London, 1941, p. 60. On Lynch, see Litten, *Persien*, pp. 66-69, 98; Wilson, *The Persian Gulf: An Historical Sketch from the Earliest Times to the Beginning of the Twentieth Century*, Oxford, 1928, p. 265. Sir Percy Sykes, the British resident in the Gulf before the war, states that the British government agreed to pay Lynch up to £2,000 per annum to cover his losses in return for carrying the mails. Sykes, *Ten Thousand Miles in Persia or Eight Years in Iran*, New York, 1902, p. 245 n1.

[24] Hesse (consul, Bagdad) to Bethmann Hollweg, Feb. 4, 1910, *AA*, Persien Nr. 1, vol. 62, reel 62/174-75.

[25] On Wönckhaus, see Eugene Staley, "Business and Politics in

77

at the turn of the century was not great, for there was little of value or bulk to be exported for which there was any demand elsewhere in the world. There was, however, considerable expectation that once the land along the Tigris and Euphrates was irrigated and a railroad constructed to connect Bagdad with the Gulf the area might prove to be commercially very active.

In 1900, the much publicized Bagdad-Berlin railroad being built by German capital had proceeded only as far as Konia in south-central Anatolia, the terminal point of the original concession. Negotiations were under way to extend the line to Bagdad, and a concession for this route was granted by the Ottoman government to a German-led syndicate in 1902. Ballin correctly foresaw that the logical terminus of a southern extension of the line from Bagdad must be Basra, an undeveloped port on the Shatt-al-Arab river twenty miles above the northern end of the Gulf. No one could predict how many years it would take the railroad to reach Basra, but Ballin proposed that the HAPAG be there to meet it. Once the railroad made its way into the Tigris-Euphrates valley, immense quantities of building materials would have to be shipped by water to Basra and then along the rivers to the construction sites. And once completed, the railroad would be an enormous stimulus to business between Basra and Europe. Until such time as the railroad reached Basra, Ballin contemplated the intro-

---

the Persian Gulf: the Story of the Wönckhaus firm," *Political Science Quarterly*, XLVIII, no. 3 (Sept. 1933), 367-85, based largely on interviews with Wönckhaus. This material is recapitulated in condensed form in Staley's *War and the Private Investor: A Study in the Relations of International Politics and International Private Investment*, Chicago, 1935, pp. 40-51. See also Esmaïli, *Golfe persique*, p. 72, and Vadala, *Golfe persique*, pp. 34-37. On Wönckhaus' business success, see *AA*, Türkei Nr. 165, vol. 29, reel 456/00857-62. The Wönckhaus "Nachlass" itself is unfortunately fragmentary and of limited value.

duction of only a limited freight and passenger service to the Gulf. Late in June 1900, he confided in his friend, Paul Count Wolff Metternich, then an official at court and later German ambassador to the Court of St. James, that he intended to plant the HAPAG flag in the Gulf. Metternich reported this "interesting" conversation to chancellor Bülow, who enthusiastically endorsed Ballin's plans. Metternich and Bülow, like Ballin, were anxious for Germany to secure a tangible position in the Gulf before the railroad was completed. Both Metternich and the chancellor believed that the appearance of Ballin's merchantmen in the Gulf would arouse less suspicion than would German warships, but would, presumably, be as effective in securing entrée for Germany in the region.[26]

Ballin's intention to extend the HAPAG to the Gulf was not effected until 1906, however. The reasons for the delay are unclear, but it seems likely that it was occasioned by the line's difficulties with J. P. Morgan, which lasted throughout 1901-02, and its involvement in the Russo-Japanese War in 1904-05. It was only in the spring of 1906 that Ballin returned to his plan of establishing a connection to the Gulf. He then sent one of his veteran captains to Persia to investigate the freight market and the possibility of the HAPAG's attempting to obtain a concession from the sultan for river shipping on the Tigris. Ballin's agent reported favorably on the trade prospects, but advised that the HAPAG should not attempt to win a place in the river traffic, since the sultan was not likely to allow a third party to enter a market already concessioned to Lynch and to the line owned by the Ottoman government.[27] Since these reports substantiated Ballin's own ex-

[26] Metternich to Bülow, June 24, 1900, *GP*, XVII, no. 4,978, pp. 8-14. The original document is filed in *AA*, Türkei Nr. 165, vol. 9, but was not included in the microfilm selection of this file made by the University of California (series I, reel 453).

[27] Capt. Paul Wiehr to HAPAG, Aug. 25, 1906, *AA*, Türkei Nr.

pectation of the commercial future of the Gulf, he decided to advance into the area, even though a number of HAPAG directors were dubious of the wisdom of the venture. An *Arabisch-Persischer Dienst* was organized at the HAPAG, Robert Wönckhaus & Co. were appointed the line's agents in the Gulf, and by the summer of 1906 Ballin was ready to send out his first ship. He did not expect to make a profit from this new service until the railroad reached Basra. The advantage in anticipating the railroad was that the British firms in the Gulf, themselves trying to wring a profit from their operations, were financially weak and could not withstand the HAPAG's competition. The German line, fortified by its profitable business in other parts of the world, was therefore in a position to capture the Gulf market and then bide its time until a lively freight trade developed.[28]

On July 16, 1906, the HAPAG's *Canadia* departed from Hamburg laden with 3,500 tons of cargo consisting primarily of matches, champagne, chinaware, sugar, glass, and wood. German merchants in the Gulf greeted the ship's arrival at Basra on September 5th, delighted now to be released from their dependence on British carriers, especially since the HAPAG announced that its freight charges from Basra to European ports would amount to ten to twenty shillings per ton compared to the forty shillings charged by British lines.[29] The *Canadia* sailed for Hamburg on September 18th, its holds filled with rice, dates, and miscellaneous cargo.[30] The German government was as

---

165, vol. 26, reel 455/00697-701. See also Richarz (consul, Bagdad) to Bülow, Aug. 27, *ibid.*, 455/00689-91.

[28] Heyking (Prussian minister to the Hanseatic cities and the Mecklenburgs) to Bülow, April 25, 1906, *ibid.*, reel 455/00405-07.

[29] Vadala, *Golfe persique*, p. 34.

[30] On the first HAPAG ships in the Persian service, see *AA*, Türkei Nr. 165, vol. 26, reel 455/00734-35; Karl Schneider, "Der Hafen von Bassorah in Vergangenheit und Gegenwart," *Asien*, VII, no.

pleased by Ballin's enterprise as were Basra's merchants. Ballin had not consulted Berlin in deciding to inaugurate a connection to the Gulf, but after making his plans he informed the Prussian minister in Hamburg, Baron Heyking, who in turn passed the information on to Bülow. The chancellor was happy to have the news and wrote in the margin of Heyking's report: "*Ja.* I'm very pleased. This can only hurt the British."[31]

Ferdinand Haller, the chief of the HAPAG's Arabian-Persian division, has left an estimable picture of the undertaking.[32] The line put its oldest freighters at Haller's disposal, and these ships slowly made their way from Hamburg, calling at various ports in the Mediterranean and Red Seas before passing Muscat and entering the Gulf. Duty in the Persian division was wearisome and unpopular, and both officers and crews had to be rotated frequently. The passenger trade in the Persian Gulf was always secondary to that in goods. There were very few travelers bound for such steamy harbors as Djibouti, Lingeh, Bushehr, and Port Sudan. But Jidda, where HAPAG ships regularly called, opened some possibilities for development, for it lay only twenty miles from Mecca, and Mecca meant pilgrims. Ballin called in professors from the Oriental seminar of the Hamburg *Kolonialinstitut* for advice, and the HAPAG's advertisements for the pilgrimage service which he soon established were fetchingly printed in the dull green color revered by the Shi'a Mohammedans who dwelled at the head and along the eastern coast of the Gulf. The pilgrimage business did not prove a great success,

---

6 (March 1908), 84-85; London *Times*, *The Times Documentary History of the War*, 11 vols., London, 1917-20, III, 98; *Hansard*, 4th ser., CLXIX, cols. 293-94.

[31] Heyking to Bülow, April 25, 1906, *AA*, Türkei Nr. 165, vol. 26, reel 455/00405-07.

[32] Haller "Nachlass." See also *Nauticus*, X (1908), 337-38, for details of the Persian service supplied by the HAPAG.

however. Armed guards had to be posted on board to prevent Arab and Persian zealots from falling on one another, and competition from Greek lines cut deeply into the HAPAG's profits.[33]

The export trade from Europe to the Gulf was predominant one of sugar. "The Persian drinks sugar with tea, and the Arab cooks his coffee with sugar," Haller claimed. Other goods exported for sale in the Near East were coffee, matches, woolen goods, and window panes. On return trips, the holds of HAPAG vessels were tight with such orientalia as opium, dates, rugs, camel's hair, and mother-of-pearl for Bohemian button factories. When the HAPAG founded its Persian line the sugar trade was largely in the hands of a French concern which shipped its products with Strick & Co. Belgium was also the center of a flourishing refined sugar industry, but Strick and other British shipping companies refused to handle this considerable trade unless the sugar first was shipped to England. This process was cumbersome and expensive, much sugar was spoiled in transit, and, as a result, Belgian sugar was priced out of the Persian market. Soon after 1906, the Hamburg-American Line contracted to transport Belgian sugar direct from Antwerp to the Gulf, and the outcome of this arrangement was a sugar war between Anglo-French and Belgian-German combines.[34] This struggle, like the passenger rate wars in the north Atlantic, was financially ruinous for all concerned, and the HAPAG and Strick & Co. eventually arrived at an agreement for sharing the European sugar trade with the Gulf.

It was not long before German sugar producers entered the Persian market, a move which further increased the

[33] In some cases the HAPAG may have transported the pilgrims free of charge in order to create good will. See Esmaïli, *Golfe persique*, p. 73.

[34] *Zeitschrift*, VI, no. 12 (June 5, 1907), reprinting an interview with Ballin published in the May 27th *Frankfurter Zeitung*.

HAPAG's business at Basra and other ports. The demand for lump sugar was particularly great, but German factories produced only crystalline and granulated varieties, while the Persian consumer preferred cubes. In 1913, a German firm developed machinery which would not only produce cubes, but cubes which contained the standard amount of sugar yet ingeniously appeared much larger. This inflated German commodity quickly proved more popular than the smaller cubes of rival manufacturers. Cookies were also an important import: here the Germans won an edge because their products were sweeter than those baked in England.

The British were concerned by the appearance of German traders in the Persian Gulf for both political and economic reasons. The maintenance of British influence in southern Persia was considered in London to be an absolutely essential prerequisite for the defense of India.[35] Such a view had been advanced with great vigor by George Nathaniel Curzon in his popular *Persia and the Persian Question*, published in 1892, and in the next decade in Captain Alfred T. Mahan's *The Problem of Asia*, which was widely read in England.[36] To both writers, Russia was the power whose designs in the Gulf were feared, but after 1900, with the increase of German influence in Turkey, the construction of the Bagdad railroad, and the foundation of a German bank in Teheran, British observers began to grow wary of German ambitions as well. This attitude became particularly noticeable after 1907, when Anglo-Russian rivalry was alleviated by a convention which divided Persia into three sections; a sphere of

[35] See Rosa Louise Greaves, *Persia and the Defense of India: A Study in the Foreign Policy of the Third Marquis of Salisbury*, London, 1959.

[36] *The Problem of Asia and Its Effect upon International Politics*, Boston, 1900, esp. chap. ii.

83

influence for Russia in the north, one for Great Britain in the south, and a neutral strip in between.[37]

British shipowners active in the Persian Gulf viewed the appearance of the Hamburg-American Line in the area with hostility, for they doubtless knew of Ballin's earlier success in challenging his rivals in the north Atlantic. Their fears were quickly confirmed, since the HAPAG soon wrested from the British a number of valuable contracts through its offer of lower freight rates.[38] Questions were raised in the Commons as to whether the government was aware of the HAPAG's invasion of this former British market.[39] The presence of the HAPAG in the Gulf was also regarded by the British as one further, and very significant, indication of Germany's intention to establish itself politically, as well as commercially, in the Near East. The British ambassador in Constantinople wrote in April 1906 that "another symptom of Germany's interest in Persian affairs, which we cannot afford to overlook and which would seem to be part and parcel of some policy for a definite end, is the recent establishment by the Hamburg-American Company of a service of steamers to the Persian Gulf."[40] Ballin himself was under

[37] For this change in British opinion, see the Bombay *Times of India* for Oct. 31, 1906, included in Richarz to Foreign Office, Nov. 16, *AA*, Persien Nr. 1, vol. 22, reel 419/0519; Wilson, *SW. Persia*, p. 133; Chirol, *Fifty Years*, pp. 159, 170. Anglo-German relations at this time with regard to Persia are treated in George Monger, *The End of Isolation: British Foreign Policy 1900-1907*, London, etc., 1963, pp. 119-23.

[38] See *AA*, Türkei Nr. 165, vol. 23, reel 455/00405-07; vol. 26, reel 455/00734-35; vol. 29, reel 456/00029-30; *Zeitschrift*, VI, no. 17 (Aug. 20, 1907), 162-63; Martin, *German-Persian Relations*, pp. 150-51; Esmaïli, *Golfe persique*, p. 73 n30.

[39] *Hansard*, 4th ser., CLXIX, question by Rees, answer by Grey, Feb. 14, 1907, cols. 293-94.

[40] O'Conor to Grey, April 24, 1906, *BD*, IV, no. 328, 381-82. See also Listemann (vice consul, Bushehr) to Bülow, May 15, 1906, enclosing a *Times of India* notice of May 2, *AA*, Türkei

fire in the British press as being one of the principals behind the *Deutsche Orientbank* in Teheran, which was widely regarded in Great Britain as the primary agent of German penetration in Persia.[41] Since the Gulf was an unpleasant place in which to live and since trade there was slight, British officials were suspicious that the HAPAG and Wönckhaus were subsidized agents of the German government, involved in the locale less for economic than for political reasons.[42]

There is nothing to indicate that these notions of collusion were grounded in fact. The Hamburg-American Line received no subsidy from the German government for its new service.[43] Wönckhaus & Co. and the HAPAG often made joint and separate appeals to Berlin for diplomatic protection of their interests, and their requests received attention.[44] But beyond such ordinary relations between

---

Nr. 165, vol. 25, reel 455/00571-76; and Metternich to same, July 24, 1906, noting such charges in the *Daily Mail* (*ibid.*, 455/00628).

[41] Martin, *German-Persian Relations*, pp. 114-15.

[42] For such conspiratorial views of the Germans' activity, see Philip Graves, *The Life of Sir Percy Cox*, London and Melbourne, 1941, pp. 133-34; Sir Arthur Hardinge, *A Diplomatist in the East*, London, 1928, p. 276; London *Times Documentary History of the War*, III, 98; Chirol, *Fifty Years*, pp. 131-48; and Staley, "Business and Politics," 373, 382-83. See also Sir Arnold T. Wilson, *Loyalties: Mesopotamia 1914-1917: A Personal and Historical Record*, London, 1930, pp. 74-75, in which Wilson reports the prevalence of such a view and then rejects its accuracy. Cf. Wilson's *The Persian Gulf*, p. 13. The British were particularly suspicious of Thomas Brown, the Wönckhaus agent in Lingeh. On Brown's relations with the HAPAG, see Wönckhaus "Nachlass," folder entitled "Notizen Brown," containing letters from Brown to Robert Wönckhaus for the period 1907-13; and also *AA*, Türkei Nr. 152, vol. 64, reel 419/0023-25.

[43] On this point, see *AA*, Türkei Nr. 165, vol. 26, reel 455/00648-49, 00651, 00654, 00659-61.

[44] For an example, see *ibid.*, vol. 28, reel 455/00855-59.

businessmen abroad and their home governments, there was no connection which warrants these firms having been considered political emissaries of Berlin. Germans in the Gulf seem to have been content to leave political affairs to the British. Like their counterparts in China, these Germans admired the capability of Englishmen as colonial administrators and acknowledged the valuable service the British navy performed in policing the pirate- and brigand-infested Gulf to the benefit of merchants of all nations.[45]

As many of Ballin's advisers had warned, the HAPAG's business in the Persian Gulf proved unprofitable, and in 1908, only two years after the *Canadia*'s initial trip, the HAPAG seriously considered abandoning the service. Ballin instructed the German Foreign Office that the line's Persian operations were costing 500,000 marks per year and declared that unless the government had a "very special" (*ganz besonderers*) interest in its maintenance the line would dissolve its connection to the Gulf. The reply from Berlin was that had Ballin consulted the government in 1906 it would have advised against establishing a service to the Gulf. But now that the line was in operation its maintenance was considered to be both economically and politically desirable (*handelspolitisch erwünscht*).[46] The Gulf line therefore was continued, and apparently the HAPAG and its British rivals came to an agreement on freight rates to Basra and other ports.[47] Ballin's ships gradually won an increasing share in the trade to and from the Gulf, and finally in 1911 the Persian branch was able to present its first black balance sheet.

[45] Haller "Nachlass," pp. 10-11; Chirol, *Fifty Years*, p. 174.

[46] Lucius (Geschäftsträger, Prussian ministry, Hamburg) to Bülow, Jan. 31, 1908, *AA*, Türkei Nr. 165, vol. 28, reel 455/00866-67.

[47] Metternich to Bülow, Feb. 13, 1908, and Lucius to same, Feb. 18, both in *ibid.*, reel 455/00869-72.

Within five years of opening its service to the Persian Gulf, the Hamburg-American Line thus had demonstrated its ability to invade with success a British overseas market. But the Gulf trade remained small in volume and seemed unlikely to grow until the railroad connection from Bagdad to Basra was built. There was little doubt that the German-controlled Berlin-Bagdad railroad consortium would be granted a concession to extend the track from Bagdad to Basra. Negotiations to that end had been under way between the Ottoman, Persian, and German governments since the turn of the century. The construction of a rail link between the Gulf and inland trading centers was of crucial importance to the Hamburg-American Line. As long as the railroad to Basra remained unbuilt, the British, together with their Ottoman associates, enjoyed a great advantage in the entire Gulf trade, since their competitors could transport cargoes only as far as Basra, from which point goods destined for the interior had to be transferred to British or Turkish river steamers. The British often created delays and obstructions for the forwarding of goods unloaded from German ships, hoping thereby to discredit the German lines with their customers and cause business to return to British steamship companies in service between Europe and the Gulf.[48] Once the railroad was completed, however, German traders would no longer be dependent on British or Turkish river steamers. The situation was one which seemed promising for compromise. If Great Britain would share its position on the rivers with German firms, Germany might consent to British participation in the administration of the rail-

[48] Wönckhaus to Zimmermann (under secretary, Foreign Office), May 22, 1913, *AA*, Türkei Nr. 152, vol. 61, reel 418/00448-50; Jagow to Lichnowsky, May 29, *ibid.*, vol. 62, 418/00520-23 (*GP*, 14,748).

87

road. In 1913, negotiations between Germany, England, and Turkey to regulate the waterways and railroads from Bagdad to Basra were begun.[49]

The position of the two north European powers in an extremely complicated year of negotiations may here be summarized. Germany was insistent that it build the Bagdad-Basra line and that it be exclusively a German enterprise, with no financial or managerial participation by the British. Germany had conceived the railroad and it was only fair that it be allowed to complete it. The British, on the other hand, insisted that the Anglo-Ottoman monopoly on the Tigris be left intact and that in addition they be given a share in the railroad, as well as in the management of the modern harbor which was to be built, primarily by the Germans, at Basra.[50] Germany countered that in that case it must have a voice in the Tigris monopoly.

As negotiations progressed, both parties showed a willingness to compromise. Germany agreed to give the British two directorships on the railroad as well as the right to participate in the harbor construction project at Basra. In return, the German government asked to be awarded one

---

[49] The Bagdad-Basra negotiations, insofar as the HAPAG was involved, can be traced in *ibid.*, vols. 57-77, reels 418-20. Some of this material is printed in *GP*, XXXI, chap. ccxlv. The British documents are found in *BD*, X, chaps. xci-xciv. For background see the following: Maybelle K. Chapman, *Great Britain and the Bagdad Railroad 1888-1914*, Northampton, Mass., 1948; John B. Wolf, *The Diplomatic Background of the Bagdad Railroad*, Columbia, Mo., 1936; and Martin, *German-Persian Relations*. The older study by Edward Meade Earle, *Turkey, the Great Powers, and the Bagdad Railway: A Study in Imperialism*, New York, 1923, is still of some interest.

[50] Kühlmann to Bethmann, May 30, 1913, *AA*, Türkei Nr. 152, vol. 61, reel 418/00442-43 (*GP*, 14,742). See also Felix Somary, *Erinnerungen aus meinem Leben*, Zurich, n.d., pp. 93-94; and H. F. B. Lynch, "Railways in the Middle East," *Imperial and Asiatic Quarterly Review*, 3d. ser., XXXI, no. 62 (April 1911), 225-49.

directorship in the new Tigris navigation company which was to be formed by amalgamating the Lynch firm and a number of smaller British and Turkish carriers. The foreign minister, Gottlieb von Jagow, confessed that the German demand, much like Sir Edward Grey's on behalf of British interests, was motivated by a desire "to conciliate public opinion and to be able to mollify German shipping and trade circles." The German government itself would be content with no more than a statement by England that there would be no discrimination against German freight on the rivers, Jagow declared, but the pressure being exerted by Germany's mercantile interest forced him to ask for formal participation in the river navigation combine.[51]

Ballin was informed of the compromise under consideration and he attacked it as being unfavorable to Germany's interests. Leaving the river route—the cheapest means of transporting bulk goods—in the hands of a virtual Anglo-Turkish monopoly was a grave error which Germany would later regret.[52] Jagow asked Ballin for a "brief expression" of his views on the matter, and Ballin answered on June 3, 1913, heatedly and at length.[53] He criticized the British claim to a riverine monopoly as going "entirely too far." British influence in the area was already so great that goods bound for German ships at Basra or cargo unloaded from these vessels destined for locations along the rivers were often delayed by British carriers.

[51] Jagow to Lichnowsky, May 29, 1913, *AA*, Türkei Nr. 152, vol. 62, reel 418/00523-27 (*GP*, 14,748). For the influence of public opinion on Grey, see Kühlmann to Bethmann, May 20, *ibid.*, 418/00442-43 (*GP*, 14,742); and Lichnowsky to same, Dec. 20, 1913, *GP*, XXXVII (1), no. 14,805, p. 292.

[52] Haller "Nachlass," pp. 22-23.

[53] Jagow to Ballin, May 29, 1913, *AA*, Türkei Nr. 152, vol. 62, reel 418/00520-23; Ballin to Jagow, June 3, *ibid.*, 418/00556-60 (*GP*, 14,751).

The mere presence of a German director on the board of the Anglo-Turkish river shipping company constituted no guarantee for nondiscriminatory treatment of German interests, nor should a pledge to this effect by the British government be relied on. The only solution, Ballin concluded, was for Germany to participate directly in the Anglo-Turkish monopoly by owning part of the company's shares. The HAPAG and Wönckhaus & Co. would be willing to put some of their ships at the disposal of the new concern.[54]

Jagow forwarded Ballin's memorandum to ambassador Lichnowsky in London, noting that it should be given "earnest consideration."[55] Ballin's insistence that Germany acquire an active role in the river monopoly was subsequently reflected in a draft agreement drawn up on June 21st by Jagow, with the assistance of HAPAG officials and the head of the *Deutsche Bank*, Arthur von Gwinner. This proposal provided for the acquisition of 10 per cent of the shares of the river monopoly by Germany in addition to one place on the board. In return for this, Germany agreed not to "encourage or support claims on the part of German subjects to participate in any enterprises of navigation on the Tigris and Euphrates rivers."[56]

The draft was sent to the Kaiser, who was at Kiel for the annual regatta. William II accepted it, whereupon Jagow instructed his staff to obtain Ballin's approval. Ballin, who was also at Kiel, was not entirely satisfied with the draft, feeling that it would not adequately protect German shipping interests in the Gulf. William was unhappy at this opposition, and Ballin, sensing the Kaiser's dis-

[54] Jagow to London embassy, June 4, 1913, *ibid.*, reel 418/00561-64.

[55] *ibid.*

[56] Draft convention, *ibid.*, vol. 62a, reel 418/00641-42 (*GP*, 14,754).

pleasure, made what one onlooker described as a "very comic retreat action," acknowledging that the draft contained more concessions from the English than he had dreamed possible.[57] In spite of Ballin's assurances to William, his misgivings persisted, and he wrote to his friend, Maximilian Harden, that the Persian situation was "most unpleasant." Ballin agreed, however, to offer no further opposition to an Anglo-Turkish predominance on the rivers provided the HAPAG was enabled to quote as favorable direct rates from European ports to Bagdad as the British lines operating in the Gulf.[58]

Like Ballin, other German businessmen were dissatisfied with the proposed agreeement, and protests were raised in the press and on the floor of the Reichstag that by its terms Germany would receive too little, Great Britain too much. Jagow took notice of these complaints, and in July 1913, ambassador Lichnowsky informed Grey that "the idea of a monopoly for river transport is extremely unpopular with the shipping interest in Germany, and it is only with the greatest difficulty that the opposition of this large and powerful interest can be overcome, [even] if they get more than a nominal share in the new river navigation company."[59] Jagow then upped Germany's demands to a 20 per cent share in the river company's shares, at the same time declaring himself willing to give England a like 20 per cent interest in the harbor company. The British government in turn pronounced this inflated demand unacceptable, but it did agree to increase the German share

[57] Treutler (imperial entourage) to Bethmann, June 29, 1913, *ibid.*, reel 418/00674-75 (*GP*, 14,757).

[58] Minute by Alwyn Parker (assistant clerk, British Foreign Office), July 5, 1913, *BD*, x (2), no. 114, pp. 167-68; Ballin to Harden, July 20, 1913, Harden "Nachlass."

[59] Note of July 16, 1913, *AA*, Türkei Nr. 152, vol. 64, reel 419/00085-91.

to 16 2/3 per cent. Jagow, doubtless interpreting this as a sign of weakness, held out for 20.

Throughout the course of the negotiations in the summer and winter of 1913-14, the HAPAG was active in advising the German government on the Persian situation. At Jagow's request, Ballin went to Berlin on several occasions to furnish information on technical points under consideration.[60] In Ballin's absence, the HAPAG's interests were represented by Haller and his assistants or by officials of the *Deutsche Bank*, which cooperated very closely with the HAPAG on this matter. In November 1913, Stephen Lynch, who had steadfastly opposed any compromise by Great Britain on the question of river transport, died, an event which greatly facilitated the subsequent course of negotiations. In mid-December, a mutually satisfactory formula was reached. This draft agreement provided for a 20 per cent share in the river monopoly for Germany, with the German share to be subtracted from Turkey's interest so that Great Britain would retain a 50 per cent share. England was granted, in return, two places on the board of directors of the Bagdad Railway Company as well as a 40 per cent interest in the harbor at Basra.[61]

William II and the German Foreign Office were delighted at England's acceptance of the German demands, and the

[60] Jagow to Ballin, Sept. 3, 1913, and Ballin to Jagow, same date, *ibid.*, reel 419/00015-17; Zimmermann to Bülow (Prussian minister, Hamburg), Jan. 15, 1914, *ibid.*, vol. 68, 419/00562-63; Ballin to Zimmermann, Jan. 19, *ibid.*, 419/00579; Jagow to Ballin, June 12, 1914, *ibid.*, vol. 76, reel 420/00441-43. For criticism of the complications which Ballin's advice caused the Foreign Office, see Friedrich Rosen, *Aus einem diplomatischen Wanderleben*, 4 vols. in 3, Berlin, 1931-59, II, 182.

[61] The text of the agreement is printed in *GP*, XXXVII (1), 453-65, and in *BD*, X, 398-406. See Ross J. S. Hoffman, *Great Britain and the German Trade Rivalry 1875-1914*, Philadelphia, 1933, p. 159, which shows British and German shipping tonnage at Basra in 1913 as 254,714 and 55,149 tons respectively.

two governments, in concert with the sultan, began work ironing out a number of minor issues preparatory to drawing up the final, definitive agreement. Negotiations proceeded smoothly, and an Anglo-Turkish-German agreement was initialed on June 15, 1914, with the formal ratification scheduled to take place in August. On July 30th, less than a week before England declared war on Germany, the instrument was forwarded to ambassador Lichnowsky, who was authorized to sign it in the name of the Kaiser.

We have followed Ballin through the course of his advance: the reorganization of the Hamburg-American Line in 1886, its slow victory over the North German Lloyd, its gradual displacement of all European and American competitors in the Atlantic, until by the turn of the century it had become the largest steamship company in the world. Once in this position of preeminence, the HAPAG had worked its way around the world and in 1914 spanned the globe with a vast network of routes. Its field had truly become the world.

This impressive record had been achieved only through great struggles, and the HAPAG's principal antagonists, once it had won out over the Lloyd, had been its British competitors. During the years of its development, the Hamburg-American Line had acquired the grudging admiration but also the jealousy, and occasionally the enmity, of those British lines from which it had drawn off more and more passengers and freight. Paralleling the growth of Anglo-German friction in international shipping was, however, a well-intentioned and remarkably successful attempt on the part of shipping leaders on both sides to find solutions to their problems. Ballin, the Lloyd, and

93

foreign competitors worked out pools to regulate the Atlantic business, and though relations between pool members were often frayed, the combinations managed to preserve a delicately adjusted compromise. Similarly, in China and in the Persian Gulf, the shipping interests of Germany and Great Britain, supported by their governments, worked out satisfactory arrangements which enabled both to prosper. None of these settlements approached perfection; had war not come in 1914 there would doubtless have been more friction in these and other areas—the Atlantic pools would certainly have collapsed only to be pasted together again, and further conferences would have proved necessary to settle new problems. But the fact remains that international shipping was one area in which Anglo-German rivalry was mitigated by adroit compromise. Although it was Ballin's very success which was responsible for much of this rivalry, it was also he who worked hard to promote good feeling and mutually advantageous agreements among competitors in world shipping.

Even though British businessmen could often find solutions to their difficulties with German competitors, and though the governments of both nations were disposed to mollify economic friction between Englishman and German, the notion of an inevitable and insoluble economic rivalry between the two countries won credence in a large part of the British population. The rivalry in international shipping, because it was such a significant area of British economic power and because it was a visible contest between sleek liners and imposing merchant fleets, inclined many Englishmen to believe that their prestige was being questioned and their security undermined. Shipping circles in London and Liverpool and a number of statesmen became concerned at the displacement of British by German shipping, while an irresponsible press made use of the fact to alarm the public. The British, we know today, need not have been so concerned, for careful studies made after the First World War have shown that Great Britain was in fact successfully withstanding Germany's competition on the seas.[62] In the mood of the moment, however, things German became suspect. The inability to differentiate between the German merchant with his ship and the German empire itself was not limited to the untutored Persian natives who simple-mindedly labeled Wönckhaus & Co. "Germany." Ballin's swift and elegant transatlantic liners, with their galling capture of the coveted Blue Ribbon of the Atlantic, and his flotillas of drab, purposeful freighters were regarded as constituting just as grave a menace to British security as Admiral von Tirpitz' great battleships. "Ballin has declared war on the world," London's *Daily News Leader* proclaimed on the last day of January 1914, ". . . and if our claim to rule the waves is threatened, this threat comes not from the German dreadnoughts but from Herr Ballin."[63]

The British attitude toward German shipping and particularly toward the Hamburg-American Line, though encouraged to hysteria by Germanophobe press lords and pundits, was not altogether irrational. There *were* several grounds on which an Englishman might indict the HAPAG's fleet of being little more than a governmental convoy in disguise. First of all, it was alleged, the Hamburg-American

[62] See Hoffman, *German Trade Rivalry*, p. 219, and S. G. Sturmey, *British Shipping and World Competition*, London, 1962, chap. i. For differences of opinion on this point within the British shipping industry, see J. H. Welsford, *The Great Shipping Problem*, Liverpool, n.d., and Charles Boothe, *Fiscal Policy and British Shipping from the Free Trade Point of View*, Liverpool, 1909. See also Marcel Brunet, *La brèche maritime allemande dans l'empire colonial anglais*, Paris, n.d.

[63] Quoted in Kaspar Pinette, *Albert Ballin und die deutsche Politik: ein Beitrag zur Geschichte von Staat und Wirtschaft 1900-1918*, Hamburg, 1938, p. 72.

Line's ships had been built or were being run on government subsidies, or both. There is no evidence that the HAPAG at any time received building subsidies, though it had been granted a small operational subsidy from 1900 to 1904 for carrying the China mail. Much was made of this, however, and charges persisted both in England and on the continent that the HAPAG was the economic creature of the German state.[64] Closely connected with the subsidy issue was the allegation made frequently in England—again one which was true but vastly exaggerated—that the HAPAG's liners were designed for conversion in time of war into fast auxiliary cruisers.[65] In still other areas it appeared that Ballin's HAPAG and the imperial government were suspiciously close. There were the emigrant *Kontrollstationen* on the German-Russian border at which, British steamship officials charged, frontier police overtly helped HAPAG agents force emigrants to contract for passage on German rather than British ships.[66] Hamburg-American Line ships were frequently chartered by the German government for service as troop carriers, and the concern's interests were sedulously represented by the imperial government and by German consular offi-

[64] On the question of shipping subsidies, see Bernhard Huldermann, *Die Subventionen der ausländischen Handelsflotten und ihre Bedeutungen für die Entwicklung der Seeschiffahrt*, Berlin, 1909; R. Ibbeken, *Das aussenpolitische Problem Staat und Wirtschaft in der deutschen Reichspolitik 1880-1914* . . . , Schleswig, 1928; Friedrich P. Seigart, *Die Subventionen der Weltschiffahrt und ihre sozial-ökonomischen Wirkungen*, Berlin, 1930; and W. Greve, *Seeschiffahrts-Subventionen der Gegenwart*, Hamburg, 1903. For Ballin's opposition to subsidies, see *Zeitschrift*, I, no. 21 (May 20, 1902), 179-80, 183-84.

[65] The HAPAG admitted that some of its liners had been constructed for such conversion but denied that it was paid any sort of premium by the government for doing so. See *Zeitschrift*, II, no. 18 (Sept. 20, 1903), 143-44; also *Hamburger Nachrichten* (Oct. 16, 1905).

[66] See pages 41-42.

cials all over the world. Berlin, moreover, appeared to be aiding the line by establishing a complex series of preferential railroad and shipping rates, which in fact were designed more to help German railroads and ports than domestic shipping lines.[67] Finally, what Englishman could fail to notice the well publicized and really quite remarkable friendship between Wilhelm Hohenzollern, king of Prussia and German emperor, and *Generaldirektor* Ballin of the Hamburg-American Line?

[67] Sir Francis Oppenheimer, *Stranger Within: Autobiographical Pages*, London, 1960, pp. 158-59, 217. Oppenheimer was a British commercial attaché stationed in Germany.

CHAPTER IV

Prussians and Politicians

N AN AGE of unabashed materialism such as the late nineteenth century, close friendships between princes and men of business were by no means unusual. First at Marlborough House and later at Buckingham, Edward VII delighted in the company of a mercantile and banking aristocracy— names such as Cassel, Rothschild, and Hirsch come to mind, a commercial elite conspicuous for its German-Jewish element. These men were more than royal favorites: they were integral and popular members of English landed society. A somewhat commercial atmosphere could occasionally also be detected at the Berlin Schloss, at Potsdam and Rominten, where a number of German plutocrats could be observed mingling with the landed east Elbian aristocracy. Some courtiers whose incomes were derived from industrial operations, such as Guido Prince Henckel von Donnersmarck and Karl Baron von Stumm-Halberg, bore impressive but rather recent titles. Many more businessmen who appeared at William II's court, and particularly those who were active in banking, commerce, and light rather than heavy industry, were bourgeois Jews, though some had submitted to baptism after having succeeded in business, and on a few an ennobling *von* had been bestowed. There were, to name only a few, the great banker industrialist, Fritz von Friedländer-Fuld, the Rathenaus, father and son, James Simon, patron of the arts, a long file of distinguished bankers—Paul von Schwabach, Carl Fürstenberg, Max Warburg, and several of the Mendelssohn Bartholdys—and Albert Ballin.

Being on familiar terms with the monarch did not mean, however, that these Jewish giants of German finance and industry figured as members of Prussian society. They were —in contradistinction to their counterparts in Great Britain—merely royal favorites and not fixtures of the aristocratic establishment. They saw William II during the day at luncheons and hunting parties, where the company was almost invariably masculine and often predominantly military. Very rarely did a Jew drawn from the world of business, or members of his family, secure an invitation to the formal court soirées which were the pivot around which Berlin society, and indeed that of the empire, revolved.[1] Inclusion in such social affairs of state was, with few exceptions, reserved to the diplomatic corps, high government officials, and the Prussian nobility, with a few additional peers from the other German states.[2] It is vital for an understanding of what follows that the relationship between William II and Ballin and other Jewish businessmen be understood in terms of the peculiar constraints and limitations to which they were subject by the canons of Prussian society.

British society was more fluid, and in the case of Queen

[1] A daughter of Gerson Bleichröder, William I's banker, was presented at court, but a special effort had to be made to insure her finding dancing partners, not because she was unattractive but because she was Jewish. See Johann Heinrich Count Bernstorff, *Memoirs of Count Bernstorff*, trans. Eric Sutton, New York, 1936, p. 27.

[2] The narrowness of the Prussian court under William II is best described in Mathilde Gräfin von Keller, *Vierzig Jahre im Dienst der Kaiserin: ein Kulturbild aus den Jahren 1881-1921*, Leipzig, 1935; Robert Graf Zedlitz-Trützschler, *Zwölf Jahre am deutschen Kaiserhof*, Berlin and Leipzig, 1924; Marie Princesse Radziwill, *Lettres de la Princesse Radziwill au Général de Robilant 1889-1914: une grande dame d'avant guerre*, 4 vols., Bologna, 1933-34; and the sketch in Fedor von Zobeltitz, *Chronik der Gesellschaft unter dem letzten Kaiserreich*, 2 vols., Hamburg, 1922, II, 71-74.

99

Victoria's son there was nothing remarkable about attachments to Jews or men of affairs, for Edward VII was not a man who questioned the source of his pleasure. Victoria's German grandson, who did not share many of the indulgent and cosmopolitan tastes of his royal uncle, did not take so uncomplicated a view of society. William II's attitude toward Jews was curiously ambivalent. Bernhard von Bülow, who knew the Kaiser perhaps as well as any man did and who found much to criticize in him, considered the Kaiser "in no way" prejudiced against Jews, an opinion confirmed by numerous other contemporaries.[3] On the other hand, his correspondence and conversation exhibited unmistakable, though only occasional, traces of anti-Semitism.[4] William seems to have had a rather selective prejudice: with wealthy Jews prominent in business and finance his relations were almost uniformly good, even cordial. At the same time, the Berlin press lords and the leadership of the Socialist party, both largely Jewish

[3] Bülow, *Denkwürdigkeiten*, 4 vols., Berlin, 1930-31, I, 297; II, 385; Walter Görlitz, ed., *Der Kaiser . . . : Aufzeichnungen des Chefs des Marinekabinetts Admiral Georg Alexander v. Müller über die Ära Wilhelms II.*, Berlin, 1965, p. 151; Axel Count Schwering (pseud.), *The Berlin Court under William II*, London, 1915, pp. 224-25. See also Eugen Schiffer, *Ein Leben für den Liberalismus*, Berlin-Grunewald, 1951, p. 100; and the interesting remarks and press quotations in the *Sigilla Veri* (*Ph. Stauff's Semi-Kürschner*) . . . , 5 vols., Erfurt, 1929-32, I, 371.

[4] See Robert A. Kann, "Emperor William II and the Archduke Francis Ferdinand in Their Correspondence," *American Historical Review*, LVII, no. 2 (Jan. 1952), 323-51, who attributes the Kaiser's anti-Semitic remarks not to conviction but to a desire to please the well-known prejudices of the Habsburg heir-apparent; Houston Stewart Chamberlain, *Briefe 1882-1924 und Briefwechsel mit Kaiser Wilhelm II.*, 2 vols., Munich, 1928, II, 226; *GP*, xxv (2), no. 8,881, p. 574. See also Arthur N. Davis, *The Kaiser as I knew Him*, New York and London, 1918, pp. 161, 167; Lady Norah Bentinck, *The Ex-Kaiser in Exile*, New York, n.d., pp. 107-08; Schiffer, *Ein Leben*, pp. 135-37; and Kuno Graf Westarp, *Konservative Politik im letzten Jahrzehnt des Kaiserreiches*, 2 vols., Berlin, 1935, II, 299.

in composition and usually very hostile to the Kaiser, were frequent objects of imperial malediction. Friedrich Schmidt-Ott, a Prussian official and confidant of William, commented on this inconsistency in his sovereign's thinking. Once midway in a diatribe by His Majesty against the Jews, Schmidt dared to remind him of his Semitic friends, Ballin and Franz Mendelssohn, whereupon William declared that he did not consider them to be Jews at all. And after his abdication, the Kaiser even alleged that he had been unaware that Ballin had in fact been a Jew.[5]

Much of the Prussian aristocracy was unenthusiastic about the Kaiser's friendship with Jews and criticized him for debasing the crown by associating with such men. Because of his frequent appearances with Ballin and other wealthy Jews, William more and more was linked with the new society of riches, and he became the butt of many puns in aristocratic circles. S.M.—*Seine Majestät*—was scurrilously declared to stand for "SEMI-Imperator" or even for "Siegfried Meyer." The German Kaiser and king of Prussia, at least one noble disdainfully observed, was really only a parvenu.[6] Many Junkers who were in attendance at court, and others who resided permanently on their estates, believed that their old social, economic, and political hegemony was being undermined by a new elite based on wealth not associated with land. Simple prejudice, inherited from centuries of German history in which Jews had been regarded as inferior in the eyes of both law and society, was responsible for much of the antipathy of the conservative aristocracy toward Jews. By the nineteenth century, due to emancipation edicts and the alarming

[5] Schmidt-Ott, *Erlebtes und Erstrebtes 1860-1950*, Wiesbaden, 1952, p. 195; Harry Graf Kessler, *Tagebücher 1918-1937*, Frankfurt, 1961, p. 386; Görlitz, ed., *Der Kaiser*, p. 151.

[6] [Edgar Vincent] Viscount D'Abernon, *The Diary of an Ambassador*, 3 vols., Garden City, 1929-31, ii, 210-11.

permissiveness of modern society, there seemed to be an actual, demonstrable, and serious cause for alarm. Jews seemed to be acquiring greater influence at court and in the Wilhelmstrasse, they seemed to be beginning to succeed in marrying off their daughters to aristocratic landlords and *Geheimräte*, and they seemed to be acquiring wealth beside which the old agricultural fortunes appeared increasingly insignificant. Their politics, their economic views, and their social ambitions all seemed perversely calculated to challenge the ancient traditions by which Prussia, and thus Germany, was governed.

Ballin's relationship with William II and with Prussian and German society and politics is illustrative of the peculiar and difficult role which Germany's Jewish notables played in the last decades of the empire. What is true for Ballin seems to have been the case for other German Jews—all, certainly, were similarly subjected to an inferior status in the social and political order. It appears likely that the attitudes and activities of Gentile businessmen were close to those of their Jewish competitors, since they too were excluded (if somewhat less rigidly) from the highest levels of society and politics. Distinctions must, of course, be drawn not only between the Gentile and Jewish businessman, but between those in various regions of Germany, and between those engaged in different types of enterprise. An attempt is made here to outline only the position of the Jewish banking and commercial elite as reflected in Ballin's experience.

Ballin and the Kaiser had been born within eighteen months of one another, Ballin in August 1857, William in January 1859. Though they had nothing in common through inheritance or circumstance, their personalities were much alike, as were their interests and inclinations. William II, himself gracious and winning in discourse, was doubtless taken by Ballin's acknowledged gifts as a witty and tactful conversationalist and by his ease in society. Ballin, for his part, was impressed by William's faculty for quickly penetrating to the essentials of any subject under discussion. In the arts, both had traditional turns of mind, attached to old forms and standards and hostile to innovation. Both knew how to exercise a near-hypnotic spell on other men. Like Ballin, William was disposed to rush from optimism to despair, from benign amiability to impulsive anger. The two men shared a number of common interests and aspirations: ships and the sea, a restless love of travel, and an ambition to see Germany and its merchant marine achieve a worthy *Weltstellung*. They might therefore have been expected to find enjoyment in each other's company.

More importantly, both partners found a pragmatic virtue in the friendship. Ballin was a virtuoso in the arts of *Repräsentation*, and because of William's weakness for pageantry and glamour he was able to utilize this talent to great advantage. Though a man of only moderate wealth, Ballin had at his disposal a fleet whose elegance and immensity knew no peer in all the world. His entertainments aboard these floating palaces were sumptuous affairs, the refinements and graceful execution of which did not escape the Kaiser's discriminating eye. Ballin was also useful to William II. He was par excellence a source of information, a man with sound and influential contacts in many of the world's capitals and shipping centers, a man through whom overtures to Germany could be made and through whom hints to other powers could be dropped with a certainty of their obtaining the ultimate ear desired. On home territory as well, Ballin could perform a similar service. His acquaintance with important men extended to many fields, and he could, and did, introduce the Kaiser to many interesting and significant figures who otherwise

103

might never have reached the imperial presence.[7] The ships of the Hamburg-American Line always stood at the Kaiser's disposal, and more than once William chartered a liner for a cruise in the North Sea or the Mediterranean when his own *Hohenzollern* was in drydock. For many years, the HAPAG made several cabins on each of its cruise ships available at no cost to persons designated by the emperor.[8] To Ballin, as to almost any German of his time, the Kaiser's friendship was welcomed because of the signal honor it bestowed; for a humble Jew it was a rare accomplishment in which Ballin took an understandable satisfaction and a deep pride. In a more practical sense, being on a good footing with the Kaiser was valuable to Ballin, since it enabled him to present his views, and his appeals, to the highest political authority in the land.

Ballin was not uncritical; he was aware of the Kaiser's faults of character and judgment. He knew that William often chose his associates without judicious reflection and from them received much erroneous counsel. Always anxious to shield his imperial master, Ballin was inclined to attribute the Kaiser's transgressions less to undesirable qualities in the man than to the evil forces which encompassed him. "The poor Kaiser," he frequently lamented, lacked not the intelligence to overcome his problems but the will to stand up to his servants in the government and at court.[9] William's absurd animadversions of omnipotence

[7] Both Carl Fürstenberg and Max Warburg, for example, met the Kaiser through Ballin. Hans Fürstenberg, *Carl Fürstenberg: die Lebensgeschichte eines deutschen Bankiers*, Wiesbaden, n.d., p. 439; Warburg, *Aus meinen Aufzeichnungen*, n.p., 1952, p. 30.

[8] *Zeitschrift*, III, no. 4 (Feb. 20, 1904), 31; see also William II's *Ereignisse und Gestalten aus den Jahren 1878-1918*, Berlin, 1922, p. 90. For an interesting reaction to such an invitation, see Jonathan Steinberg, *Yesterday's Deterrent: Tirpitz and the Birth of the German Battle Fleet* (London, 1965), p. 54 n64.

[9] Theodor Wolff, *Der Marsch durch zwei Jahrzehnte*, Amsterdam, 1936, p. 255.

and omniscience were mere histrionics which were to be received politely but not with credulity, although Ballin himself sometimes became transported by the Kaiser's fiery rhetoric.[10] More often, however, he was well aware of the deleterious effect at home and abroad produced by William's shocking tactlessness, and he often deplored the Kaiser's thoughtless exuberance of expression.[11] It was, however, one thing to be conscious of the ruler's short-comings and quite another to do something about them. Ballin was an accomplished courtier, well aware of his own peculiar status and of William's singular personality. He therefore did not offer the Kaiser gratuitous advice, and, when asked for his opinion, he spoke out, but only as frankly as the Kaiser's mood and the attendant circumstances allowed. William listened patiently and with attention.[12]

The Kaiser's friendship with Ballin was the subject of wide comment and did much to enhance not only the

[10] See, for example, Ballin's favorable reaction to William's bombastic speech to his army at Döberitz in 1908 ("Let them come. We are ready.") in Ballin's article in the *Hamburgische Correspondent* (June 22, 1908), included in Ballin to Bülow, June 23, *AA*, Preussen 1 Nr. 1, no. 4m, vol. 1, reel 166/00839-40. See also Treutler (imperial entourage) to Foreign Office, June 21, *ibid.*, 166/00835-36.

[11] For Ballin's misgivings about the Kaiser's personality, see Ballin to Warburg, Aug. 29, 1910, Warburg "Nachlass," 2302/9/802; same to Harden, Sept. 3, 1910, Harden "Nachlass"; Bjarne Aagaard, "The Life of Albert Ballin," *Fairplay* (Jan. 26, 1922), 396; Wolff, *Marsch*, p. 255; Huldermann, p. 295.

[12] William's receptivity to Ballin's opinions and his failure to act on his advice is treated in Max Warburg's funeral oration on Ballin in Warburg "Nachlass," 3988/–/39, part of which is printed in the *Hamburgische Correspondent* (Nov. 13, 1918); Warburg, *Aufzeichnungen*, p. 25; Bülow, *Denkwürdigkeiten*, III, 7; Bogdan Graf von Hutten-Czapski, *Sechzig Jahre Politik und Gesellschaft*, 2 vols., Berlin, 1936, II, 154; Joachim von Kürenberg, *War Alles Falsch?: das Leben Kaiser Wilhelms II.*, Bonn, 1951, p. 99; Wolff, *Marsch*, pp. 255-56; Fürstenberg, *Lebensgeschichte*, p. 435; Bernstorff, *Memoirs*, p. 102; Huldermann, pp. 291-92.

managing director's personal prestige but that of the Hamburg-American Line as well. William's affection for the HAPAG and the North German Lloyd had begun early in life. Prince Bülow recalled the young man's exclaiming excitedly (and in too loud a voice) about the two maritime rivals as early as 1875, and later, as Kaiser, William followed the fortunes of both companies with the greatest interest. He even took pleasure in speaking of the HAPAG as his own creation and prided himself as having been personally responsible for the line's success.[13] Often the Kaiser's intervention in the Hamburg-American Line's relations with its competitors—as in the case of the Morgan trust negotiations—was helpful in promoting a settlement favorable to the line. This royal concern for the HAPAG and for its leader, though undoubtedly comforting to the line's stockholders, was not without its disadvantages. The Kaiser was fond of sending unsolicited advice and technical drawings to Ballin, material which, we are told, was given earnest consideration in Hamburg.[14] William's meddling was sometimes very impolitic and disturbed the HAPAG's relations with foreign governments and clients. A member of the HAPAG's board forthrightly declared that "Ballin's friendship with the Kaiser hurt more than it helped the Hamburg-American Line."[15]

[13] Anne Topham, *Chronicles of the Prussian Court*, London, n.d., p. 130; Bülow, *Denkwürdigkeiten*, III, 255; Carl August Schröder, *Aus Hamburgs Blütezeit*, Hamburg, 1921, pp. 207-08.

[14] See Admiral Georg von Müller, chief of the Naval Cabinet, to unnamed, April 23, 1912, *AA*, Marine-Kabinets, xxxi.c., vol. 1, reel 18/00606-08; *Zeitschrift*, III, no. 11 (June 5, 1904), 83-84; Huldermann, pp. 280-83.

[15] Huldermann, p. 292. For an example of the difficulty William caused the HAPAG, see Norman Rich and M. H. Fisher, eds., *The Holstein Papers* . . . , 4 vols., Cambridge, 1955-63, I, 178-79; Bülow, *Denkwürdigkeiten*, I, 48-49; Zedlitz-Trützschler, *Zwölf Jahre am Kaiserhof*, p. 200. Throughout William's reign, there were reports that he had sizeable investments in HAPAG stock. I

The person who first introduced Ballin to the Kaiser is unknown, though it may have been Prince Henckel von Donnersmarck. The occasion of their initial encounter is also obscure; it can be that they met as early as 1891, though the earliest record of their acquaintance dates only from 1895. The 1895 meeting proved rather unpleasant for Ballin, inasmuch as William—in what General Waldersee described as a "painful scene"— bluntly refused to entertain a plan which Ballin had drawn up for the festivities accompanying the opening of the *Nordostsee* canal.[16] This episode was soon forgotten, however, and relations between the two men became increasingly close. After Ballin's appointment as managing director in 1899, the Kaiser and his entourage became his guests at the annual HAPAG dinner preceding the lower Elbe regatta, Germany's great sailing event held in Hamburg every June immediately before Kiel Week. In 1905, William began to dine at Ballin's own house when in Hamburg. It was then a modest dwelling, but Ballin soon exchanged it for a mansion in the Feldbrunnenstrasse. This residence provided him with a suitable backdrop for entertaining the Kaiser, and so regular did the imperial visits become that one English newspaper christened Ballin's establishment "Klein Potsdam."[17] Sometimes the Kaiserin was present at these affairs; more

---

have not been able to find either a confirmation or a denial by the line on this point.

[16] See Heinrich O. Meisner, ed., *Denkwürdigkeiten des General-Feldmarschalls Alfred Grafen von Waldersee*, 3 vols., Stuttgart and Berlin, 1923, II, 343-44; also Hans Mohs, *General-Feldmarschall Alfred Graf von Waldersee in seinem militärischen Wirken*, 2 vols., Berlin, 1929, II, 427; Huldermann, p. 277-78.

[17] Ballin's guest book for his successive houses in Hamburg and his country seat in Hamfelde, Holstein, covering the years 1902-18, is preserved in the HAPAG archive. For a description of Ballin's dinners honoring the Kaiser, see Görlitz, ed., *Der Kaiser*, pp. 155-56.

often she stayed behind in Berlin. Auguste Viktoria was an Anglophobe and something of an anti-Semite. She never shared her husband's affection for Ballin and was troubled by their friendship.[18] When apart, Ballin and the Kaiser exchanged letters, a correspondence which William found useful and which he encouraged.[19] Prior to 1914, Ballin saw the Kaiser no more than a half dozen times a year in society, and perhaps equally frequently on business or political matters. The remarkable aspect of their friendship was not therefore its intimacy—for it never approached the relation William had with his close friends such as Max Egon Prince von Fürstenberg or Philipp Prince zu Eulenburg—but the fact that Ballin was the only Jew, and one of the few businessmen, whom William saw regularly and whose friendship he obviously valued and enjoyed.

Ballin's position at court was entirely dependent on his relationship with the Kaiser; with the Junker aristocracy which composed the royal entourage he had almost no connections. The only figure in William's retinue with whom he had a really close association was Admiral Georg von Müller, the chief of the Naval Cabinet (*Marinekabi-*

[18] For the Kaiserin's hostility to Ballin, see Merck "Nachlass," "Erinnerungen," Anlage 10, pp. 234-35; Wolff, *Marsch*, p. 248. On Auguste Viktoria (the name was frequently spelled Auguste Victoria), whose influence has been underrated, see Keller, *Vierzig Jahre*; Edith Keen, *Seven Years at the Prussian Court* (London, 1916); Zedlitz-Trützschler, *Zwölf Jahre am Kaiserhof*; the memoirs of her sister, Princess Friedrich Leopold of Prussia, *Behind the Scenes at the Prussian Court*, London, 1939; Andreas Dorpalen, "Empress Auguste Victoria and the Fall of the German Monarchy," *American Historical Review*, LVIII, no. 1 (Oct. 1952), 17-38; and Görlitz, ed., *Der Kaiser*, pp. 204-05.

[19] Almost all of William's letters to Ballin were destroyed in Ballin's lifetime. See the letter of former chancellor Wilhelm Cuno, Ballin's successor at the HAPAG, to Max Warburg, Aug. 11, 1927, in folder 149, "Cuno-M. M. Warburg um 1921 bis 1932," HAPAG archive. See also Merck "Nachlass," "Erinnerungen," p. 198; Wolff, *Marsch*, p. 254; Huldermann, p. 292.

nett) from 1906 to 1918, a man who was born neither a Prussian nor a noble.[20] Most of William's courtiers appear to have treated Ballin with respect and attention—which was the behavior to be expected toward a royal favorite and a man of importance in his own right—but with suspicion, for Ballin was to them the prototype of the socially ambitious and politically dangerous Jewish plutocrat.

On the social front, there were many Jews who strove for a place in society commensurate with their wealth and who believed that it could be secured if only one lived in state and entertained with premeditation. The wives of Carl Fürstenberg and Paul von Schwabach were noted for the weekly salons over which they presided, at which Jewish businessmen and aristocratic army officers and government officials mixed.[21] Ballin detested this sort of involvement and maintained that the social ambitions of wealthy Jews only increased anti-Semitism.[22] Albert and Marianne had no such aspirations, and while their parties in the Felbrunnenstrasse house were noted for their elegance, the guests themselves were usually old Hamburg and Berlin friends. The immense affairs on HAPAG liners during the regatta and at Kiel Week were to the Ballins business affairs in a social setting, designed to discharge

[20] See Görlitz, ed., *Der Kaiser*, and also his *Regierte der Kaiser?: Kriegstagebücher, Aufzeichnungen und Briefe des Chefs des Marine-Kabinetts Admiral Georg Alexander von Müller 1914-1918*, Göttingen, 1959. Ballin knew and respected the Minister of the Royal Household, August Count zu Eulenburg, a Junker. Rudolf Vierhaus, ed., *Das Tagebuch der Baronin Spitzemberg: Aufzeichnungen aus der Hofgesellschaft des Hohenzollernreiches*, 2d edn., Göttingen, 1960, p. 548; Wolff, *Marsch*, p. 255.

[21] Fürstenberg, *Lebensgeschichte*, pp. 56, 334, 398-99; Zobeltitz, *Chronik*, II, pp. 253-55.

[22] Ballin to Harden, April 11, 1911, Harden "Nachlass." Cf. Werner Freiherr von Rheinbaben, *Viermal Deutschland: aus dem Leben eines Seemanns, Diplomaten, Politikers 1895-1954*, Berlin, 1954, p. 76.

109

HAPAG obligations, render favors to valued clients or pro-spectively helpful legislators, and to pay a courtesy to the Kaiser. To outside observers, however, they might easily have been regarded as Ballin's bid for social status. Even the very ships on which his receptions took place—to William II and the general public inspiring proof of Ger-many's commercial and technological accomplishments—were to much of the Prussian aristocracy only the effete and sensuous emblems of a decaying empire. A prominent general complained of the *Imperator* that "to me the whole get-up, including the sumptuous Hamburg-style meals . . . , appeared as a typical manifestation of the new Germany, with its huckstering, obtrusive manners more a snobbism than a symbol of true German ability. To others it seems just so." The Kaiser's intimate, Philipp zu Eulen-burg, disparaged the HAPAG's great *Deutschland* in much the same way.[23]

There were, to be sure, some German aristocrats who had no prejudices against rich Jews, or who managed to overcome them for the sake of lavish entertainment, a handsome dowry, or interesting company. Some of these nobles were Prussians, but more seem to have been drawn from the other German states. It is perhaps symptomatic of this distinction that virtually all of Ballin's aristocratic friends—men such as the grand duke of Oldenburg, Philipp Prince zu Hohenlohe-Schillingsfürst, and several distinguished counts, Metternich, Brockdorff-Rantzau, Bernstorff, and many others—were not Prussians. The more broad-minded of Germany's nobility enjoyed the society of the Ballins, Friedländer-Fulds, and Fürstenbergs and returned their favors without ever reflecting that they

[23] Hugo Freiherr von Freytag-Loringhoven, *Menschen und Dinge wie ich sie in meinem Leben sah*, Berlin, 1923, pp. 172-73; Eulenburg, *Mit dem Kaiser als Staatsmann und Freund auf Nordlandsreisen*, 2 vols., Dresden, 1931, II, 178, 233. Cf. Spitzem-berg, *Tagebuch*, p. 542.

were Jews, or at least without deliberately reminding themselves of the fact.[24]

The political position of the Jews in imperial Germany
was as uncertain as the place which they had managed to
establish for themselves in Wilhelmine society. Just as
the Prussian aristocracy exercised a virtual monopoly in
court society, its control of politics was unassailable,
though not uncontested. The aristocracy's inordinate
political power was derived from the peculiar construction
of the Prussian electoral system and from the great prominence awarded to Prussia by the imperial constitution. The
Conservative (*Deutschkonservative*) party, which represented the Junkers in both the Prussian and imperial par-
liaments, was frankly—and at times officially—anti-
Semitic.[25] In political terms, the "Jewish peril"—to employ
the vocabulary of William II's good Anglo-Prussian friend
Daisy, Princess of Pless—loomed on two fronts as far as
Junker Conservatives were concerned. The commercial
middle class, whose wealthiest and most articulate members
so often were Jews, as well as Jewish newspaper magnates, were attracted not to the Conservative party but to
those parties such as the National Liberals which called for
a lower tariff and a franchise which would grant the
moneyed interest a greater measure of participation in
politics. Even more disturbing to Conservatives was the
fact that relatively indigent Jews, so it seemed, had formed
the backbone of the socialist terror from Lassalle in the
1860's on down to Bernstein and Luxemburg at the

[24] Magnus Baron von Braun to author, Feb. 3, 1964, and in
his *Von Ostpreussen bis Texas*, Stollhamm, 1955, p. 79. See also
Wolff, *Marsch*, p. 246.

[25] See the 1892 Tivoli program of the party in Wolfgang Treue,
Deutsche Parteiprogramme 1861-1954, Göttingen, etc., 1954, pp.
74-76; also Peter G. J. Pulzer, *The Rise of Political Anti-Semitism
in Germany and Austria*, New York, etc., 1964, pp. 118-20. Cf.
Westarp, *Konservative Politik*, I, 198-99; and Schiffer, *Ein Leben*,
p. 102.

present.[26] Though the Conservatives were powerless to keep Jews from becoming active in parliamentary politics, they were successful in preventing many from being appointed to high positions in the Prussian and imperial governments. Ballin himself was one of their victims, for he was mentioned several times for cabinet posts only to be ruled out on at least one occasion for fear of antagonizing the Conservatives.[27]

There was also hostility between the Conservatives and the leaders of German commerce on economic questions, and it was here that Ballin found himself most at odds with Junkerdom. Social snobbery he could bear easily, but business was Ballin's life, and economic policies which were counter to the interests of German commerce were too intolerable to be swallowed without protest. The economic differences between Ballin and the Conservatives were quite unbridgeable. Agrarian protectionism, one of the cornerstones of Conservative policy, clashed with his demand for low tariffs, if not for free trade. The Hamburg-American Line had a vital interest in the lucrative grain trade with North America, which made up a great part of its freight operations. High import tariffs would render foreign grain uncompetitive in the German market, and once American grain could be undersold it would cease to be imported. As a result, of course, the HAPAG's freight loadings would decline. The same situation

[26] See the testimony on this point of the Princess of Pless in her *What I Left Unsaid*, New York, 1936, pp. 170, 254; also Henry Wickham Steed, *Through Thirty Years 1892-1922: A Personal Narrative*, 2 vols., Garden City, 1924, I, 32-33; Schwering, *Berlin Court*, p. 225; Max Warburg, "Zur Gründung des Überseeklubs," address of June 17, 1922, printed copy in the Hamburg Staatsbibliothek. On anti-Semitism and the German press, see Sir Valentine Chirol, *Fifty Years in a Changing World*, London, 1927, p. 268.

[27] *Berliner Tageblatt* (June 24, 1901); Bülow, *Denkwürdigkeiten*, II, 385; *Sigilla Veri*, I, 371.

112

applied to the importation of meat from the western hemisphere.[28] The HAPAG therefore publicly insisted on a downward revision in the tariff and entertained legislators, educators, and other influential groups to create support for its campaign against the Conservative party and its strong agricultural lobby, the *Bund der Landwirte*.[29]

Taxation policy was another issue over which Ballin and most German businessmen clashed with the Junkers. The Conservative party stubbornly refused to agree to any plan of tax reform which would require the agrarian interest to contribute a more equitable share toward the costs of government. In 1909, Ballin joined a number of commercial and industrial leaders in forming the *Hansa Bund*, which was to help elect Reichstag deputies who would press for tax and tariff reforms to which the Conservatives were opposed.[30] In addition, he was engaged for many years in a quarrel with the Prussian Conservatives because of their attempt to impose duties on shipping on the Elbe and other inland waterways, a form of taxation which Ballin claimed was prohibited under the 1871 imperial constitution.[31]

If Ballin and the Conservatives were economically at odds, there were at the same time personal and ideological forces which tended to draw him and the greater figures of the party together. His relations with Germany's political chieftains after 1900 reveal this tie and also indicate the

[28] See the *Hamburger Correspondent* (June 6, 1893), reporting complaints by the conservative *Kreuzzeitung* on this point.

[29] HAPAG, Annual Report, 1904; for the line's purposeful entertaining, consult the *Zeitschrift*.

[30] *Zeitschrift*, VIII, no. 13 (July 5, 1909) 61.

[31] Annual Report, 1903. See also Ballin's article in the *Handels-Zeitung des Berliner Tageblatts* (Aug. 25, 1909), and the commentary on it in the *Hamburger Fremdenblatt* (Aug. 26 and Sept. 3); also Adolf Goetz, *25 Jahre Hamburgische Seeschiffahrtspolitik*, Hamburg, 1911, pp. 286-94.

avenues and opportunities for wielding political influence which were available to a man officially unconnected with the government.

Ballin's acquaintance with Bismarck and his first two successors, General Leo von Caprivi and Chlodwig Prince zu Hohenlohe-Schillingsfürst, was fleeting, and it was not until Bernhard von Bülow took office in 1900 that Ballin and the Conservatives were brought into political contact. There is evidence of Ballin's acquaintance with Bülow from the mid-1890's, though it is possible that they knew each other earlier in Hamburg, for Bülow had been born in Flottbek, just outside the city, and maintained a residence there until his death. From 1903 on, the two men corresponded occasionally and saw one another frequently in Hamburg or in Berlin. Bülow, with his enthusiasm for hyperbole and classical allusion, apostrophized his friend as *Albertus Magnus*. The chancellor's affection for Ballin appears to have been genuine and Bülow paid him the extraordinarily rare compliment of a charitable portrait in his controversial memoirs.[32] For his part, Ballin enjoyed the witty prince and his talented and exuberant wife and he entertained them often. He was, however, concerned at the effect which Bülow's blandishments might have on the very impressionable Kaiser.[33] In 1903, after Bülow had served for three years as chancellor, Ballin characterized him as a "misfortune," and declared to Field Marshal Waldersee that the chancellor was "completely spoiling the Kaiser, constantly telling him the grossest flatteries and thereby leading him to have an ex-

[32] See particularly the summation of Ballin's character in the *Denkwürdigkeiten*, III, 284-85, and also Sigmund Münz, *Fürst Bülow der Staatsmann und Mensch: Aufzeichnungen, Erinnerungen und Erwägungen*, Berlin, 1930, p. 210.

[33] Hermann Freiherr von Eckardstein, *Die Entlassung des Fürsten Bülow*, Berlin, 1931, pp. 69-71; Waldersee, *Denkwürdigkeiten*, III, 176; Spitzemberg, *Tagebuch*, pp. 548-49.

travagant opinion of himself."[34] Friedrich von Holstein, Bülow's intimate in the Foreign Office, retailed this criticism to Bülow, but the chancellor's good relations with Ballin were undisturbed.[35] Ballin apparently overcame his qualms about Bülow; in any case, he did not raise the charges again, though the chancellor's efforts to ingratiate himself with William II remained unbounded.

Ballin and Bülow constantly disagreed on economic policy, for Bülow supported the Conservatives on tariff matters during most of his administration. It was not until 1909, just before Bülow fell, that the two men joined forces against the agrarians, who refused to agree to tax revision necessitated by the increasing cost of Germany's naval construction program. As Bülow noted, however, he and Ballin were otherwise in agreement, and the economic difficulties between the two men were balanced by the similarity of their views on purely political matters.[36] The cornerstone of the Prussian conservative tradition was allegiance to the monarchy, and this was a principle to which Ballin wholeheartedly subscribed. He was a monarchist by conviction and he was frankly suspicious of all republicans. "The essential thing," he wrote to Maximilian Harden in 1909, ". . . is the throne; the republicans (I have seen too much of them behind the scenes) are loathesome (*widerlich*)."[37] Like both the chancellor and the Conservatives, Ballin was an energetic opponent of Social Democracy, and he congratulated Bülow for his adamant stand against the socialist leader, August Bebel, who for years held one of Hamburg's Reichstag seats.[38] On the all-

[34] Waldersee, *Denkwürdigkeiten*, III, 220.

[35] Rich and Fisher, eds., *Holstein Papers*, IV, 234-35.

[36] Huldermann, p. 294.

[37] Harden "Nachlass," letter of Nov. 1, 1909.

[38] Telegram of Dec. 11, 1903, Bülow "Nachlass," partially printed in *Denkwürdigkeiten*, II, 10.

115

important issue of parliamentary reform, Ballin sided with the Conservatives. In his speech to his employees on the Kaiser's birthday in 1907, an annual HAPAG rite, Ballin declared himself against any alteration in the Prussian franchise, and at about the same time he branded the proposals for constitutional reform made by the Progressive deputy, Friedrich Naumann, as "enormously stupid."[39] Bülow, moreover, had always encouraged and supported the Hamburg-American Line's attempt to plant the German flag around the world. In the decisive 1907 Reichstag elections, Ballin therefore joined in a move by the *Zentralverband Deutscher Industrieller* to establish an election fund to help Bülow and his Conservative allies in their battle at the polls with the Centrists, Social Democrats, Guelfs, and Poles.[40]

Bülow's "Block" carried the election, but the chancellor's continuation in office was contingent on his ability to resolve the many controversies, notably those centering on electoral and fiscal reform, which were the subject of current debate. Ballin realized this, and much as he had come to like the chancellor, he was by no means at a loss for men whom he considered suitable replacements should Bülow prove unable to overcome his problems. As early as January 1908, Ballin had decided on Adolf Baron Marschall von Bieberstein, then ambassador to the Porte, a man whom he greatly admired and whose name he suggested to the Kaiser. A courtier, on hearing of Ballin's suggestion, observed that "it is quite remarkable that Ballin is already allowing himself to dispose of Bülow's place in such a manner."[41] William II only winced at Ballin's idea,

---

[39] *Zeitschrift*, VI, no. 4 (Feb. 5, 1907), 32, also printed in Goetz, *Seeschiffahrtspolitik*, pp. 277-82; Bülow, *Denkwürdigkeiten*, II, 464.

[40] George D. Crothers, *The German Elections of 1907*, New York, 1941, pp. 162, n165.

[41] Spitzemberg, *Tagebuch*, p. 480. For Ballin's high regard for Marschall, see *ibid.*, p. 548.

however, for he had never liked Marschall. Ballin's proposal of Marschall in 1908 was premature, but after the Kaiser's unfortunate *Daily Telegraph* interview at the end of October of the same year, speculating on a successor for the discredited chancellor became a public pastime. Very soon after the scandal occurred, Ballin was approached by a number of people—none of whose names we know—who entreated him to speak plainly to William so that in the future he would be more circumspect. Ballin declined the request, holding that to do so would be an unpleasant assignment which properly belonged to someone else.[42]

Ballin's behavior in the winter of 1908-09 indicates very clearly that he sympathized with the chancellor, who as the head of the government was responsible for the fact that the interview had been approved by the Foreign Office for publication, and not with the Kaiser, whose tactlessness accounted for the incendiary observations contained in it. At the same time, the unfortunate affair put Ballin in a delicate position no matter whether the fault were the Kaiser's, Bülow's, or that of some unobservant functionary in the Foreign Office. Could he openly sympathize with the chancellor and at the same time preserve his good standing with William II? Ballin apparently decided to tell Bülow and the Kaiser what each wanted to hear, hoping that neither would get wind of his words of commiseration to the other. According to Professor Theodor Schiemann, one of the Kaiser's intimate friends, Ballin had at first not blamed the chancellor for the fiasco, but later, informed by William of some incriminating details, declared to the distraught man that "the chancellor has betrayed Your Majesty."[43] To Bülow, if we can believe the

---

[42] Merck "Nachlass," "Erinnerungen," p. 72.

[43] Klaus Meyer, *Theodor Schiemann als politischer Publizist*, Frankfurt, 1956, p. 160. A similar report is given by Eckardstein

chancellor's version, Ballin spoke quite differently: "Ballin said to me then, 'I don't read a tenth part of the incoming mail or the letters presented to me for signature. No leader of a great concern can do that!' "[44] Ballin's *Doppelspiel* went undetected, and the incident in no way troubled his cordial relations with either man.

The *Daily Telegraph* affair caused Ballin, very briefly, to question his former contentment with the political system by which Germany was ruled. The interview had made evident not only the incapacity but also the irresponsibility of the throne, as well as the fact that the bureaucracy was unequal to the task of preventing the Kaiser's idiosyncratic diplomacy from damaging Germany's relations with its neighbors. The only recourse was to put more authority in the hands of the Reichstag. Ballin, together with Max Warburg, hoped that as a result of the *gaffe* some sort of constitutional reform would be introduced to limit the crown's power and increase that of the parliament. The two men intended that Friedrich Naumann, whose call for reform Ballin had ridiculed only the year before, become the leader of a reform movement in the Reichstag. It was essential that Bülow not be forced to resign, for then the responsibility for the affair would appear to have been his alone and his resignation would bury the matter without any constitutional steps having been taken to prevent a similar debacle from occurring in the future.[45] Though

---

in his *Entlassung Bülow*, pp. 52-53, 69-70. See also Helmuth Rogge, *Holstein und Harden: politisch-publizistisches Zusammenspiel zweier Aussenseiter des wilhelminischen Reichs*, Munich, 1959, p. 436.

[44] Bülow "Nachlass," Merkblatt K, 119a, written in Oct. 1920. The pagination scheme used here is that devised by Friedrich Freiherr Hiller von Gaertringen in his *Fürst Bülows Denkwürdigkeiten: Untersuchungen zu ihrer Entstehungsgeschichte und ihrer Kritik*, Tübingen, 1956.

[45] Warburg to Naumann (Draft), Nov. 3, 1908; Warburg to

there was also reform agitation in the Reichstag by liberals and Social Democrats, no bills proposing constitutional changes were introduced, and a highly agitated William retired from public notice to avoid the mounting outrage in both England and Germany at his asinine behavior. Within a few weeks the furor created by the interview was much abated. The Kaiser, for once remorseful, resolved to retain Bülow in office, a decision which prompted Ballin to wire the chancellor how "happy and heartfully thankful" this development made him.[46] Ballin's enthusiasm for strengthening the Reichstag, it should be carefully noted, did not survive the immediate crisis. By mid-November, there are no further traces in his correspondence of any interest in constitutional reform.

The reasons for Ballin's failure to persevere with his 1908 reform intentions are unclear. It seems probable, however, that in the winter of 1908-09 Ballin felt that the Kaiser's apathy and depression, which set in immediately after William realized how unpopular his indiscretion had made him, indicated that he would not repeat his performance. Though William did and said many foolish things after his recovery and return to public affairs in the late spring of 1909, none, perhaps, were as epic as the *Daily Telegraph* fiasco. Ballin may have concluded that the experience had mellowed William, and from 1909 on there is nothing to indicate that he felt that the Kaiser's behavior was alarming enough to warrant changes in the constitution which would reduce the crown's prerogatives. It would be only late in 1918, as the empire's extinction

Ballin, same date, both in Warburg "Nachlass," 1014/9/801. See the commentary on this correspondence by the friend of both men, Eduard Rosenbaum, "A Postscript to the Essay on Albert Ballin," Leo Baeck Institute of Jews from Germany, *Year Book*, IV, London, 1959, 269.

[46] Telegram of Nov. 17, 1908, Bülow "Nachlass."

became imminent, that Ballin was again enlisted in the cause of constitutional reform.

Although Bülow was allowed to continue as chancellor, the *Daily Telegraph* incident seriously weakened his position, for the Kaiser believed that he had been disloyal, the Reichstag—depending on the party—that he had been very negligent or very stupid. Ballin tried again without success to persuade William that ambassador Marschall was the man of the hour: when the moment for Bülow's departure should arrive, it was he who should become chancellor, with August Count zu Eulenburg, Minister of the Royal Household, and Field Marshal Colmar von der Goltz as somewhat superannuated alternatives.[47] Theobald von Bethmann Hollweg, the Prussian interior minister, was also a man whom the Kaiser might keep in mind for the post.[48] Interestingly, rumors current in Berlin placed Ballin himself among those said to be under consideration as Bülow's successor.[49] Many years later, the exiled Kaiser declared that he had indeed wanted to name Ballin chancellor in 1909 but that "obvious reasons" had prevented his doing so.[50]

By late spring 1909, Bülow's fall had become increasingly likely, not only because of the lingering distaste at-

[47] For Ballin's role in the succession crisis see Rogge, *Holstein und Harden*, pp. 409, 443, 451-52, 458-66; Otto Hammann, *Um den Kaiser*, Berlin, 1919, pp. 80-81; Eckardstein, *Entlassung Bülow*, p. 70; Görlitz, ed., *Der Kaiser*, p. 102. See also Karl Nowak and Friedrich Thimme, eds., *Erinnerungen und Gedanken des Botschafters Anton Graf Monts*, Berlin, 1932, p. 147.

[48] Müller diary notes for Dec. 11, 1908, in Görlitz, ed., *Der Kaiser*, p. 102.

[49] See, for example, the laconic entry in Schiemann's journal for March 10, 1909: "Reichskanzlerkandidaten, Kapp, Bethmann-Hollweg, Ballin," in Meyer, *Schiemann*, p. 166; also Ernst Jäckh, *Kiderlen-Wächter der Staatsmann und Mensch: Briefwechsel und Nachlass*, 2 vols., Berlin and Leipzig, 1924, II, p. 32.

[50] Bernhard Guttmann, *Schattenriss einer Generation 1888-1919*, Stuttgart, 1950, p. 247.

tached to his role in the *Daily Telegraph* imbroglio but also because of Conservative opposition to an estate tax scheme which he had introduced to solve the government's fiscal problems. The Conservatives deserted Bülow's "Block," a move which Ballin castigated as "deceitful," "vulgar and stupid."[51] On June 24th, the government's proposed legislation was defeated by a narrow vote, and on July 14th the chancellor resigned. Ballin at once telegraphed Bülow to pay tribute to the support which the former chancellor had given to German overseas trade and promised that the next HAPAG liner would be christened the *Fürst von Bülow*. The prince responded to this handsome gesture by inviting Ballin, General Helmuth von Moltke, and other loyal friends to a farewell dinner in the chancellor's palace. The Kaiser and Kaiserin, with whom Ballin had dined the previous evening, were also present, invited, doubtless, only because the dictates of etiquette prescribed their inclusion. A few days later, Bülow left Berlin for Hamburg, where Ballin was waiting on the station platform to welcome the fallen chancellor and to take him to dinner, after which the two friends sat up until past midnight over cigars and brandy.[52]

Ballin was fond of referring to Bethmann Hollweg, whose appointment as chancellor had been arranged by his predecessor, as "Bülow's revenge."[53] Ballin and Bethmann had little in common—the Hohenfinow academic

[51] Ballin to Harden, June 29 and July 2, 1909, Harden "Nachlass"; same to Warburg, May 3, 1909, Warburg "Nachlass," 1014/9/801. For Ballin's advice to Bülow at this time, see Ballin to Warburg, July 9, 1909, Warburg "Nachlass," 1014/9/801. Cf. same to Fürstenberg, July 6, in Fürstenberg, *Lebensgeschichte*, p. 482, and Loebell to Ballin, June 18, 1909, in Harden "Nachlass." Loebell is probably Friedrich Wilhelm von Loebell, chief of the imperial chancellery.

[52] *Berliner Tageblatt* (July 15 and 16, 1909); Bülow, *Denkwürdigkeiten*, III, 5-6, 371.

[53] Eckardstein, *Entlassung Bülow*, p. 80.

121

agrarian, well-meaning but very slow-moving, contrasted with the volatile, cosmopolitan merchant of Hamburg. No real personal rapport ever developed between the two men, for Ballin found the chancellor's tendency to procrastinate a very dangerous attribute in a man entrusted with such great authority. Bethmann, Ballin complained to Harden, unfortunately possessed "all the qualities which honor a man but ruin a statesman."[54] In a similar vein, he remarked to another acquaintance that Bethmann was an uncommonly articulate man but one whose failure was that he did not realize that politics was a dirty business and therefore one which could not be pursued by honorable means.[55] Bethmann apparently thought highly of Ballin, for he consulted him frequently on matters of state and entrusted him with private diplomatic business abroad. Ballin, in turn, forwarded the correspondence or views of his friends to the chancellor whenever he felt that Bethmann was in need of guidance or information.[56]

To Ballin, a chancellor of Bethmann's stamp constituted a double misfortune. First, Bethmann's torpor, like Bülow's unctuous flattery, had a disastrous effect on the Kaiser. Instead of controlling the excitable monarch, the chancellor did nothing and thereby encouraged William to commit new *faux pas*.[57] In the second place, the chancel-

[54] Letter of March 6, 1910, Harden "Nachlass." The description of Ballin's "hostile attitude" toward Bethmann in Hutten-Czapski, *Sechzig Jahre*, II, 134, is overdrawn for the peacetime years. For favorable judgments of Bethmann by Ballin, see Ballin to Harden, July 4, 1910, Harden "Nachlass"; Spitzemberg, *Tagebuch*, p. 548. See also Bülow, *Denkwürdigkeiten*, III, 106.

[55] Magnus Baron von Braun to author, Feb. 3, 1964. See also Spitzemberg, *Tagebuch*, p. 548.

[56] Ballin to Warburg, April 16, 1913, Warburg "Nachlass," 3072/265/802; same to Harden, Aug. 9, 1910, Harden "Nachlass."

[57] Ballin to Warburg, Aug. 28, 1910, Warburg "Nachlass," –/25a/Privat.

lor's passivity was hardly sufficient to cut through what Ballin described as the "stupefying atmosphere" which pervaded Berlin. At the end of August 1910, he wrote despairingly to Harden that the German government was one characterized by "delay everywhere because of questions and considerations—no action. Willing to move but not capable of doing so because qualms are always being raised. . . . The German nation really cannot keep on getting excited about the Zeppelin: it must have deeds. I've written this to Bethmann Hollweg, but with a certainty that it will do no good."[58] If Bethmann could not muster enough initiative to control his government, then the Foreign Office would be able to pursue a policy independent of any sort of executive supervision. This would be intolerable, for the direction of the Wilhelmstrasse 76, as far as Ballin was concerned, was dangerously irresponsible and narrow-minded to the point of idiocy.

The German Foreign Office, like the Prussian officer corps, was to Ballin an arrogant enclave—"a club," he said, "into which one must be admitted by and through birth."[59] Ballin might have been able to stomach the Wilhelmstrasse, bastion of privilege that it was, had he not been convinced that it was also very largely a special preserve for aristocratic incompetents. The Foreign Office's ineptitude, Ballin claimed, deserved comparison only with its Austrian equivalent, and he had a very low regard for Austria in general and Viennese bureaucrats in particular.[60] Being a sealed social cloister of marginal intelligence, the Foreign Office seemed to be blind to everything except Prussian conservatism and agrarianism. The worst of these

[58] Letter of Aug. 18, 1910, Harden "Nachlass." See also same to same, Sept. 16, 1910, in *ibid*.

[59] Same to same, March 22, 1914, *ibid*.

[60] Ballin to Harden, July 30, 1913; see also same to same, Dec. 8 and 15, all in Harden "Nachlass."

123

cataracts was the fact that the department had no real awareness of economic factors and therefore paid scant attention to the views of German businessmen in the formulation of policy.[61] On hearing, for example, that minister von Wangenheim's reports from Mexico City contained items of interest for the business community, Ballin expressed his pleasure that "for once, finally, a minister is not 'too big' to bother himself with economic affairs."[62] In its aristocratic seclusion from economic issues and other timely questions, the Wilhelmstrasse drifted along in its self-created vacuum. "It seems," Ballin wrote to Harden in 1913, "as though one is determined in Berlin to remain on the lonely heights, beyond party and above the demands of the hour. Where the voyage is supposed to be going, no one knows."[63]

Many German diplomats, particularly those filling staff positions in Berlin, were as critical of Ballin as he was of them. Some of the Wilhelmstrasse's objections to the head of the HAPAG, like those of the conservative circles from which the department for the most part was recruited, grew out of its inbred, aristocratic prejudices against Jews, rich businessmen, and commoners. German diplomats, with a measure of justification, also took umbrage at the Kaiser's conversations on foreign affairs with Ballin to which government representatives were often not invited. The Wilhelmstrasse likewise protested the unofficial diplomatic missions which Ballin undertook on behalf of William II, although it frequently called on him to serve as an intermediary in delicate negotiations with England.[64] There

[61] Same to same, Nov. 1, 1909, Sept. 27, 1913, *ibid.*; Bülow, *Denkwürdigkeiten*, III, 178.

[62] Spitzemberg, *Tagebuch*, p. 451. See also Bülow, *Denkwürdigkeiten*, III, 178.

[63] Ballin to Harden, Nov. 14, 1910, Harden "Nachlass."

[64] See Richard von Kühlmann, *Erinnerungen*, Heidelberg, 1948, p. 347; E. F. Willis, *Prince Lichnowsky, Ambassador of Peace*,

were also officials who, like some of Ballin's associates in the Hamburg-American Line, felt that the HAPAG's expansion in colonial areas reaped little in the way of profits but did much to impede the establishment of better Anglo-German relations.[65]

In Ballin's opinion, some German diplomats—especially those who were not Prussians—were better than others. Baron Marschall von Bieberstein, a Badener who served as ambassador to the Porte from 1897 to 1912, struck him as the most competent of Germany's representatives abroad, and he therefore had favored his elevation to the chancellorship in 1908-09. Toward the Swabian Alfred von Kiderlen-Wächter, Bethmann's secretary of the Foreign Office from 1910 to 1912, Ballin was of two minds. He found Kiderlen's policies shortsighted, his "frivolous impetuosity" and coarse manners embarrassing. Yet he was, for all his faults, a man superior to the average official.[66] Counts Johann Bernstorff and Ulrich Brockdorff-Rantzau, both Holsteiners, Anton Count Monts from Bavaria, Paul Count Wolff Metternich, a mediatized Rhinelander, Richard von Kühlmann, no Junker, and Otto Hammann were all friends and all men whose judgment Ballin considered sound. All but Hammann were usually stationed far from Berlin, however, and were frequently slighted by the Foreign Office, which was inclined to disregard its ambassadors' reports when these dispatches clashed with its

Berkeley, 1942, p. 227; Wolff, *Marsch*, pp. 247-48, 264; A. von Tirpitz, *Politische Dokumente*, 2 vols., Berlin, etc., 1924-26, I, 163-64.

[65] Rich and Fisher, eds., *Holstein Papers*, IV, 424-25, and Norman Rich, *Friedrich von Holstein: Politics and Diplomacy in the Era of Bismarck and Wilhelm II*, 2 vols., Cambridge, 1965, II, 800.

[66] Ballin to Warburg, Jan. 3, 1913, Warburg "Nachlass," 3072/265/802. See also Johann Heinrich Count Bernstorff, "Ein Lebensbild Albert Ballins," *Deutsche Einheit*, VIII, no. 46 (Nov. 13, 1926), 1084-86, and *Memoirs*, p. 100; Spitzemberg. *Tagebuch*, p. 549.

preconceived notions of foreign affairs.[67] The situation grew worse under Kiderlen's successor, the sterile Gottlieb von Jagow, a man whom Ballin disliked greatly. The *Staatssekretär*, the scion of an ancient Prussian house and a snob, for his part was not very fond of Ballin.[68] Near the end of the war, after many of the men in question had been ignominiously cashiered, Ballin bitterly described what he would have done with Jagow, Bethmann, and other Wilhelmstrasse officials had they been HAPAG employees: ". . . for Bethmann, there would hardly have been a position at all, at the most that of librarian; Jagow barely a messenger boy, Zimmermann at most a porter; Stumm, 'as a borderline case' and half feebleminded, immediately to be dismissed."[69] More and more, Ballin looked back wistfully to the *Bülowzeit*. Throughout Bethmann's eight-year administration, Ballin remained the prince's partisan and tried to persuade the Kaiser to recall Bülow to his old office, a plan which the former chancellor himself persistently encouraged.[70]

Ballin, then, was both attracted and repelled by the conservative aristocracy which had effective command of German society and politics. The fact that he established himself on a close footing with William II, Bülow, and subsidiary figures in the government, as well as the nature of his relations with these men, leaves no doubt that Ballin, though anxious neither for office nor honors, wanted to make his influence felt in Wilhelmine politics. There

[67] German diplomatic correspondence abounds in examples of this practice. The best example I have encountered concerns Hugo Prince Radolin, ambassador in Paris from 1900 to 1910, in Radziwill, *Lettres*, III, p. 206.

[68] Theodor Wolff, *Der Krieg von Pontius Pilatus*, Zurich, 1934, p. 317, and his *Marsch*, p. 247.

[69] Note of Oct. 20, 1918, in Bülow "Nachlass," Notizen 1918 (II), 7.

[70] Eugen Zimmermann to Bülow, Jan. 26, 1913, and Nov. 8, 1914, in *ibid.*, file no. 131; Bülow, *Denkwürdigkeiten*, III, 115.

were many other middle class men who for differing reasons were opposed to Prussian conservatism and to the powerful sway which its adherents exercised in affairs of state. Being men of less distinguished connections, however, they could not expect to bring about changes in government policy by fraternizing with the aristocrats who composed the leadership of the state. Instead, they entered parliamentary politics. These middle class dissidents were represented in the Reichstag primarily by the National Liberal party, and to a lesser extent by the Free Conservatives, Catholic Centrists, and Progressives. Many members of these parties, and not a few of their leaders, were men who had made their mark in the world of business and who in most cases shared Ballin's views on economic questions. In spite of the similarity of their economic views and social origins, Ballin declined to be drawn into an active partnership with parliamentary liberalism. There is no indication that he ever formally joined or made financial contributions to any political party, liberal or conservative.

The reason for Ballin's aloofness from the liberals was his conviction that their politics were bad and their parliamentary activity well intentioned but ineffectual. In terms of policy, Ballin's sympathy for liberalism was at best only partial. While he subscribed to the liberals' economic demands for laissez-faire and more equitable taxation, he could not agree with their political aspirations —exactly the opposite of his relationship with the Conservative party. Prior to the war, except for the brief moment in the wake of the *Daily Telegraph* incident, Ballin was opposed to any alteration in the Prussian franchise, the great issue over which liberals and conservatives clashed. He insisted instead that talented businessmen stand as candidates for the Reichstag and, if elected, introduce measures favorable to Germany's economic

127

interests.[71] Ballin himself never considered running, for to him parliamentary politics were too wearisome, too slow, and too removed from the real seat of power. The Wilhelmine Reichstag had almost no authority in the formulation or execution of foreign policy, while it was precisely in this area that Ballin's personal predilections and most of the HAPAG's business interests lay.[72] Diplomacy was the province of the crown, the chancellor, and the Foreign Office, and with all three he possessed varying degrees of contact. Ballin chose to work where he felt his activity would prove most effective—outside the Reichstag. The HAPAG, of course, did entertain legislators on its ships during Kiel Week and on other occasions, but Ballin made only one attempt to enlist a parliamentary figure as his spokesman. During the war, he encouraged Siegfried Heckscher, the head of the HAPAG's labor relations division, to run on the Progressive ticket for a Reichstag seat with the expectation that, if successful, Heckscher would serve as the HAPAG's mouthpiece. On taking his seat, however, Heckscher found Ballin's directives distastefully conservative, and relations between the two men quickly became acrimonious. Heckscher proved to be of almost no use to the line.[73]

It may be that no effective cooperation could develop between Ballin and parliamentary liberals because of his identification in the popular mind with William II and therefore with the Kaiser's arch-conservative entourage.

[71] *Zeitschrift*, VI, no. 4 (Feb. 5, 1907), 32; Ballin to Harden, Aug. 28, 1910, Harden "Nachlass."

[72] A Reichstag deputy, Eugen Schiffer, declared that the body regarded foreign policy as *Geheimwissenschaft*. Schiffer, *Ein Leben*, pp. 24-25; see also Fürstenberg, *Lebensgeschichte*, p. 470.

[73] Merck "Nachlass," "Erinnerungen," pp. 25-26. See also Heckscher's article on Ballin in *Roter Tag* (Jan. 3, 1922), in *ibid.*, II, Konv. 4, as well as correspondence between Merck and Heckscher in II. Konv. 5.

It was one thing to be a monarchist—and most German liberals favored preserving the crown—but quite another to be a royal favorite. It was not always possible for the liberal observer to perceive Ballin's incompatibility with much of what Prussian conservatism embodied nor the Junkers' opposition to his political activity, for he saw only the repeated meetings with the Kaiser, the lavish dinners and gigantic receptions aboard HAPAG ships and at the managing director's residence in Hamburg. Part of Ballin's isolation from parliamentary liberalism was probably due to this suspicion and to Ballin's inability to find any of the middle of the road parties compatible. But the fundamental cause was Ballin's impatience with parliamentary politics and his reservations about the desirability of constitutional reform.

Ballin consequently had few acquaintances among Reichstag liberals, and his only close parliamentary connection was Gustav Stresemann, who became the National Liberal leader after Ernst Bassermann's death in 1917.[74] The two men first met in 1913, when Stresemann, recently defeated for reelection to the Reichstag, and Ballin were instrumental in forming the *Deutsch-Amerikanischer Wirtschaftsverband*, the object of which was to promote transatlantic commerce. During the war, when Stresemann once again sat in parliament, the friends corresponded frequently and were constantly in touch through mutual acquaintances, one of whom was Peter Franz Stubmann,

[74] For correspondence between the two consult the Stresemann "Nachlass." Stresemann's appreciative eulogy of Ballin is printed in his *Reden und Schriften: Politik—Geschichte—Literatur 1897-1926*, 2 vols., Dresden, 1926, I, 206-11. See also Felix Hirsch, "Stresemann, Ballin und die Vereinigten Staaten," *Vierteljahrshefte für Zeitgeschichte*, III, no. 1 (Jan. 1955), 20-35; Marvin L. Edwards, *Stresemann and the Greater Germany 1914-1918*, New York, 1963; Donald Warren, Jr., *The Red Kingdom of Saxony: Lobbying Grounds for Gustav Stresemann 1901-1909*, The Hague, 1964.

another National Liberal deputy, who later became Ballin's biographer. With the leaders of German light industry, most of whom supported the National Liberals, Ballin had very limited dealings. Walther Rathenau of the *Allgemeine Elektrizitäts Gesellschaft*, like Ballin a Jew, was a friend, but not a close one.[75] In the ranks of the Progressives, Heckscher was the only Reichstag member with whom Ballin was in contact. The party, he declared, had "learned nothing" since Eugen Richter's death in 1906.[76] The Free Conservatives, who usually represented the interests of heavy industry, were unsatisfactory to Ballin because of their cooperation with the Conservatives on tax and tariff questions. Although he was a member of the *Bund der Industriellen* and though many industrialists were active in the *Hansa Bund*, Ballin had virtually nothing to do with the coal and iron magnates of the Rhineland and Silesia other than Prince Henckel von Donnersmarck and Eduard Arnhold, whom he knew either socially or through mutual philanthropic interests. Only with Hugo Stinnes did Ballin have substantial business relations, for Stinnes was a member of the HAPAG board during the war and had ambitions of entering the shipping business on his own. Ballin found the Rhinelander an entrepreneurial genius, but also crafty, grasping, and offensive. "As some children cannot let alone a piece of cake, or some men a beautiful woman," Ballin warned, "so Stinnes cannot let business alone; he wants to make everything his own, even if it should happen to belong to someone else."[77] Finally, Ballin had little taste for the

[75] See Rathenau, *Briefe*, 2 vols., Dresden, 1926, and *Politische Briefe*, Dresden, 1929, in which there are occasional letters to Ballin and to Gustav Steinbömer, a mutual friend.

[76] Ballin to Harden, July 2, 1909, Harden "Nachlass."

[77] Harden, *Köpfe*, IV, 425, quoted in Hans W. Gatzke, *Germany's Drive to the West (Drang nach Westen): A Study of Germany's Western War Aims during the First World War*, Baltimore, 1950, p. 42.

130

amorphous Catholic Center party after it joined with the Conservatives to sabotage Bülow's tax legislation in 1909. Although Ballin recognized that there were talented men among the Centrists, he did not have a particularly high regard for the party's rising light, Matthias Erzberger, advising Bülow that while Erzberger had talent he lacked depth.[78]

Considering Ballin's ragged relationship with his employees, his friendship with the Kaiser, and his political conservatism, it is hardly surprising that he and the Social Democrats viewed each other with undisguised hostility.[79] In the Reichstag, the HAPAG and its leader were constantly under attack, most often because of the line's treatment of its workers. Parliamentary debates were strewn with socialist demands for higher wages for seamen and dockworkers, for better working conditions and shorter hours. Socialist deputies protested vehemently against the Hamburg-American Line's practice of hiring relatively cheap foreign and non-union help, either to perform jobs which German hands were capable of doing, or, worst of all, to serve as strikebreakers. Ballin himself, as the most prominent of Germany's shipping magnates and a man plainly opposed to the political and economic demands of the proletariat, was not unnaturally singled out as the archenemy. Socialist criticism of Ballin became especially vituperative after it became known in the fall of 1904 that the HAPAG was assisting the tsar in his war with Japan. Just before Admiral Rozhdestvenski's fleet sailed for the Far East, a socialist paper proclaimed that the HAPAG chief was "now the autocrat of Germany, in spite of the monarchy, the constitution, and the law. In this country today, one really obeys Ballin more than all legal factors. This is so because Herr Ballin dares to play

[78] Bülow, *Denkwürdigkeiten*, III, 209; Stubmann, pp. 191.
[79] See pp. 31-36.

131

the role of a Russian viceroy in Germany. And 'Russian' is now trumps in the German Empire."[80] This antagonism did not abate with time. A royal governess recalled an incognito visit to a radical socialist meeting in Potsdam in 1913 at which the speaker declared that an economic as well as a political revolution was necessary. If only the throne collapsed, political power would pass into the hands of "even more dangerous criminals" such as Ballin and Krupp von Bohlen und Halbach.[81]

Charges against Ballin were by no means restricted to the industrial Social Democrat proletariat. Some non-socialist artisans and handicraftsmen, who blamed their declining economic position on Germany's industrial revolution, saw in Ballin the eponym of those modern economic forces which had brought them privation and ruin. Many of these workers looked to the crown for protection and redress, and they were therefore alarmed when they noted the influence which Ballin seemed to enjoy at court. "It has come to the point," one critic lamented, "that our highest echelons are Ballinized (*verballinisiert*), that foreigners from Palestine and America enjoy entrée even at the uppermost steps of the throne, while the simple, hardworking German people, our craftsmen, small businessmen, our peasantry—those classes which have built up our *Volk* in sober, honorable loyalty—their path has been made difficult."[82]

Ballin thus found himself in a sort of political no man's land. He could not accept Prussian conservatism, though

[80] *Deutsch-Soziale Blätter* (Sept. 10, 1904), a violently anti-Semitic sheet, later published as the *Deutsches Blatt*.

[81] Keen, *Seven Years*, pp. 235-36.

[82] *Reichstag*, XI. Legislaturperiode, I. Session, erster Sessionsabschnitt (1903/04), vol. 1, 11. Sitzung, Jan. 14, 1904, remarks by Böckler, cols. 275-77. For the Deutsche Reform Partei to which Böckler belonged, see Westarp, *Konservative Politik*, I, 21.

its devotion to the monarchy, to law, order, and the rights vested in property were identical to his own. The Junkers, however, were prejudiced and arrogant; they were often inferior diplomats and bureaucrats, and they were fixedly attached to an economic point of view totally at variance with Ballin's. To middle class liberals, whose economic aspirations and social origins he shared and with whom he might have made effective use of his contacts and abilities, Ballin remained distant. He could not agree with their demands for constitutional reform and he found that parliamentary politics, which constituted the arena of the liberals' political activity, was a plainly insufficient agent in the battle for influence. For the lower orders, Ballin showed a patrician concern but no real sympathy; for Social Democracy, only detestation. He remained a man without a party.

Ballin by no means regarded his alienation from parliamentary politics as a disadvantage, for there were other means of furthering one's aims. The large pressure groups, such as the *Flottenverein*, the *Bund der Industriellen*, or the *Kolonial Gesellschaft* served such a function, and many of Ballin's business friends placed their names, resources, and energies at the disposal of such organizations. Ballin belonged to all three of these associations, and to many others, but he made no attempt to attain a commanding position in any of them. He was unhappy when he found himself in a body in which his authority was not readily admitted. And if debate became extended or committee work necessary, he quickly grew impatient. The pressure groups, like the Reichstag, were too ponderous, though they were often quite successful in realizing their aims.

Ballin preferred to work independently rather than become entangled in large bodies, and to him the proper channel through which a man got what he wanted was by presenting and discussing his views with those authorities who had sufficient power to take immediate and effective action toward their fulfillment. It was more practical to be able to open palace and ministerial doors and ask favors, or to urge changes through administrative fiat, than to wait on the laborious machinery of the Reichstag to pass new laws or revise old ones. Even when the Reichstag acted, who could be sure its legislation would be approved by the *Bundesrat* or accepted by the Kaiser? In order for Ballin to get what he wanted, it was important to him to cultivate men—such as bankers, government dignitaries, and writers—who not only shared his outlook but who were also in a position to make those in authority aware of it. Or he might work for the appointment of fellow business-men to high executive positions in the government. So, for example, in 1906 Ballin recommended to the Kaiser that the vacant colonial secretaryship be filled by a busi-nessman, and it seems that as a result of his suggestion Bernhard Dernburg of the *Darmstädter Bank* was named to the post.[83] To these men, in return, Ballin could offer his own influence both at home and abroad, as well as the enjoyment of his superb ships. To act independently was Ballin's nature, and he had great confidence that because of his tact, shrewdness, discretion, and charm he would be successful when he dealt with other men. The Hamburg-American Line, after all, had been built not only by his enterprise, but also by his talent for persuasion and negotiation.

[83] Heinrich Schnee, *Als letzter Gouverneur in Deutsch-Ostafrika. Erinnerungen*, Heidelberg, 1964, pp. 80-81, based on information given to Schnee in 1924 by the former vice-president of the Reichs-tag, Hermann Paasche. In their memoirs, neither Paasche, chan-cellor Bülow, nor William II mention Ballin's role in Dernburg's appointment. They do not, however, attribute the inspiration to anyone else, and there seems no reason to doubt Schnee's state-ment.

It is not surprising that Ballin chose to pursue his aims in such a manner, for he knew most of the great men of Germany and not a few in foreign capitals. If influence could be wielded through person-to-person contact, he was in an excellent position to wield it. Ballin's great advantage was, of course, his friendship with the Kaiser. On an inferior level, there was his association with Bülow, Bethmann, and other high officials in Berlin. The nature of Ballin's connection with some of these men has already been described; his relationship with other political leaders will be treated in the chapters which follow. Outside the government, Ballin could count on two groups of friends who were of considerable influence in Wilhelmine Germany. These were Germany's leading bankers and journalists. Ballin often did his work entirely alone, going straight to the Kaiser or chancellor, but sometimes he joined these men in attempts to convince the government to take certain lines of action and often he used them as a means of circulating his own views.

The financial lords of the German empire were, like Ballin, men of conservative political opinions. They, too, wanted a flourishing but sound economy, one in which both the volume and the reliability of loans and investments would be assured. The financial structure of the state had therefore to be modernized and political affairs kept stable. This could be done, they believed, by being reasonably liberal in economic matters and by restricting political change to measures clearly necessary in the interests of national stability. Many of Ballin's banker friends were Jews, drawn closely together in Hamburg, Frankfurt, and Berlin, and often vacationing together in Swiss and German mountain resorts. These bankers had elaborate connections in government departments and with leaders of German commerce and industry. Their influence abroad, particularly in England and the United States, was also

135

significant, for many of the great German banking firms were family partnerships, with brothers or cousins overseeing London or New York branches. Ballin's most intimate friend, and a man whom he resembled in many ways, was Max M. Warburg, the senior partner of his family's famous banking house in Hamburg. The two men were virtually in a state of continuous communication, by letter, by conference, and by a private telephone line which ran between their neighboring office buildings. Though Ballin and Warburg occasionally disagreed on matters, their views were usually remarkably similar and they often cooperated to make Berlin aware of their position on economic and political questions. A good friend of both men was Carl Fürstenberg, the energetic and immensely successful head of the *Berliner Handelsgesellschaft*, and all three frequently made recommendations to the government in unison. Max von Schinckel of Hamburg's *Norddeutsche Bank* was a close, if sometimes annoying, associate; Adolf von Hansemann of the *Disconto-Gesellschaft*, a more helpful one. Finally, Ballin had many dealings with Arthur von Gwinner and Karl Helfferich of the *Deutsche Bank* in Berlin, especially after the HAPAG and the bank developed mutual interests in the Near East.[84]

Ballin was on good terms with many publishers and writers, though he professed that "to keep journalists from going amuck and awry and on the straight and narrow is harder than capturing a swarm of fleas."[85] He numbered among his friends the *Zukunft*'s redoubtable Maximilian Harden, the acerbic and unflagging critic of the many

[84] On Ballin's relations with these financiers, see the Warburg and Harden "Nachlässe," as well as the Ballin-Schinckel correspondence in the HAPAG archive; also Warburg, *Aufzeichnungen*; Fürstenberg, *Lebensgeschichte*; and Schinckel, *Lebenserinnerungen*, Hamburg, n.d.

[85] Bülow, *Denkwürdigkeiten*, II, 351.

136

woes which he believed ailed Germany. From 1909, the two exchanged letters frequently or were kept in touch through their mutual friend Fürstenberg.[86] Ballin's favorite among Hamburg's numerous newspapers was the *Correspondent*, an Anglophile daily which was pro-Bismarck and anti-socialist, anti-agrarian, and anit-Jesuit, and to which he contributed an occasional article on political or economic affairs. Ballin was intimately associated with Bernhard Huldermann, the head of the journal's commercial section and subsequently a HAPAG director and Ballin biographer, less closely with Felix von Eckhardt, the paper's editor after 1907, and with Fedor von Zobeltitz, its Berlin correspondent.[87] The editor of the distinguished *Berliner Tageblatt*, Theodor Wolff, knew Ballin well, and the HAPAG chief was also acquainted with Robert Mosse, the paper's owner. He also knew Therese Simon-Sonnemann, the proprietress of the *Frankfurter Zeitung*, as well as a number of the paper's Hamburg correspondents, particularly Bernhard Guttmann and Gustav Mayer.[88]

Still other ties in the field of journalism were Dr. Landau, the editor of the influential Berlin *Börsen-Zeitung*, the brothers Ullstein, who owned a string of dailies and a publishing house, and August Scherl, the reclusive pro-

[86] See, in addition to the Harden "Nachlass," Harry F. Young, *Maximilian Harden, Censor Germaniae: The Critic in Opposition from Bismarck to the Rise of Nazism*, The Hague, 1959.

[87] Ernst Baasch, *Geschichte des hamburgischen Zeitungswesens von den Anfängen bis 1914*, Hamburg, 1930, pp. 122-49; conversation of author with Dr. Eduard Rosenbaum, London, March 18, 1961; Zobeltitz, *Ich habe so gern gelebt: Lebenserinnerungen*, Berlin, 1934, p. 152.

[88] See Wolff, *Marsch*, and his *Krieg von Pontius Pilatus*; Guttmann, *Schattenriss einer Generation*; Fürstenberg, *Lebensgeschichte*, p. 514; Gustav Mayer, *Vom Journalisten zum Historiker der deutschen Arbeiterbewegung: Erinnerungen*, Vienna, 1949.

prietor of a publishing empire headed by the *Lokal An-zeiger* in the capital.[89] Though most of these newspaper-men were more liberal than Ballin, they liked him and rel-ished his conversation. Ballin was a valuable acquaintance to newspaper owners and editors, for he could share inside information on economic and political affairs with them. The HAPAG, moreover, was likely to spend part of its advertising budget, a modest one, in their columns.[90]

The uses to which Ballin put his connections in the publishing field are not easy to trace, for only his letters to Landau and Harden have survived. It seems clear, how-ever, that Ballin's first concern was that German news-papers give the HAPAG a good press, and to further this end the line's very active "Literary Bureau" circulated items to friendly newspapers. The press as a channel of political influence was to Ballin a secondary but not un-important consideration. There were many areas—tariff questions, colonial policy, emigration regulation and the like—in which the HAPAG's affairs were necessarily con-nected with political decisions. Ballin undoubtedly hoped to influence such matters through the press. He himself contributed signed articles only rarely, but he often allowed interviews, and what he had to say was the subject of com-ment at home and abroad.

Business, not politics, was Ballin's primary interest, and that of his banker friends. Ballin and men like him were therefore inclined to be content with a regime which indi-cated a willingness to give support, to protect, and to ad-

[89] On Landau, see the Landau "Nachlass," described in the bibliography.

[90] *Zeitschrift*, I, no. 27 (Sept. 10, 1902), 228, notes that the line's annual advertising expenditure ran between 75,000 and 150,000 marks. See also *BAB*, 1913 advertising bill of nearly 30,000 marks with Scherl, Ullstein, and Mosse.

vance Germany's economic position. Political power was not Ballin's goal, but the opportunity to propose, to warn, to counsel—in a word, to influence—was, and he found that influence was easily to be had without the least traffic with parliamentary figures. Power lay not in the Reichstag, but with the crown, the bureaucracy, the captains of finance and industry, with the molders of public opinion, and it was therefore to these forces that Ballin turned. The external bases of power might be left unaltered provided that the newer forces of wealth were respected. It did not matter by whom policy was fashioned or executed so long as it was satisfactory to the economic interest. The desideratum was a government whose tariff and taxation policies were moderate, which would not unnecessarily disturb the nation's internal social or political structure, and which would support German trade while avoiding any sort of conflict with foreign powers. Ballin believed that these aims could be successfully pursued, simultaneously and indefinitely. Depressions were periodic but business always recovered; the Prussian bureaucracy was often harsh, opinionated, and ignorant, but these failures were at least partially compensated for by the efficiency and orderliness which it promoted in the day to day clockwork of government. There were troublesome demands by socialists and other strident critics for a reconstitution of German society and government, but these voices, although aggravating, were still those of a minority. There were complications abroad, often alarming ones, but peace somehow was maintained. There was certainly no cause for desperate measures. The old system, with all its faults and anachronisms, could be made satisfactory enough with a little assiduous cultivation.

There were, however, real crises from time to time, and when, because of political, economic, or diplomatic difficulties, Germany, or German business, fell into serious trouble, Ballin tended to lash out at two enemies whom he felt were responsible. First, he inveighed against the economic obscurantism, the incompetence in foreign affairs, and the Anglophobia of the Prussian aristocracy. To most liberals and every radical, the logical way to eliminate the noxious prerogatives of this class was to alter, or overthrow, the system which enabled the Junkers to rule the empire. To such a radical solution Ballin and his friends could never reconcile themselves, for such a move, though it would rid Germany of a politically unsound elite, might also open the gate to the second peril against which Ballin railed. This was socialism, which, if not kept firmly in check, might engulf Germany. If the machinery of government were tampered with, who could predict how extensive the changes might become? Would reformist, bourgeois governments be able to protect business against the increasingly predatory claims of the working class? If the existing political structure was to be altered, the best and safest way to do so was not by constitutional revision but by the intensification of business-class influence on the shapers of government policy. If Ballin and his friends were willing to let the aristocracy control the organs of government, it was because they believed that state policy could be affected in their interest by personal influence, propaganda, and the lavish expenditure of money. Not all evils could be overcome in this way, but those which persisted were certainly preferable to liberal and socialist visions of reform. Businessmen therefore were unfortunately content to remain, in Max Warburg's phrase, *Nur-Kaufleute*, and to leave politics to the Junker *Nur-Politiker*, while neither made much effort to understand the other.[91] Theodor Wolff noted this distinction in Ballin. "He hardly bothered himself with questions of internal politics if they did not concern economic affairs,"

[91] Warburg, "Zur Gründung der Überseeklubs," 2-4.

Wolff wrote. "He understood the necessity of basic and timely [political] reforms, but he avoided becoming involved, excusing himself with the rather lame insistence that such things were beyond his competence."[92]

Events in and after 1914 demonstrated that this attitude was only wishful thinking. Ballin made his views prevail often enough—in the Morgan trust crisis and in the Bagdad railroad affair, to take two important examples—to be encouraged to believe that his method of wielding influence was effective and that it could also be successfully employed in great matters of state such as armaments and foreign relations. As we shall see, this proved to be an exaggerated expectation. It was this mistaken evaluation of the efficacy of his influence that led Ballin to accept the German state as it existed. Men like Ballin, Warburg, Fürstenberg, and the others, for all their technical ability and imagination, for all the critical faculties which made them aware of both the opportunities and the dangers breeding in Germany's development, were not disposed to alter the world in which they lived and were unconvinced that any substantial changes were necessary. Only as the Great War neared its catastrophic end did Ballin and his friends perceive that a thorough constitutional reform in Prussia was the only means whereby Germany could be put on a really secure foundation.

In the first decade of the new century, the domestic situation became more disturbed. Socialism, either re-

---

[92] Wolff, *Marsch*, pp. 252-53. See also Ballin's statement in 1907 that the fact that the Reichstag contained so few businessmen was "partly our own fault, for we were so busy with business that we had no time for politics." *Zeitschrift*, VI, no. 4 (Feb. 5, 1907), 32. Cf. Arthur Rosenberg's remarks in Germany, Nationalversammlung, *Das Werk des Untersuchungsausschusses*, 4. Reihe, "Die Ursachen des deutschen Zusammenbruchs im Jahre 1918," 12 vols., Berlin, 1925-29, VII (1), 248; the excellent analysis in Schiffer, *Ein Leben*, pp. 155-58; and Fürstenberg, *Lebensgeschichte*, pp. 470-71.

visionist or orthodox, won new adherents, while the aristocracy clung all the more intractably to its old prerogatives. The government seemed increasingly incompetent, autocratic, and unpopular, and increasingly incapable of coping with the domestic problems which confronted it. Ballin himself was always inclined to look beyond rather than within Germany and was largely, though never completely, unaware of the crisis looming at home. More and more, Ballin found that his attention was being drawn not to difficulties in Germany but to the nation's isolated position in Europe. He was particularly concerned by a problem which was rapidly becoming critical. Germany and the great power against which his own success had been measured now seemed to be irresistibly bound on conflict, a conflict which threatened to sweep away everything which he had created and in which he believed. It was Great Britain on which Ballin turned his gaze, with an eye that was at once envious, admiring, and extremely apprehensive.

142

CHAPTER V

A Place in the Sun

T HE SPAN of almost two decades—from October 1899 to November 1918—during which Ballin served as managing director of the Hamburg-American Line was, except for the war years, an enormously successful period in the company's history. For Ballin personally, however, these were years of difficulty and frustration, and of mounting concern. The first of his worries was the fact that his health was poor. Ballin's constitution, never strong, deteriorated after he passed his fiftieth birthday. His vacations—now at Sils Maria, now at Madonna di Campiglio, but more and more in the company of other Jewish businessmen at Professor Dapper's sanatorium above Bad Kissingen—became longer and more frequent. Ballin bought a modest villa in Holstein, not far from Bismarck's estate at Friedrichsruh, to have a retreat from the hectic pace of Hamburg. Life, it seemed, was really just "one damn thing after another," as a tag which he kept in a small frame on his desk proclaimed. He abandoned the classics to take up detective thrillers. Plagued by insomnia, in middle age the overworked and nervous man developed a need for opiates to combat the pressures which buffeted him on every side and drained away his energy.

In the second place, the HAPAG's expansion in both size and geographical extent, though a product of Ballin's entrepreneurship, also discomforted him, for it made it increasingly arduous for him to maintain the sort of personal supervision over the line which he felt was both desirable and necessary. "Every extension of a concern is a curse

143

to its leader," he liked to say.[1] The line's finances, once a relatively simple, local affair, had now become the concern of Berlin banks and thousands of stockholders on both sides of the Atlantic. Ballin had little enthusiasm for the anonymity and democracy to which modern corporations fell victim once they passed under the control of finance capitalism. He noted sadly that fiscal exigencies had saddled the once independent Krupps with a directorate, and he deplored "the impotence which . . . is imposed on us through the democratization of trade and commerce as a result of the general transformation of these great enterprises into joint-stock companies."[2]

The third problem with which Ballin had to contend, and the one which troubled him most between 1899 and 1918, was the deteriorating and finally tragic relationship between Germany and Great Britain, one which was closely related to the success of German businesses such as the Hamburg-American Line.[3]

At the turn of the century, there was almost no place on which England and Germany could establish a cordial footing. Ideologically, there was a latent distaste in Great

[1] Bjarne Aagaard, "The Life of Albert Ballin," *Fairplay* (Jan. 5, 1922), 147.

[2] Ballin to Harden, April 6, 1910, Harden "Nachlass."

[3] The most useful introduction to Anglo-German relations under William II are the relevant chapters in William L. Langer, *European Alliances and Alignments 1871-1890*, 2d edn., New York, 1956, and *The Diplomacy of Imperialism 1890-1902*, 2d edn., New York, 1956, both containing exemplary bibliographies. There is no comprehensive account for the period after 1902, though there is much suggestive material in Georg W. F. Hallgarten, *Imperialismus vor 1914* . . . , 2d edn., 2 vols., Munich, 1963. Much new archival material, some of it published, has made a revision of these works imperative. It has been begun, on the British side, in J. A. S. Grenville, *Lord Salisbury and Foreign Policy: The Close of the Nineteenth Century*, London, 1964, and in George Monger, *The End of Isolation: British Foreign Policy 1900-1907*, London, etc., 1963.

Britain for the conservative and military Prussian tradition. The Germans, in turn, wryly suggested that the English were elegant but archaic, and intellectually pedestrian as well, endowed with fine manners but incapable of transcending their worldliness. On the highest level, relations between the closely kindred houses of Hohenzollern and Hanover, particularly after Edward VII's accession in 1901, were characterized by very little fraternity and considerable rancor. In diplomatic affairs, though an attempt was made from 1898 to 1901 to form an alliance, there was much hard feeling in England toward Germany's pro-Boer sentiments in the war laboriously being fought in South Africa. There were, besides, two other fields in which Germany and England had entered into intense competition. One was the armament race between their navies; the other was the commercial and industrial rivalry in which the two empires were embroiled.[4]

[4] The only general treatment of Anglo-German naval rivalry, Sir Ernest Woodward, *Great Britain and the German Navy*, New York, 1935, is dependable but concentrates on England. The best approach is through the naval figures connected with the contest. Essential are Tirpitz' *Erinnerungen*, Leipzig, 1919, and *Politische Dokumente*, 2 vols., Stuttgart, etc., 1924-26, and Fisher's *Memories*, London, etc., 1919, as well as his correspondence, edited by A. J. Marder as *Fear God and Dread Nought: The Correspondence of Admiral of the Fleet Lord Fisher of Kilverstone*, 3 vols., Cambridge, Mass., 1952-59. Among the secondary literature, see especially Marder's *From the Dreadnought to Scapa Flow: the Royal Navy in the Fisher Era 1904-1919*, 3 vols. to date, London and New York, 1961- . On Tirpitz, see Jonathan Steinberg, *Yesterday's Deterrent: Tirpitz and the Birth of the German Battle Fleet*, London, 1965, and his "The Kaiser's Navy and German Society," *Past & Present*, no. 28 (July 1964), 102-10. Walther Hubatsch, *Die Ära Tirpitz: Studien zur deutschen Marinepolitik 1890-1918*, Göttingen, 1955, and his "Der Kulminationspunkt der deutschen Marinepolitik im Jahre 1912," *Historische Zeitschrift*, CLXXII, no. 2 (Oct. 1953), 291-322, are valuable rehabilitations of Tirpitz. On the commercial rivalry, see Ross J. S. Hoffman, *Great Britain and the German Trade Rivalry 1875-1914*, Philadelphia, 1933; Angelike Banze, *Die deutsch-englische*

The mighty German navy of 1914 was the work of Admiral Alfred von Tirpitz, who from 1897 to 1916, as secretary of the Imperial Naval Office, conceived it, built it, and directed its operations. Within a year of Tirpitz' appointment, the first of a series of naval laws providing for the systematic construction of a number of warships was passed and the keels of a great German fleet were laid with dispatch. At irregular intervals during the next fifteen years, the admiral would ask for—and always get—approval of both Kaiser and Reichstag for increases in his fleet. Tirpitz' new ships for the most part were large, heavily armed battleships and cruisers of limited sailing range, and he stationed them in the North Sea behind Helgoland. Tirpitz' strategic planning for his navy depended on a "risk theory" which he devised.[5] The theory was predicated on a belief that England was Germany's implacable enemy, determined to wipe its rival's commerce and its navy off the seas when the moment became advantageous. Germany could never hope to have a fleet as large as England's, but it could strive for a ratio of capital ships—the proportion shifted from time to time, but it usually fell at 2:3—which would make Germany strong enough to inflict serious damage on the British fleet should the two powers become involved in hostilities. Tirpitz believed that Germany could more easily afford a navy than could Great Britain, and that financial considerations would prevent the British from maintaining a lead greater than that calculated in the "risk theory." Once the desired ratio had been achieved, the British would think twice before pitting its navy against Germany's. If, however, it

Wirtschaftsrivalität: ein Beitrag zur Geschichte der deutsch-eng-lischen Beziehungen 1897-1907, Berlin, 1935; and Raymond J. Sontag, *Germany and England: Background of Conflict 1848-1894*, New York, 1938.

[5] See Tirpitz, *Erinnerungen*, chaps. vii, ix, and xi.

was foolish enough to do so it would be severely battered. At that juncture, according to Tirpitz' schedule, the other naval powers, all of them jealous of Britain's overweening naval strength, would attack the crippled British fleet in order to deliver the *coup de grâce.*

Although the rationale of Tirpitz' theory was to protect Germany against England, building a fleet might so arouse British ire that the Royal Navy would strike out at Germany *before* Tirpitz' plans could be completed. Tirpitz himself was well aware that his building plans might expose Germany to danger before the fleet became strong enough to deter England. "In the creation of our seapower," he admitted, "we never hoped for Britain's applause."[6] It was a gamble Tirpitz was prepared to take. The admiral knew, however, that he would encounter opposition in Germany from those who realized the risk inherent in his naval ambitions. He was therefore very careful to woo German public opinion, constantly emphasizing the necessity of building a battle fleet and glossing over the danger of collision with England such a program would entail.

Winning William II's endorsement of a greater navy was of special importance, for once it was obtained there would be no royal opposition to construction bills, and, more positively, the naval movement would win a certain social cachet, and enormous publicity, as a result of the crown's association with it.[7] William proved, as usual, an easy conquest, and he readily agreed to Tirpitz' plans. The Kaiser's naval aspirations arose from his ambivalent feelings toward England. On the one hand he feared the British; on the other, he was consumed with envy and

[6] *ibid.,* p. 176; see also Tirpitz' *Politische Dokumente,* I, 7.

[7] There is no satisfactory study of the Kaiser's relationship to German navalism, nor are his numerous biographies illuminating. William's own account can be found in his *Ereignisse und Gestalten aus den Jahren 1878-1918,* Leipzig and Berlin, 1922, pp. 193-205.

determined to make Germany Britain's peer, if not its superior on the high seas. William did not believe that the differences between Germany and Great Britain had inevitably to lead to a reckoning by arms. Such an unfortunate conflict was, at the turn of the century, not foreseeable. War, however, was at least a possibility which out of prudence had to be entertained. German trade and Germany's overseas domains, he declared, would be imperiled without the protection of a navy. "In spite of the fact that our fleet is still not what it should be," the Kaiser proclaimed in 1901, "we have gained a place in the sun for ourselves. It will be my duty to see that this place in the sun remains in our possession uncontestedly in order that its rays be able to work beneficially on trade and commerce abroad, on industry and agriculture at home . . . , for our future lies on the water. The more Germans who go forth on the water . . . the better it is for us."[8] It is not unlikely that personal considerations also played a part in the Kaiser's enthusiasm for a fleet. If an important and inordinately wealthy empire such as Germany was made strong enough to play its proper part in world affairs, all Europe would have to pay due homage to its ruler and make use of his extraordinary talents. Finally, a navy, with its great ships and billowing ensigns—to say nothing of an additional wardrobe of resplendent uniforms—would provide William with a background at once glamorous and ferocious.

The German middle class, like its sovereign, was quickly won over by Tirpitz' arguments for a strong navy.[9] The prevalence of neo-Darwinian notions of an armed struggle between nations as well as men, in addition to the specialized testimony of Admiral Mahan, gave

[8] *Berliner Tageblatt* (June 19, 1901).
[9] On the German bourgeoisie and the navy, see especially Steinberg, "Kaiser's Navy," and his *Yesterday's Deterrent*, pp. 36-46.

intellectual respectability to the view that a navy was absolutely essential for survival in a world of superpowers. In the early 1890's, the navies belonging to Great Britain, France, and the United States far outdistanced Germany's and were being increased in size and strength. In comparison, Germany's fleet was a bathtub armada, at best an instrument of coastal patrol and certainly not an arm of international defense. If Germany failed to take its place on the sea, it would become the prey of the strong. With its quickly growing population, Germany could no longer subsist on native-grown foodstuffs. A navy strong enough to keep the sea lanes open was therefore a necessary bulwark against starvation. It was also essential for prosperity. Men and women everywhere in Germany depended on a lively overseas traffic in manufactured goods and raw materials for the pursuit of their livelihoods. The claim that a fleet was required for both physical and economic survival was therefore one of wide appeal. There was no reason why the nation should not have a large navy. Germany was rich, strong in men and colonies, a force in European diplomacy. National dignity demanded a navy commensurate with Germany's enormous wealth and prestige, with the ingenuity of its middle class and its industrial potential, and with its imperial commitments.

Tirpitz' argument that Great Britain was Germany's enemy was not difficult to accept. The irresponsible diatribes in the British press—a press characterized by Ramsay MacDonald as being edited "in such a way as to bring the technique of journalism to a high pitch of excellence and its honours to the lowest depths of disgrace"—did much to turn Germans to Tirpitz.[10] If the admiral's strategical talents are open to question, there can be no

---

[10] Ludwig Stein, ed., *England & Germany: By Leaders of Public Opinion in Both Countries*, London, 1912, p. 95.

doubt that he had superlative gifts as a propagandist. Tirpitz took advantage of the incendiary editorials in London papers, citing them as convincing proof that there was indeed a British conspiracy against Germany. The Anglo-Japanese alliance of 1902 and the Entente Cordiale with France two years later were particularly ominous developments, for if Britain felt compelled to abandon its traditional policy of splendid isolation against whom was it allying? And against whom were the significant increases in the British navy intended? In 1905, a really serious crisis developed between the two powers in Morocco which momentarily threatened to lead to war, but which was eventually settled by diplomacy. There seemed reason to suspect, and to prepare for, further difficulties with the British.

The German middle class, once firmly behind Tirpitz, worked hard to promote the fleet. It organized pressure groups such as the Navy League (*Flottenverein*), created in 1898 to promote enthusiasm for a navy, and spread Tirpitz' ideas in the official statements of municipal *Handelskammern* and in the columns of bourgeois newspapers. International trade and shipping interests were well represented in the naval movement, and nowhere did Tirpitz have a more loyal following than in Hamburg.

Prior to the mid-1870's, Hamburg's interest in naval protection had been limited to keeping the mouth of the Elbe open in time of war, for in 1870 the French had succeeded in sealing off the river for a period of several weeks. During the last quarter of the century, Hamburg merchants—especially Adolph Godeffroy and Adolph Woermann—began to send their ships farther afield, first down the African coast and then to the Indian and Pacific oceans. At the same time, the city played an important role in encouraging the German government to annex overseas territories which offered promise of being commercially exploited.[11] As the tentacles of Hamburg's trade extended, its businessmen became increasingly concerned that this foreign commerce be adequately protected. Several years before the first Naval Law was passed in 1898, the Hamburg *Handelskammer* publicly called for the introduction of such a measure, and on its adoption the HAPAG wired the Kaiser expressing "great pleasure" that the bill would at last provide for the "strengthening of the war fleet necessary for Germany's welfare."[12] The Hamburg chapter of the Navy League was very active, much to the gratification of General August Keim, the national president.[13] The local membership roster was notable: in addition to Ballin, such distinguished and influential names as Woermann, Blohm, Laeisz, Krogmann, and Siemers were included, as was that of Paul Count Wolff Metternich, then Prussian minister to the Hanseatic cities and the Mecklenburgs and later German ambassador in London.[14] The Hamburg chapter called for a fleet which would be "strong enough to protect Germany's growing overseas trade and its fledgling colonies with force and might, and at all times watch over the honor of the empire in distant seas."[15]

[11] Ballin's memorial address praising Woermann's business acumen is printed in Stubmann, pp. 139-41. For Hamburg's role in German colonialism, see E. Kehr, *Schlachtflottenbau und Parteipolitik* . . . , Berlin, 1930, pp. 236-45; Mary Evelyn Townsend, *The Rise and Fall of Germany's Colonial Empire 1884-1918*, New York, 1930; Kurt Himer, *75 Jahre Hamburg-Amerika Linie: 1. Teil, Adolph Godeffroy und seine Nachfolger bis 1886*, Hamburg, n.d.; Otto Mathies, *Hamburgs Reederei 1814-1914*, Hamburg, 1924.

[12] *Jahresbericht der Handelskammer zu Hamburg* (1896), pp. 9-10; *ibid.* (1897), pp. 10-11. The *Handelskammer* soon became disenchanted because of the high costs of the new navy. See *ibid.* (1900), pp. 12-13.

[13] Keim, *Erlebtes und Erstrebtes: Lebenserinnerungen*, Hanover, 1925, p. 117.

[14] *Hamburger Nachrichten* (Feb. 11, 1900).

[15] *ibid.* On the Hamburg chapter, see file 614-2/1, "Deutscher Flottenverein," Staatsarchiv, Hamburg.

Ballin was among Tirpitz' first supporters and publicly expressed his agreement with the risk theory.[16] He served on the governing committee of the Hamburg branch of the Navy League and belonged in addition to related groups such as the Navy League Abroad, the *Hamburgischer Verein Seefahrt*, and the *Kolonial Gesellschaft*, in all of which he held office.[17] The HAPAG provided the League with considerable help. When the body met in convention in Hamburg, hundreds of members were invited to cruise the Elbe on the line's steamers, and at other times visiting League delegations were accorded similar favors.[18] Although ordinary League dues were one mark per year, Ballin annually contributed twenty, while the Hamburg-American Line made a yearly donation of 300 marks to the League's coffers.[19]

During the first ten years of Tirpitz' regime, Ballin cooperated with the bearded admiral, sending him reports on various naval matters and items of related interest. In 1898, shortly after Tirpitz took office, Ballin became involved in a plan whereby the HAPAG would serve as the agent through which Germany would obtain a naval base in the Virgin Islands. According to a scheme devised by Tirpitz and a number of Danish real estate

[16] See an article by Ballin in the *Hamburgischer Correspondent* (Jan. 6, 1900).

[17] For Ballin's memberships, see Harry R. Rudin, *Germans in the Cameroons 1884-1914: A Case Study in Modern Imperialism*, New Haven, 1938, pp. 172-73; Pauline R. Anderson, *The Background of Anti-English Feeling in Germany 1890-1902*, Washington, 1939, p. 167 n99; *Zeitschrift*, II, no. 5 (May 5, 1903), 38-39.

[18] See, for example, *Zeitschrift*, V, no. 10 (May 20, 1906), 99. Cf. *ibid.*, I, no. 9 (Dec. 10, 1901), 69, for a disagreement between the HAPAG and the League.

[19] "Hamburgischer Landesverband des deutschen Flottenvereins: Mitglieder Verzeichnis" (1909-13), in file 614-2/1, folder III/6 no. 4, "Akten betreffend Personalien des hamburgischen Landesausschusses und der hamburgischen Geschäftsstelle," Staatsarchiv, Hamburg.

speculators, the Hamburg-American Line, which already had installations on St. Thomas, would gradually acquire substantial blocks of land on St. John until finally the island was virtually in its ownership. When this had been accomplished the German government would purchase the island from Denmark. The HAPAG's participation was necessary so that in the crucial early stages Washington would not suspect that Germany was bent on direct annexation. Ballin agreed to help Tirpitz only if the German government approved the operation. Chancellor Hohenlohe and William II, on being informed, were both opposed and the plan was quickly abandoned.[20] In the summer of 1899, Ballin and Tirpitz again collaborated in an attempt to form a Franco-German consortium to help finance a canal across the Panamanian isthmus. Once again, however, the matter dissolved when the government refused to take any interest.[21]

To Ballin, the construction of a German fleet was necessary, or at least desirable, for several reasons. First, and of only marginal importance in his calculations, was a moral element. "The fleet is also the bearer of another, higher mission," he wrote after discussing the strategic advantages of a strong navy. "It is, as it were, the embodiment of the national purpose (*Gedanken*) of a 'greater Germany' and of imperial power."[22] Secondly, the presence of a German navy might lead to the opening up of trading regions to home merchants. "The commandant of a war-

[20] Alfred Vagts, *Deutschland und die Vereinigten Staaten in der Weltpolitik*, 2 vols., New York, 1935, II, 1,425-30; Charles Callan Tansill, *The Purchase of the Danish West Indies*, Baltimore, 1932, pp. 397-453.

[21] Vagts, *Deutschland und die Vereinigten Staaten*, II, pp. 1,495-99.

[22] *Hamburger Nachrichten* (Feb. 27, 1900). In a similar vein, Ballin once spoke of the "cultural" mission which had been entrusted to the HAPAG. See *Zeitschrift*, V, no. 3 (Feb. 5, 1906), 21-22.

153

ship in foreign ports is an agent for mercantile interests in the mother country," Ballin declared.[23] The navy's essential mission, however, was the defense of Germany's position in Europe as well as the protection of its trade and colonies overseas. On this point, Ballin's views were identical to those of Tirpitz and the Kaiser.

From the perspective of a shipping executive such as Ballin, the extension of an oceanic carrier into distant waters meant that extra security was required. A firm which widely spread its connections might thereby protect itself against adverse conditions in a particular market area, but in doing so it also exposed itself to the danger of financial and physical overextension. After 1900, a war or a revolution anywhere in the world could mean that the HAPAG's trade in that region would be halted, its merchantmen subject to confiscation or destruction, its crews to impressment or death. The line's continued viability therefore depended on keeping the world's markets safely open to its ships. The freedom of the seas, as well as law and order in the ports of trade, had to be guaranteed. The German merchant marine required assurance that its vessels could pass from home ports to destinations abroad unmolested by foreign navies or by marauding pirates. Now that Germany had become a colonial power it could maintain a fleet based on widely scattered points from Helgoland to Lüderitz to Tsingtao.

Ballin's conception of the reasons why a German navy had to be built and the role which it was to play were well expressed in an article, "War Fleet and World Trade," which appeared in the *Hamburger Nachrichten* on February 27, 1900. In this piece, Ballin enunciated all the arguments for navalism which were then being circulated in Germany by propagandists for the second Naval Law under consideration in the Reichstag. He began by denying

---

[23] Kehr, *Schlachtflottenbau*, p. 214.

154

that the construction of a battle fleet was tantamount to pursuing a "policy based on prestige and adventure." It was, rather, one of necessity for a nation whose agriculture could no longer nurture an exploding population and whose economy depended on the import of foreign raw materials to keep its working class employed. If the navy was necessary for economic survival, it was also imperative for political reasons. Indeed, Ballin argued that in the twentieth century it was no longer possible to differentiate between economic and political considerations. He continued:

We are not thinking about a war between any particular powers, although a cosmopolitan statesman will not hide from himself that in any future war the fleet will play an entirely different role than before because now the whole world instead of continental Europe has become the arena of politics. Without a strong fleet, Germany will be very much reduced as a power for friend and foe alike in a future war; with a strong fleet the German empire will hold the balance in its hand for a long time perhaps. But in time of peace as well, Germany needs a powerful war fleet. If England, France, Russia, and the United States of America make greater efforts from year to year to strengthen and increase their navies, so the German empire, as a competitor in world markets, dares not content itself with a modest instrument and should put an end to the miserable makeshift fleet of the last fifteen years. In the brutal struggle of nations for light and air, strength alone counts in the final analysis. Diplomatic dexterity and clever political moves, alliances and declarations of neutrality—in the long run all these have value and effectiveness only if real power stands behind them. Germany has an incomparable land army, but beyond

155

the seas only its warships can create respect for it. Without the support of a strong fleet, whose iron core can only be made up of battleships, Germany has no real power against the tiniest exotic state which permits might to go before right and which, in possession of a few modern armored ships, can sneer at obsolete, impotent cruisers. Behind every German [merchant] vessel abroad must stand the German battleship!

There is a paradox in the fact that Ballin supported Tirpitz, for certainly it must have been clear to him—as a regular reader of London papers and a man with countless acquaintances in England—that German navalism was increasing British suspicions and causing Anglo-German relations to deteriorate. It is, I think, remarkable that Ballin and men like him did not for many years pause to subject the British specter which Tirpitz raised to the tests of experience and common business sense. Though no one could deny that there was hostility in Great Britain toward Germany, must it lead to an armed conflict in which Tirpitz' fleet would be Germany's savior? In spite of the many crises and incidents, the conflicting aims and antagonistic policies which had marred their relations in the past, the two nations had, after all, managed to coexist peacefully for many years. Occasionally, to be sure, British warships or orders from London had interferred with German merchantmen in order to prevent loadings or deliveries of suspected contraband. But experience would have demonstrated that the British had done nothing to prevent Germany from accumulating colonies or establishing trading connections from the Atlantic to the Pacific. As has already been indicated in the case of the Persian Gulf and China, German overseas merchants appear to have been content for the British to serve as a police force for the benefit of all nations. There was ample evidence in reviewing the past to see Russia as Britain's principal foe, and France—not Britain—as Germany's. Good business sense would have presented as strong a case for the mutuality, rather than the hostility, of Anglo-German interests. Ballin and other businessmen, better than anyone else in Germany, knew that the prosperity of both nations depended to a large extent on the perpetuation of the immense triangular trade between the two countries and the overseas world. Briton and German therefore had every reason to cultivate cordial relations with one another. The two peoples, Ballin often argued, had a common destiny to bring mankind out of economic and intellectual backwardness, and to manifest to the world the virtues and advantages of the Anglo-Saxon community. It was to be a partnership, not a rivalry.

In any event, whether one believed—as did Tirpitz—that England was dangerous, or—as Ballin and his business friends—that England was Germany's natural partner in economic development, building a fleet was not the proper course of action. If the British, according to Tirpitz' allegation, were really intent on curbing Germany, could they not do so at once rather than allow their rival to build up its maritime force? In 1900, the ratio of ships for which Tirpitz was aiming was not expected to be reached for almost twenty years—if at all, for contrary to the admiral's assurances, the British parliament seemed quite resolved to absorb the German naval increases by making proportionate reinforcements in the Royal Navy, no matter what the cost. Was there therefore anything to be gained by trying to implement the "risk theory"? If, on the other hand, Great Britain was Germany's partner, then everything which made relations between the two powers difficult should be avoided. Since the colossal German navy which Tirpitz proposed was unlikely ever to reach the strength relative to Britain's navy called for by the

157

admiral's strategy and since the thought of such a fleet's being constructed was so profoundly disquieting to the British, the German navy should be limited to a size which the British found tolerable. In return, Germany might expect to receive concessions from Britain in other matters in which the two nations had differences. Berlin should therefore sponsor a policy of conciliation with the British. Compared to Tirpitz' building mania, such an approach to England would be much less costly, would offer Germany the prospect of concessions from London, and would hold much more hope of eliminating the danger of conflict.

Ballin, however, does not appear to have reasoned along such lines. If he had any reservations about the wisdom of Tirpitz' plans from 1897 to about 1908 he kept them to himself. Perhaps, like his colleague at the North German Lloyd, Heinrich Wiegand, he believed that Tirpitz could be restrained or got rid of if he proved too fervent. Wiegand was also an admirer and early advocate of Tirpitz' program, but on the occasion of the admiral's appointment to the Imperial Naval Office he had written that if Tirpitz "actually comes forward with unbounded plans, which in my judgment is out of the question, there will still be time to move against him (*Front zu machen*)."[24] It seems more likely, however, that Ballin was caught up in the general swell of enthusiasm for a navy and could find justification for his support of Tirpitz by reflection on the arguments concerning economic survival and political power advanced in his newspaper articles in 1900. For years, he did not concern himself with the effect Tirpitz' program was having in England, and when finally he was brought face to face with the real

[24] Arnold Petzet, *Heinrich Wiegand: ein Lebensbild*, Bremen, 1932, p. 217.

cause of Anglo-German friction he was unable to do anything to alleviate it.

It was not until about 1908 that Ballin began to question the wisdom of continuing to support Tirpitz.[25] Three factors were crucial in leading him to desert the admiral. First, and most important, was Ballin's conviction that by 1908 Germany had quite enough ships to maintain its European position and protect its interests and possessions abroad, and therefore the fleet had only to be modernized, not expanded. Years later, he admitted that even these men-of-war had not been necessary for the protection of German commerce.[26] Certainly, building more would serve only to enrage the British. Writing in 1915 to Maximilian Harden, Ballin reflected on his change of mind.

> You speak of Tirpitz. . . . Tirpitz had the great fortune that England did not take advantage of an opportune moment to halt the development of the German fleet by force. In my opinion [this was] an enormous error on England's part. But Tirpitz did not use this good luck as a statesman would have. By 1908-09, he had fortunately got by the danger zone. At any time [thereafter] he could have negotiated with England as one power to another. But he did not wish to negotiate. He wanted no settlement, he wanted only to build ships. He put obstacles in the way of every understanding with England, even though at the time every intelligent man had to admit that limitless construction (*unlimitierte Baufrei-*

[25] After 1908, I can find no record of Ballin's having favored naval increases save a curious reference in Admiral von Müller's diary in December 1911, for which I am unable to offer any explanation. See Walter Görlitz, ed., *Der Kaiser . . . : Aufzeichnungen des Chefs des Marinekabinetts Admiral Georg Alexander v. Müller über die Ära Wilhelms II.*, Berlin, 1965, p. 102.

[26] Friedrich von der Ropp, *Zwischen Gestern und Morgen: Erfahrungen und Erkenntnisse*, Stuttgart, 1961, pp. 93-94.

159

heit) on the part of both sides was a race which England was always destined to win because of its much greater resources."[27]

The second factor which separated Ballin from Tirpitz was his belief that an attempt to construct a navy such as the admiral wanted would be financially ruinous and would therefore lead Germany into serious social and political problems. This consideration became especially important after 1905, when both nations began to construct *Dreadnought*-class battleships, which were much more expensive to build. "Our relations to England are causing me great concern," Ballin wrote to Harden in July 1909. "Please use your maximum influence for support of an agreement on the question of naval construction. It is a necessity for both nations, and this necessity should offer to practical men the basis for a fair compromise. Otherwise the life will certainly be knocked out of us, and in two years what will we have for this accelerated naval construction—a new financial catastrophe or a war?"[28] By September, Ballin was writing to Harden that "so much is certain: if we do not come to an understanding we must very quickly proceed to a new financial reform, and with this reform [domestic] developments can take a most serious turn."[29] William II and some influential German naval figures believed, however, that England, and not Germany, would be unable to bear the financial strain imposed by its naval estimates, and this opinion encouraged Tirpitz to refuse any compromise with England.[30] Ballin agreed that England, France, and Russia

[27] Letter of Jan. 10, 1915, Harden "Nachlass."

[28] Letter of July 21, 1909, *ibid*.

[29] Letter of Sept. 21, 1909, *ibid*. For financial qualms in other quarters, see Kehr, *Schlachtflottenbau*, pp. 291-93.

[30] Hubatsch, *Ära Tirpitz*, p. 91. See also Capt. Erich von Müller (naval attaché, London) to Tirpitz, Nov. 9, 1913, *AA*, Eng. Nr. 71b, vol. 77, reel 340/00394-400.

could not stand the burden any more easily than Germany, but the result, he predicted, would not be that England would give in but that this economic tension, together with political friction, would only accelerate the outbreak of war. "In a few years, this must lead to a catastrophe," Ballin wrote to former chancellor Bülow on June 1, 1914, "for to all these nations the armaments with which they have had to gird themselves (*as a result of Germany's example*) are economically intolerable."[31]

The third factor in Ballin's decision to withdraw his support for a greater German navy was the fact that in the summer of 1908 Max Warburg introduced him to Sir Ernest Cassel, one of the great financial lords of the City and a man born, like Ballin, a German and a Jew.[32] Few private citizens in England commanded more attention than Cassel, less because of his personal power in investment banking than because he was an intimate of King Edward VII and was besides a fixture in the social world of Britain's governing aristocracy. His views could therefore be interpreted as very probably a mirror of those which prevailed in the government. At the time that Ballin met Cassel, the Englishman's thoughts on Anglo-German relations were disturbing. Cassel was pessimistic about the future and even spoke of a *Kriegsnotwendigkeit* because of Germany's astonishing economic advances and the ceaseless augmentation of its navy.[33] Late in 1908,

[31] Letter in Bülow "Nachlass." The passage in italics was underlined by Bülow in red pencil.

[32] On Cassel, see Brian Connell, *Manifest Destiny: A Study of Five Profiles of the Rise and Influence of the Mountbatten Family*, New York, 1946, pp. 53-87; Paul H. Emden, *Money Powers of Europe in the Nineteenth and Twentieth Centuries*, London, n.d., pp. 331-42; Sigmund Münz, *King Edward VII at Marienbad: Political and Social Life at the Bohemian Spas*, London, 1934; Cyrus Adler, *Jacob H. Schiff: His Life and Letters*, 2 vols., New York, 1928.

[33] Felix Somary, *Erinnerungen aus meinem Leben*, Zurich, n.d., pp. 95, 110-11.

161

the connection between London and Berlin, already disturbed earlier in the year by a letter by William II concerning naval armaments addressed to Lord Tweedmouth, the first lord of the Admiralty, was further disaffected by the Kaiser's foolish admission of German hostility toward England in his *Daily Telegraph* interview. This contretemps only increased Cassel's gloom, though he told Max Warburg that he did not think that war was "likely" at the moment.[34]

Although by 1908 Ballin was beginning to turn away from Tirpitz, there were many Germans who rejected his argument that navalism was responsible for the broadening gulf between England and Germany. Instead, they attributed it to the penetration of German commerce and industry into markets which had formerly been dominated by the British. It may be, in fact, that a majority of the German population felt that England's hostility to Germany could be traced primarily to trade rivalry rather than naval competition.[35] It would certainly have been possible to arrive at such a conclusion by reading official trade statistics and listening to the rumblings, at once morose and belligerent, of the London press. The navy and its allies went out of their way to discredit international trade and award it the onus of being responsible for England's illfeeling toward Germany. Tirpitz needed to stress the economic rivalry between Germany and England not only to provide a persuasive *raison d'être* for the annual construction of new warships, but also to deflect and inundate

[34] Cassel to Warburg, undated but about Oct. 26, 1908; Warburg to Ballin, Oct. 31, 1908, both in Warburg "Nachlass," 1014/9/801.

[35] This was Hans Delbrück's opinion, expressed in his *How to Improve Anglo-German Relations*, New York, 1912, p. 1; see also the opinions collected in Stein, ed., *England & Germany*, most of which confirm Delbrück's view.

162

the voices of those who argued that it was actually navalism which was making an enemy of England.[36]

In addition to the navy, there was another group in Germany which held commercial tension to be the decisive factor in Anglo-German discord. While it was not an important segment of opinion, it is of interest because it was more specific and charged that the race for merchant marine tonnage was at the bottom of the antagonism. Granted the argument, the Hamburg-American Line, being the most successful of the German lines, was therefore the party most at fault for the deterioration of relations. From there, the attack centered unavoidably on Ballin, merchant extraordinary and menace to peace.

The most vociferous of Ballin's critics on this score was his old enemy, Walter Freyer, former president of the Hamburg ship officers' union.[37] To Freyer, Ballin was not only a remorseless foe of organized labor, but of any person, corporation, or nation which stood in the way of his powerful ambition.[38] Freyer, who possessed at best a circumscribed literary talent, wrote a novel, *The Struggle for the Ocean*, which was published in the spring of 1914.[39] This epic of avarice, devastation, and death concluded with Germany and England on the verge of war due to the unscrupulous machinations of one Moritz Bebacher, "Napoleon of the Sea," a titan among Germany's shipping magnates. Though Ballin helped publicize

[36] Looking back after the war, Tirpitz declared that the trade rivalry had been the essential cause of England's hatred for Germany but that the German fleet had been seized upon as the arch villain in order to make a more dramatic impact on the British mind. See Tirpitz, "Ballins politische Anschauung," in the *Deutsche Allgemeine Zeitung* (April 2, 1922), and also his *Erinnerungen*, pp. 167-72, and *Politische Dokumente*, I, 91-92.

[37] See pp. 34-35.

[38] Freyer "Nachlass," I, pp. 2-10.

[39] *Im Kampf um den Ozean: Seeroman*, Leipzig, 1914.

the work by bringing a libel suit against its author, sales were disappointing, and the only effect of Freyer's polemics was that a number of Ballin's friends facetiously dubbed him Moritz. Freyer's attack was similar to one which had appeared in 1910 under the title "Veritas." This exposé of Ballin was the work of Georg Schröder, apparently a polemicist of small reputation. Schröder argued that the proliferation of the HAPAG's tonnage was not only commercially questionable but also likely to lead to war with England. Ballin, he declared, had so trampled on his rivals that "Germany had made an enemy of the whole world through the HAPAG, that is, through Ballin."[40] At the same time, the term *Ballinismus* was coined by Ballin's foes to describe a policy characterized by complete ruthlessness.[41]

Insubstantial and unimportant as these detractors were, there was an undeniable element of truth in their charges that Ballin was ruthless and that the HAPAG's growth was dictated by ambition as well as by sensible business calculation. Even among the line's officials there were voices of discontent, and more than one of Ballin's associates criticized what seemed to be his insensate determination to force the HAPAG forward.[42] They questioned Ballin's judg-

[40] Included in Schröder, *Fiasko! Die deutsche Politik des Wahnsinns: Ballin gleich Deutschlands Tragödie . . .* , Hamburg, n.d., p.16.

[41] Adolf Goetz, *25 Jahre hamburgische Seeschiffahrtspolitik*, Hamburg, 1911, pp. 195-96.

[42] Max von Schinckel, *Lebenserinnerungen*, Hamburg, n.d., p. 268; Eduard Rosenbaum, "Albert Ballin: A Note on the Style of His Economic and Political Activities," Leo Baeck Institute of Jews from Germany, *Year Book*, III, London, 1958, p. 265; Petzet, *Wiegand*, p. 33; Merck "Nachlass," "Erinnerungen," pp. 28-30; Erich Murken, *Die grossen transatlantischen Linienreederei-Verbände, Pools und Interessengemeinschaften bis zum Ausbruch des Weltkrieges . . .* , Jena, 1922, pp. 530-31; Kurt Himer, *Geschichte der Hamburg-Amerika Linie: 2. Teil, Albert Ballin*, pp. 46-47; Freyer "Nachlass," II, pp. 13, 47-48. There were also

ment and agreed that his passion for ship building and expansion was excessive and could lead to financial trouble for the line and difficulties with England. In reply to these critics, Ballin defended himself by noting that if the line was to serve the world's increasing trade it must be prepared to build ships to carry the goods or hang back and surrender the business to other lines which were willing to assume the risk involved. That being the case, he elected the more adventurous alternative.[43] Ballin knew that he and the Hamburg-American Line were contributing to the growing tension between Germany and England, a thought he found morbid and distressing and one which he did not like to discuss.[44] An associate, Siegfried Heckscher, once told Ballin that the HAPAG's continuous construction of large liners increased the danger of war with England. Ballin agreed, Heckscher wrote, "but he declared at the same time that it was impossible for him to bring technological developments and successful competition to a halt."[45]

Ballin refused to believe, however, that aboveboard economic rivalry could permanently alienate two great nations whose commercial intercourse was so fundamentally responsible for their mutual prosperity. Indeed, in the Anglo-Germany community of business and businessmen lay the hope for better relations. There was a fundamental difference between economic and armament rivalries, for the one was a positive response to an expanding world

---

complaints by otherwise well satisfied stockholders. See *Zeitschrift*, XI, no. 7 (April 5, 1912), 40-41.

[43] *Zeitschrift*, VII, no. 7 (April 5, 1908), 49-50; XI, no. 7 (April 5, 1912), 40-41.

[44] Siegfried Heckscher, "Albert Ballin," *Roter Tag* (Jan. 3, 1922).

[45] *ibid*. See also Gustav Mayer, *Vom Journalisten zum Historiker der deutschen Arbeiterbewegung: Erinnerungen*, Munich, 1949, p. 153.

market, the other a negative policy, both futile and unnecessary, grounded in fear, vanity, and megalomania. The intensifying antagonism between Germany and England was essentially due, Ballin believed, to factors which were not the work of merchants and traders but of misguided princes, ambitious admirals, and inept diplomats. He did not deny that economic competition had in some cases led to political friction and bad feelings between the two powers, but these were problems which could be cleared up once the contest in armaments had been eliminated. If the British and German people had come to the crossroads, it was because the expansionist naval program pursued by Admiral Tirpitz and his confederates in Berlin had terrified England and convinced the British that their very continuance as a world power was being contested. It was a situation which, if not arrested, could lead to the most awesome consequences. There were many Germans in high places who agreed with Ballin, but there were also many others who would have to be convinced that it was Tirpitz, and not Ballin and other businessmen, who was leading Germany into the shadow of war.[46]

There were, Ballin reasoned, two things that he could do. First, he could join with other men in England and Germany who were also concerned about the declining

[46] For views similar to Ballin's on the naval question, see Wilhelm Widenmann, *Marine-Attaché an der kaiserlich-deutschen Botschaft in London 1907-1912*, Göttingen, 1952, p. 40; Karl Nowak and Friedrich Thimme, eds., *Erinnerungen und Gedanken des Botschafters Anton Graf Monts*, Berlin, 1932, p. 196; Ernst Jäckh, *Kiderlen-Wächter der Staatsmann und Mensch: Briefwechsel und Nachlass*, 2 vols., Berlin and Leipzig, 1924, II, 155; Kühlmann, *Erinnerungen*, pp. 334, 346-47, 373-79; Tirpitz, *Politische Dokumente*, I, 91-92; Somary, *Erinnerungen*, pp. 93-94. For similar British opinion, see the views expressed by Balfour, Spender, Garvin, and Rothschild in Stein, ed., *England & Germany*, and also J. E. C. Montmorency, *Francis William Fox: A Biography*, London, 1923, pp. 93-95.

166

goodwill between their countries. Secondly, and more importantly, an attempt could be made to influence the Kaiser, the chancellor, and the Wilhelmstrasse to moderate Tirpitz' plans in order to come to a naval agreement with England. Ballin's attempt to smooth relations between London and Berlin involved him almost continuously in Anglo-German diplomatic affairs from 1908 to 1914.

About 1905, a number of businessmen in both Germany and England began to organize themselves into formal bodies to supplement private efforts already in progress to improve Anglo-German relations. The initiative seems to have been almost entirely British. Sir Alfred Mond, a financier, industrialist, and politician of German descent, summed up the feelings of the British business community: "They are convinced that it is high time that businessmen generally, however reluctant they may be to enter the political field, should in both countries exercise their undoubted right to tell politicians and diplomatists that a way must and shall be found to make a reality of our mutual desire for friendly relations."[47] The most publicized such group was the Anglo-German Friendship Society, established in 1905 by an elderly but energetic Quaker, Thomas Fox, who served as secretary.[48] The Society, which received the blessing of both Bülow and the Kaiser, held banquets and sponsored reciprocal visits by parliamentarians and journalists, while the British branch encouraged the public to give German passen-

[47] Stein, ed., *England & Germany*, pp. 59-60.
[48] Montmorency, *Francis Fox*; Kühlmann, *Erinnerungen*, pp. 329-30. For private efforts by English businessmen at this time to improve relations, see Hallgarten, *Imperialismus vor 1914*, II, 1-6; Bernhard Fürst von Bülow, *Denkwürdigkeiten*, 4 vols., Berlin, 1930-31, II, 190-96.

ger ships a hospitable welcome when in port. Ballin, who in 1905 had not yet become seriously concerned about Anglo-German relations, was not a charter member, though he may have joined the Society later. In 1910, Sir Ernest Cassel established the King Edward VII Endowment in memory of his good friend, who died in May of that year. The fund, ostensibly for no loftier purpose than to help Germans financially stranded in England and Englishmen in similar straits in Germany, had as its real purpose the general amelioration of relations between the two nations.[49] Ballin worked actively for the Endowment, sitting on its board along with Max Warburg and the coal tycoon and art collector, Eduard Arnhold. Through Ballin's offices, the Kaiser and Kaiserin were pleased to serve on the Endowment's honorary board, and Ballin entreated Harden to put in a good word for it in the *Zukunft*.[50]

Ballin's campaign for Anglo-German naval talks got under way in the summer of 1908. In June, apparently at the behest and certainly with the knowledge of the Kaiser, Ballin went to London to discuss Anglo-German affairs with Cassel. Sir Ernest informed him that Edward VII was very concerned by Germany's naval building program and added that someday England, joined by France and Russia, might have to inquire at what point Berlin intended to stop this construction. Ballin's blunt reply was that Germany would resist such a "Fashoda" with all its

[49] Eduard Arnhold, *Ein Gedenkbuch*, Berlin, 1923, p. 298.

[50] On the Endowment, see Ballin to Warburg, Aug. 13, 1910, and Warburg to Ballin, Aug. 15, 1910 and June 5, 1911, all in Warburg "Nachlass," 2302/9/802; Warburg, *Aus meinen Aufzeichnungen*, n.p., 1952, p. 25; Arnold, *Gedenkbuch*, pp. 297-302; Eduard Rosenbaum, "A Postscript to the Essay on Albert Ballin," Leo Baeck Institute of Jews from Germany, *Year Book*, IV, London, 1959, 269.

might.[51] A somewhat more cordial exchange followed when the conversation turned to the difficult personal relations between William II and Edward VII, a situation which Cassel and Ballin hoped that they might be able to improve.[52] Sir Ernest concluded the discussion by proposing that the two nations attempt to negotiate their differences.

Although there was an informal diplomatic interchange concerning Anglo-German naval rivalry during the winter of 1908-09, Ballin was not involved. Cassel wrote repeatedly to Ballin in the spring of 1909 to warn him again, according to Bülow, that German navalism was the "Alpha and Omega of English mistrust as well as of all English machinations against us."[53] Ballin expressed Sir Ernest's concern, which he fully shared, to Bethmann and sent Bülow a memorandum by Walther Rathenau in which Rathenau appealed for efforts on the part of both governments to overcome their problems.[54] Ballin sounded out the Kaiser during Kiel Week in June 1909 about the prospect of further negotiations. He proposed that he be empowered to initiate feelers with the British via Cassel, with the expectation that these efforts would eventually lead to formal talks between Admiral Tirpitz and Sir John Fisher, the first sea lord. Ballin was anxious that Tirpitz himself conduct the negotiations because he believed that the admiral constituted the principal stumbling block to a naval agreement. At the same time, Ballin argued, Tirpitz delighted in meddling in politics and dreamed of scoring a diplomatic coup. Why not, then, let the admiral conduct the talks with England? He would thereby have the re-

[51] Huldermann, pp. 208-11; Tirpitz, *Politische Dokumente*, I, 67-68.

[52] William II to Bülow, July 6, 1908, *AA*, Eng. Nr. 83, secr., vol. 3, reel 71/00419-20.

[53] Bülow, *Denkwürdigkeiten*, II, 427.

[54] *ibid.*, II, 427-28.

sponsibility of establishing his diplomatic reputation by securing an agreement. But since the British would not agree to any solution which did not conform to their naval plans, Tirpitz would be forced to compromise in order to obtain their signature. If Tirpitz refused, the burden of failure would rest squarely on him.[55] The Kaiser favored a discreet step in this direction, and Ballin thereupon met with Tirpitz and Admiral von Müller, chief of the Naval Cabinet, to work out details. It was agreed that Ballin would first discuss the possibility of a commercial agreement with Cassel and then intimate to him that Germany was by no means opposed to arriving at a naval convention with England. He might then ask in what form Great Britain would conceive of such an understanding.[56] Ballin wrote to Cassel to say that he would like to discuss the *Flottenfrage* with him "for my personal information." Cassel invited him to come to London.

The second meeting between the two men took place in June 1909.[57] Ballin began the discussion by inquiring if Cassel still felt that formal negotiations should be begun between Berlin and London. Cassel, to Ballin's surprise, declared that the situation had changed so in the interim that England could no longer agree to commit itself to a naval agreement with Germany. The reason cited by Cassel for this change of opinion was the recent increases which France and the Habsburg empire had announced for their navies. In addition, Cassel noted, Great Britain's trade position was being damaged by German enterprise

[55] *ibid.*, III, 6.

[56] Memo by Müller, June 26, 1909, printed in Hubatsch, *Ära Tirpitz*, pp. 87-88. See also Görlitz, ed., *Der Kaiser*, p. 76.

[57] For Ballin's 1909 conversation with Cassel, see a memorandum by Ballin, July 10, 1909, in *AA*, Marine-Kabinets, xxxi.b., vol. 2, reel 18/00058-65; also Ballin to Admiral von Heeringen, chief of the Admiral Staff, July 6, 1909, *ibid.*, 18/00049-50. The July 10 memo is partially printed in Huldermann, pp. 216-22.

and ingenuity. England, he reasoned, could not do anything to correct this economic problem, but its naval supremacy could be maintained by appropriating more money to guarantee a sufficiently powerful navy. Ballin replied very pointedly that if England did so, Germany would be forced to follow suit and a senseless armament race would be the inevitable result. He also made it clear that Germany would have to insist, as a part of any settlement, that England maintain its traditional free-trade policy, so valuable to Germany's commerce.

The conversation was broken off at this point for a few hours. When Ballin returned to Cassel's house he found the Englishman in a more conciliatory mood. Ballin surmised that Sir Ernest had been impressed by his forthrightness on Germany's position concerning armaments and had acquainted the British government that Berlin could not be intimidated into giving up its construction program. Cassel disposed of the free trade question by noting that, in his opinion, any turn to protection by England was very unlikely. He was at pains to emphasize to Ballin that Great Britain's insistence on maritime supremacy did not mean that some sort of mutually acceptable naval ratio could not be reached. England was, moreover, prepared to make concessions on a number of other issues. Therefore, Cassel concluded, it would be useful if talks on these points were held.

On his return to Germany, Ballin went at once to Berlin and submitted a report on his conversation to the Kaiser on July 10th.[58] William II indicated that he would approve further soundings provided that they were conducted in secrecy. He congratulated Ballin on the skillful manner in which he had handled his delicate mission.[59]

[58] Tirpitz, *Politische Dokumente*, I, 164.
[59] Müller's notes dated July 15, 1909, on Ballin's memo of July 10, *AA*, Marine-Kabinets, xxxi.b., vol. 2, reel 18/00058-65.

Tirpitz, to whom Ballin had forwarded a memorandum covering his trip to London, was less pleased. Already alarmed by what he feared to be government weakness on his naval plans, the admiral was upset that Ballin had needlessly, and without any authority from Berlin, broached the free trade question. The British, Tirpitz argued, could easily regard this as an affront.[60]

A decision in Berlin as to what step should now be taken was complicated by chancellor Bülow's fall from office on July 14th, four days after Ballin's conference with the Kaiser. At Tirpitz' insistence, the new chancellor was informed of Ballin's mission.[61] The news was communicated to Bethmann on August 4th at a meeting on board the *Hohenzollern* at Swinemünde attended by the chancellor, Ballin, and Admiral von Müller. Bethmann's reaction was that while a naval agreement was very desirable, overtures for such a purpose could not come from Germany. Since Germany was the weaker power in maritime strength, any move for negotiations on Berlin's part could be interpreted as an admission of weakness.[62] Müller pointed out that there was no point in negotiations, even if the British were willing to take the initiative, unless the German government defined the maximum concessions it was prepared to make. This, Müller argued, was a technical matter which only Tirpitz could formulate. Ballin should inform Cassel that Berlin considered the moment favorable for negotiations but that first the two men should meet again to work out details and to give Tirpitz time to make his calculations.[63] Ballin, presumably

[60] Tirpitz to Müller, July 17, 1909, *ibid.*, reel 18/00066-67; see also Tirpitz, *Politische Dokumente*, I, 164.

[61] Müller to Tirpitz, July 27, 1909, *AA*, Marine-Kabinets, xxxi.b., vol. 2, reel 18/00069; same to Ballin, same date, 18/00070.

[62] Müller to Tirpitz, Aug. 4, 1909, *ibid.*, reel 18/00073-75.

[63] *Ibid.*

with Bethmann's consent, telegraphed Cassel to inquire if he could see him; Sir Ernest cordially replied that he would be happy to receive him at any time he chose. Ballin thereupon asked Bethmann what reply he should make.[64]

The new chancellor concurred with William II that Ballin was indeed a skillful diplomat, but he was disturbed that the Imperial Chancellery as well as the Foreign Office had up to now participated only peripherally in this matter. Bethmann did not intend to be dismissed as a figurehead, and he therefore determined to put affairs firmly into official hands. The chancellor, according to Bülow, declared that Anglo-German relations were "*his* department" and "*his* specialty."[65] The Kaiser yielded. "You see," William observed to Ballin, "it won't work. I can't risk a chancellor-crisis just a few weeks after appointing Bethmann Hollweg. But how ambitious the fellow is! I hope that he will come to a good end with England."[66] On August 17th, Bethmann called Ballin to Berlin and informed him that in the future naval talks would be conducted through regular diplomatic channels. Tirpitz, much to his exasperation, was similarly excluded.[67]

For the rest of 1909 and on into 1910, the two powers exchanged feelers on the naval question through their ambassadors, but no formal negotiations were entered into and the dangerous situation remained unresolved. King Edward VII died in May 1910, and hope arose that the Kaiser would be able to establish a more pleasant relation-

[64] Ballin to Bethmann, undated but written on Aug. 11, 1909, and same to Müller, same date, *ibid.*, reel 18/00076-79.

[65] Bülow "Nachlass," Notizen 1918 (II), pp. 83-84. See Bülow, *Denkwürdigkeiten*, III, 5-7, for a similar, or perhaps the same, episode.

[66] Bülow "Nachlass," Notizen 1920 (II), p. 147. Cf. Bülow, *Denkwürdigkeiten*, III, 7.

[67] Tirpitz, *Politische Dokumente*, I, 165-68.

ship with George V. Harden urged Ballin to make a private survey of British public opinion to determine whether or not talks might be resumed. The monarch's death, however, removed Cassel from a position of influence at court, for George V, at first at least, did not share his father's intimacy with the banker.[68] Ballin was aware of this diminution of Cassel's influence, and he replied to Harden that now that Edward was dead, private negotiations would serve no purpose and that any future Anglo-German talks had best proceed through official channels.[69] Within a year, however, Ballin and Cassel found themselves once again involved in an effort to keep the peace between their two countries.

[68] See Somary, *Erinnerungen*, p. 96, for Cassel's complaints at his lack of influence.
[69] Ballin to Harden, Aug. 9, 1910, Harden "Nachlass."

CHAPTER VI

Peace or War with England?

I N THE spring of 1911, a new exacerba-
tion of Anglo-German relations occurred
which interrupted the attempts being
made to compose differences between London and Berlin. This most recent embarrassment between the two
powers came as a result of Germany's ambition to secure a
position of influence in Morocco.[1] Great Britain and Germany had first become embroiled over Morocco in 1905,
when William II created a diplomatic scandal by landing
—from a HAPAG ship—at Tangier and proclaiming that
Germany stood for the independence of Morocco and the
open door there for the trade of all nations. The Kaiser's
gesture was the result of his government's displeasure at
the way in which France, with England's acquiescence,
was attempting to reduce the sultan of Morocco to vassa-
lage. Germany's move was intended to make both the
French and the British aware that Germany intended to
have a voice in any changes in Morocco's status. The result
of William's action was a conference held at Algeciras
early in 1906 which affirmed his demands but which also
awarded France extensive police and fiscal powers in the
sultanate. The settlement worked out at the conference
specifically allowed the other Great Powers to intervene in
Morocco to protect the persons and investments of their
nationals. This compromise was reinforced in February

[1] On the Moroccan crises of 1905 and 1911, see Eugene N.
Anderson, *The First Moroccan Crisis 1904-1906*, Chicago, 1930;
George Monger, *The End of Isolation: British Foreign Policy
1900-1907*, London, etc., 1963, chap. viii; Irma C. Barlow, *The
Agadir Crisis*, Chapel Hill, 1940.

1909 by a Franco-German agreement, in which France's political and Germany's economic interests in Morocco were recognized.

From 1906 to 1911, Germany greatly extended its economic activities in the area. In 1909, the Düsseldorf metallurgical firm of Mannesmann Brothers established a subsidiary, *Marokko-Mannesmann & Co.*, to exploit ore deposits in southern Morocco. At the same time, Max Warburg set up a *Hamburg-Marokko Gesellschaft*, which apparently was to be a holding company through which mining investments in the sultanate would be managed.[2] As Germany's economic role was thus expanding, France was simultaneously enlarging its police powers, a move made necessary by endemic native rebellions. In May 1911, a French force took Fez, the capital. Germany protested that the occupation of Fez was contrary to the Algeciras compromise and was in fact a thinly veiled attempt to establish a protectorate in Morocco. Discussions were begun between Kiderlen-Wächter, the secretary of the Foreign Office, and Jules Cambon, France's talented ambassador in Berlin, to work out a settlement.

Kiderlen quickly became exasperated. He and others in the Foreign Office felt that the Quai d'Orsay was not sufficiently aware that France would have to compromise. The head of the African *Abteilung* of the Foreign Office, Baron Langwerth von Simmern, persuaded the secretary and chancellor Bethmann Hollweg to confront France with a *coup de théâtre*. Langwerth's plan of action was to send German warships to Agadir in southern Morocco. The expectation was that such a move would frighten Paris into conceding to Germany *part* of the French Congo, in return for which Germany would withdraw its bothersome op-

[2] F. W. Pick, *Searchlight on German Africa: The Diaries and Papers of Dr. W. Ch. Regendanz. A Study in Colonial Ambitions*, London, 1939, pp. 6-7.

position to France's political authority in Morocco. Before Langwerth's stratagem could be carried out, however, a pretext needed to be found and William II's consent had to be obtained.

The pretext was manufactured without delay. Langwerth had Dr. Wilhelm Regendanz, one of Warburg's employees, draw up a petition in which German firms active in southern Morocco appealed to Berlin for help against marauding natives. The petition was a fiction. There was no immediate danger to German interests in the vicinity, and nothing, in any case, that warships lying at Agadir (where no Germans whatsoever were resident) could do to protect them. Having drawn up his petition, Regendanz then set about finding firms which would be willing to sign it—without examining the text. This was considered a necessary precaution in order to insure that the affair be kept secret. In spite of the irregularity of the request, M. M. Warburg & Co. and ten other firms active in Morocco affixed their names to the document.[3]

William II approved the government's plan for using the Moroccan situation to obtain compensation for Germany in equatorial Africa.[4] After some initial reluctance, he agreed in theory to the dispatch of men-of-war to Agadir.[5] Now that the pretext for intervention had been prepared, the only thing which remained was to secure the Kaiser's consent for the actual ordering of warships to Morocco in the immediate future. At the end of June 1911, William was attending the Lower Elbe Regatta in Hamburg on board the *Hohenzollern*. Among his guests were Beth-

[3] *ibid.*, pp. 14-18. Most of the eleven firms had some sort of corporate interrelationship. *Marokko-Mannesmann* was not included.

[4] See William's marginalia on a telegram from Bethmann, dated July 10, 1911, *GP*, XXIX, no. 10,600, pp. 177-78.

[5] Ernst Jäckh, *Kiderlen-Wächter der Staatsmann und Mensch: Briefwechsel und Nachlass*, 2 vols., Stuttgart, etc., 1924, II, 122.

mann, Kiderlen, and Ballin. The chancellor and the secretary were worried that now that everything was in order all might collapse on the Kaiser's refusal to allow German warships to be dispatched. On June 25th, Bethmann therefore informed Ballin of the government's plans and asked him to "prepare" the Kaiser.[6] Neither Ballin nor the Hamburg-American Line had any business interests in Morocco, but Warburg had kept Ballin informed of developments in the area, and it may be that Heinrich Baron von Ohlendorff, a member of the HAPAG board who had interests in Morocco and who had signed Regendanz' circular, also spoke to him on the subject. Ballin agreed to work on William, and the result was that on the following day Kiderlen was able to send a laconic wire to his under secretary, Arthur Zimmermann, informing him that the Kaiser had consented that men-of-war might be sent.[7] Consequently, on July 1, 1911, the *Panther*, a small gunboat, steamed into Agadir and dropped anchor. It was replaced three days later by a light cruiser, the *Berlin*, which remained in port until late November.

The *Panther*'s arrival in Agadir created a furor in London and Paris, and before July was out there were warnings by Lloyd George and others that Europe was perilously close to war.[8] None of the Great Powers, however, were willing to become involved in hostilities because of Morocco, and the Germans and the French, the latter firmly supported by Great Britain, therefore attempted to work out a diplomatic settlement. Ballin, who was consulted from time to time by the German government from

[6] Pick, *Searchlight on German Africa*, p. 20.

[7] *GP*, XXIX, no. 10,576, p. 152.

[8] For Ballin's fear that England would sooner or later force Germany into war, see Gustav Stresemann, *Reden und Schriften: Politik—Geschichte—Literatur 1897-1926*, 2 vols., Dresden, 1926, I, 209. See Lloyd George's Mansion House speech of July 21, 1911, in *BD*, VII, pp. 391-92, and in the London *Times* (July 22).

the *Panther* incident to the final resolution of the matter in November 1911, felt at first that although the situation was dangerous, Germany should not retreat from its position.[9] By August, however, he was beginning to become alarmed by Kiderlen's insistence that Germany be given the *entire* French Congo, a demand that was unacceptable to the French and profoundly disturbing to the British. Ballin therefore decided that the Franco-German negotiations should be terminated and the Algeciras compromise reaffirmed as the basis on which Moroccan affairs were to be handled.[10] Kiderlen and Cambon continued to discuss the matter, but their attempts at settlement foundered on German insistence on having all of the French Congo. In September, Ballin broke with Kiderlen. The reasons are not clear, but it is likely that the collapse of the Berlin stockmarket on September 2d because of the continuing war scare was largely responsible. Ballin now wrote to his friends that he was sick of the whole business, that Kiderlen was vastly overrated and that his policies were leading Germany into a fiasco.[11]

Since the French government showed no signs of yielding to his demands, Kiderlen finally agreed to reduce his claims, and in mid-October he and Cambon arrived at a compromise by which France would be given even more extensive rights in Morocco than those provided for at Algeciras. In return, Germany's economic interests in the sultanate were to be recognized. France was also to surrender about 100,000 acres in the French Congo lying along the Cameroon border. Bethmann and Kiderlen personally informed Ballin of the envisioned compromise, and Ballin wrote to Warburg that he was happy that the

[9] Ballin to Warburg, July 29, 1911, Warburg "Nachlass," -/25a/Privat.

[10] Ballin to Ernst Francke, Aug. 23, 1911, Stubmann, p. 193.

[11] Ballin to Harden, Sept. 9, 1911, Harden "Nachlass"; same to Francke, Sept. 8 and 15, Stubmann, pp. 193-95.

"*Marocco-Komödie*" was finished.[12] Only the formulation of the final treaty remained, and this was accomplished on November 4th.[13] Even though a peaceful and territorially advantageous settlement had been reached, Ballin continued to regard Kiderlen's Moroccan adventure as a regrettable blemish in the career of an able man.[14]

Although the Moroccan crisis had created an atmosphere which would add to the difficulty of arranging an Anglo-German naval agreement, its peaceful settlement made it possible for Germany and England to reopen negotiations. Almost immediately after the conclusion of the Franco-German agreement in November 1911, rumors began to appear in the press that London would soon send a delegation to Berlin to discuss the naval armament question. There was some truth in these reports, for there were indeed several private efforts then being made in both Germany and Great Britain for a resumption of discussions, efforts which would culminate in the mission to Germany in February 1912 undertaken by Viscount Haldane of Cloan, the British minister of war. One champion of renewed negotiations was Francis William Fox of the Anglo-German Friendship Society, who mistakenly believed that a suggestion along such lines which he made to Sir Edward Grey, the British foreign secretary, in December 1911 led directly to the Haldane Mission.[15] Felix Somary, a German banker and a friend of Ballin's, like-

[12] Ballin to Warburg, Oct. 11, 1911, Warburg "Nachlass," -/25a/Privat.

[13] The treaty is printed in *GP*, xxix, nos. 10,772-73, pp. 413-22.

[14] Ballin to Warburg, Jan. 3, 1913, Warburg "Nachlass," 3072/265/802; same to Harden, Jan. 4, 1912, Harden "Nachlass."

[15] Great Britain, Foreign Office, Germany, political, 1911, file 371/1129, Fox to Grey, Dec. 21, 1911, with minutes by Grey and Crowe; *ibid.*, 1912, file 371/1372, same to same, Jan. 20, 1912; Crowe to Fox, Jan. 27, Public Record Office, London. Cf. J. E. C. Montmorency, *Francis William Fox: A Biography*, London, 1923, pp. 25-26, 119-22.

wise asserted an earnest but fraudulent claim to having been the initiator of Haldane's journey.[16]

The question of who first brought up the suggestion that negotiations be resumed was a subject of controversy to the participants in the Haldane Mission, and the dispute has been continued by those historians who have attempted to reconstruct the negotiations.[17] British statesmen by and

[16] Somary, *Erinnerungen aus meinem Leben*, Zurich, n.d., pp. 93-96.

[17] The literature on the Haldane Mission is enormous. The most recent general treatment is in Sir Ernest Woodward, *Great Britain and the German Navy*, Oxford, 1935; the most voluminous is B. D. E. Kraft, *Lord Haldane's Zending naar Berlijn in 1912: de duitsch-engelsche Onderhandelingen over de Vlootquaestie, 1905-1912*, Utrecht, n.d. An older study by Bernadotte Schmitt in Louis Paetow, ed., *The Crusades and Other Historical Essays Presented to Dana C. Munro* . . . , New York, 1928, pp. 245-88, is still of use. See also E. C. Helmrich, "Die Haldane Mission," *Berliner Monatshefte*, 12. Jg., no. 2 (Feb. 1934), 112-43; Emile Bourgeois, "La Mission de Lord Haldane à Berlin, Février 1912," *Revue des deux Mondes*, xxxv (Oct. 15, 1926), 881-910; the peripheral but very important study by Walther Hubatsch, "Der Kulminationspunkt der deutschen Marinepolitik im Jahre 1912," *Historische Zeitschrift*, CLXXVI, no. 2 (Oct. 1953), 291-322; F. Uppleger, *Die englische Flottenpolitik vor dem Weltkrieg*, Berlin, 1930. The documents on the mission published by the two governments involved appear in *BD*, VI, chap. xlix, and in *GP*, XXXI, chap. ccxliii. Among the substantial memoir and biographical literature particular reference should be made to Tirpitz' *Politische Dokumente*, 2 vols., Stuttgart, etc., 1924-26, and *Erinnerungen*, Leipzig, 1919; Walter Görlitz, ed., *Der Kaiser* . . . : *Aufzeichnungen des Chefs des Marinekabinetts Admiral Georg Alexander v. Müller über die Ära Wilhelms II.*, Berlin, 1965; Wilhelm Widenmann, *Marine-Attaché an der kaiserlich-deutschen Botschaft in London 1907-1912*, Göttingen, 1952; Bethmann's *Betrachtungen zum Weltkrieg*, 2 vols., Berlin, 1919-21; Richard B. Haldane, *Before the War*, London, etc., 1920, and *An Autobiography*, London, 1929; Huldermann's biography of Ballin; and the important biography by General Sir Frederick Maurice, *Haldane: the Life of Viscount Haldane of Cloan* . . . , 2 vols., London, 1937-39. A recent biography by Dudley Sommer, *Haldane of Cloan: His Life and Times 1856-1928*, London, 1960, although utilizing some unpublished family papers, is poorly written and very incomplete.

large believed that the initiative had come from Germany, while exactly the opposite opinion was entertained in Berlin. The reason for these attitudes is that in 1912 neither the British nor the German governments were anxious to publicize their desire for negotiations since the other power, as well as public opinion at home—always touchy on such matters—might interpret such an overture as a sign of weakness. Nor was the conduct or the aftermath of the Mission such as to prompt either side to claim the inspiration for it later. The Haldane Mission proved to be one of the least adroit diplomatic interchanges in the history of Anglo-German relations prior to the Great War. The preparation for it was, at best, lamentably insufficient. Too many issues—armaments, colonial demands, political formulae—were introduced, no agenda established for determining the relative importance of the points to be discussed, responsible and experienced negotiators were excluded in favor of private parties or uninitiated officials, and neither government was internally agreed on its aims or on the extent to which it was prepared to make concessions. It was, all told, a sorry example of the old diplomacy.

The first move appears to have been a private letter which Ballin, acting without the knowledge of the German government, addressed to Sir Ernest Cassel at the very beginning of 1912.[18] Ballin proposed that when Sir Ernest came to Germany in March for a meeting of the King Edward VII Endowment he bring his friend, Winston Churchill, the new first lord of the Admiralty, for negotiations on the naval question. The hope which Ballin and

[18] Ballin's letter is missing, but some indication of its contents can be gleaned from Cassel's reply, dated Jan. 9, 1912, and from Ballin's letter of Jan. 13 to Admiral von Müller, in *AA*, Marine-Kabinets, xxxi.b., vol. 2 reel 18/00136-37. Cassel's letter is partially printed with some minor alterations in Huldermann, pp. 246-47.

others favoring a naval agreement entertained—one which was defined with increasing precision as negotiations progressed—was that in return for limiting the size of its navy, Germany would receive a political agreement, preferably a pledge by Britain that it would remain neutral if Germany became involved in a war on the continent. On receipt of Ballin's letter, Cassel spoke to Churchill. The first lord declined Ballin's suggestion because, as Cassel wrote to Ballin, "he feels that the office to which he was recently appointed has very peculiar limitations which would not permit a visit such as you describe at the present time."[19] The only manner in which Churchill thought that he might suitably come to Germany would be if he were to accompany King George V on a state visit to Berlin. Sir Ernest noted that he himself believed that Great Britain was prepared to go "*very far*" by way of compromise if Germany would voluntarily limit the size of its navy, new increases in which were expected soon to be proposed in a *Novelle*, a budgetary authorization for additional spending under an existant legislative act, in this case the Naval Laws of 1898 and 1900. Ballin furnished Admiral von Müller, the chief of the Naval Cabinet, with copies of his correspondence with Cassel and urged that the German government invite the British monarch to come to Germany so that Churchill could find a place in the royal entourage. Müller advised him that the matter was one with which Bethmann or William II would have to deal and he forwarded the Ballin-Cassel correspondence on to the chancellor.[20]

The British government meanwhile decided to send Cassel to Germany to determine whether Ballin's enthusi-

[19] Letter of Jan. 9, 1912, in *AA*, Marine-Kabinets, xxxi.b., vol. 2, reel 18/00133-36.

[20] Müller's notes on Ballin to Müller, Jan. 13, 1912, *ibid.*, reel 18/00136-37; Bethmann to Müller, Jan. 16, 18/00132.

asm for naval talks was in fact shared by officials in Berlin. Sir Ernest arrived in the capital on January 29th and met with Ballin at once. Ballin then saw Bethmann and went on to the palace to ask William to grant the British financier an audience, since, Ballin declared, Sir Ernest had come to Germany on a matter of "great importance."[21] The Kaiser ordered Cassel to be summoned without delay, and the Englishman presented William with a note expressing Britain's notion of the conditions under which negotiations might take place. Germany would have to recognize England's superiority on the sea and consequently agree not to increase its present naval construction program. In return, London would look with favor on Germany's colonial ambitions and would welcome "reciprocal assurances" prohibiting either power from joining coalitions designed to commit aggression against the other.[22]

As soon as Cassel left, William called in Bethmann and the two men, with Ballin possibly also in attendance, drafted a reply to Cassel's note. The German answer accepted the British propositions, but only provided that the 1912 *Novelle*, soon to be submitted to the Reichstag, be construed as part of Germany's "present" construction program.[23] The German reservation of the forthcoming *Novelle* was an important condition, inasmuch as this act was to provide for a third squadron to be placed in active service. Cassel advised Ballin that Germany's position on the *Novelle* would prove a liability in any negotiations and inquired if some formula could not be arrived at

[21] William II, *Ereignisse und Gestalten aus den Jahren 1878-1918*, Leipzig and Berlin, 1922, pp. 122-23; Churchill, *The World Crisis*, 5 vols., New York, 1923-29, I, 96-97.
[22] Cassel's note is printed as Anlage I to a memo by Bethmann, dated Jan. 29, 1912, in *GP*, XXXI, no. 11,347, p. 98.
[23] *ibid.*, Anlage II. For Ballin's support of the *Novelle*, see Görlitz, ed., *Der Kaiser*, p. 102.

which would at least slow the tempo of the ship construction provided for by the *Novelle*. If not, Great
Britain would be compelled to make immediate provision for the increase of its own fleet. In general, however,
Cassel was pleased by the results his feelers had yielded,
while the German government, interested in following up
his overture, urged that Sir Edward Grey, rather than
Churchill, come to Germany for conversations.[24]

Bethmann was prepared to examine the possibility of
alterations in the naval building tempo only if England
would adopt a "friendly orientation" in its policy toward
Germany. On February 4th, the chancellor sent a rather
vague statement embodying that phrase to Ballin for trans-
mission to Cassel and the British government.[25] Ballin
entrusted the chancellor's note to Bernhard Huldermann,
the general secretary of the Hamburg-American Line and
one of his trusted aides. Ballin also gave Huldermann a
personal letter for Cassel in order to furnish his British
friend with a more accurate picture of the German attitude than did the accompanying official note. Ballin
wrote to Sir Ernest that he was not optimistic about the
prospect of negotiations. He warned that Germany's
acceptance of limitations in its naval strength would be
contingent on Great Britain's agreeing to a "strongly
enunciated neutrality agreement" rather than to such
meaningless diplomatic declarations as "reciprocal assurances" used in Cassel's original message for the
Kaiser.[26] In other words, if Germany was voluntarily to

[24] See Cassel's third undated wire to Ballin printed in French in
GP, XXXI, no. 11,350, p. 102, and in English in Churchill, *World
Crisis*, I, 99-100.

[25] Bethmann to Ballin, Feb. 4, 1912, in Huldermann, pp. 249-50;
Bethmann's message is in *AA*, Marine-Kabinets, xxxi.c., vol. 1,
reel 18/00384, and is printed in *GP*, XXXI, no. 11,351, pp. 103-04,
and in Tirpitz, *Politische Dokumente*, I, 280-81.

[26] Ballin's undated letter to Cassel is printed in Huldermann,
pp. 250-52.

limit its navy, Great Britain would have voluntarily to resign its freedom to intervene at will in any continental war, offensive or defensive, in which Germany might become involved.

Huldermann left for London on February 6th and on the following day gave Cassel the German note and Ballin's letter. The English financier did not comment on the message from Ballin, but he did declare that he found the German note somewhat "evasive," though he was apparently satisfied that it constituted a reasonable basis for further negotiation.[27] Sir Ernest thereupon consulted with Lord Haldane, who had meanwhile been selected by the British cabinet to represent Great Britain in the negotiations. Haldane had long been a student of German philosophy and literature, he was proficient in the language, and he was known to favor an Anglo-German understanding. On the other hand, while the war minister was well versed in questions affecting the army, he knew very little of naval affairs, and the British government seems to have done nothing to repair this deficiency before sending him to Berlin. Haldane realized that there were obstacles in the way of reaching a definitive agreement with Germany, but he agreed with Cassel that the climate was certainly favorable and the opportunity to make an investigation of the prospects should not be lost. The minister noted that England could offer Germany what it had promised France and Russia: neutrality only if Germany were the attacked and not the attacker—not at all what Berlin had described as its desideratum for a political agreement. Cassel sent a report on Haldane's observations to Ballin, who in turn sent the

[27] Huldermann's record of his two conversations with Cassel are printed in *ibid.*, pp. 252-55.

message on to Bethmann and to the Kaiser.[28] William relayed it to Admiral von Tirpitz, who was very displeased at the narrow conception of a political agreement entertained by the British. He insisted that the feebleness of the English offer meant that Germany must not abate in its efforts to reach a 2:3 naval ratio with Great Britain.[29] The admiral, as well as his colleague Kiderlen-Wächter, resented the fact that negotiations had been arranged without his having been consulted, and he was displeased that Berlin had used Ballin and Cassel as intermediaries.[30] The mission, launched in an atmosphere charged with suspicion and complaint, was from the beginning burdened with what seemed to be irreconcilable demands.

In London, Haldane was rather unenthusiastically preparing for his forthcoming trip. At Ballin's urging, Sir Ernest agreed to accompany the war minister. The third member of the delegation would be Haldane's brother John, a distinguished physiologist, whose presence would lend some credibility (which Cassel's certainly did not) to London's announcement that the minister was going to Germany to investigate German education on behalf of a parliamentary committee then deliberating reforms for the University of London. "I start with Johnnie and Sir Ernest Cassel to-morrow morning," Haldane wrote to his mother on February 7th. "I am now quite prepared, but my mission is a very difficult one and I am far from

[28] Ballin to William II, Feb. 7, 1912, *AA*, Marine-Kabinets, xxxi.c., vol. 1, reel 18/00388-90, also printed in Tirpitz, *Politische Dokumente*, I, 281-82.

[29] Tirpitz to Müller, Feb. 8, 1912, *AA*, Marine-Kabinets, xxxi.c., vol. 1, reel 18/00394-96, also printed in Tirpitz, *Politische Dokumente*, I, 282.

[30] Tirpitz memo of conversation with Bethmann, Feb. 6, 1912, in *Politische Dokumente*, I, 282-83; Jäckh, *Kiderlen-Wächter*, II, 155.

sanguine of success. . . . I find myself the centre of many hopes and wishes, more than I feel that I am likely to be able to satisfy. But it is a memorable task and is well worth putting my strength into."[31]

Haldane and his party arrived in Berlin on February 8th and met Bethmann Hollweg for lunch at the British embassy. The two men had a cordial exchange concerning the neutrality agreement Germany wanted and the naval limitations which Great Britain expected to secure through negotiations. The obstacles standing in the way of an accord were openly admitted by both sides, but both Haldane and the chancellor were encouraged by each other's candor and readiness to leave nothing untried to bring about a settlement.[32] At the conclusion of his luncheon conference, Haldane saw Ballin and Cassel and expressed his satisfaction at the friendly reception accorded him by the chancellor. Now that the negotiations were actually under way, Ballin and Sir Ernest announced that they would leave Berlin on the following day. Haldane insisted however that Cassel remain in the capital, and the Kaiser, on being informed by Ballin of Haldane's desire, readily agreed.[33] Ballin also postponed his departure from Berlin and continued to remain in close contact with Cassel, though an attempt was made to conceal the fact that both men were in Berlin. The British delegation was kept out of public view as much as possible, and Sir

[31] Sommer, *Haldane*, p. 260. See also Grey to Sir Edward Goschen, Feb. 7, 1912, *BD*, VI, no. 496, p. 668; same to same, same date, no. 497, pp. 668-69.

[32] Haldane's diary of his talk with Bethmann on Feb. 8th is printed in *BD*, VI, no. 506, pp. 676-79; the chancellor's scanty notes are in his *Betrachtungen*, I, 50-51. See also Goschen to Sir Arthur Nicolson, Feb. 9, *BD*, VI, no. 502, pp. 672-73; same to Grey, same date, no. 500, pp. 667-71.

[33] Ballin to William II, Feb. 8, 1912, *GP*, XXXI, no. 11,358, pp. 111-12.

Ernest and Haldane were quartered in different hotels, seeing each other only at night.[34]

Haldane's conversation with Bethmann on February 8th had posed no problem, for the chancellor was sincerely anxious to mend the feud between England and Germany. The real test, and the decisive moment of Haldane's trip, came on the next day, when the British minister saw Admiral Tirpitz and the Kaiser. At this meeting, Haldane was given a copy of the forthcoming *Novelle*, the provisions of which were discussed at length. William II, over Tirpitz' objections, agreed in principle that some alteration of the tempo for ship construction under the new law might be introduced, but only provided Great Britain would sign a satisfactory political agreement.[35] According to Haldane's account, the question of increases in German naval personnel—later to become a very decisive point—was mentioned only in passing. Tirpitz, however, remembered Haldane's declaring rather more positively that the British government was "indifferent" (*ganz gleich*) on this item.[36] In any case, Haldane was not very encouraged by his encounter with Tirpitz.

Bethmann, who was generally mistrustful of Ballin's private diplomacy even when availing himself of his services, was determined that Ballin and Cassel leave Berlin before the negotiations progressed any farther. Though Haldane wanted Cassel to stay, the Kaiser, changing his mind overnight, ordered that the two men retire from the

[34] Sir Almeric Fitzroy, *Memoirs*, 2 vols., London, n.d., II, 765, diary entry of Nov. 10, 1921, following a conversation with Haldane.

[35] Haldane's diary, first entry for Feb. 9, 1912, *BD*, VI, no. 506, pp. 679-81; Tirpitz, *Politische Dokumente*, I, 286-89. Cf. Hubatsch, "Kulminationspunkt," 313.

[36] Haldane's diary, Feb. 8-9, 1912, *BD*, VI, no. 506, pp. 676-82; Tirpitz, *Politische Dokumente*, I, 287; *Erinnerungen*, p. 190.

capital.[37] Ballin departed for Hamburg on the 9th, and Sir Ernest returned to England. On arriving home, Ballin wrote to William II to report that Haldane had observed to him that he was "very pleased, though at the same time he felt that one *might have done more* in view of the great concessions which one expected from England." The Kaiser's marginal comment on the passage which he himself underlined was terse: "*Donnerwetter, das ist stark!*"[38] Haldane saw Bethmann again on February 10th, and the two drew up a "Sketch of a conceivable Formula" for a political agreement. Since the armament question had not been settled, Haldane was unable to consent to a political agreement such as the chancellor wanted. The British minister therefore rejected Bethmann's demand for an unqualified pledge of neutrality by England, and the final draft contained only a vacuous promise by both powers to observe at least benevolent neutrality if either was attacked in a war of aggression.[39] Haldane left for London on the following day, after having promised Bethmann that he would inform him of the reaction of his cabinet colleagues to the provisions of the *Novelle*. He assured Ballin that a decision would be forthcoming within a week or so.[40]

At this juncture, spirited discussions were in progress in both capitals between those, such as Cassel, Haldane, Bethmann, and Ballin, who believed that a compromise was essential and must be worked out, and those, particularly Tirpitz and Churchill, who raised fears that compro-

[37] Goschen to Nicolson, Feb. 9, 1912, *BD*, VI, no. 502, pp. 672-73; same to same, Feb. 10, no. 504, pp. 674-75.

[38] Ballin to William II, Feb. 9/10, 1912, in *AA*, Marine-Kabinets, xxxi.c., vol. 2, reel 18/00399-401. See also William to Ballin, Feb. 9, in Widenmann, *Marine-Attaché*, p. 238.

[39] Haldane's second diary entry for Feb. 9, 1912, and appendices, *BD*, VI, no. 506, pp. 681-85.

[40] *ibid.*; William II, *Ereignisse und Gestalten*, p. 128.

190

mise might mean a restriction of diplomatic freedom or an abdication of the right to self-defense. On February 22d, a new and troublesome factor was introduced into the negotiations. Sir Edward Grey informed ambassador Metternich that the Admiralty, on examining the *Novelle* brought back by Lord Haldane, was disturbed that the personnel increases provided for seemed to be in excess of a normal complement for the third squadron, for whose construction the *Novelle* was being introduced. A formal memorandum which the foreign secretary simultaneously handed Metternich stated the British objections and noted that the German increases in personnel would have to be met by a corresponding augmentation in British crews.[41] The note implied that this question would have to be settled before further progress could be made toward arranging a political agreement.[42]

The sudden introduction of the personnel issue was perplexing and irritating to the Germans, since Haldane had made no objection on this point while in Berlin. The Kaiser became infuriated on reading Grey's note, declaring that it meant that the British government had repudiated Haldane and that it was nothing less than an attempt to force Germany to abandon the *Novelle* entirely. William added with his usual rhetorical vehemence that "in the name of the German people as emperor and in the name of my armed might as supreme commander I must reject out of hand such a monstrosity as being incompatible with our honor."[43] The German government, in much calmer

---

[41] Undated memo by Grey to Metternich, enclosed in Grey to Goschen, Feb. 24, 1912, *BD*, VI, no. 524, pp. 697-99, also printed in Tirpitz, *Politische Dokumente*, I, 304-05. See also Metternich to Bethmann, Feb. 22, *GP*, XXXI, no. 11,370, pp. 128-30, also printed in Tirpitz, *Politische Dokumente*, I, 296-98; and a memo by Grey, same date, *BD*, VI, no. 523, pp. 696-97.

[42] Grey to Goschen, Feb. 24, 1912, *BD*, VI, no. 524, pp. 697-99.

[43] William to Bethmann, Feb. 27, 1912, in Tirpitz, *Politische*

language, protested London's precipitous shift to the personnel question as the central issue standing in the way of an agreement.[44] Haldane explained to Metternich that he had not objected to the proposed personnel increases while in Berlin since he was not a specialist in naval affairs and therefore could not have foreseen the Admiralty's objections. Only on his return to London had naval officials scrutinized the figures in the *Novelle* and found them unsatisfactory.[45] The Kaiser instructed Bethmann very emphatically that no concessions whatsoever were possible on the personnel issue.[46]

Even though the negotiations had thus taken a decidedly unpromising turn, Bethmann was determined that the talks continue so that the friendly tone injected into Anglo-German relations by the Haldane Mission might be maintained, even if no substantial arrangement could be made with England. The chancellor therefore entreated Ballin to do what he could through "discreet private support" to keep the exchange going.[47] Ballin was persuaded that England's peculiar behavior on the personnel issue was attributable not only to the Admiralty's qualms but also to the intrigues of the French, who feared that a *rapprochement* between London and Berlin would wreck the Entente Cordiale. He agreed with the Kaiser that the

---

Dokumente, I, 306-08. See also same to Kiderlen, Feb. 28, in *GP*, XXXI, no. 11,378, pp. 141-42.

[44] Bethmann to Metternich, March 4, 1912, *GP*, XXXI, no. 11,381, pp. 148-53, also printed in Tirpitz, *Politische Dokumente*, I, 315-17, and in *BD*, VI, no. 529, pp. 704-06, with a hostile minute by Crowe, Acland, and Grey.

[45] Metternich to Bethmann, March 1, 1912, *GP*, XXXI, no. 11,380, pp. 145-48; same to Foreign Office, March 7, no. 11,390, p. 159.

[46] Two telegrams by William to Bethmann and Metternich, both dated March 5, 1912, in Tirpitz, *Politische Dokumente*, I, 317, also printed in *GP*, XXXI, nos. 11,386-87, pp. 155-56.

[47] Bethmann to Ballin, March 8, 1912, in Huldermann, p. 258.

shift in the British position to the personnel question was essentially a repudiation of the preliminary soundings made by Lord Haldane. In order to obtain a clarification of London's point of view and to express his own feelings to Cassel, Ballin dispatched Huldermann to the south of France, where Sir Ernest was on vacation. Huldermann was given a letter to Cassel in which Ballin declared that Germany had made all the concessions possible on the naval question. Ballin requested Cassel to return to London with all speed in order to be able to watch developments more closely.[48] Cassel, in reply, assured Huldermann that the French were not trying to spoil the agreement. It was true, Sir Ernest admitted, that Churchill and other specialists were not satisfied with the personnel increases in the *Novelle* and that Haldane, in accepting the *Novelle* as a basis for discussion, had trespassed into a technical area in which he was insufficiently versed. Cassel stressed, however, the British government's—and particularly Churchill's—desire to reach an agreement, and expressed satisfaction that the Haldane Mission had produced a more favorable atmosphere in which to continue the search for a solution to Anglo-German difficulties. He agreed to Ballin's request that he depart for England at once.[49]

On Huldermann's return to Hamburg, Ballin himself left for Paris and London to see what he could find out about the situation. Conversations with financial leaders in the French capital confirmed Cassel's assurances that the French would do nothing to prevent an Anglo-German entente.[50] Once in London, Ballin conferred with am-

[48] Paraphrase by Huldermann of undated letter by Ballin to Cassel, *ibid*., pp. 258-61.

[49] Huldermann's notes of his conversations with Cassel in Marseilles, March 9-10, 1912, in *ibid*., pp. 261-63.

[50] Undated letter from Paris by Ballin to Bethmann, in *ibid*., p. 164.

bassador Metternich, Haldane, and Churchill. The opinion he derived from these talks, he advised Bethmann, was that the essential stumbling block was indeed the personnel increases, which were twice as great as the British had anticipated. Ballin was nonetheless optimistic that a settlement would be reached. All the signs were favorable. Both George V and the cabinet were disposed to conclude such an agreement. Ballin was especially encouraged by a conversation of several hours' duration which he had with Churchill on March 14th or 15th.[51] He reported that the first lord felt that naval specialists could work out solutions to the technical problems of personnel and ship increases. Churchill had then declared that he hoped that Germany might be moved (*bewegen*) through a political agreement to moderate its fleet program. There is nothing in the record to indicate that by such an agreement Churchill—or anyone else in the British cabinet—favored anything more than a promise that England would not intervene in the event Germany was forced to fight a defensive war on the continent. Ballin, however, seems to have interpreted the first lord's statement to mean that Great Britain would be willing to grant the *unconditional* neutrality agreement desired by Germany, and moreover to do so *before* the technical points regarding ships and personnel were settled. Churchill left no record of his conversation with Ballin, but what he undoubtedly meant was that he hoped that the expectation of Germany's securing a *conditional* neutrality agreement from the British would be sufficient lure to Berlin for it to go ahead and adjust the technical questions still outstanding. Be-

[51] Two letters by Huldermann to Bethmann, dated March 14 and 15, 1912, both enclosing wires from Ballin in London, in *AA*, Marine-Kabinets, xxxi.c., vol. 2, reel 18/00540, 00544-46. Bethmann forwarded this correspondence on to the Kaiser, *ibid.*, 18/00542.

cause of his erroneous interpretation of Churchill's position, Ballin was, of course, very pleased with the results of his discussion and felt that there was nothing more that he could accomplish in London. He declined an invitation to dine with prime minister Asquith and Grey and left for Germany, confident that the final negotiations could be left to naval specialists and to regular ambassadorial channels.

Returning to Germany on March 17th, Ballin went at once to Berlin to report his findings to William II. Admiral von Müller, who was present at the meeting, described Ballin's encounter with his sovereign.

> Ballin back from England where he spoke and ate with Haldane and Churchill. At 11 AM report at the palace in the presence of Valentini and myself. Ballin entered the star chamber with the words: "Your Majesty, I bring the alliance with England!" Ballin apparently very taken in (*eingenommen*) by the diplomats. Navy and especially Tirpitz disturbers of peace, "want war." Is convinced of the good will of the English cabinet. Decision of English cabinet on our neutrality proposal on its way; will arrive in the afternoon. Envisions already a defensive and offensive alliance in development.[52]

The only point on which Ballin proved correct was that the British answer would come that afternoon. Later in the day, a telegram did in fact arrive from Metternich, but its contents utterly contradicted everything that Ballin had said to the Kaiser.[53] The German ambassador announced that he had been informed by Grey in a formal statement

[52] Hubatsch, "Kulminationspunkt," 315-16, also printed with a few unimportant changes in Görlitz, ed., *Der Kaiser*, p. 117. See also unsigned telegram, almost certainly Ballin to Müller, March 17, 1912, in *AA*, Marine-Kabinets, xxxi.c., vol. 2, reel 18/00548.

[53] Metternich to Foreign Office, telegram in two parts, March 17, 1912, *GP*, xxxi, nos. 11,403-04, pp. 181-85.

that Great Britain could not accept the personnel increases envisioned by the *Novelle* and, as a result, could offer Germany nothing more than a non-aggression declaration by way of a political agreement. The two powers thus were deadlocked. The suspense was broken, the attempt to negotiate had failed. The news was received almost with relief by William II and his entourage. "Now, at least," Admiral von Müller wrote, "we know where we stand."[54] Both the Kaiser and Bethmann wired the news to Ballin, who had left Berlin immediately after his audience to return to Hamburg. William's message was rather curt, but the chancellor expressed his appreciation for Ballin's efforts and urged him "not to forget the Wilhelmstrasse on your next visit to Berlin."[55] Cassel wrote to say that the British government had authorized him to advise Ballin that the negotiations concerning a political agreement might be renewed after the *Novelle* had been adopted and the British public had had a few months time in which to get used to the new increases in the German navy.[56]

The collapse of the negotiations was a serious blow to Ballin, for the Haldane Mission had, he thought, promised to lead to the realization of his goal of an Anglo-German understanding. Instead, the conversations had yielded nothing. Ballin should not have been surprised, however, for he was well aware both of the problems involved as well as of the opposition to compromise which existed in influential quarters of both governments. From the beginning he was convinced that England wanted an agreement and he persisted doggedly in this view even after Berlin proved unable to offer any acceptable reduction in

[54] Hubatsch, "Kulminationspunkt," 316.
[55] William to Ballin, March 19, 1912, *AA*, Marine-Kabinets, xxxi.c., vol. 2, reel 18/00554; Bethmann to same, same date, in Huldermann, pp. 266-67.
[56] Ballin to William II, March 19, 1912, *AA*, Marine-Kabinets, xxxi.c., vol. 2, reel 18/00553-55.

196

the naval personnel question. It is difficult not to agree with Ballin's admirer, Admiral von Müller, that he was "taken in" by the numerous, and quite sincere, affirmations made to him by Cassel, Churchill, and Haldane that Great Britain earnestly desired to reach an agreement with Germany. In Ballin's eager mind, the professions of Anglo-German friendship made to him in London were misconstrued as a sign, if not a guarantee, that the British were ready to offer the extensive, unilateral concessions necessary to remove the weighty impediments which lay in the way of a *rapprochement*. He was simply blinded by a noble but, under the circumstances, a foolish hope.

The negative outcome of the Haldane Mission also affected Ballin personally, for he worried that his false assessment of the British position had cost him William II's confidence. In mid-April, Ballin wrote to the Kaiser that he had suffered from the impression that "the rather unhappy course of my work of many years in England had gained me Your Majesty's displeasure," but that he had been relieved to have had a letter from him indicating that this notion was unfounded.[57] William may not have been impressed by Ballin's powers of observation on this occasion, but the two men remained good friends and the Kaiser was to use Ballin again more than once as a private emissary.[58] Ballin's efforts in 1912 to promote a naval compromise with England did nothing, however, to ingratiate him with the Kaiserin, who was a firm supporter of Admiral von Tirpitz and an outspoken critic of Great Britain.[59]

The Haldane Mission increased Ballin's alienation from

[57] Same to same, April 11, 1912, *ibid.*, reel 18/00615.

[58] Cf. Bogdan Graf von Hutten-Czapski, *Sechzig Jahre Politik und Gesellschaft*, 2 vols., Berlin, 1936, II, 134.

[59] Widenmann "Nachlass," pp. 34, 49; Theodor Wolff, *Der Marsch durch zwei Jahrzehnte*, Amsterdam, 1936, pp. 248-50; Tirpitz, *Politische Dokumente*, I, 324-25.

Tirpitz. When he asked himself why England's response to Germany's proposals had been negative, the fault did not seem to lie so much with London as with Berlin, and more particularly with Tirpitz. Six months after the Haldane negotiations had been terminated, the aristocratic diarist and courtier, Baroness Spitzemberg, reported a conversation her son had recently had with Ballin. According to her report, Ballin's view was that among those who had prevented an understanding with England "before all to be blamed was Tirpitz, whom Ballin hates and regards as the Kaiser's evil spirit, as do others. The only thing is that His Majesty, who really does not like him and who is even afraid of him, at the same time has a sort of superstitious dread of letting him go out of remembrance of the disaster which Bismarck's dismissal brought in its wake."[60] Ballin continued to believe that an accommodation with England was possible but that Tirpitz would thwart any attempt to bring one about. On June 1, 1914, he wrote to former chancellor Bülow that "The political situation is causing me great concern. In my opinion, Germany cannot bear the enmity of France, Russia, and England if these three powers continually grow more cordial. One can still have England today but Tirpitz does not want it. His strong and unscrupulous personality, complicated even more by an insurmountable hostility to the Wilhelmstrasse, would make every negotiation over the fleet question impossible or lead it to certain failure."[61]

The lamentable outcome of the Haldane Mission made Ballin resolve "from the bitter experience of recent times" to have nothing more to do with politics.[62] This was idle

[60] Rudolf Vierhaus, ed., *Das Tagebuch der Baronin Spitzemberg: Aufzeichnungen aus der Hofgesellschaft des Hohenzollernreiches*, 2d edn., Göttingen, 1960, p. 548. See also Ballin's letter to Harden of Jan. 10, 1915, quoted on pp. 159-60.

[61] Bülow "Nachlass."

[62] Ballin to Harden, April 27, 1912, Harden "Nachlass."

talk, and he was repeatedly in England in the two years which elapsed between Haldane's trip to Berlin and the outbreak of the Great War to discuss political matters with Cassel and with his acquaintances in the British government. Occasionally, during this period, Bethmann used Ballin as a channel through which to settle minor incidents which troubled relations between the two nations.[63]

Early in 1914, Ballin and Cassel were again at work to promote a resumption of the negotiations broken off in March 1912. Ballin wrote to Sir Ernest that he was "sure" that if Tirpitz and Churchill could ever get together the admiral could be persuaded to come to an understanding on Germany's naval construction program, strange reasoning for one who believed Tirpitz to be the primary barrier to Anglo-German harmony. Cassel reported in reply that Churchill was enthusiastic at the prospect of grappling with Tirpitz. Ballin suggested to Berlin that the first lord be invited to Kiel Week in June, but William II vetoed the plan on a point of protocol and declared that the Asquith government must first ask whether Churchill might come, in which case he was to be assured that he "would be greeted with pleasure."[64] Before matters progressed further, however, Ballin—presumably on orders from Berlin—decided that "because of the nature of circumstances" it would be better if Churchill did not come.[65] The British had independently reached the same conclusion, and the first lord stayed in England.[66]

[63] For an example, see *AA*, Marine-Kabinets, xxxi.c., vol. 2, reel 18/00138-45; Churchill, *World Crisis*, I, 113.

[64] Treutler to Foreign Office, April 27, 1914, in *AA*, England Nr. 71b, vol. 77, reel 340/00445; Müller to Treutler, same date, *ibid.*, 00440.

[65] Bülow (Prussian minister to the Hanseatic cities and the Mecklenburgs) to Stumm, June 16, 1914, in *AA*, England Nr. 78, no. 3, reel 72/00715-16.

[66] Churchill, *World Crisis*, I, 189-91.

199

Churchill's absence did not prevent Kiel Week of 1914 and the Elbe regatta which preceded it from being the last imperial spectacle of prewar Germany. On June 14th, the HAPAG's *Vaterland*, sister ship to the mighty *Imperator*, began her maiden voyage for New York, while six days later, in the presence of the Kaiser, a third leviathan, the *Bismarck*, was christened. On the 21st, Albert and Marianne Ballin entertained William II and his entourage at a gala luncheon in the Feldbrunnenstrasse, after which the Kaiser and Ballin left for Kiel. Here, on board the *Hohenzollern*, William proudly observed the maneuvers of his formidable array of battleships and the imposing silhouettes of the HAPAG's liners, the greatest in the world. Ballin always found the regatta and Kiel Week somewhat exhausting and he was happy to be able to retire to his villa at Hamfelde for a few days' rest. Here, at 6:35 P.M. on June 28th, he received a telegram from the HAPAG's main office which read in part: "News just received from the *Hohenzollern* that the Austrian heir apparent murdered in Sarajevo. Flags on all ships at half-mast."[67]

For the next five weeks peace hung in the balance as Austria demanded satisfaction from Serbia for its alleged complicity in the assassination plot. Ballin was very fearful that this local quarrel might engulf all the nations of Europe in a disastrous war.[68] He did not at once hasten back to Hamburg or head for Berlin, however, but remained at his country estate and early in July departed for Professor Dapper's sanatorium for further rest. His vacation was soon interrupted by an appeal for help from Berlin.

[67] The wire is filed in *BAB*.
[68] Ballin to Warburg, July 14, 1914, Warburg "Nachlass," -/25a/Privat; Haldane to Grey, July 5, 1914, in Sommer, *Haldane*, pp. 299-300.

For years, the German government—sometimes with good cause, sometimes merely to strengthen its position against internal opposition—had expressed concern that Russia, England, and France were on the verge of signing an alliance with each other directed against Germany. This apprehension, heightened by the Entente Cordiale of 1904, the Anglo-Russian agreement of 1907, and the continuous military conversations between Paris and London, was intensified in the spring of 1914 when rumors began to spread that Russia and Britain were negotiating a military pact.

The first sign of trouble came on May 22nd, when the *Berliner Tageblatt*, edited by Ballin's friend Theodor Wolff, published a letter which Wolff said he had received from a "trustworthy Parisian personnage."[69] Wolff's informant advised him that Russia was trying to persuade England to enter into a naval convention and that this agreement would be but the first step leading to an eventual "alliance." This was a serious matter, the correspondent warned, and its significance was not realized in the Wilhelmstrasse.

On the contrary, the Foreign Office took the matter in dead seriousness. And well it might, since, in fact, it was the Foreign Office and not an anonymous Frenchman who had passed the word to Wolff. The ministry had derived the information from one of its agents, a certain Benno von Siebert, second secretary of the Russian embassy in London, who had access to letters addressed to Sergei Sazonov, the Russian foreign minister, by his ambassador in London, Count Benckendorff.[70] In two

[69] For partial texts of the article, see *GP*, xxxix, 617-18, note; *BD*, x, 791.

[70] Wolff, *Marsch*, p. 259; *The Eve of 1914*, New York, 1936, pp. 379-86, 440-41. Siebert later published the documents he had filched as *Diplomatische Aktenstücke zur Geschichte der Entente-*

communications, written just a few days before the *Tageblatt* published its letter, the ambassador reported that Grey and Asquith had agreed that talks between naval officers of both countries might begin shortly, but that Grey had made it clear that such conversations would in no case lead to any agreement committing England to action in the event of war. Benckendorff emphasized that he felt no firm "alliance or any other public agreement" with England was possible, and quite correctly pictured Grey's attitude as anything but enthusiastic.

The Wilhelmstrasse's reaction to Siebert's intelligence was that the talks must be frustrated, if possible before they even started. It hoped that its launching of rumors that such talks were soon to occur would be circulated in the British press and that the British would realize that an Anglo-Russian naval convention would only provoke countermeasures by Germany.[71] The rumors would also bring forth criticism of such negotiations by those in England who were hostile to military engagements with continental powers. For a while, it appeared that the Foreign Office's stratagem would have the desired effect, for the London press publicized the *Tageblatt* letter, with the result that Grey was questioned in Commons on June 11th as to whether the government was indeed holding, or preparing to hold, discussions with St. Petersburg.[72] Grey replied indirectly to his inquisitors that no negotiations were in progress which "would restrict or hamper the

---

politik der Vorkriegsjahre, 2 vols., Berlin and Leipzig, 1921. The letters in question are found in II, 812-15. Cf. Otto Hoetzsch, ed., *Die internationalen Beziehungen im Zeitalter des Imperialismus*, 8 vols., Berlin 1931-36, Reihe I, III, 21-22, for the correct date of the second letter.

[71] See Jagow to vom Rath, May 25, 1914, *GP*, XXXIX, no. 15,876, pp. 617-18.

[72] *Hansard*, 5th series, LXIII, questions by King and Byles, June 11, cols. 457-58.

freedom of Government . . . to decide whether or not Great Britain should participate in a war."[73] At the same time, Grey's private secretary assured ambassador Lichnowsky that no military pact with Russia existed or would be entered into.[74] The foreign secretary, anxious to stress the solidarity of the Triple Entente, admitted to Lichnowsky that England and Russia had "from time to time" discussed naval questions of mutual interest.[75] The Manchester *Guardian* was dissatisfied with Grey's statement in the Commons and on June 12th called for more specific questions to be addressed to the secretary. Apparently Grey privately assured the newspaper, somewhat more plainly, that no agreement existed and that "no negotiations" for one were in progress. The *Guardian*, in any case, declared that Grey had come forward to its satisfaction with the categorical denial it had demanded, and no more questions were asked in parliament.[76] Lichnowsky was equally content and advised Bethmann that Grey's assurances to the *Guardian* "left nothing to be desired as to exactitude."[77]

Bethmann agreed with Lichnowsky, but Gottlieb von Jagow, the secretary of the Foreign Office, was perplexed.[78] On the one hand, he had Siebert's persistent

[73] *ibid.*, col. 458.

[74] Lichnowsky to Bethmann, June 12, 1914, *AA*, England Nr. 83, secr., vol. 3, reel 71/00415.

[75] Same to same, July 9, 1914, *GP*, xxxix, no. 15,887, p. 639. See also Grey to Goschen, June 24, and to Sir Horace Rumbold (counsellor of embassy, Berlin), July 6, 1914, *BD*, xi, nos. 4, 7, pp. 4-6, 24-25. Grey's *Twenty-Five Years 1892-1916*, 2 vols., New York, 1925, prints the dispatch to Goschen but provides no additional information.

[76] The text of the *Guardian* article is printed in *GP*, xxxix, 625-26.

[77] Wire of June 13, 1914, in *AA*, England Nr. 83, secr., vol. 3, reel 71/00418.

[78] Bethmann to Lichnowsky, June 16, 1914, *ibid.*, reel 71/00426; Jagow, *England und der Kriegsausbruch*, Berlin, 1925, p. 20.

reports that talks were being planned, on the other Grey's vague but equally persistent declarations, backed by the German ambassador, that they were not. Weighing the evidence, Jagow decided that Grey was not telling the truth. Even more disturbing news was coming meanwhile from Siebert to the effect that the Russian naval expert who was to negotiate the agreement was already in London.[79] On June 15th, Jagow saw Sir Edward Goschen, the British ambassador, and delivered what he later described as a "feeler which at the same time should warn" (*ein Fühler der zugleich warnen sollte*).[80] The secretary declared that he had been shaken by the *Tageblatt* letters but that Grey's statement in the Commons had reassured him. He was relieved to know that the rumors were false, for had they not been—here was Jagow's "warning"— Germany would have had no choice but to increase its armaments in view of a worsened international position. Goschen did not report what he said in return, but presumably Jagow did not get any definite information out of him about the conversations with Russia. Jagow thus delivered his warning, but his "feeler" netted him nothing. He did not believe Grey and he had no confidence in Lichnowsky's judgment. In his quandry, Jagow turned to Ballin.

On July 15th—a month had meanwhile elapsed, since Jagow had been married in mid-June and gone to Switzerland for a honeymoon—the secretary wrote to Ballin at Professor Dapper's.[81] In the interim, of course, the international situation had been disrupted by the as-

---

[79] Siebert, *Diplomatische Aktenstücke*, I, 821-22. The Anglo-Russian talks began at some undetermined point between June 12 and July 7.

[80] Jagow, *England und der Kriegsausbruch*, pp. 19-20.

[81] The original document is in *AA*, England Nr. 83, secr., vol. 3, reel 71/00445-47, and is printed in *GP*, XXXIX, no. 15,888, pp. 640-43.

sassination at Sarajevo. Jagow began by apologizing for his invasion of Ballin's vacation but noted that the *Tageblatt* disclosure had raised a serious problem in Germany's relations with England, a field in which, he added diplomatically, Ballin was particularly well versed. Jagow did not confess to Ballin that his department had planted the rumors in the *Tageblatt*, nor did Wolff inform him of the source of the article.[82] Jagow explained that he wanted the talks to be stopped and that the best way to do so would be to persuade a member of the British cabinet to take a stand against the Anglo-Russian negotiations. Could not Ballin let a warning (*Warnruf*) slip across the North Sea to Haldane to the effect that the navy and the Foreign Office were very disturbed and foresaw a new naval scare as the inevitable result of the rumors. The Anglo-Russian talks, Jagow concluded ominously, could lead to "dangerous consequences."

Ballin left at once for Berlin. Jagow, or possibly Ballin himself, proposed that he go in person to London rather than writing to Haldane. Ballin was commissioned, as Jagow's letter specified, to investigate the state of the Anglo-Russian naval talks and to warn his highly placed London connections against the deleterious effect they would have on England's relations with Germany. The chancellor asked Ballin also to make an extensive probing of his English friends' views as to what course England would take in the event that the Serbo-Austrian situation led to a general war on the continent.[83] It may be that William II himself was responsible for Ballin's selection to perform this mission; Ballin's friend Carl Fürsten-

[82] See Wolff, *Marsch*, pp. 259-60. Ballin suspected that the *Tageblatt* story did not in fact originate in Paris, *ibid*., p. 264.

[83] Memo by Stumm, July 16, 1914, in *AA*, England Nr. 83, secr., vol. 3, reel 71/00447; Merck "Nachlass," "Erinnerungen," pp. 148-49.

205

berg thought so, as did Winston Churchill.[84] Since Ballin's undertaking was to be entirely private, Lichnowsky was not informed and first learned of the incident only in 1915.[85] Ostensibly on a business trip to arrange a fuel oil contract, Ballin arrived in London on July 20th.

Ballin, together with Grey and Lord Morley, lord president of the council, had dinner at Lord Haldane's on Thursday, July 23d, the day on which Austria dispatched its ultimatum to Serbia. The accounts of what was said at this dinner—a point later to be of considerable importance—are fragmentary and conflicting.[86] Haldane's version, one written many years later, held that both he and Grey told Ballin that while relations between England and Germany were very good at the moment, "their maintenance was dependent on Germany's not attacking France. In such a case Germany could not reckon on our neutrality." The two British statesmen at the same time assured him that England had no obligation of any sort toward France or Russia.[87] According to the report which Ballin sent to Jagow, the talk centered on rumors of

[84] Hans Fürstenberg, *Die Lebensgeschichte eines deutschen Bankiers*, Wiesbaden, n.d., p. 553; Churchill, *World Crisis*, I, 207-08.

[85] "Zuschrift" by Jagow and Stumm, dated Jan. 1928, in *Die Kriegsschuldfrage*, VI, no. 4 (April 1928), 397-98; Paul Herre, "Fürst Lichnowsky und die Kriegsschuldfrage," *ibid.*, no. 2 (Feb. 1928), 189-90; Edward F. Willis, *Prince Lichnowsky, Ambassador of Peace: A Study of Prewar Diplomacy*, Berkeley, 1942, pp. 227-28.

[86] Ballin's letter to Jagow of July 24th describing this dinner is in *AA*, England Nr. 83, secr., vol. 3, reel 71/00475-78, and printed in *GP*, XXXIX, no. 15,889, pp. 643-45. Grey and Morley do not describe the meeting in their memoirs. Haldane's account appears in his *Autobiography*, Garden City, 1929, p. 288, while Grey commented on it indirectly in a memo of April 1915, printed in George M. Trevelyan, *Grey of Fallodon*, London, 1937, p. 284.

[87] Max M. Warburg, *Aus meinen Aufzeichnungen*, n.p., 1952, p. 25.

the Anglo-Russian naval negotiations, with both Grey and Haldane denying that any convention had been signed and attributing the *Tageblatt* reports to "uneasy French friends." Ballin's message to Jagow reported these assurances and said nothing more. But in a letter addressed to Lord Haldane on August 1st, Ballin recalled what he remembered as having been said on the question of British neutrality.[88] "Last week," he wrote, "you gave me in your clear manner the impression that England would only be induced to make a martial intervention if Germany were to *swallow up* France, in other words, if the balance of power were to be greatly altered by German annexation of French territory." Ballin had thus left the dinner with a view of England's position in a Franco-German war which was fundamentally at odds with what Haldane later claimed he told him.

Two evenings later, on July 25th, Ballin dined with Churchill. He now proposed to the first lord the formula of a war-without-annexation against France which he mistakenly believed would be acceptable to Grey and Haldane. Churchill's response, though more guarded, did not dissipate Ballin's belief that the formula might be accepted by the British. Churchill left a record of his conversation with Ballin.

> He said the situation was grave. . . . [The maintenance of peace] all depended on the Tsar. What would he do if Austria chastised Serbia? A few years before there would have been no danger, as the Tsar was too frightened for his throne, but now again he was feeling himself more secure . . . and the Russian people besides would feel very hardly anything done against Serbia. Then he said, "If Russia marches against Austria, we must march:

[88] The letter is printed in Haldane, *Autobiography*, pp. 290-91 (italics mine).

207

and if we march, France must march, and what would England do?" I was not in a position to say more than that it would be a great mistake to assume that England would necessarily do nothing, and I added she would judge events as they arose. He replied, speaking with very great earnestness, "Suppose we had to go to war with Russia and France, and suppose we defeated France and yet took nothing from her in Europe, not an inch of her territory, only some colonies to indemnify us. Would that make a difference to England's attitude. Suppose we gave a guarantee beforehand." I stuck to my formula that England would judge events as they arose, and that it would be a mistake to assume that we would stay out of it whatever happened.[89]

Finally, Ballin was no doubt encouraged that a solution such as he had in mind could be worked out because of the manifest pacifism of large segments of the English population and because of the fact that many financial leaders in the City, with whom he probably talked during his stay in London, were opposed to any involvement in a continental war.[90]

The misunderstanding between Ballin and the British was partly the result of the vague language used by both sides to avoid stating the facts with clear, if sanguinary, precision. But Ballin's failure correctly to have assessed the opinion of the cabinet was essentially due—as it had been in the case of the Haldane Mission—to his tendency to be carried away by his own desire for an Anglo-German accommodation and by the earnestness and sincerity with which the Englishmen to whom he talked declared that they wanted to avoid war. He was quick to interpret what

[89] Churchill, *World Crisis*, I, 207.
[90] See Lord Morley, *Memorandum on Resignation*, London, 1928, pp. 5-6, and Wolff, *Marsch*, p. 260.

British statesmen told him in the most favorable light, and he conveniently submerged any references which were gloomy or admonitory. So far as Ballin recalled, none of the English ministers with whom he had discussed matters had declared positively that England would intervene in the event of a German attack on France. Indeed, Haldane had indicated that England might do nothing if Germany made no annexations, while Churchill had spoken vaguely of judging events as they arose—a proposition which, if optimistically construed, could also mean that the British would stay out. It is singularly unfortunate that Ballin's mission was a private one, for had it not been he would doubtless have seen Lichnowsky, who was most emphatic in his belief that England would never, and under no circumstances, countenance an offensive war by Germany against France.[91]

Ballin returned to Hamburg on July 27th but was prevented from going directly to Berlin by a fever which he had contracted while in London. It is almost certain from the subsequent course of events, however, that Ballin informed Bethmann or Jagow of his belief that a non-annexation formula regarding France might keep England out of the war. For two days after Ballin's return to Germany, the chancellor summoned ambassador Goschen and proposed just such an arrangement. Bethmann told Goschen that "as far as he was able to judge the keynote of British policy, it was evident that Great Britain would never allow France to be crushed. Such a result was not contemplated by Germany. The Imperial Government was ready to give every assurance to the British

[91] See, for example, Lichnowsky's report to Bethmann on May 29, 1914, in *GP*, xxxix, no. 15,878, pp. 619-20. Luigi Albertini has discussed Ballin's misunderstanding of the British position in his *The Origins of the War of 1914*, trans., Isabella M. Massey, 3 vols., London, etc., 1952-57, II, 412-13.

Government that, provided Great Britain remained neutral, Germany aimed at no territorial acquisitions at the expense of France in the event of a victorious war."[92] This German overture, other passages of which agreed to guarantee Belgian neutrality only after the war and then only under certain conditions, was promptly and pointedly rejected by London.

The situation was now acute, for Austria had declared war on Serbia on the 28th, and Russian intervention to aid the Serbs appeared to be imminent. If Russia entered the war, Germany would be obliged by its 1879 alliance to come to Austria's defense, a move which would require France to take up arms. Since Bethmann's attempt to provide for British neutrality had failed, Germany was now faced with the prospect of war with England as well as with France and Russia.

On Saturday, August 1st, Germany declared war on Russia after the tsar failed to reply to a German ultimatum ordering Russian demobilization on the Polish frontier. Within ten days, all the major powers of Europe, honoring the pledges made under the system of alliances, had separated into two hostile camps. Former chancellor Bülow passed through Hamburg early on the first, and Ballin went at once to the Hotel Atlantic to talk to his old friend. Bülow reported that Ballin seemed "shocked not only by the war, but almost still more by the enormous ineptitude through which we had 'blundered' (*hineingetapert*) into it, and he predicted misfortune for the further course of events if coachman Bethmann stayed on in the driver's seat."[93] After seeing Bülow, Ballin left for Berlin to confer with Jagow and the chancellor.[94] Even on

[92] Goschen to Grey, July 29, 1914, *BD*, XI, no. 293, pp. 185-86.
[93] Bernhard Fürst von Bülow, *Denkwürdigkeiten*, 4 vols., Berlin, 1930-31, III, 142, 167-68.
[94] Bülow's account of Ballin's presence in the *Reichskanzlei* on

Saturday, Ballin clung to his hope that it would be "possible for England to preserve a friendly neutrality in return for certain guarantees. . . ."[95] On the same day, Ballin wrote to John Walter, one of the principal owners of the London *Times* and one of his guests at Kiel Week only a month before. This letter, which was actually composed by Otto Hammann, press director of the Foreign Office, with a view to publication, assigned Russia the "full weight of responsibility" for leading Europe into war and insisted that William II had struggled valiantly to maintain peace.[96] Two days later, on August 3d, Ballin returned to Hamburg, only to learn that at that very moment the Kaiser's armies were crossing the Belgian frontier. Even so, Ballin seems to have believed that England and Germany would not go to war with one another.[97]

On August 4th, Great Britain declared war on Germany. Ballin was not only dismayed; he was incredulous. Eleven

---

August 1st as Bethmann drew up the declaration of war on Russia has been much repeated. Jagow, who was there, denied that Ballin had been present. It is not impossible, though I think it doubtful, that Ballin saw Bülow in Hamburg early on the first, made the four-hour train trip to Berlin and consulted with Bethmann before the declaration was dispatched at 7 P.M. See Bülow, *Denkwürdigkeiten*, III, 142, and Friedrich Thimme, ed., *Front wider Bülow: Staatsmänner, Diplomaten und Forscher zu seinen Denkwürdigkeiten*, Munich, 1931, p. 210.

[95] Ballin to Haldane, Aug. 1, 1914, Haldane, *Autobiography*, pp. 271-73.

[96] Ballin's letter is printed in Henry Wickham Steed, *Through Thirty Years 1892-1922: A Personal Narrative*, 2 vols., Garden City, 1924, II, 17-18. See also *AA*, Weltkrieg, vol. 11, reel 1820/847574-76, for a letter of Haldane to Ballin on the same date. For the subsequent history of the letter to Walter, see Steed, *Thirty Years*, II, 16-25; London *Times*, *The History of the Times*, 4 vols., London, 1935-52, IV (1), 192-93, IV (2), 1064-65; interview of Ballin in the New York *World* (April 14, 1915); London *Times* (April 15, 19-20, 23-24, 1915).

[97] Bjarne Aagaard, "The Life of Albert Ballin," *Fairplay* (Jan. 26, 1922), 397.

211

days after the war between Germany and England had begun, Admiral von Müller noted in his diary that Ballin "still does not understand how England came to war against us and believes that a great part of the English people are against this war."[98] Only later did Ballin perceive how mistaken his observations in England had been and how his ardent hope for Anglo-German peace had led him falsely to believe that it would, somehow, be maintained. Ballin felt, his good friend Carl Fürstenberg wrote, that he had contributed to the break between the two nations in that his optimistic reports from London had encouraged Jagow, Bethmann, and others to act more recklessly than they might otherwise have.[99] Now—too late— he realized that years before he should have been more forcible in his warnings that German navalism conceived by Tirpitz could only end in war. "My ships did not need the protection of a German fleet," he confessed in 1915, "and I should have emphatically said so to the Kaiser. But I could never summon the courage to do so. . . . We were all too weak toward the Kaiser. No one wished to disturb his childlike, happy optimism, which could shift at once into an almost helpless depression if anyone criticized one of his pet projects [Lieblings-Themen]. And among these, the fleet was the greatest. Now we have the result of our lack of courage!"[100]

The news of the English declaration of war affected Ballin deeply, emotionally and physically. Bjarne Aagaard, a Norwegian shipowner who had seen him on August 3d, called on Ballin again the next day. "I could see," Aagaard

---

[98] Walter Görlitz, ed., *Regierte der Kaiser?: Kriegstagebücher, Aufzeichnungen und Briefe des Chefs des Marine-Kabinetts Admiral Georg Alexander von Müller*, Göttingen, 1959, p. 47.

[99] Fürstenberg, *Lebensgeschichte*, p. 554.

[100] Friedrich Baron von der Ropp's account of a conversation with Ballin in his *Zwischen Gestern und Morgen: Erfahrungen und Erkenntnisse*, Stuttgart, 1961, p. 94.

recalled, "that he had had no sleep and that the intervening hours had brought radical changes in his face, had made him an old, bent man."[101] Neither Ballin's merchant friends in Hamburg nor the citizenry at large shared his forebodings, however. The mood of the city was prayerful, resolute, and optimistic. Church bells tolled away all afternoon on the fourth, while after nightfall the streets filled with young people chanting "We want war!"[102] Ballin's business associates were cheerful, though there was some confusion during the first few days in becoming adjusted to the realities of living in a world at war. Ballin, once again, found himself set apart from his colleagues, for he saw no cause for rejoicing. "We were too confident," Max Warburg later confessed, "so much so that Ballin again and again shook his head at us."[103] Ballin himself turned now with disgust and remorse to face new problems created by a war he loathed and whose bitter end he was not to live to see.

[101] Aagaard, "Life of Ballin," 397.

[102] For the sentiment of Hamburg at the outbreak of the war, see the recollections of three of Ballin's friends: Carl August Schröder, *Aus Hamburgs Blütezeit,* Hamburg, 1921, p. 279; Warburg, *Aufzeichnungen,* pp. 34-35; Aagaard, "Life of Ballin," 397.

[103] Warburg, *Aufzeichnungen,* p. 34.

213

CHAPTER VII

The Phantom Fleet

NGLAND'S declaration of war on Germany on August 4, 1914, deactivated the Hamburg-American Line. The British fleet immediately took up position in the English Channel and in the North Sea, restricting all but the most intrepid German craft to the triangle of water enclosed by Helgoland, the Belgian coast, and the Jutland peninsula. German ships abroad trying to make for home were barred by the British from passing into the area. Freight bound for Germany in German ships and goods destined for export from German ports piled up in warehouses; passengers on both sides of the Atlantic exchanged their berths on German ships for space on neutral liners.

There seemed little for the HAPAG to do but to create a moth ball fleet and station it permanently on the Elbe. Rust, not competition, now became the danger with which the line had to contend. Ballin was miserable, for his mind was not one happily involved in mundane problems of maintenance and repair. "At the moment," he wrote despairingly to Frau Maximilian Harden on August 26th, "my life's work lies in shreds. I cannot cry hurrah, but I do derive some pleasure from the magnificent discipline and accomplishment of the General Staff. There are only two organizations which are beyond reproach; they are the Prussian army and the Catholic church. I once also included the HAPAG, but that was a vain conceit."[1]

[1] Harden "Nachlass." See also Ballin's letter to Ernst Francke, Aug. 17, 1914, in Stubmann, p. 211.

The problems confronting the Hamburg-American Line during the Great War were grim and their solution essentially negative: retrenchment and conservation became the order of the day. Ballin worked manfully and often under very difficult circumstances to save his line and he accomplished much.

The first task facing Ballin was the disposition of the HAPAG's 25,554 employees, most of whom had been left without work to perform once the war began. Almost half were immediately called to the colors, while 4,000 HAPAG men stationed abroad or caught on ships in enemy ports were interned by the Entente powers. To the families of hands who went to war, the line paid monthly allotments and allowed those who occupied company housing to stay on rent-free. Other families, who found themselves in real need, were given fuel and food at nominal prices or without any charge.[2] There were still some 8,000 workers to be provided for. The HAPAG kept a skeletal force—at reduced salaries—to run its offices and to keep its ships on the Elbe in repair, and it sought to find jobs for its employees in converting the old emigrant depots in Hamburg and Emden into hospitals; the company's cavernous baggage rooms were made over for use by the Red Cross.[3] There was even talk of the line's erecting a P.O.W. camp in the Hamburg suburb of Lokstedt, though apparently the plan was given up. Those employees who were skilled in journalism were handed over to the *Reichsmarineamt* press

[2] *Bericht und Rechnungslegung* for the meeting of the stockholders of the Hamburg-American Line, April 29, 1921, comprising balance sheets for 1914-20, HAPAG archive. See also *Kriegs-Zeitschrift*, no. 1 (Feb. 20, 1915), 5; *Holtzendorff-B*, I, folder 11, "Personal der Hapag im Reichsdienst, 1914/15," notes for Nov. 22, 1914.

[3] On salary reductions, in effect from August 22, 1914, see Merck "Nachlass," "Erinnerungen," p. 165; *ibid.*, II 8 Konv. 5, "Briefe von Kollegen . . . ," *Direktor* Thomann to Merck, June 21, 1915.

bureau. The HAPAG appealed to the army for defense contracts for its machine shops and eventually was entrusted with projects such as the conversion of railroad freight cars into rolling hospitals.[4]

These emergency measures provided for all the line's employees except for about 1,000 *Angestellte.* Many of these white-collar workers were transferred to the *Reichseinkauf-Gesellschaft,* a corporation established immediately after the outbreak of the war under the aegis of the HAPAG.[5] While in Berlin on August 1, 1914, Ballin had proposed that a body be established which would be responsible for the importation of food to feed Germany's civil population during the war. It was little short of a crime, he declared, that nothing had been done prior to the war to stockpile grain and other necessary produce, but the government had insisted on rushing Germany into war without ensuring that the nation was prepared. Ballin claimed that had Germany made Austria delay its ultimatum to Serbia by four weeks he could have secured more than enough food.[6]

[4] For these projects, see letters of *Direktor* Storm to Ballin, March 29, 1915; Stellmacher to same, July 31; Ballin to Stellmacher, Aug. 2, in *BAB.* See also *Holtzendorff-B,* I, folder 11, notes for Nov. 22, 1914; *ibid.,* folder 20, "Arbeiten in den Werkstätten der Hapag," notes for Nov. 11, 1914, and a letter of *Direktor* Warnholtz to Holtzendorff, March 5, 1915.

[5] On the *Reichseinkauf* and its successor, the *Zentral-Einkaufs-Gesellschaft,* see August Skalweit, *Die deutsche Kriegsernährungs-wirtschaft,* Stuttgart, etc., 1927, much of which is taken without acknowledgement from the memoirs of Clemens von Delbrück, *Die wirtschaftliche Mobilmachung in Deutschland . . . ,* Munich, 1924.

[6] Unsigned and incomplete letter of Jan. 9, 1915, identified as being one by Ballin to Admiral von Capelle in a letter by Ballin to Bethmann, also of Jan. 9, both in *Holtzendorff-A,* II. See also Ballin to Holtzendorff, Oct. 6, 1916, in *Ballin-Holtzendorff, Private*; same to Harden, Jan. 10, 1915, Harden "Nachlass." In 1912, at the request of the army, Ballin had the HAPAG draw up a plan for provisioning the army as well as the civilian population in the event of war, but nothing came of the matter. Ballin later

On August 2d, secretary Clemens Delbrück of the Imperial Interior Ministry (*Reichsamt des Inneren*) sent one of his assistants, *Geheimrat* Frisch, to Hamburg to consult Ballin as to the quickest means of importing food and fodder supplies, which were already in short supply. Two days later, as a result of this conversation, the *Reichseinkauf-Gesellschaft* was formally established with headquarters in Hamburg, and from the beginning it was largely under the control of HAPAG officials. It was not protected by a state import monopoly and therefore had to compete with other government agencies, private firms, and war profiteers. Ballin's original plan was that the HAPAG would manage the *Reichseinkauf* for a commission, but he subsequently decided that the line would serve without compensation. There were, however, periodic complaints in the German press that the HAPAG was charging the government a handsome fee for its services, an accusation which Ballin categorically denied.[7]

The *Reichseinkauf*, as Ballin had predicted on its establishment, rapidly expanded its operations. In January 1915, the imperial government decided to take the body more firmly in hand and moved the central office to Berlin. The *Reichseinkauf* was then dissolved and a new organization, the *Zentral-Einkaufs-Gesellschaft* (*ZEG*) was established and Frisch was put in charge. What had begun in August 1914 as a department of the HAPAG had within five months become a government-owned corporation employing over 8,000 people. After the move to Berlin, the HAPAG continued to act as one of the principal procuring agents for the *ZEG* and may also have rented it warehouse space in Hamburg. Rumors persisted that the

---

devised a similar plan for the German navy. See Huldermann, pp. 307-09, and *Holtzendorff-A*, x, report 505, Oct. 17, 1916.

[7] *Holtzendorff-A*, II, report 94, Dec. 22, 1914, and letter of Ballin to Capelle, Jan. 9, 1915.

line was deriving huge profits from its dealings with the
ZEG, but it seems unlikely that much money was made
through this connection. In any case, the first HAPAG Annual Report issued after the war denied that any profit had
been made in the line's business with either the *Reichseinkauf* or the *ZEG*.[8] Ballin was determined that the *ZEG*
itself should not make a profit, and he condemned
the leaders of the government sponsored *Kriegsgesell-
schaften*, who, he argued, were intent not on furthering
Germany's war effort, but were merely anxious to advertise
their capabilities by piling up huge earnings for their
agencies.[9]

Once Ballin had taken care of his employees he turned
to his second problem, that of disposing of the HAPAG's
ships. The war had caught the line's fleet scattered around
the world in allied, in enemy, and in neutral ports. On
July 20, 1914, secretary Jagow, on William II's order,
warned the HAPAG that Austria would very shortly
send an ultimatum to Serbia. Since events were likely to
move very swiftly once the ultimatum was dispatched,
Jagow felt that the Hamburg-American Line should be
prepared to safeguard its ships in the event of war. On
receipt of this news, Ballin postponed the departure from
Cuxhaven of several liners and ordered others to proceed
directly to German ports.[10] Even so, of the line's 175
major passenger and freight ships, only 80 lay at anchor in
German ports at the beginning of hostilities. Twelve
HAPAG vessels berthed in Entente harbors were immediately

[8] *Bericht und Rechnungslegung* for stockholders' meeting, April
29, 1921.

[9] Ballin to Schinckel, Aug. 15, 1915, *Ballin-Schinckel*; same to
Holtzendorff, Aug. 16, 1915, *Ballin-Holtzendorff, Private*.

[10] Wedel (imperial entourage) to Foreign Office, July 20, 1914,
in *AA*, Weltkrieg, vol. 2, reel 1817/845658; Jagow to Wedel, same
date, 1817/845671. See also Bülow "Nachlass," Notizen 1920
(I), p. 7.

seized by the enemy. The other 83 ships were tied up in neutral ports, with the greatest concentration in the United States, where 35 were riding at anchor. Included among these was the HAPAG's flagship, the magnificent *Vaterland*, the world's largest ship and one valued at almost 36,000,000 marks on the company's books. Altogether about 200,000,000 marks worth of ships flying the HAPAG ensign lay in neutral ports thousands of miles from Hamburg.[11] Ballin estimated that the wartime cost of keeping his virtually inactive fleet intact came to between two and three million marks a month, of which a third was applied to the maintenance of ships in neutral ports.[12]

There were two solutions to the problem. The first, bringing the ships back to German ports, seemed impossible because of the blockade which Great Britain had imposed and because of the inability or unwillingness of the German navy to break through this blockade. A more realistic solution appeared to be to dispose of the HAPAG's ships either by sale or by offering them for charter to neutral powers.[13]

Selling the line's ships raised a number of questions which not only affected the HAPAG's balance sheet but the war aims of the German empire as well. No one knew how long the hostilities would last nor the course they would

[11] Resumé of HAPAG tonnage at the end of Aug. 1917, enclosed between two letters by Ballin, both dated June 22, 1918, in *Ballin-Holtzendorff, Private*.

[12] Ballin to Tirpitz, Oct. 22, 1914, HAPAG-V.

[13] Ballin and the German government were also involved in an unsuccessful attempt to secure guarantees from Britain for HAPAG ships which would be used to bring German citizens overseas back to Germany, to send Russian internees to Sweden, and to transfer captured Russian soldiers to P.O.W. camps in Germany. See *Holtzendorff-B*, I, reports 3, 5, and 9, Aug. 20, 22, and 29; Holtzendorff to Ballin, Sept. 1, 1914; folder 2, "Guido Vertrag;" folder 14, "Heimsendung der Tsingtao-Leute;" folder 15, "Rücksendung von Seeleuten."

219

take. But it was plain to Ballin that immediately after the war there would be a tremendous market for ships, since all over the world demand would exist for large quantities of goods, imports of which had been prevented or restricted by the war.[14] The HAPAG, therefore, would be unwise to dispose of its ships, particularly since it would be very difficult, as long as the war lasted, to acquire material or labor to build new merchantmen as replacements. On the other hand, the HAPAG could ill-afford the enormous maintenance costs of its inactive fleet, a fleet which, after all, would become increasingly obsolete the longer the war lasted. Moreover, as an increasing number of neutral powers moved into the Entente camp, the question arose as to whether the HAPAG could risk refusing to sell its ships abroad, only to watch them later be seized by Germany's new enemies.

The decision whether or not to sell the ships was not an easy one, nor was the HAPAG a free agent in making up its mind what to do, for the German navy also had an interest in the HAPAG's ships lying in neutral waters. The avowed purpose of the submarine attacks on Entente vessels which Germany began on the war's outbreak was to starve England until it was forced to sue for peace. To do this, the ships which provisioned the British isles had to be sunk. If, however, the HAPAG sold its ships to neutrals who in turn used them to bring food and material to England, then the navy's entire objective was subverted. As the war continued, the line became increasingly insistent on the sale of its ships in countries which appeared to be slipping toward the Entente. At the same time, the German navy, putting its trust in unrestricted submarine warfare to

[14] Memo by Ballin, "Lage der Schiffahrt nach dem Kriege," dated May 8, 1915, in HAPAG-V. Ballin acknowledged, however, that this post-war trade boom would be only temporary and would be followed by a period of attenuated commerce, limited credit, and general hard times for international trade.

220

defeat England after the war on land in the west proved to be a stalemate, opposed with mounting intransigence any ship sales to the diminishing number of neutral powers.

In October 1914, the United States government indicated to the HAPAG that it was interested in acquiring part of the line's fleet lying in American ports. Admiral Tirpitz heard of the offer and immediately expressed a desire to know whether or not the HAPAG actually had any intention of disposing of these vessels.[15] To clarify the line's position, Ballin composed a lengthy memorandum to the admiral in which he weighed all the factors for and against such a sale.[16] Selling the ships would insure the line against eventual loss should the United States join the Entente and seize the ships as alien property, a possibility which in 1914 seemed very remote but which Ballin regarded as a factor which nonetheless had to be considered. A sale would also relieve the line of the costs of maintaining its idle ships. There were, however, a number of considerations which militated against a sale. The principal disadvantage was the fact that the HAPAG would later need these ships to participate in the post-war freight boom. Disposing of the vessels would also greatly help the United States' shipping industry take over former German markets in South America and Asia and would have the undesirable psychological effect of making Ballin's British competitors believe that the HAPAG was in desperate financial condition, which it was not. Moreover, transferring the HAPAG's ships to the American flag would not, in Ballin's opinion, help Germany's war effort, for he correctly believed that Great Britain and France would act energetically to "protest" the Americans' using these ships to replenish Germany's dwindling stocks of foodstuffs

[15] *Holtzendorff-B*, I, folder 6, "Verkauf deutscher Schiffe in New York," notes for Oct. 22, 1914.
[16] HAPAG-V, dated Oct. 22, 1914.

and raw materials.[17] On reviewing all these factors, Ballin found that there was no reason as yet to sell the ships, particularly in view of Tirpitz' opposition to such a move. In the fall of 1914, moreover, there appeared to be some possibility that he could find ways to charter many of the HAPAG's ships in America. Chartering the ships would be much more desirable than selling them, since by a charter contract the line would be provided with income and could have its vessels back at the expiration of the term agreed to in the contract. To the navy, however, chartering the ships was as dangerous as selling them, since by either method neutral powers might use them to arm and provision the enemy.

The most promising opportunity to charter HAPAG ships was presented by the work undertaken after the war began by Herbert Hoover and his associates for the relief of Belgium.[18] Once its troops conquered Belgium, Germany became responsible for feeding the civilian population, a difficult task since Germany itself was short of food and therefore could not export edibles to Belgium. The Ger-

[17] Great Britain and France both informed Washington that they would seize such vessels. In Feb. 1915, the HAPAG sold a freighter lying at Port Arthur, Texas, the *Dacia*, to an American citizen. The ship was transferred to American registry and dispatched to Bremen or Rotterdam with a cargo of cotton bound for Germany. It was seized by a French warship in the North Sea and eventually awarded to France by a French prize court. The intervention of the Entente in the *Dacia* case and the decision of the court made American citizens wary of further purchases of German ships. For a thorough discussion, see Arthur S. Link, *Wilson: The Struggle for Neutrality*, Princeton, 1959, pp. 82-91, 179-87.

[18] On Belgian relief, see the two series of recollections by Hoover, *The Memoirs of Herbert Hoover*, 4 vols., New York, 1951-64, and the more elaborate *An American Epic*, 4 vols., Chicago, 1959-64. An essential collection of documents has been gathered by George I. Gay and H. H. Fisher, *Public Relations of the Commission for Relief in Belgium: Documents*, 2 vols., Stanford, 1929, hereafter cited as Gay-Fisher.

mans, in fact, were forced to requisition food in Belgium in order to feed their occupying armies. They could do nothing to help other than to open the port of Antwerp to all neutral ships bearing foodstuffs. While the Entente powers were concerned by the plight of the Belgian population, they were reluctant to send food, since this would not only relieve Germany of feeding the Belgians but would also aid it in sustaining its own troops in the occupied area. At the end of 1914, the German government declared its willingness to stop taking food from the Belgians, but simultaneously imposed a monthly cash levy of $7,500,000 on the defeated kingdom.

The reluctance of the belligerent governments to assist the Belgians forced the relief of the nation on interested individuals and private organizations. Soon after the German armies had completed their drive to the sea and placed almost all of Belgium behind their lines, a Belgian Relief Commission was established under Hoover's leadership and began the work of supplying the Belgians with food. The securing of adequate provisions was a considerable financial undertaking, the monthly food charges running between eight and twelve million dollars. The Belgians themselves could not raise the sum; the government in exile at Le Havre had very little cash, while Belgian citizens at home were unable to convert their notes into the gold necessary for food purchases on the international market. Neither Germany nor France would contribute, and the Commission therefore depended almost entirely on the generosity of private American donors to finance its efforts. Operating on this sort of voluntary charity was difficult, and what Hoover wanted was a regular monthly allotment from all three belligerents.

Early in 1915, after weeks of negotiation, Hoover obtained French and English agreement to support the Commission financially, provided that Germany would

223

guarantee that in the future it would impose neither food nor monetary requisitions on Belgium. Berlin issued a note renouncing food levies which was satisfactory to the Entente, but on the question of money payments Germany refused to budge. Karl Helfferich, the able and ambitious secretary of the Imperial Treasury (*Reichsschatzamt*), declared that an abandonment of the Belgian financial contribution was "wholly and absolutely" impossible.[19] Hoover thereupon turned to Max Warburg and Ballin. Warburg promised to do what he could to induce Helfferich to change his mind. On February 5, 1915, Hoover met Ballin in Berlin for an extended conversation on Belgian affairs. He found Ballin a "humane man" and reported that Ballin had agreed to exert his influence on Helfferich and Bethmann to give up Germany's financial exactions on Belgium, "as he considered that the whole problem of these captured people was the most important problem which was before the German people at the present time. . . ."[20] It is not clear whether Ballin actually saw the chancellor in Hoover's behalf; we know only that Bethmann requested and later received a memorandum from Ballin written on February 6th containing his views on the Belgian situation.[21] In any case, before the chancellor received Ballin's note, he saw Hoover and, like Helfferich, refused to give up Germany's monetary exactions.[22] On February 9, 1915, however, the Ger-

[19] Memo of Hoover, Feb. 6, 1915, of a conversation with Helfferich on Feb. 4th, Gay-Fisher, I, 245-47.

[20] *ibid.*, 248-49.

[21] Letter of Ballin to Holtzendorff, Feb. 8, 1915, in *Holtzendorff-A*, II. The text of this report is missing, but it apparently dealt with the Belgian war aims question, rather than with the problems of the Commission. See also Ballin's letter to Holtzendorff of Oct. 13, 1915, in *ibid.*, V.

[22] Hoover's memo of a conversation on Feb. 7, 1915, with Bethmann and the American ambassador to Germany, James W. Gerard, Gay-Fisher, I, 252-55.

man government agreed to advance the Commission
$5,000,000, though it persisted in continuing its fiscal
levies on the Belgians. Nine days later, the British government announced that it would grant Hoover's Commission
a million pounds per month, and Paris likewise consented
to extend its financial aid.[23]

Hoover now had the necessary funds with which to
buy food, and his problem next became one of obtaining
ships to bring his purchases across the Atlantic to Antwerp
and Rotterdam. Belgium's own merchant fleet was plainly
insufficient to meet the Commission's requirements. Hoover
had succeeded in acquiring a number of Dutch and Belgian
vessels of limited freight capacity, but it was imperative that
more, and larger, craft be procured. Ships, however, were
in short supply. Germany's vast merchant fleet had completely retired from intercontinental trade, and German
submarines had reduced the number of Entente merchantmen available. Neutral shipping was overworked trying to
fill the gap and keep abreast of the huge orders of war
goods placed by the belligerents. There existed, besides,
an unwillingness on the part of some of the Entente's military leaders to allow British or French vessels to be used
to alleviate a situation which Germany had created and
for whose solution it should now be held solely responsible.[24]

When Hoover went to Berlin in February 1915 to plead
for the cessation of Germany's financial demands on Belgium, he had also broached to Ballin the possibility of
chartering some forty HAPAG ships then at anchor in the
United States. Such an arrangement offered Ballin great
opportunities, for not only would the ships earn money,
but once securely across the Atlantic to Rotterdam, they

[23] *ibid.*, 257-67; Hoover, *American Epic*, I, 72-77, and *Memoirs*,
I, 165-70.
[24] Hoover, *American Epic*, I, 121-23, and *Memoirs*, I, 178.

could proceed on to Hamburg, where they could be safely tied up until the war's end.[25] Ballin therefore welcomed Hoover's overtures and admitted to him that the HAPAG would be happy to have the business.

During February and March 1915, Hoover and other officials of the Commission moved constantly between Paris, London, and Berlin, ironing out the obstacles to using the HAPAG's ships. On April 6th, the HAPAG's Berlin agent, Arndt von Holtzendorff, sent Ballin a copy of an agreement reached between the Commission and the British government.[26] By the terms of this paper, the vessels would be transferred to a firm in a neutral country, but as soon as they ceased to be exclusively employed by the Commission the ships were to be returned to their German owners. Another stipulation provided that the crews be entirely of neutral composition, while the British guaranteed that the German-owned ships would not be interfered with by its warships so long as they were "solely and absolutely" employed in transporting food for the Commission. The British government insisted as a final condition that the Belgian Relief Commission not pay more than 4s. per dead weight ton to the neutral firm chartering the ships and that no additional payment of any sort be made to the HAPAG. Within a few days, a representative of the Commission was in Berlin to negotiate with Ballin the transfer of a number of HAPAG ships in New York to the Royal Dutch Lloyd under the conditions set forth in the British note.[27] Ballin agreed to the con-

[25] Memo written in 1917 by Ballin for Helfferich, in Hulder-mann, p. 319.

[26] *Holtzendorff-B*, VI, memo entitled "Employment of German ships by the Commission for Relief in Belgium," dated March 16, 1915, also printed in Hoover, *American Epic*, I, 135-36, and in Gay-Fisher, I, 324.

[27] J. Beaver White to Hoover, April 17, 1915, Gay-Fisher, I, 325-26.

ditions imposed in the note, but only with the provision that the 4s. per ton figure be raised to 6s. The 4s. rate, he declared, had been arrived at by the British because this was the minimum figure at which a tramp steamer could operate and still make a profit. But Ballin held that the HA-PAG's freighters, because of the particular nature of the Commission's business and the risks attendant on trade during wartime, could not undertake the work at anything less than 6s. per ton.[28] After three weeks of acrimonious debate between Ballin and Helfferich, the Imperial Treasury agreed to pay the HAPAG a 2s. per ton differential.[29]

Once Ballin had been assured that the price would be satisfactory, the negotiations could proceed. In August, a series of conferences were held in Cologne which resulted in a formal contract signed on the 26th by Ballin and Herr Wilminck, the head of the Dutch Lloyd. By the terms of the convention, the Hamburg-American Line would transfer to the Dutch firm title to 21 of its ships in the United States, South America, and the Dutch West Indies, which would then be used by neutral crews for a period of at least six months to transport food to Belgium. The two lines would split any profit made on the Relief Commission's business, while the HAPAG, meeting a condition imposed by the British, would guarantee the Dutch Lloyd a minimum profit of 6d. per ton.[30]

Even though Ballin had succeeded in having his price met, he declined to deliver his ships to the Dutch Lloyd until both the Central Powers and the Entente had given

[28] *Holtzendorff-B*, VI, Ballin to Holtzendorff, July 19, 1915.

[29] *ibid.*, and Helfferich to Holtzendorff, July 24, 1915, in *ibid.*; Ballin to Holtzendorff, July 14, and report 209, July 17, both in *Holtzendorff-A*, IV.

[30] *Holtzendorff-B*, VI, copy of an agreement dated Aug. 26, 1915. See also the minutes of a conference held on the same day by Ballin and Dutch Lloyd officials, *ibid.*

Hoover formal assurances that the HAPAG vessels would in no way be interfered with by their warships.[31] On being approached, the German government offered Hoover nothing more satisfactory than a tacit agreement that German submarines would not attack relief ships, at the same time reserving the right to inspect them to insure that the ships were in fact laden with provisions and not with contraband. If, by accident, an innocent ship was sunk, Germany would reimburse the Commission only if German submarines could be proved to have been responsible. Russia and England gave the requested pledge with no hesitation, though the British, like the Germans, insisted on inspection rights. France, in spite of the constant entreaty of the Commission, refused to join its allies. The French government, according to Hoover, was hopeful that the HAPAG might be driven into bankruptcy if it could be prevented from obtaining the Commission's business. Negotiations with France dragged on through 1915 and into the spring of 1916, with Hoover and the British exerting all possible pressure on Paris to alter its position. Their efforts proved vain.

By the time the matter had proceeded this far, Ballin himself had become somewhat less enthusiastic about the charter of his ships to Hoover's Commission. On March 23, 1916, Holtzendorff reported that Ballin was now suspicious that the negotiations were a "trick" on the part of England. "The English," Holtzendorff wrote, explaining Ballin's views, "naturally do not want to give up their own tonnage to the Commission and also hope that our U-boats will fire on our own steamers."[32] Ballin, moreover, was discouraged by the fact that in war one could not operate

[31] *ibid.*, Ballin to Holtzendorff, Nov. 6, 1915. See page 226 for such an assurance already given by the British.

[32] *Holtzendorff-A*, VIII, second series of notes for March 23, 1916.

one's business by oneself. The British dictated the freight rate the HAPAG could charge Hoover; the German navy was trying to hedge the business about with impossible conditions; the French would give no guarantees, the Germans only unsatisfactory ones, that the ships would not be attacked while in the Commission's service. Unattractive as the deal with Hoover was, however, Ballin nevertheless remained interested in it, but only because it was the sole prospect at the moment for putting HAPAG ships to work. He was therefore very irritated when the North German Lloyd, which heretofore had had nothing to do with the Commission, now pushed forward to claim a share of the chartering business for its own ships tied up in American ports. In very harsh language, Ballin informed the Lloyd that the affair was one to which the HAPAG did not intend to admit any competitors.[33]

If Ballin was now lukewarm about doing business with the Relief Commission, the German government had become positively hostile to such an undertaking. The Interior Ministry and the occupation *Generalgouvernement* of Belgium were opposed to the charter, while Admiral Henning von Holtzendorff, the chief of the Admiral Staff (*Admiralstab*) and a brother of Ballin's representative in Berlin, insisted that an effort be made clearly to determine that Ballin's ships were the *only* vessels which the Commission could find available to do its work. If British ships could instead be forced into service, this tonnage would no longer be available to Great Britain for its war effort against Germany.[34] Ballin, in reply, rather sharply informed the government that the HAPAG's business with

[33] Heineken to Ballin, May 30, 1916, Ballin to Heineken, May 31, *Ballin-Heineken*, II: *Holtzendorff-A*, IX, notes for May 31 and June 1, 1916.

[34] *Holtzendorff-A*, VIII, second series of notes for March 22, 1916; report 396, April 21.

Hoover was not the Admiral Staff's affair and that if it persisted in intruding in the matter the line would withdraw from the negotiations.[35]

On June 6th, the Foreign Office advised Holtzendorff that Baron von der Lancken, head of the political department of the *Generalgouvernement*, was of the opinion that Hoover could obtain his ships elsewhere and that the whole business was a swindle concocted by Hoover and Sir Edward Grey. Lancken furthermore intended to say so to the Interior Ministry, the Admiral Staff, and the Supreme Command (*Oberste Heeresleitung*).[36] Two days later, doubtless aware that he was only anticipating the government's reaction to Lancken's report, Ballin asked Berlin not to consent to the release of HAPAG ships for use by the Relief Commission.[37] On June 9th, the Interior Ministry did in fact inform Ballin that at the time there was no need for the line's ships to become involved, since Hoover had enough tonnage on hand to make his food deliveries during the summer months. "Whether in a few months," the communiqué concluded, "relations will have changed so that the release of the ships is in the Fatherland's interest can lie in abeyance."[38] Herr Wilminck of the Dutch Lloyd gave formal advisement of this decision to Hoover.[39] Bemoaning that "stupidity is an essential concomitant of war," Hoover turned elsewhere to look for his ships.

At the same time that Ballin was attempting to arrive at a charter contract with the Belgian Relief Commission, he was also making efforts to charter or sell his ships to

[35] Ballin to Heineken, June 5, 1916, *Ballin-Heineken*, II.
[36] *Holtzendorff-A*, IX, notes for June 6 and 7, 1916.
[37] Ballin to Heineken, June 9, 1916, *Ballin-Heineken*, II.
[38] Lewald to Ballin, June 9, 1916, *Holtzendorff-B*, IV.
[39] Wilminck to Hoover, July 1, 1916, in Gay-Fisher, I, 330-31.

interested parties in North and South America. As the war continued into 1916, the financial strain of wartime inactivity became more and more burdensome for the Hamburg-American Line. And as Germany's intensifying submarine warfare claimed a number of American merchantmen among its victims, the danger increased that eventually the United States would join the Entente and seize the HAPAG's ships before they could be sold or chartered. If the United States entered the war, Ballin noted pessimistically, the Americans and the British would force the remaining neutral powers in the western hemisphere to choose sides.[40] He was therefore anxious to sell as many of his ships as possible and to do so without delay.

As early as February 1916, just before Germany announced that armed merchantmen would be regarded as men-of-war and therefore be liable to attack without warning, Ballin began to have forebodings of American intervention and even went so far as to draw up a telegraph code by which Holtzendorff could at once inform him of the United States' declaration of war. The navy, at the same time, ordered the HAPAG to make plans to wreck the engines of its ships in America to prevent their being of any use in the event of seizure.[41]

Ballin's efforts to dispose of the HAPAG's floating assets in the Americas foundered, as had his negotiations with the Belgian Relief Commission, on the opposition of a number of authorities within the German government. When he attempted to offer for charter a number of ships tied up in Chile belonging to the Kosmos Line, a Hamburg concern in which the Hamburg-American Line had a large interest, the Admiral Staff forbid such a move, holding that it would only strengthen the enemy's

[40] *Holtzendorff-A*, x, notes for Sept. 14, 1916.

[41] *ibid.*, VII, report 338, Jan. 28, 1916; report 340, Jan. 30; notes for Feb. 3 and 4; Ballin to Heineken, Feb. 7, *Ballin-Heineken*, II.

position.[42] In November 1916, the Guaranty Trust Company of New York City demanded additional security for the HAPAG's notes which it was holding. The *Disconto-Gesellschaft*, which for many years had been the HAPAG's financial agent and which controlled a substantial block of the line's stock, declined to increase its loans to the HAPAG so that the Guaranty's demands could be met.[43] If the interest on the American loans was not paid, the HAPAG would be forced to watch helplessly as its assets in the United States were attached by the line's creditors. The obvious means of raising the needed sums was to sell some of the ships lying in the port of New York. The Admiral Staff agreed to the plan but made its implementation conditional on Helfferich's approval. Helfferich, now secretary of the Interior, was opposed and declared that if approval were given to Ballin, every steamship company in Germany would demand permission to dispose of its ships abroad.[44]

In March 1917, the HAPAG, certain that America's entry into the war could be only a matter of weeks away and foiled in its attempts to sell or charter its ships there, gave the order to its captains in the United States to cripple the engines of their ships. The order was duly carried out. No sooner had this been accomplished than ship brokers made offers to buy these damaged ships, one of which was the disabled *Vaterland*, at reduced prices.[45] Now that the ships were not in running condition, Helfferich consented to their sale, but the Admiral Staff imposed a number of conditions—the engines must be so extensively damaged

[42] *Holtzendorff-A*, VII, notes for March 9, 10, and 11, 1916.
[43] *ibid.*, X, notes for Nov. 28, 1916.
[44] *ibid.*, and reports 534 and 537, Dec. 3 and 6, 1916.
[45] *ibid.*, XII, report 609, March 19, 1917. *Ibid.*, vol. XI, covering the period from Dec. 1916 to March 1917 is missing, but *Holtzendorff-B*, XII, report 663, June 16, 1917, gives a resumé of negotiations during this interval.

that repairs would take at least six months, buyers must promise not to use the ships before the end of the war, etc.—which Ballin rejected as impossible or utterly unrealistic.[46] The conditions were eventually retracted, but before the sale could be carried out Germany and the United States had gone to war. Ballin was enraged at the obstruction in Berlin which had caused the plan to miscarry. He blamed Helfferich, whose ability he acknowledged but whom he disliked, for having spoiled the sale, though, as Arndt von Holtzendorff pointed out to him, it was really the Admiral Staff which was to blame.[47]

Contrary to Ballin's prediction, the neutral powers of the western hemisphere did not all at once follow the United States into the war. There were, however, disturbing signs that it would be only a matter of time, for both Panama and Cuba declared war on Germany within a week of Washington's action and seized six small ships belonging to the Hamburg-American Line. Thirty-odd ships flying the HAPAG ensign remained in neutral ports in the area. Ballin was certain that the Latin and South American republics coveted these German vessels and would not find a declaration of war on Germany too high a price to pay for them. There was, of course, no possibility of German retaliation. The temptation to seize these ships as enemy property, if they could not be purchased, would therefore become overpowering.[48]

Most of these vessels lay at anchor in Argentina, Brazil, and Chile, and elaborate and quite unsuccessful negotiations were opened with the governments of each of these states to sell the HAPAG's ships. In all three nations, the line found prospective purchasers for its ships, but Ballin

[46] Ballin to Holtzendorff, March 23 and 29, 1917; report 611, March 21, in *Holtzendorff-A*, XII.

[47] *ibid.*, reports 662 and 663, June 15 and 16, 1917; notes for June 20.

[48] Memo by Ballin, May 5, 1917, *BAB*.

233

met with formidable opposition from the German government. Junior officials in the Foreign Office were the first to raise objections, but Ballin was able to overcome this opposition by having Holtzendorff protest to secretary Richard von Kühlmann, who was a good friend of both men.[49] The Admiral Staff, which apparently was reluctant to make a point-blank refusal to Ballin, procrastinated and tried to feign that the responsibility for the decision lay elsewhere. Finally, in January 1918, Admiral Holtzendorff advised his brother that any sale of HAPAG ships in Argentina was out of the question, since such sales, in the Admiral Staff's opinion, would only increase the Entente's merchant fleet, thus defeating the purpose of unrestricted submarine warfare.[50] In Chile and Brazil, the course of events was almost identical: purchasers made offers but the Admiral Staff refused to allow any sales. Because of the obstruction of the German government, of the HAPAG's 175 capital ships in August 1914, only 9 were sold during the course of the war.

―――――――

At the outbreak of hostilities in August 1914, the Hamburg-American Line decommissioned 80 large and several hundred small ships in home ports. They lay thereafter at anchor, awaiting the war's end. Meanwhile they had to be maintained. The German government relieved the HAPAG of some of these vessels under the provisions of an 1870 law which made all merchantmen available in wartime for military service. Immediately after Germany went to war, the navy began to inspect the HAPAG's ships

[49] For Ballin's problems with the Foreign Office, see *Holtzendorff-B*, XII, report 732, Oct. 23, 1917; Ballin to Holtzendorff, Nov. 1; report 742, Nov. 2; HAPAG to Delfino (HAPAG agent, Buenos Aires), Nov. 2.

[50] *ibid.*, XIV, reports 805 and 809, Jan. 17 and 21, 1918.

to determine which ones would make suitable additions to the German fleet. The great *Schnelldampfer*, fast enough to elude enemy men-of-war, were at once picked as auxiliary cruisers. These swift liners had been designed by navy specifications, with their coal bunkers situated so as to protect their engines and otherwise arranged so that armor and other structural improvements could be quickly added.[51] Slower vessels and freighters were reserved by the navy for use as supply ships. At the war's onset, Ballin had no expectation that hostilities would last more than a few months and he therefore objected to his elegant liners being outfitted with armor plate and guns and also to the navy's intention to dismantle some HAPAG ships in order to obtain scarce items needed for warships under construction.[52] In spite of Ballin's protests, the navy made its selection and took over several dozen vessels. The line's steamer *Königin Luise* was the first German merchant marine ship to be sunk on active service, when, on August 5, 1914, it was surprised by British cruisers while laying mines in the mouth of the Thames. The German government agreed to reimburse the line for any ships lost in military service, and in October 1914 awarded it 5,000,000 marks as an advance against future losses.[53]

Ballin did not find this arrangement at all generous. In October 1914, he appealed to Admiral Tirpitz to have the government do something which would enable German shipping companies to remain intact during the war —which after the Marne deadlock looked as though it

[51] *Zeitschrift*, II, no. 18 (Sept. 20, 1903), 143-44.

[52] *Holtzendorff-B*, I, folder 8, "Hilfskreuzer," notes for Nov. 22 and 23, 1914; report 91, Dec. 16; Ballin to Holtzendorff, Dec. 18; Huldermann to Holtzendorff, Dec. 20; folder 25, "Hilfskriegsschiffe," report 120, Feb. 24, 1915; Ballin to Holtzendorff, Feb. 25.

[53] *ibid.*, I, folder 3, "Rückzahlung des Reiches für versenkte Schiffe und Charter-Schiffe," notes for Oct. 16, 1914; London *Times* (Aug. 6, 1914).

might be a long one—and emerge in the post-war market in a financially competitive position. This could be done either by allowing the sale of ships overseas, to which Berlin was opposed, or by a monetary grant or interest-free loans to shipping firms.[54] On December 22d, the Hamburg-American Line and the North German Lloyd submitted a joint report to Bethmann Hollweg which noted that the cost of keeping the two lines in operation during the war came to four million marks per month. Since both corporations were virtually deprived of their prewar sources of income, they asked for a loan of 50,000,000 marks at 2.5 per cent interest and an outright grant of fifty to seventy million marks.[55]

The government responded in April 1915 by offering each line a monthly loan of two million marks at 4 per cent interest, to be paid back in ten equal installments beginning two years after the conclusion of hostilities. Any discussion of an outright grant was ruled out by the government until the end of the war, and could then be considered only if Germany made a favorable peace and received a sizeable indemnity from the Entente. Ballin was displeased by what he considered to be a niggardly offer and instructed Holtzendorff to express to Helfferich his judgment that "he should have been better treated now that, in difficulty, he for the first time asked the government for something."[56]

In May, Ballin presented a new proposal to Tirpitz.[57] The HAPAG, Ballin argued, could not afford to sit idly by

[54] Ballin to Tirpitz, Oct. 22, 1914, HAPAG-V.

[55] The HAPAG-Lloyd proposal and the government's reaction to it is described in an unsigned letter by Ballin to Tirpitz, May 2, 1915, in *Ballin-Heineken*, II.

[56] *Holtzendorff-B*, I, folder 23, "Zahlungen für verlorene Schiffe," notes for April 22, 1915.

[57] See Ballin to Tirpitz, May 2, 1915, *Ballin-Heineken*, II.

and wait to see what sort of peace Germany would be able to make. The line had already lost 15 ships in the navy's service and had received 19,000,000 marks in compensation for them, a sum which the navy considered adequate. According to Ballin, to rebuild these lost ships after the war would cost 30,000,000 marks and they would not be ready until two or three years after the conclusion of hostilities, by which time the post-war trade boom would already have waned. As it was, the HAPAG's losses in income in the first nine months of the war came to 100,000,000 marks, not including the value of the ships requisitioned by the navy or seized by the enemy. Ballin proposed to Tirpitz that the HAPAG and the Lloyd each build three merchant ships designed as auxiliary cruisers during the next five years, for which each line would receive 42,000,000 marks. Once these ships were commissioned, the two lines would pay the government a sum equal to 4 per cent on the principal, while the principal itself would be paid back in ten annual installments. In return, the two lines would agree to put the ships at the government's disposal in wartime without fee and without claim in the event of loss or damage. Ballin's demand for an outright grant made in December 1914 was dropped. Heineken of the Lloyd, however, felt that Ballin's plan smacked of state socialism, a charge which his rival was quick to deny. Ballin agreed that the two firms might conceivably get by without state aid but appealed to Heineken's concern for the Lloyd's stockholders, who, like their HAPAG counterparts, were not likely to be receiving dividends anytime in the immediate future. "Besides," Ballin concluded, "I am of the opinion that the state has the duty to help out two great national corporations in view of their huge losses caused by the war. You know that I have always resisted any government aid,

237

but here it seems to me to be a question of a bounden duty and obligation on the part of the state."[58]

Ballin's plan was rejected by the government, which declined to do more than continue the 2,000,000 mark monthly loans to the two lines. Helfferich, in whose hands the matter rested, was never willing to grant the loans for periods longer than a half year, and the periodic renewal negotiations, usually in March and September, occasioned much controversy between the HAPAG, the Lloyd, and the government. In the spring and again in the fall, Ballin would go to Berlin to arrange for an extension, and the government, though consistently granting his requests, always sought to hem its generosity with conditions which Ballin would then have to work his way around.[59]

The government loans kept the HAPAG's huge buildings in Hamburg open, its ships in a fair state of repair, and permitted the line to meet its reduced payrolls at home and abroad. With its maintenance costs covered by these loans, by the sale of nine of its ships abroad, the compensation payments made for a number of its ships sunk early in the war while on government service, and by rigorous economies in Hamburg, the HAPAG was able to invest its prewar capital surplus in a number of enterprises whose work was not so adversely affected by the war. HAPAG funds were placed in warehouse concerns, airplane companies, the Zeppelin works, and in hotel and insurance corporations. The income from these investments almost

[58] Same to Heineken, May 5, 1915, *ibid.*

[59] Among the government's demands were the raising of interest on the loans and the acquisition of large blocks of HAPAG and Lloyd stock in return for its assistance. See Ballin to Heineken, Aug. 8, 1916, in *ibid.*; same to same, Oct. 9, 17, and 20, and Heineken to Ballin, Oct. 16, 1916, in *ibid.*, III; *Holtzendorff-A*, X, notes for Sept. 15 and Oct. 14, 1916; Ballin to Schinckel, Sept. 7, 1915, in *Ballin-Schinckel*.

allowed the line to break even. It did not, however, enable it to replace the ships lost during the war or to renovate old vessels so that they would be economical carriers once the war was over. In the four years from 1914 to 1918, the Hamburg-American Line, after making allowance for interest and mortgages due, made a profit of 12,869,865 marks, a figure which prior to the war would have been regarded as a fair return for only twelve months' operations. From this net gain, 13,107,131 marks were paid out in insurance and depreciation, leaving the line with a net deficit of 237,266 marks for the war years.[60]

In August 1915, Ballin returned to his attempts to wring a direct cash grant from the government. Such a payment would not only make it possible for the HAPAG to build new ships and recondition old ones, but it would relieve Ballin of the necessity of constant haggling with Helfferich for the extension of government loans. Ballin now asked that a war indemnity bill to benefit the German shipping industry be presented to the Reichstag. What the HAPAG and the Lloyd needed was not only a sum to replace their lost ships at home and abroad, but indeed one which would compensate them for the value of the freight and passenger business lost during the war.[61]

Throughout the winter of 1915-16, Ballin worked hard on government officials and naval figures to enlist support

[60] The financial position of the HAPAG during the war is cloudy, for the company, as one whose income was largely derived from foreign operations, was excused by law from submitting annual reports while hostilities lasted. Almost the only source of information is the *Bericht und Rechnungslegung* prepared for the April 1921 stockholders' meeting, which gives the above figures. A calculation by *Direktor* Johannes Merck gives a wartime deficit of 1,637,439 marks. See an undated memo by Merck, included in Merck "Nachlass," II Konv. 5.

[61] Ballin to Jonquières (*Ministerialdirektor*, Interior Ministry), Aug. 19, 1915, in *Holtzendorff-B*, I, folder 38, "Kriegsentschädigung der Rheedereien."

239

for his demands.[62] In January 1916, he persuaded Tirpitz to agree in principle to his claims, though the admiral insisted that he could support such a measure only after the conclusion of the war.[63] The matter of compensation became even more pressing in February, when the German government, fearful that the United States was on the verge of joining the Entente because of the sinking of its merchantmen by German submarines, informed Ballin that the HAPAG might summarily be ordered to destroy the engines of its ships in American ports.[64] At a conference with Tirpitz and representatives of the Foreign Office and Interior Ministry, Ballin argued that the HAPAG could not possibly consent to such an order's being given unless the government would compensate the line for the losses involved. Tirpitz answered that the HAPAG would of course be indemnified but that, once again, the sum to be paid would necessarily depend on what sort of peace Germany secured. If Germany was able to dictate the peace, the line would be generously served.[65] The crisis with America was averted, however, and, as already noted, the engines were not destroyed until March 1917.

The opinion of the civil branch of the government was no more encouraging than that of the navy. Helfferich's position, based on the same reasoning as Tirpitz', was that no relief bill could be passed before the end of the war. The HAPAG, he held, had no *right* to compensation, but its claims would certainly be sympathetically enter-

[62] Ballin's activity in this period is covered in both series of Holtzendorff papers and in the correspondence between Merck, Thomann, and Hopff of the HAPAG and Stapelfeldt of the Lloyd in Merck "Nachlass," II 8 Konv. 5, "Briefe von Kollegen . . . ," and also in *ibid.*, "Erinnerungen," pp. 171-74.

[63] *Holtzendorff-A*, VII, notes for Jan. 10, 1916.

[64] *ibid.*, notes for Feb. 3, 1916.

[65] *ibid.*

tained.[66] The best the Interior Ministry could do, Helffe-rich informed Ballin, was to offer the shipping companies interest-free construction loans in addition to the 2,000,000-mark monthly loans begun in April 1915. The HAPAG would be well advised to accept such an offer, the secretary warned, for the longer the war lasted the more difficult it would be to continue paying the monthly loans.[67] Ballin, however, rejected Helfferich's proposal, for it would, in his opinion, really benefit shipbuilding firms rather than carriers. Besides, if the HAPAG was granted sub-stantial construction loans at this juncture, its chances of eventually obtaining an indemnification from the govern-ment might be jeopardized.[68]

Although the government and the navy opposed Ballin's indemnification scheme, there was considerable support for such a measure in the Reichstag. In April 1916, one of Ballin's friends, Peter Franz Stubmann, a National Liberal deputy, informed Holtzendorff that he thought that the Reichstag could be persuaded to pass an indemni-fication bill for the shipping industry.[69] Working through Stubmann, Ballin and Holtzendorff began at once to in-fluence legislators in favor of such a measure. In order to win the support of the National Liberals and Conserva-tives, the HAPAG joined the *Sechserverband*, an annex-ationist group composed primarily of agrarians and heavy industrialists.[70] On May 11, 1916, a joint resolution was adopted by the National Liberal, Progressive, Conserva-

[66] *ibid.*, VIII, report 374, March 21, 1916; *ibid.*, X, report 504, Oct. 12, 1916.

[67] *ibid.*, IX, report 473, Aug. 17, 1916.

[68] Ballin to Holtzendorff, Oct. 11, 1916, in *ibid.*, X; same to Heineken, Oct. 9, *Ballin-Heineken*, II.

[69] *Holtzendorff-A*, VIII, report 384, April 8, 1916; report 389, April 14.

[70] *ibid.*, notes of May 11, 1916.

tive, and Center parties which called on the government "to take all suitable measures for the maintenance and outfitting of German merchantmen and above all to help the German steamship companies in the construction of merchantmen by placing at their disposal generous amounts of money,"[71] With only the Social Democrats opposed, the Reichstag in June passed an act approving in principle future legislation to benefit specific industries and businesses by means of government indemnities. The shipping industry was listed as one in whose behalf such a bill would be introduced.

In the fall of 1916, the Reichstag began to discuss the provisions of an indemnification act specifically to aid the shipping industry. Ballin's friend, the National Liberal leader Gustav Stresemann, served as an energetic spokesman for the HAPAG's interests, rounding up votes in his own party and using his influence on members of other factions as well as on government officials.[72] The government, which was simultaneously drafting its own bill, continued to resist an indemnification, and its opposition was reflected in an elaborate measure which Bethmann Hollweg laid before the Reichstag in February 1917. It provided for up to 300,000,000 marks in *loans*, one-half of which were to be interest-free and to be paid back within twenty years following the construction of the ships made possible by the loans. The other half would bear 6 per cent interest. The loans were to be applied only to the construction of ships which were primarily freighters.

[71] Paul Kollbach, *Deutsche Handelsflotte und Versailler Vertrag*, Berlin, 1929, pp. 27-28.

[72] Stresemann to Ballin, Dec. 7, 1916, Stresemann "Nachlass," Politische Akten, vol. 157, reel 3063/129735-40; same to same, March 25, 1917, *ibid*., vol. 189, reel 3076/134888-93; same to same, April 2, 3076/134956-61; same to same, March 7, 1917, *ibid*., vol. 192, reel 3076/135413-15. See also *Holtzendorff-A*, x, notes for Nov. 27, 1916.

Almost immediately after the government's proposed law was made public, the United States broke off diplomatic relations with Germany because of its declaration on January 31, 1917, of unrestricted submarine warfare. It seemed very likely that a state of war would follow at any moment. The HAPAG was now faced with the loss of its 35 ships in the United States, ships which would cost 155,000,000 marks to replace, to say nothing of another 40 vessels scattered in neutral ports elsewhere in the western hemisphere. Clearly the increasing desperation of the line should win more sympathy for its claims for financial relief. Ballin at least thought so.[73] On April 6, 1917, the United States declared war on Germany, and while the HAPAG's ships were not at once seized, little hope remained that the line would ever be able to sell them during the war or recover them at its conclusion.[74] As far as Ballin was concerned, the line's case for an indemnity from the government—not merely a loan—had become unassailable.

The government realized that the entry of the United States into the war created a new situation and that its February bill for compensation to steamship companies would have to be reconsidered. The bill was therefore withdrawn and negotiations begun again between the shipping industry, the Reichstag, and the government. Secretary Count Rödern of the Treasury, who was piqued because he felt that the HAPAG was not proceeding decorously through ministerial channels but was trying instead to force the bill's introduction by stirring up the

[73] Ballin to Heineken, Feb. 10, 1917, *Ballin-Heineken*, III.

[74] Later in 1917, the HAPAG's assets in the United States, including 35 capital ships totaling 234,056 tons, were confiscated as alien property. On Nov. 10, 1918, A. Mitchell Palmer, alien property custodian, estimated the value of the line's holdings in the United States at $100,000,000. See the *New York Times* (Nov. 11, 1918).

Reichstag, refused to consent to an indemnification law before the war had ended. To grant compensation to one branch of the economy at this time, Rödern told Ballin, would result in a flood of claims from all others, and there was simply not enough money to satisfy everyone. Rödern did, however, agree that the interest-free construction loans proposed by the government would not have to be repaid in the event that no indemnity measure benefitting the shipping companies was passed after peace was concluded.[75] Ballin, in reply, wrote a letter to Rödern, extraordinary in its tone considering the fact that Germany was at war, in which his disgust and exasperation were plainly expressed. "I wish," he complained, "that the leaders of the shipping industry had been heard, and I think it absolutely one of the greatest errors that in this most stupid of all wars (*in diesem dümmsten Kriege*) which the history of the world has ever seen that experienced businessmen were paid so little attention."[76] After some haggling, Rödern backed down and agreed to an indemnity.

Up to this point, only the imperial government had been involved in the negotiations for the indemnity bill, but now the Prussian Finance Ministry insinuated itself into the deliberations. The Ministry demanded that if an indemnification was awarded, a commission be established which would exercise control over the funds granted to the shipping industry.[77] Ballin was alarmed by this proposal because it would increase the government's intrusion in the HAPAG's affairs. Even though the indemnity bill seemed likely to be tethered by a number of undesirable "man-traps" (*Fussangeln*), it was better than nothing, and

[75] *Holtzendorff-A*, XII, notes for May 31, 1917.
[76] *Ganz vertraulich* letter of June 8, 1917, in Stresemann "Nachlass," Politische Akten, vol. 171, reel 3066/131953-56.
[77] *Holtzendorff-A*, XII, report 660, June 13, 1917.

Ballin wrote to Holtzendorff that if the bill could not be forced through the Reichstag there would be nothing left to do but to liquidate the HAPAG.[78]

In June 1917, a second bill was presented by the government which Ballin, somewhat unenthusiastically, decided that he could support. It was this bill which, after some delay, became law.[79] This draft agreed to pay the ship lines an indemnity equal to the prewar value of all ships which were primarily freighters that had been lost in action or damaged by the enemy. The government, moreover, would reimburse the lines for the costs of reconditioning freighters forced to sit out the war. A cash payment, rather than a loan, was thus provided. The payments were to be made *after* the war, a point which Ballin surrendered, for by 1917 neither material nor labor was available for ship construction. Rebuilding the HAPAG's fleet would have to wait for the peace. Since shipbuilding costs had risen greatly during the war, the measure provided that the government would pay from 20 to 70 per cent of the increased costs of ships built to replace those lost or damaged in the war if such ships were constructed within the first nine years after the conclusion of hostilities. The Prussian Finance Ministry's demand for government control of the compensation funds was partially satisfied by paragraph eight, which provided for the establishment of a *Reichsausschuss* with vague powers for this purpose. The Center's question of whether or not—and, if so, how extensively—the government should participate

[78] Ballin to Holtzendorff, June 14, 1917, *ibid.*
[79] The law is printed in Germany, Reichstag, *Anlagen zu den stenographischen Berichten*, XIII. Legislaturperiode, II. Session, vol. 322, document 1,122, pages 1,904-07. The negotiations leading to its passage are conveniently digested in Kollbach, *Deutsche Handelsflotte*, pp. 24-38. See also Heinz-Hellmut Kohlhaus, "Die HAPAG, Cuno und das deutsche Reich, 1920-1933," diss., Hamburg, 1952.

in the earnings of ships built with the indemnity funds and whether or not any limitation should be placed on their use was to be deferred for decision until after the war.[80]

In spite of very persistent lobbying in Berlin by Ballin, activity which irritated both Rödern and Helfferich, the draft bill did not become law during the July session, for it was swamped by the onrush of more immediate problems resulting from Bethmann's resignation on July 14th and Erzberger's Peace Resolution five days later. The draft bill was referred to a committee until the fall session, and Ballin sent out word to his friends that they should curtail their efforts for the time being.[81] In September, the bill was reported unaltered out of the committee, and Ballin at once went to Berlin to be on hand until the measure was adopted or rejected. The Social Democrats and Progressives, supported by Helfferich, attempted in vain to attach new conditions to the bill, but it passed its third reading in the Reichstag on October 11, 1917. The Bundesrat accepted the measure exactly a month later and it became law. The bill was not, from Ballin's point of view, a perfect measure, particularly because the indemnity did not cover the HAPAG's passenger ships which had been lost. "Men fail to realize," he had observed earlier in 1917, "that trade follows the [merchant] flag less than it does the passenger liner."[82] He also did not look forward to the prospect of a government board's being established to administer the bill, and he felt that the construction cost differential was insufficient.

Ballin's reservations notwithstanding, the shipping indemnification law of November 11, 1917 constituted a

[80] *Holtzendorff-B*, XII, notes for Oct. 4, 1917.
[81] Ballin to Holtzendorff, July 30, 1917, *Holtzendorff-A*, XIII.
[82] Ballin to Stresemann, June 10, 1917, Stresemann "Nachlass," Politische Akten, vol. 171, reel 3066/131957-62.

substantial achievement for him, for it was the first of hundreds of acts to provide relief for specific trades and industries which had been ruined or adversely affected by the war. And when the United States and South American governments seized many of the line's ships during the remaining year of the war, Ballin could at least take comfort that there would be money available, if only the war would end, to replace the freighters among these old standard-bearers with new and finer ships. The Kaiser wired Ballin his congratulations on the bill's passage, and Ballin, delighted that he could now leave a city he had come thoroughly to detest, returned to Hamburg more content than he had left it, reassured that the HAPAG would be better served in peace than it had been in war.

CHAPTER VIII

A Voice in Berlin

AFTER THE war began, Ballin's health plainly deteriorated and his nervousness and insomnia became more pronounced. His face, once so animated, assumed a perpetually morose expression, and he depended increasingly on veronal and other drugs to provide calm by day and sleep at night. Ballin began to spend long weekends at his estate in Holstein or at Professor Dapper's sanatorium in the mountains above Bad Kissingen. He relied on his longtime secretary, Fräulein Kluge, to keep him informed by letter and telephone of developments in the main office. Now that the Hamburg-American Line's overseas business had come to a standstill, Ballin found that its affairs could be managed from a distance.

Berlin, rather than Hamburg, gradually became the locus of Ballin's activity, and when not in Holstein or at Dapper's he was as often to be found there as in Hamburg. *Reichseinkauf* and *Zentral-Einkaufs-Gesellschaft* business frequently necessitated his presence in the capital, and his advice on other matters was sought almost continuously by government officials. The negotiations between the steamship companies and the government which resulted in November 1917 in the shipping indemnity bill kept him in Berlin month after month. Ballin did not enjoy his stays there, for although he had many friends in Berlin he disliked what he considered to be the artificiality and avariciousness of the city and its society.

As the HAPAG's freedom of action became increasingly subject to government interference because of the war, the line's Berlin office acquired added importance. Immediately after the war's outbreak, Ballin decided to convert the HAPAG's idle ticketing office and travel bureau in Berlin into a much smaller organization which would be entrusted with the task of serving as a listening post and as a lobby which might influence government policy in the line's favor. Arndt von Holtzendorff, who for some years had managed the Berlin office, was assigned to direct this work.

Holtzendorff, who resembled a cherubic, demilitarized Hindenburg, was a lawyer by training whom Ballin had met casually during a summer vacation. Impressed by Holtzendorff's charm and good judgment, Ballin offered him a position with the HAPAG.[1] Early in August 1914, the two men worked out a system whereby Holtzendorff would keep Ballin informed by reports, supplemented by notes and letters. When Ballin was in Berlin, Holtzendorff maintained extensive records of his chief's conversations with government officials and friends as well as his opinions on a variety of subjects. Between August 1914 and November 1918, Holtzendorff sent 968 reports to Hamburg, in addition to many memoranda and letters. Ballin occasionally gave his agent directions by return mail, but more often he contacted Holtzendorff by telephone. Almost every day, some form of communication occurred between the two.

Holtzendorff was an ideal choice for this role, for not only was he a genial personality sure to please anyone with whom he came in contact, but was as well a man of excellent connections. His brother, Henning, was a distin-

[1] Conversation with Holtzendorff's son, General Hans Henning von Holtzendorff, Hanover, Aug. 12, 1963; Stubmann, p. 117. For a description of Holtzendorff, see Ernst Jäckh, *Der goldene Pflug: Lebensernte eines Weltbürgers*, Stuttgart, 1954, p. 189.

guished admiral who in September 1915 was called out of retirement to become chief of the Admiral Staff. Through marriage, the brothers were distantly related to Admiral Georg von Müller, who served as chief of the Naval Cabinet from 1906 to 1918. Holtzendorff's relations with his brother were easy, although they frequently disagreed on policy, and he could see him at will. Müller was similarly available, as were a number of junior officers in the *Reichsmarineamt* and on the Admiral Staff. Holtzendorff was also an intimate of Arthur Zimmermann, under secretary of the Foreign Office from 1911 to 1916 and then briefly secretary. The two took daily walks and horseback rides through the Tiergarten very early in the morning, during which Zimmermann discussed official matters with remarkable indiscretion. Karl Helfferich, successively secretary of the Imperial Treasury and the Interior Ministry, was also a good friend, and Holtzendorff frequently dropped in at Helfferich's office to discuss affairs of interest to Ballin. A Prussian by birth, Holtzendorff's inclinations were aristocratic and conservative, but he did not stand on ceremony and counted among his acquaintances many men of humble origin and very liberal politics.

Soon after Germany went to war, Ballin decided that Holtzendorff should establish a circle which would meet frequently for dinner and conversation, with invitations going to men whom Ballin wished to influence or from whom he wanted to derive information. In doing so, Ballin was following a trend which developed in wartime Berlin of forming social groups which gathered periodically for refreshment and political discussion. These assemblies took varied forms. Some, like the *Deutsche Gesellschaft 1914*, were large and formally organized, with high dues and programs with scheduled speakers.[2] There were many

---

[2] For the *1914*, see H. von Moltke, *Erinnerungen, Briefe, Doku-*

smaller circles, such as the sixteen-member *Mittwoch-Gesellschaft*, of which Ballin was a member. Wednesday was also the day for Hans Delbrück's *Mittwoch-Abend*, an association of moderate conservatives.[3] Other cliques were dependent on the powers of attraction and the finances of their founders. Ernst Jäckh, the indefatigable advocate of countless causes, had his own circle. Its membership easily was the most ecumenical, including —in addition to a handful of distinguished statesmen— such assorted figures as Max Planck, Albert Einstein, and Rabindranath Tagore.[4] There were many other such groups. Stresemann had one; a woman, Baroness Schröder, *née* Mary Donahue of San Francisco, presided over a regular salon of pro-American guests.[5] All these associations represented some shade of political opinion, from the militantly Pan-German *Donnerstag-Gesellschaft* founded late in the war to the moderate Delbrück circle.

---

mente 1877-1916, Stuttgart, 1922, pp. 443-45; Kuno Graf Westarp, *Konservative Politik im letzten Jahrzehnt des Kaiserreiches*, 2 vols., Berlin, 1935, II, 11-12; Hans W. Gatzke, *Germany's Drive to the West (Drang nach Westen): A Study of Germany's Western War Aims during the First World War*, Baltimore, 1950, pp. 136-37.

[3] Heinrich Schnee, *Als letzter Gouverneur in Deutsch Ostafrika: Erinnerungen*, Heidelberg, 1964, pp. 158-61; Friedrich Meinecke, *Strassburg, Freiburg, Berlin 1901-1919: Erinnerungen*, Stuttgart, 1949, pp. 162-71; Ludwig Stein, *Aus dem Leben eines Optimisten*, Berlin, 1930, p. 229; Jäckh, *Goldene Pflug*, p. 188.

[4] Jäckh, *Goldene Pflug*, pp. 184-93.

[5] *Holtzendorff-A*, II, report 113, Feb. 9, 1915; Jäckh, *Goldene Pflug*, p. 189. On Baroness Schröder, see Franz Rintelen von Kleist, *The Dark Invader: Wartime Reminiscences of a German Naval Intelligence Officer*, New York, 1933, pp. 185-86; and Walter Görlitz, ed., *Regierte der Kaiser?: Kriegstagebücher, Aufzeichnungen und Briefe des Chefs des Marine-Kabinetts Admiral Georg Alexander von Müller*, Göttingen, 1959, p. 114. For Stresemann's and Ballin's involvement in a group denominated the *Continental-Gesellschaft*, see a memo from Stresemann's office of Aug. 18, 1916, in Stresemann "Nachlass," Politische Akten, vol. 173, reel 3065/130868.

The first of the Holtzendorff evenings was held in the fall of 1914. Holtzendorff was the host, but it was Ballin who ran the affairs. At the time the gatherings were inaugurated, Holtzendorff and his wife lived in the *Kaiserhof* hotel and entertained their guests in the establishment's restaurant. Ballin wanted Holtzendorff's social efforts to be kept as free from publicity as possible, and, after much searching, an apartment was found in the Viktoriastrasse, just off the Tiergarten and equidistant from the Reichstag and the Wilhelmstrasse. It was a distinguished address and an elegant residence. Among the Holtzendorffs' new neighbors were old Emil Rathenau, Carl Fürstenberg, and the Brockdorff-Rantzau twins. The apartment itself, according to August Count zu Eulenburg, who had spent his life at court, was a "little palace."[6] Ballin supervised every detail; it was as though he had a new ship to put into commission. He had definite ideas about how the evenings should be organized, from the table arrangement to the selection of the guests themselves. Informality was to be the keynote, and neither speeches nor set topics of conversation were to be imposed on those present. Every attempt was to be made to avoid giving the circle a definite political character. The guests were not to be chosen because they represented a point of view shared by Ballin or Holtzendorff; they were there because they were influential, because they had done or could perform favors for Ballin, or because they were reliable sources of information. Holtzendorff was allowed some latitude in issuing his invitations, though his lists were usually submitted to Ballin in advance. Ballin did not hesitate to delete or add names. As far as he was concerned, anyone was eligible for inclusion, with the only restriction being that when he himself was present

[6] *Holtzendorff-A*, IV, report 194, June 27, 1915.

there be no Social Democrats on hand.[7] Holtzendorff's job was not to reconcile the divers opinions of those who gathered at his board. Such an effort would lead only to an argumentative free-for-all—a "political *Bierabend*," Ballin called it.[8] Holtzendorff was to circulate discreetly among his guests, asking questions, occasionally promoting talk on subjects of interest to Ballin, without, he was warned, letting his guests realize that they were being pumped.[9] Particularly should Holtzendorff avoid giving the impression that the circle had been set up to further the HAPAG's own interests, although this was certainly one of the functions of the parties in the Viktoriastrasse. Ballin wrote that ". . . it would be a shame for your *Abende* if the false impression arose that they did not serve national issues but private interests. Both aims are easily capable of being combined."[10]

Holtzendorff's guests came at irregular intervals, but generally there were two evenings a month. The number invited likewise varied, and though both Ballin and Holtzendorff preferred a small gathering of eight to ten, the group often swelled to twenty and sometimes even to thirty. Ballin himself came only rarely, as did such high personages as Bethmann Hollweg and secretary Jagow. But almost every other figure of importance in Berlin supped at least once at Holtzendorff's table. A file of secretaries and under secretaries turned up: Helfferich, Delbrück, Rödern, Zimmermann, Richter, Wahnschaffe, and others. Two officials, low in rank but high in influence, also figured repeatedly in Holtzendorff's registers: Captain Grasshoff, chief of the *Auslandsabteilung* of the

[7] *ibid.*, II, report 127, March 13, 1915; Jäckh, *Goldene Pflug*, p. 189.
[8] Ballin to Holtzendorff, May 10, 1915, *Holtzendorff-A*, III.
[9] *Holtzendorff-B*, XIII, report 769, Dec. 7, 1917.
[10] Ballin to Holtzendorff, Dec. 6, 1917, *ibid.*

Admiral Staff, and Major Deutelmoser, a liaison officer in charge of press and censorship relations between the Supreme Command and the Wilhelmstrasse. The court was represented frequently by Count Eulenburg and Admiral Müller. Party leaders—Westarp, Bassermann, Stresemann, Erzberger, Naumann—also attended. Jäckh described the distinction of Holtzendorff's circle with his customary inflation: "Without naming names, it can be said in summary that every *Reichskanzler*, every *Reichsminister* . . . every court chamberlain, every party leader . . . every allied ambassador, the leading economic and academic figures, everyone who occupied decision-making positions—met one another there, not all together, but intermittently, because practice best confirms the principle to have at a discussion table no more than the number of muses, no less than the number of graces; at best, Plato's eight."[11]

The care which Ballin and Holtzendorff took in their arrangements and invitations bore fruit, for the evenings proved an immensely valuable source of information. The guests were likewise delighted with the excellent food and drink, the easy informality, and the distinguished company they encountered *bei* Holtzendorff.[12] Eugen Schiffer, a National Liberal deputy, declared that Holtzendorff's circle was just what Ballin had intended it to be: a neutral place where questions of the day could be freely discussed with leading figures in the government.[13]

Like the other groups, Holtzendorff's circle quickly acquired a political reputation. It was regarded in many

[11] Jäckh, *Goldene Pflug*, pp. 189-90.
[12] For the favorable testimony of a number of highly placed government officials, see *Holtzendorff-A*, II, notes for Jan. 24, 1915; *ibid.*, IX, notes for June 18, 1916; Clemens von Delbrück to Holtzendorff, May 11, 1917, in *ibid.*, XII; Jäckh, *Goldene Pflug*, p. 189.
[13] *Holtzendorff-A*, IX, report 452, July 18, 1916.

quarters as little short of subversive, pro-English, anti-annexationist, and defeatist. Naval officers were particularly outspoken in their criticism of the Viktoriastrasse group. The former naval attaché in London, Captain Wilhelm Widenmann, branded the Holtzendorff assembly as "the center of everything defeatist. . . ."[14] Admiral Tirpitz was only vaguely aware of the evenings in the Viktoriastrasse and confused them with Hans Delbrück's circle or with the *Bund Neues Vaterland*, both moderate groups opposed to the extent of the admiral's war aims.[15] Had Tirpitz known more, he would doubtless have joined Widenmann in his condemnation. Ballin was anxious that Tirpitz come to one of Holtzendorff's affairs, but the admiral politely declined to attend any "political evenings."[16] The army was likewise a center of opposition to the Holtzendorff group, although a number of high ranking officers frequently were present. General Gustav von Kessel, one of the Kaiser's adjutants, responded to an invitation from Holtzendorff by asserting that he was "too good a patriot and too old a Prussian to go over to the defeatists!" Kessel charged that Holtzendorff's circle stood for "peace at any price" and stiffly criticized Ballin for his deficient hostility toward England.[17] Kessel, who was a seasoned courtier, was doubtless influenced in this view by a criticism of private political discussion

[14] Widenmann "Nachlass," "Erinnerungen," pp. 157-58.

[15] *Holtzendorff-A*, v, notes for Oct. 29, 1915. See also Lujo Brentano, *Mein Leben im Kampf um die soziale Entwicklung Deutschlands*, Jena, 1931, p. 323. For Tirpitz' criticism of Ballin's attitude toward the war in 1914-15, see his *Erinnerungen*, Leipzig, 1919, pp. 414, 441, 460, 464.

[16] *Holtzendorff-A*, vi, report 276, Nov. 3, 1915; Ballin to Holtzendorff, Nov. 4. Tirpitz' assistant, Capt. Löhlein, head of the *Zentralabteilung* of the *Reichsmarineamt*, likewise declined to come. *Ibid.*, iv, report 177, June 5, 1915.

[17] *ibid.*, vi, report 260, Oct. 11, 1915. Kessel, however, subsequently relented and came to an evening at Holtzendorff's.

groups he had earlier heard from the Kaiser. In September 1915, two months before the general's conversation with Holtzendorff, William II had declared that he wanted the political "cliques" in Berlin eliminated. Kessel had thereupon informed William that he knew only of a *Sabbat-Clique* under Ballin's leadership, whose liquidation he felt was particularly desirable.[18]

Holtzendorff's entertainments excited suspicion in the civil branches of the government as well. Under secretary Arnold Wahnschaffe of the Interior Ministry succeeded in dispelling the fears of one of his "secret agents" that the group was subversive only by pointing out that he himself was a regular guest of Holtzendorff's.[19] At least one government figure who had no quarrel with the opinions expressed at Holtzendorff's and who found the evenings very pleasant, experienced ethical qualms at accepting invitations from the Hamburg-American Line. "I sometimes asked myself," Magnus Baron von Braun of the Interior Ministry wrote some years later, "whether it actually was right to let myself be invited to political dinners by a private business concern such as the Hapag. But, in the end, invitations from *Handelskammern*, magistrates of great cities, press organizations and the like are not much different. Nevertheless, one should be careful as a *Staatsbeamter*. Where does corruption begin?"[20]

The Holtzendorff group met throughout the war, the last dinner prior to the armistice falling on November 2, 1918. By then, the evenings in the Viktoriastrasse, though they had lost none of their fascination, were no longer very

[18] Memorandum dated Sept. 14, 1915, in A. von Tirpitz, *Politische Dokumente*, 2 vols., Stuttgart, etc., 1924-26, II, 429.

[19] *Holtzendorff-B*, I, folder 17, "Herrenabende," notes for March 30, 1915.

[20] Braun, *Von Ostpreussen bis Texas: Erlebnisse und zeitgeschichtliche Betrachtungen eines Ostdeutschen*, Stollhamm, 1955, p. 100.

256

sumptuous affairs. Whiskey vanished, first in favor of an apollonaris and champagne punch and then beer, guests were requested to supply Holtzendorff with their bread cards so that he could procure food for his board. The final indignity came in 1918, when the police insisted that even so distinguished an assembly must observe Berlin's 11:30 P.M. curfew. After the war, the HAPAG authorized Holtzendorff to continue his evenings, and his circle did not break up until his retirement in 1924.

A number of Ballin's colleagues at the HAPAG believed that his influence in Berlin both in the government and at court declined greatly after the war began. Ballin's erroneous predictions of British neutrality following his return from London at the end of July 1914 were held responsible. The waning of Ballin's own influence, they argued, had led him to make Holtzendorff his alter ego in Berlin.[21] There was some truth in this opinion, but a distinction must be drawn between court and government. With the Kaiser, as will shortly be indicated, Ballin's influence ebbed; with the government, his entrée was as extensive as ever, his advice frequently sought and sometimes heeded.

In peacetime, Ballin's politicking had been largely a public affair, at Elbe regattas, Kiel Week, and in his well-publicized meetings with William II. During the war, however, Ballin's political activities were more covert. Even Ballin's colleagues knew little of his maneuvers, but Holtzendorff's records and government documents for the war period show how close his connection with political leaders was. With less business to take care of, Ballin, secluded at Hamfelde or Dapper's, spent longer hours at his desk communicating with his friends. He had always liked to

[21] Thomann to Merck, April 26, 1915, in Merck "Nachlass," II 8 Konv. 5, folder marked "Briefe von Kollegen . . ."; *ibid.*, "Erinnerungen," pp. 150-51.

write and now at last, he said, he had plenty of time to do so. There was hardly an important government official or public figure who did not hear from him. Reports from HAPAG agents abroad were regularly forwarded to various ministries in Berlin. Letters in Ballin's elegant and precise hand flowed to Tirpitz, Brockdorff-Rantzau, Stresemann, to Bethmann, colonial secretary Wilhelm Solf, to ambassador Bernstorff, Prince Bülow, and Count Metternich, to Warburg, Harden, Fürstenberg, and many others. These men were all interested in what Ballin had to say, and in reply they asked for his opinion on issues and personalities and sometimes requested his aid to further their own interests. When Ballin came to the capital, doors along the Wilhelmstrasse stood open to him just as they had before the war. Bethmann even issued a blanket invitation to Ballin to call at the chancellor's palace whenever he was in Berlin, and expressed disappointment when he learned that he had been in town but had not come to see him.[22]

Ballin's relationship with the Kaiser, however, underwent a change after the war began. The frequency of their meetings and the intimacy of their conversations fell off. This was in part due to circumstances, for the opportunities for the two men to come together during the war years were rare. The Kaiser came to Hamburg only once, and though Ballin was frequently in Berlin, William spent more and more time at army headquarters in the field. William harbored neither anger nor resentment toward his friend because of his mistaken judgment on the eve of the war, a fact which greatly relieved Ballin.[23] An influential group in the Kaiser's entourage was, however, sharply critical of

---

[22] *Holtzendorff-A*, vi, notes for Nov. 15, 1915; Ballin to Holtzendorff, Jan. 7, 1916, in *Ballin-Holtzendorff, Private*. See also Huldermann, pp. 336-37.

[23] Theodor Wolff, *Der Marsch durch zwei Jahrzehnte*, Amsterdam, 1936, pp. 263-64; Ballin to Harden, Jan. 10, 1915, Harden "Nachlass."

Ballin for his alleged Anglophilism, his pacificism, pessimism, defeatism, and his desire to use the Kaiser to advance his own interests. This clique did everything possible to undermine Ballin's standing with his sovereign and was particularly concerned to insure that he seldom had a chance to talk to William privately.[24] It is difficult to identify with certainty more than a few members of this anti-Ballin camarilla. The Kaiserin was prominent in it, as was Friedrich von Berg after his appointment in 1918 as chief of the Civil Cabinet (*Zivilkabinett*), and General von Kessel. The Kaiser did not approve of the attacks made on Ballin by the Kaiserin and others. Holtzendorff reported to Ballin late in 1914 that Kessel had told him of the aftermath of an audience between the imperial couple and Ballin in the course of which Ballin had disagreed with the Kaiser about the conduct of the war against England. ". . . right after you left," Holtzendorff wrote, "the Kaiser spoke of you in the nicest and most charming way, and *der hohe Herr* repeatedly stressed, particularly to the Kaiserin, that he could fully understand your opinion and your standpoint, since you certainly had to represent the interests of your life's work, the greatest shipping line in the world!"[25]

Ballin was aware of the opposition to him at court and he knew that the charges of Anglophilia were damaging his standing with William II. The Kaiser, therefore, would be inclined to discount his advice. He resented the aspersions cast on his patriotism, for he felt—and quite rightly—that there was no man in Germany who in peacetime had wrested so much from the English. But such a vicious charge, Ballin noted in a letter to Harden, was the

[24] Ballin to Harden, April 17, 1917, Harden "Nachlass." Cf. Wolff, *Marsch*, p. 276; also Huldermann, p. 357.

[25] Letter of Dec. 19, 1914, in *Holtzendorff-B*, IV/V, folder entitled "Ballin und Seine Majestät"; also Huldermann, pp. 296-97.

259

"surest means of successful insinuation" against him.[26] He cried out in exasperation and despair at the Kaiser's advisers who kept him shielded behind a "Chinese wall" to protect his increasingly delicate nervous condition. The court was a cocoon of lies enveloping a helpless man, leaving Ballin—and the unpleasant truth—outside. William, kept ignorant of every detail that might upset or discourage, could therefore hardly be blamed for the somber fate which had befallen the empire.[27] "No one," Ballin lamented in March 1916, "tells him the whole truth, most people do not even tell him half the truth, and very many lie to him. That is the situation." If only, Ballin declared a year later, *he* could obtain a private audience the Kaiser would learn what the realities were, unpalatable though they might be.[28]

Ballin's exposure to the sustained efforts of the Kaiserin and others to keep him at a distance gradually altered his behavior toward William II. The anxiety which he had felt in 1916 to be allowed to speak openly to the Kaiser diminished considerably as the war went on. Thus, in the spring of 1917, when there was much discussion in Berlin concerning the choice of a successor for Bethmann Hollweg, Ballin declined a suggestion that he write to the Kaiser about the matter. "The men around the Kaiser have cut me off," he wrote to Harden, "and their anxiety that I might be able to talk openly to him about the last weeks before the war broke out have resulted in the fact

[26] Ballin to Harden, Jan. 10, 1915, Harden "Nachlass." See also the partial text of a letter by Ballin to Tirpitz of April 16, 1915, different sections of which are printed in Tirpitz, *Politische Dokumente*, II, 330-32, and in Huldermann, p. 324. See also Bogdan Graf Hutten-Czapski, *Sechzig Jahre Politik und Gesellschaft*, 2 vols., Berlin, 1936, II, 134.

[27] Wolff, *Marsch*, p. 255; Bernhard Guttmann, *Schattenriss einer Generation 1888-1919*, Stuttgart, 1950, pp. 246-47.

[28] Ballin to Holtzendorff, March 20 and July 14, 1916, in *Ballin-Holtzendorff, Private.*

that during this long period of war I have seen the Kaiser only in the company of other guests. He has been completely removed from my influence and he would be exceedingly mistrustful if now, after I have intentionally withdrawn myself from him for a long time both by the written word and in person, I suddenly wanted to take over the direction of so fateful a question."[29]

Ballin's influence in wartime Germany, then, if actively opposed and considerably limited at court, was, by his own exertions or those of Holtzendorff, still considerable. That influence Ballin put to work in the hope of bringing Germany if not victory, at least a peace that would be both honorable and lasting.

———————

From August 1914 to November 1918, Ballin wanted only one thing: a swift end to war and the immediate political and economic reconstruction of Europe. To him, the war was one between Germany and Great Britain—he had little interest in anything except the western front. The conflict was one waged by two giants, alongside whom the other belligerents were insignificant and inconsequential. It would therefore be Germany and Great Britain who would impose an eventual peace on Europe. From the beginning, Ballin argued that the longer the war lasted the less likelihood there was of Germany's deriving some profit from its sacrifices. Time would work to Britain's advantage.[30] In Ballin's opinion, economic con-

[29] Ballin to Harden, April 17, 1917, Harden "Nachlass." Cf. Wolff, *Marsch*, p. 276, which records a private conversation of three hours' duration between the two in May 1917.

[30] See Egmont Zechlin, "Deutschland zwischen Kabinettskrieg und Wirtschaftskrieg: Politik und Kriegführung in den ersten Monaten des Weltkrieges 1914," *Historische Zeitschrift*, CXCIX, no. 2 (Oct. 1964), 394-95. See also Ballin to Tirpitz, Oct. 1, 1914, in Tirpitz, *Politische Dokumente*, II, 130-31.

siderations, rather than political ones, were what made peace imperative. The war had thoroughly disrupted German trade, and as long as hostilities continued German commerce, deprived of the sea, would atrophy, while England would successfully reorient its economy to the needs of a world at war.[31]

During the first weeks of the war, Ballin would have been willing to agree to peace on the basis of a *status quo ante bellum*. But he realized that so simple a formula would be impossible, for in the west, German arms had swallowed Belgium and ravaged the north east of France, only to become bogged down on the Marne, twenty miles from Paris. And in the east, the Germans, after initial reverses, were pushing the tsar's armies back through Russian Poland. Germany, if not victorious on two fronts, had at least demonstrated its military superiority. The German government and the German people therefore would demand that peace bring with it material advantages for the Fatherland. They would have to be given something.[32] Precisely what Germany would acquire was vague, for wartime censorship regulations forbad public discussion of war aims. There were many conflicting opinions on the claims Germany was entitled to make; some Germans preferred acquisitions at Russia's expense, others claimed Belgium and parts of France as prizes of war. Still others wanted the permanent retention of every parcel of land which German arms had conquered.[33]

As far as Ballin was concerned, two principles deter-

[31] Ballin to Tirpitz, Oct. 22, 1914, HAPAG-V.

[32] Ballin to Harden, Dec. 6, 1914, Harden "Nachlass." See also Bethmann Hollweg's *Betrachtungen zum Weltkriege*, 2 vols., Berlin, 1919-21, II, 26-27.

[33] On the war aims question, see in particular Gatzke, *Germany's Drive to the West*, and Fritz Fischer, *Griff nach der Weltmacht: die Kriegszielpolitik des kaiserlichen Deutschland 1914/18*, Düsseldorf, 1961.

mined his views on Germany's war aims throughout the course of the conflict. In the first place, Germany must in the future be secured against what he now called the "eternal threat" which England's navy posed to German commerce, a threat which had been made real in August 1914 when the British bottled up Germany's merchant marine and navy behind Helgoland. England was fighting the war for the purpose of ruining Germany's overseas trade, and peace could be made only if London was willing to enter into an "iron-clad agreement" which would in the future guarantee to both Germany and England the free use of the sea.[34] Secondly, the conditions of peace must be such as would reestablish international harmony in which trade might flourish and the Great Powers—but particularly Britain and Germany—dwell in peace.[35]

These two prerequisites for peace necessitated certain specific demands by Germany on England. To secure Germany against blockade, not only was an iron-clad agreement necessary but also naval stations in Europe as well as overseas to protect German ships and to insure their free passage through the North Sea. On the other hand, to satisfy the condition that the peace terms be acceptable to Great Britain meant that these acquisitions would have to be carefully chosen, tactfully acquired, and correlated with the legitimate aspirations of the British, who, together with Germany, would guide the destinies of the post war world. The precise extent of Germany's demands would depend on the fortunes of German arms.[36] Ballin never doubted in the first months of war that the British

[34] Memorandum by Ballin, Dec. 1, 1914, in *AA*, WK Nr. 2, geh., vol. 1, reel 2104/955454-59.

[35] *ibid.*; Ballin to Ernst Francke, Oct. 31, 1914, in Stubmann, p. 212; same to Tirpitz, Oct. 1, 1914, in Tirpitz, *Politische Dokumente*, II, 130-35; same to Admiral von Capelle, Jan. 21, 1915, *ibid.*, 299-300.

[36] Ballin to Francke, Oct. 31, 1914, in Stubmann, p. 212.

people were against the conflict, and he seems to have been convinced that they therefore would gladly agree to the sort of peace he had in mind.[37] The difficulty lay not so much in London as in Berlin. William II, largely under the unfortunate influence of the Kaiserin, had sunk into an unreasoning hatred of England and was implacably resolved on total victory. With the Kaiser in such a state of mind, any efforts to negotiate a peace would be impossible.[38] Ballin, however, was confident that the statesmen would eventually realize the stupidity of their ways and would entrust the establishment of peace to businessmen of goodwill anxious to get their concerns back to work.[39]

To Ballin, the spoils of war on the continent which were most desirable lay in Belgium and along the northern French coast. Unlike the industrial titans of Germany, he was uninterested in the annexation of the Briey-Longwy coal fields in France. Ballin first elaborated his views on the war aims question in an article entitled "The Wet Triangle," which he wrote early in 1915 at the invitation of the *Frankfurter Zeitung*.[40] The text ran in part:

Germany entered this war in the first place with only one aim: to fight for a peace which would give to coming generations security for peaceful and protected development of the Fatherland. . . . In my youth, sailors used to call that part of the North Sea which stretched between Helgoland and the mouths of the [Elbe and

[37] Görlitz, ed., *Regierte der Kaiser?*, p. 47.

[38] Ballin to Bülow, Dec. 9, 1914, Bülow "Nachlass," printed in Bülow, *Denkwürdigkeiten*, 4 vols., Berlin, 1930-31, III, 198-99, with minor alterations and no date. See also Quadt (Prussian minister to the Hanseatic cities and the Mecklenburgs) to Bethmann, Nov. 12, 1915, in *AA*, WK Nr. 15, vol. 11, reel 401/00549-50.

[39] Hjalmar Schacht, *My First Seventy-Six Years*, trans. Diana Pyke, London, 1955, pp. 143, 159.

[40] *Frankfurter Zeitung und Handelsblatt* (Jan. 5, 1915).

Weser] rivers the "wet triangle." The experiences which we have had in the North Sea in recent months enable us to recognize without dispute that our ports within this "wet triangle" do not constitute the necessary prerequisites for the reinforcement of our battleships, and that for the future preservation of a successful peace it is necessary for us to come *out on the sea*!

The English have been able to place on us the heavy burden of bringing our overseas trade almost to a standstill only because this area of the North Sea turns out to be easy to blockade. The sea robber-like intimidation which England practices on the neutral Scandinavian countries and on Holland would be impossible had we had a base for our fleet which was equal to the stature and heroic valor of its brave officers and men.

Therefore we must seek a foothold for our *fleet* beyond this area of the North Sea which in the future will at least secure for us in this part of the world the same opportunities as England [now] possesses and ruthlessly exploits.

Censorship regulations required that Ballin be imprecise, and immediately after the "Wet Triangle" article appeared rumors spread that what he meant by a "foothold" was Antwerp.[41] He did indeed want Antwerp, but not by annexation. Ballin's plan early in 1915 was that although no part of Belgium should be annexed by Germany, economic and military integration between the two nations should be effected. A German port commission should be established at Antwerp, the Belgian state railways placed under German control, a naval base constructed at Zeebrugge, an indemnity paid, and a military convention entered into by the Belgian government.[42] "No annexation,"

---

[41] Tirpitz, *Erinnerungen*, p. 443. See also Stubmann, p. 240.

[42] Warburg to Ballin, Feb. 12, and Ballin to Warburg, Feb. 13, 1915, in Warburg "Nachlass," -/25a/Privat; Germany, National-

he declared, "but economic and military dependence and control on our part, especially over the ports."[43] Ballin explained the reasons for his opposition to the annexation of Belgium at a luncheon with Helfferich, secretary Delbrück, and Arndt von Holtzendorff late in March 1915. Holtzendorff recorded his arguments. "Herr Ballin stressed that in the first place one should keep his eye on war indemnities and [demand] no territorial expansion whatsoever. . . . One could see enough in the example of Austria how fatal it was when different nationalities were united in one empire. . . . Herr Ballin emphasized that the essential thing in the conclusion of peace was that one received the means to compensate our people for all the sacrifices which they had made."[44]

There was, however, a more compelling reason for Ballin's insistence that Belgium not be annexed. That reason was Great Britain. If Germany insisted on annexing Belgium, no peace with England would be possible and the war would drag on for years, while German commerce withered and the HAPAG's ships rusted at anchor.[45] "It is certainly an insane thought," Ballin wrote to Bülow in 1915, "to want to hold a land which we have treacherously invaded, and even if one does not put much value on English sentiments, one still has to understand that from purely practical considerations English policy cannot sacrifice Belgium to us."[46]

---

versammlung, *Das Werk des Untersuchungsausschusses*, 4. Reihe, "Die Ursachen des deutschen Zusammenbruchs im Jahre 1918," 12 vols., Berlin, 1925-29, XII (1), 37; *Holtzendorff-A*, II, notes for March 29, 1915; Wolff, *Marsch*, p. 265.

[43] *Holtzendorff-A*, III, notes for April 21, 1915, report 140, April 18. Cf. *ibid.*, IV, notes for June 18, 1915, in which Ballin declared that the retention of Zeebrugge would be a very *erstrebenwertes Ziel*.

[44] *ibid.*, II, notes for March 29, 1915.

[45] Ballin to Holtzendorff, May 10, 1915, in *ibid.*, III.

[46] Letter of April 7, 1915, Bülow "Nachlass."

On October 20, 1915, in a speech delivered before the *Verein Hamburger Reeder*, one which Stresemann published at once in the *Sächsische Industrie*, Ballin called for the acquisition by Germany of Boulogne and the Canary islands, proposing that the Canaries could be purchased from Spain while France could be indemnified by being given part of the Belgian coast.[47] The North Sea coast, after all, was only a segment of the world, and with his international perspectives, Ballin envisioned a peace with England which would affect areas and peoples all over the globe. As far as he was concerned, there was ample territory around the world to satisfy both Germany and Great Britain. The only sensible thing to do was to join hands in dividing it up and ruling it. It was not an unreasonable or visionary notion, he felt, for in the two decades prior to the war Germany and England had satisfied their colonial aspirations without shedding one another's blood. In China, in Persia, and in Africa, Englishmen and Germans had found that peaceful and profitable coexistence was quite possible. The two nations, in his opinion, shared a community of interest and a *Schicksalsgemeinschaft*. As a kindred people, they should join together to prevent the world from falling into the hands of the Japanese, the Slavs, the French, and the Americans. The English would prefer to cooperate with Germany rather than with Slavs and yellow men, and unless Germany and England combined forces, Yankees and Orientals might simply dump a divided Europe into their pockets. Besides, it was Germany, standing powerfully between France and Russia, who alone ensured Great

[47] Conrad Haussmann to Ballin, Oct. 25, and Ballin to Haussmann, Oct. 28, 1915, in Stresemann "Nachlass," Politische Akten, vol. 149, reel 3056/128214-17; remarks by Siegfried Heckscher, *Hamburger Correspondent* (Jan. 14, 1922). See also Stresemann's notes of a meeting with Ballin on Jan. 13, 1916, Stresemann "Nachlass," Politische Atken, vol. 161, reel 3064/130285-87.

Britain's insistence that a continental balance of power be maintained.[48] Together, the two peoples could serve as a sort of world police force.[49] Their cooperation was absolutely essential. It was senseless, Ballin held, to dream of Germany as the arbiter of the world. Berlin must work hand in hand with London, and it would be England which would be the leader of this powerful constellation and Germany which would serve as the "junior partner."[50]

As far as Ballin was concerned, the fundamental argument for a close Anglo-German association was that Germany's overseas trade could exist only at the sufferance of the British. A peace to establish this partnership would have, however, to accord something tangible to the German people in return for their sacrifices in the war. Since annexations in Belgium would be impossible if Britain's friendship was to be secured, Germany's gains —except for Boulogne—would have to lie outside Europe. Ballin found Asia Minor an inviting possibility; the Ottoman Empire could no longer justify its existence

---

[48] Ballin to Tirpitz, Oct. 1, 1914, Tirpitz, *Politische Dokumente*, II, 134; same to Holtzendorff, Sept. 13, 1915, *Holtzendorff-A*, V, in both of which Ballin went so far as to declare that had Russia overrun Germany early in the war, England would have come to Germany's aid to prevent Russia's upsetting the balance.

[49] Ballin to Holtzendorff, June 6, 1915, *Holtzendorff-A*, IV; notes for Oct. 28, 1915, *ibid.*, V. See also Tirpitz, *Politische Dokumente*, II, 131, and Huldermann, p. 326, in which the French are admitted to the charmed circle.

[50] Ballin to Haussmann, Oct. 28, 1915, Stresemann "Nachlass," Politische Akten, vol. 149, reel 3056/118216-17; *Holtzendorff-A*, V, notes for Oct. 28, 1915. Ballin's insistence that the peace must be mutually agreeable to both Britain and Germany resulted not unsurprisingly in his being accused of an insufficiency of patriotism. See *Holtzendorff-A*, V, report 243, Sept. 8, 1915; *ibid.*, IV, report 174, June 2, 1915; *ibid.*, V, Ballin to Holtzendorff, Oct. 13, 1915; Stresemann to Ballin, Sept. 24, 1916, and Ballin to Stresemann, Sept. 28, in Stresemann "Nachlass," Politische Akten, vol. 173, reel 3065/130738-43.

as an independent state, and the area offered the German people excellent opportunities for colonization.[51] Although equatorial Africa's climate and location were not as desirable, the HAPAG favored the creation by Germany of a "great middle-African colonial empire," again an acquisition to which England, it was held, would not object.[52] There was also China, a land which Ballin considered extremely vital for German commerce and one which he hoped that both Germany and England, working together, could advantageously exploit.[53] There is reason to believe, however, that Ballin's declarations concerning German colonialism were perfunctory pronouncements gauged to counteract the accusations of defeatism made against him by his enemies. So, for example, while Ballin now and then claimed to favor colonial activity by Germany in Anatolia, he was outspoken in his opposition to the *Mitteleuropa* cult which gained strength during the war.[54] Similarly, though the HAPAG went on record as supporting plans for an expanded German empire in Africa, there is nothing in Ballin's correspondence which indicates that he did anything to further such a project or indeed that he was even genuinely interested in it. What he wanted was not annexations in these areas but the establishment of strong German commercial connections, with German merchants and German merchantmen trading with them protected by the might of their state. The only adjustments of prewar Europe which Germany would have to ask to insure this protection of its trade were the economic integration of Belgium and the acquisition of Bou-

[51] *Holtzendorff-A*, II, notes for March 29, 1916; Ballin to Harden, April 7, 1915, Harden "Nachlass."

[52] Comment of HAPAG, dated April 5, 1915, to a memo of the Hamburg *Handelskammer*, in *AA*, WK Nr. 15, vol. 9, reel 401/00536.

[53] *Holtzendorff-A*, V, notes for Oct. 26, 1915.

[54] See pp. 275-76, 315-18.

logne and the Canaries. To this modest claim, he sincerely though unrealistically believed the British would consent.

Ballin's desire for a post-war Anglo-German partnership and his correlated views on Germany's war aims did not waver during the four years of hostilities. His problem was to persuade the German government to adopt a position similar to his own. This Ballin tried to do throughout the war by the letters, speeches, and articles he wrote, by his frequent trips to Berlin, and by Holtzendorff's activity in the capital. German diplomacy or German arms, or both, would have to be responsible for securing England's consent to the peace proposals advanced by Berlin.

The British might be made amenable to Germany's terms in one of several ways. First, most desirable but least likely, Germany could deal England a knockout blow on the battlefield or on the sea, crippling both its will and its ability to prolong the war. Or Germany could adopt a policy of carefully doing nothing, beyond the normal conduct of the war, which would further exacerbate Anglo-German relations, in the hope that such forbearance on its part would persuade the British that Germany earnestly desired an accommodation. The two powers could then negotiate their differences. Finally, England might be forced to break off hostilities if astute diplomacy or military force on Germany's part succeeded in breaking up the Entente by removing Russia or France from the war by means of a separate peace. Which course to pursue would depend largely on the progress of German arms and on public opinion in the Entente countries. From time to time during the war, Ballin recommended one or another of these policies to those in power, shifting his views rapidly and often contradicting a former position. Very frequently, he worked on two of the three plans of action simultaneously—never, unfortunately, with any success.

Like his fellow Germans, Ballin marvelled at the splendid progress of Germany's drive to the west in the early days of the war, and he doubtless speculated that the result might be France and England's retirement from the war followed by a general peace. He also hoped that Tirpitz' battle fleet would steam out into the North Sea and successfully engage the enemy.[55] The Germans stayed in port, however, while on land Moltke's advance was halted at the Marne early in September. The Entente had not been dealt the hoped-for knockout blow. A swift victory by arms thus ruled out, Ballin advised that Germany adopt toward England as conciliatory an attitude as possible given the state of war between the two nations. This would mean curtailing the attacks on England in the German press, and, more importantly, withholding the German navy from any engagement with the British fleet. If England were defeated on the sea, this would only increase the determination of the British to fight and would bring into power an even more belligerent government. This was to be avoided at all costs, for Ballin was convinced that the Asquith cabinet would be willing to come to an understanding with Germany provided Germany moderated its war aims and provided Tirpitz would consent to what Ballin believed would be reasonable claims for naval superiority on England's part.[56]

The British, however, were uninterested in any peace which would not restore the *status quo ante bellum*, a demand to which neither Ballin, the German government, nor the German people could agree. There was therefore nothing to do but to push on vigorously with the war.

[55] *Holtzendorff-A*, II, report 89, Dec. 14, 1914.

[56] Ballin to Tirpitz, Oct. 1, 1914, Tirpitz, *Politische Dokumente*, II, 133; Tirpitz, *Erinnerungen*, p. 265; Bülow (Prussian minister in Hamburg) to Zimmermann, Nov. 3, 1914, in *AA*, WK Nr. 2, geh., vol. 1, reel 2104/955345-49.

"England," Ballin wrote early in January 1915 to his friend, the journalist Ernst Francke, "is no doubt ready to make peace at any time, but this peace would probably have to be based on the *status quo ante bellum*. England's current willingness to make peace therefore is worthless to us, and if we do not succeed in subjecting it to strong military pressure, I do not see how we can go forward."[57]

By the time Ballin wrote to Francke, he had found that there was in fact a new military means—the submarine or U-boat (*Unterseeboot*)—through whose use such pressure could successfully be exerted on Britain. In the fall of 1914, the disappointing inactivity of the German fleet had been offset by the torpedoing of four British cruisers by German submarines. Tirpitz and the navy thereupon began to consider the U-boats, formerly regarded only as experimental craft, as the means of striking a crippling blow not only at British warships but also at the merchant fleet which supplied the islands with food.[58] Tirpitz' enthusiasm for an intense U-boat campaign was not shared by a number of other admirals, nor did Bethmann Hollweg and William II initially display any interest in Tirpitz' claims for his submarines. Kaiser and chancellor were fearful that a declaration by Germany of a submarine blockade of the British isles would arouse the resentment of Italy, the United States, and other neutral powers.

Ballin, on the contrary, had become convinced by January 1915 that a U-boat blockade of England was absolutely essential and alone offered a possibility for a rapid conclusion of hostilities. The blockade was to be given the "most brutal execution" so the British would be made aware of the futility of continuing their fight against

[57] Letter of Jan. 12, 1915, in Stubmann, p. 214.
[58] Ernest R. May, *The World War and American Isolation 1914-1917*, Cambridge, Mass., 1959, pp. 113-15.

Germany.[59] To Ballin, the submarine was Germany's fantastic deliverance and England's doom. The early success of the U-boats, he wrote to Bethmann with more passion than reason, "represents the beginning of the end of English *Weltmacht*." If Britain's leaders were wise, they would realize this and sue for peace before all was lost.[60] Ballin felt that Bethmann's qualms, and those of others, about the reaction of neutral powers were justified, but they should not be allowed to outweigh the enormous tactical advantage that a ruthless submarine blockade would give to the Central Powers.[61]

Tirpitz' plan of action against England, so enthusiastically endorsed by Ballin, was ambitious almost to the point of fantasy, for Germany possessed less than two dozen submarines, most of which were of inferior design. The admiral argued skillfully for his strategy, however, and his cajolery, backed by the increasing public demand for a more resolute war at sea against the British, forced William and Bethmann to capitulate. On February 4, 1915, an order was published declaring that after February 18th German submarines would endeavor to sink every enemy merchantman cruising off Ireland or England. Ballin hoped that the submarines would be able to sink two freighters a week, but the actual bag during February and March was somewhat less satisfying.[62] In the first six

[59] Ballin to Capelle, Jan. 21, 1915, in Tirpitz, *Politische Dokumente*, II, 299-300. Ballin, however, opposed bombing raids on London. Ballin to Harden, Jan. 10, 1915, Harden "Nachlass."

[60] Letter of Jan. 23, 1915, in *AA*, WK Nr. 2, geh., vol. 2, reel 2104/955705. Warburg expressed similar views in a letter to Ballin of Jan. 6, 1915, Warburg "Nachlass," -/25a/Privat.

[61] Ballin to Capelle, Jan. 21, 1915, in Tirpitz, *Politische Dokumente*, II, 299-300; same to Harden, Jan. 10, Harden "Nachlass"; same to Holtzendorff, Jan. 13, *Holtzendorff-A*, II. See also Warburg to Ballin, Jan. 6, Warburg "Nachlass," -/25a/Privat, and Ballin to Bülow, Jan. 13, Bülow "Nachlass," Nr. 39.

[62] Ballin to Francke, Feb. 9, 1915, in Stubmann, p. 215.

weeks following the declaration, the U-boats managed to sink some 132,000 tons of enemy shipping, or less than one-quarter of 1 per cent of the total tonnage commanded by the United Kingdom.[63] Considering Germany's limited supply of submarines, the number of ships sent to the bottom was remarkable, but Tirpitz had hardly imposed the effective blockade which he had promised in February.

By April 1915, Ballin had become disillusioned with Tirpitz. The admiral's submarines, rather than forcing England to its knees, were only intensifying its will to resist. There is no record of Ballin's having advised Berlin of his opposition to a continuation of the attempt at blockade, but there are no further references in his correspondence to his earlier satisfaction with the accomplishments of the submarine campaign. It seems clear that by April Ballin had returned to his former position that a policy of conciliation was the surest way to reach an understanding with Great Britain.[64] Anything calculated gratuitously to offend the English—such as Jagow's diatribes in the press against Sir Edward Grey—should be avoided and lines kept open for peace negotiations. Unlike Ballin, Tirpitz and Bethmann were sufficiently encouraged by the submarines' performance and were growing more confident that the United States would not intervene in the war because of the loss of American lives on torpedoed ships. They therefore allowed the attempt to blockade England to continue, the protests of neutral powers notwithstanding. The result was, as Ballin had warned, increased resolution for vic-

[63] May, *World War and American Isolation*, p. 132.

[64] In March 1915, Col. Edward M. House, who along with ambassador James W. Gerard had been entertained by Holtzendorff, expressed an interest in discussing peace possibilities with Ballin. The two men could not arrive at a mutually convenient time, but Ballin did forward to House a memorandum on the subject. This document is missing. See *Holtzendorff-A*, II, reports 131 and 134, March 21 and 24, 1915.

tory in Great Britain and the worsening of Germany's relations with the United States and other nonbelligerents.

In the spring of 1915, then, Ballin had become dissatisfied with the conduct of the war. The expected knockout blow by land had failed, a conciliatory policy late in 1914 appeared to have evoked no peace sentiment in England. Ballin had therefore shifted to a resolute course of action and had supported Tirpitz. This, too, had not brought the desired results. There was only one possibility left untried by means of which the Entente might be forced to sue for peace. The London-Paris-Petrograd alliance could not, so it seemed, be vanquished by arms, but perhaps it could be successfully assaulted by diplomacy. If one of the three nations could be detached, the other two would have neither the determination nor the ability to continue to fight for long.

The power to be "sprung" was Russia. Ballin, as will shortly be shown, was involved in negotiations for such a purpose from November 1914 until late in 1917, but he clearly regarded a diplomatic offensive against Russia as the least desirable way in which to exert pressure on England to end the war. All his life, he had had very little interest in eastern Europe, save in its endless supply of emigrants. His orientation was western, and specifically English. He condemned the *Mitteleuropa* schemes of Ernst Jäckh and Friedrich Naumann as economically senseless and politically dangerous, sure to strengthen the Entente and simultaneously saddle Germany with next to useless allies.[65] In contrast to his elaborate discussion of western war aims, Ballin evidenced almost no

[65] *Holtzendorff-B*, ii, folder 10, "Mitteleuropäischer Arbeitsausschuss (Naumann)," containing correspondence between Holtzendorff and Ballin on *Mitteleuropa* projects. See also Huldermann, pp. 367-70, and the references to Ballin in Henry Cord Meyer, *Mitteleuropa in German Thought and Action, 1815-1945*, The Hague, 1955.

concern for German claims in the east, although he went on record in favor of the retention of Courland and that part of Lithuania around Kaunas, areas which he felt more suitable for German colonization than overpopulated Belgium.[66]

The prospects for a separate peace with Russia early in 1915 did not appear to be very promising. Had the Austrian offensive against Serbia succeeded, Ballin maintained, Russia might have been forced to leave the war. The tsar himself would not be inclined to turn to Germany as long as he felt secure on his throne. As it was, Russia stood to gain nothing from signing a separate peace with Germany except a reputation for treachery. Its interests would be better served at a general peace congress.[67] In spite of his pessimism, however, Ballin put himself at the disposal of the German government to render what assistance he could to bring about an end to the war with Russia.

The first, and most significant, of Ballin's peace maneuvers with Russia was one which involved his friend, Ulrich Count von Brockdorff-Rantzau, the German minister in Copenhagen, and their mutual acquaintance, Hans Niels Andersen, a Danish shipping executive who was a close friend of King Christian X.[68] In November 1914,

[66] Ballin to Holtzendorff, Sept. 13 and Oct. 13, 1915, in *Holtzendorff-A*, v.

[67] Ballin to Bülow, Jan. 13, 1915, Bülow "Nachlass," Nr. 39, partially printed with some alterations in *Denkwürdigkeiten*, III, 212-13; same to same, March 24, 1915, Bülow "Nachlass"; same to Bethmann, Jan. 6, 1915, *AA*, WK Nr. 2, geh., vol. 2, reel 2104/955607-11. See also three letters by Ballin to Harden, Jan. 6 and 10, and May 15, 1915, Harden "Nachlass," and *Holtzendorff-A*, II, notes of March 29, 1915.

[68] The German documents on the Andersen mission are filed in *AA*, WK Nr. 2, geh. An exhaustive treatment of the mission based on these papers is Egmont Zechlin, "Friedensbestrebungen und Revolutioniersversuche: deutsche Bemühungen zur Ausschaltung Russlands im Ersten Weltkriege," *Das Parlament*, vol. 20 (May

Andersen, acting in behalf of his sovereign, approached Rantzau to offer Christian's services as a peace mediator between Great Britain, Russia, and Germany. As Andersen pointed out, Christian was willing to sound out his cousins George V and Nicholas II, but first wanted to have assurances from Berlin that the German government and William II would not rebuff an offer to negotiate if he succeeded in finding interest in such a move in London and Petrograd.[69] Rantzau referred Andersen to Ballin, who in turn informed William II of the king's offer.[70]

Bethmann and the Kaiser were cool to Andersen's report, rejecting the possibility of negotiations with Britain and preferring to treat with Russia only after a military decision had been reached in the east.[71] Nonetheless, they were unwilling to offend King Christian, and, after receiving assurances from Vienna that the Austro-Hungarian government had no objections to such a course of action, agreed to accept his offer of mediation.[72] Ballin was empowered by Bethmann to inform Andersen that Germany

---

17, 1961), 269-88. See also Aage Heinberg, *H. N. Andersen: Stifteren af det Østasistiske Kompagni*, Copenhagen, 1952, pp. 135-46, and Harold Nicolson, *King George V: His Life and Reign*, London, 1952, p. 294. An otherwise unidentified 1961 dissertation by C. V. Lafeber, "Vredes-en-bemiddelings-pogingen," referred to by Gerhard Ritter in his *Staatskunst und Kriegshandwerk*, III, p. 598 n16, treats Andersen's activities, as does W. M. Carlgren, *Neutralität oder Allianz: Deutschlands Beziehungen zu Schweden in den Anfangsjahren des Ersten Weltkrieges*, Stockholm, etc., 1962, pp. 84-89, 159-65.

[69] Memo by Ballin, Nov. 21, 1914, *AA*, WK Nr. 2, geh., vol. 1, reel 2104/955439-45.

[70] *ibid.* See also Ballin to William II, Nov. 21, 1914, *ibid.*, reel 2104/955438.

[71] Bethmann to Foreign Office, Nov. 24, *ibid.*, reel 2104/955375-76.

[72] *ibid.;* same to same, Nov. 25, 1914, *ibid.*, reel 2104/955378-79; Tschirschky (ambassador in Vienna) to same, Nov. 28, 2104/955437. For opposition in the Foreign Office to Andersen's offer, see a memo by Zimmermann, Nov. 27, in *ibid.*, 2104/955403-13.

approved Christian's overture. Andersen and Ballin met in Berlin on December 2d, after which Andersen returned to Copenhagen to put the plan into effect. Three weeks went by and Ballin received no further word from Copenhagen. Bethmann meanwhile was showing considerably more interest in the future of negotiations with Russia, a change in attitude due probably to the failure in mid-December of the Austrian campaign to take Cracow. On Christmas Day, the chancellor wrote to Ballin to inquire whether he might not be able to put out feelers to Russia through Sergei Witte, the former finance minister, now a member of the imperial council and reported to be about to reassume high ministerial office. Ballin had means of contact with Witte through one J. Melnik, who had once served the Russian statesman as a ghostwriter and translator. Melnik had also been in the pay of the Hamburg-American Line for a number of years prior to the war as its political agent in Russia.[73] After the war began, he settled in Copenhagen, where he worked with Rantzau to encourage pro-German sentiment in the Scandinavian press. From Copenhagen, Melnik sent Ballin reports on the situation in Denmark and Russia which Ballin, at the chancellor's request, forwarded to Berlin.[74] Ballin replied to Bethmann's inquiry that he felt it best to let the matter of negotiations with Russia wait until the opening of the New Year, at which time he would personally inquire of King Christian what had happened to his peace offensive in St. Petersburg.[75] Early in January 1915, Ballin sent Bernhard Huldermann, one of his confidential assistants at

[73] Ballin to Bethmann, Dec. 28, 1914, *AA*, WK Nr. 2, geh., vol. 1, reel 2104/955556-58.

[74] Same to same, Jan. 15, 1915, *ibid.*, reel 2104/955656-68; see also Melnik's reports from Copenhagen, Jan. 11, 2104/955659-66; Bethmann to Ballin, Jan. 18, 2104/955666.

[75] Ballin to Bethmann, Dec. 28 and 30, 1914, *ibid.*, reel 2104/955556-58, 955575-78.

the HAPAG, to Copenhagen to talk to both Melnik and Andersen. King Christian, it was discovered, was delaying the dispatch of a message to the tsar because he feared that his move might be misinterpreted in St. Petersburg. After some urging by Andersen and the Danish foreign minister, Erik von Scavenius, Christian finally wrote to Nicholas II on Januray 6, 1915, declaring that he was anxious to bring about peace and would value any suggestions the Russian monarch might have as to how this end might be advanced.[76]

The tsar did not reply until the end of January, attributing his delay to the fact that he had not been in Petrograd. Nicholas informed Christian that he would be happy to receive Andersen and discuss the Danish king's offer of mediation with him, though there was nothing in the letter to indicate that his response was motivated by anything deeper than a desire to be polite.[77] Andersen left for the Russian capital on February 23d, and returned to Copenhagen on March 9th, reporting that he found Nicholas moderately interested in learning William's position with regard to a separate Russo-German peace or to a general peace.[78] Christian thereupon directed Andersen to go to Germany and put himself in touch with Ballin; Scavenius, in turn, asked Rantzau to have Ballin go to Berlin to meet Andersen.[79] Andersen arrived in Berlin on March 18th. Ballin had already arranged for him to see Bethmann, and the chancellor then

[76] Rantzau to Foreign Office, Jan. 8 and 10, 1915, *ibid.*, vol. 2, reel 2104/955614-16; Ballin to Bethmann, Jan. 8, *ibid.*, 2104/955617-18.

[77] Rantzau to Foreign Office, Feb. 1, 1915, *ibid.*, reel 2104/955737-38; Jagow to German embassy, Vienna, Feb. 2, 2104/955739-40.

[78] Rantzau to Foreign Office, March 10, 1915, *ibid.*, vol. 3, reel 2105/956061-65; same to same, March 11 and 13 (2 wires), *ibid.*, vol. 4, reel 2105/956079-83, 956108-09, 956114.

[79] Same to same, March 13, *ibid.*, vol. 4, reel 2105/955115.

took Andersen to Supreme Headquarters in Charleville to talk to the Kaiser.[80] In the course of their discussion, William declared that Nicholas had been misinformed about the events of July 1914, that it was Germany who had in truth been attacked, but that he valued his old friendship with Nicholas and therefore welcomed Christian's offer to try to arrange a peace between the two empires.[81] Armed with this encouraging information, Andersen returned to Copenhagen, and on the basis of his report the Danish king decided to write again to Nicholas. A letter was sent early in April, urging the tsar to send an emissary to Copenhagen for negotiations with a German counterpart.[82] Nicholas, however, did not reply for weeks, much to Christian's irritation, and it was only on June 3d that the tsar answered that he could not entertain the Danish proposals. Nicholas gave no reason for his negative response, but Scavenius thought it was due to the fact that Italy had meanwhile entered the war on the side of the Entente.[83] The tsar's unfavorable reaction by no means marked the end of Andersen's involvement in the cause of Russo-German peace, but after June 1915 Ballin had very little to do with his schemes. He had in the interim become engaged in a more bizarre attempt to wrest a separate peace from Russia.

Ballin's second attempt to negotiate with St. Petersburg brought him into contact with a Baroness Seydlitz, the widow of a Russian officer who in 1915 was living near Christiana, where she was—among many other activities

---

[80] Geheime Aufzeichnungen by Rantzau, March 24, 1915, Brockdorff-Rantzau "Nachlass," reel 3436/232150-53.

[81] Bethmann to Treutler (imperial entourage), March 18, 1915, *AA*, WK Nr. 2, geh., vol. 4, reel 2106/956165-66; same to Jagow, March 20, 2106/956170.

[82] Memo by Bethmann, April 9, 1915, *ibid.*, vol. 6, reel 2106/956424-25.

[83] Rantzau to Foreign Office, May 30, 1915, *ibid.*, vol. 7, reel 2107/956734-36; same to same, June 3, 2107/956788-89.

—an ardent member of a theosophical group. In seances of this circle, the baroness experienced a vision in which she figured as a mediatrix of peace between Germany and Russia. This goal could be achieved, she maintained, either by strengthening the peace party in Petrograd, by bribing the war party, or by disposing of the heads of this bellicose faction, the Grand Duke Nicholas and General Dmitriev, by assassination. Her plan was to send agents to Russia, where they would contact Mme. Vyrubova, a fellow theosophist who was an intimate of the Tsarina Alexandra Feodorovna. Through Vyrubova the work of stimulating peace sentiment would be undertaken. All this would of course take money—at least 30,000 kroner for a start—and the baroness was poor, her sole means of support being a pension from her late husband's family. In looking for a source of funds to carry on her work, Baroness Seydlitz turned to her friend Ernst Jäckh, the influential German publicist.[84]

At first the baroness, who was fond of referring to herself as the *Friedensjungfrau von Orleans*, thought that she might approach Karl Helfferich, the secretary of the Imperial Treasury, for money, but subsequently she decided on Ballin, who was possessed, she said, of an "intuitive sense for the ins and outs of things" (*einen intuitiven Spürsinn für Zusammenhänge*). Consequently, on March 16, 1915, Ballin received a letter from the baroness, who styled herself Ellinor von Schütte, asking him to finance her plans and inviting him to come to Christiana to discuss details.[85] Ballin told Count Pourtalès, a former German ambassador to Russia, of the letter, and the diplomat con-

[84] The paragraph above is taken from a memorandum by Jäckh of March 28, 1915, in *AA*, WK Nr. 2, geh., vol. 5, reel 2106/956298-306. Jäckh has left an abbreviated account of the Seydlitz affair in his *Goldene Pflug*, pp. 300-13.

[85] Letter of March 15, 1915, *AA*, WK Nr. 2, geh., vol. 5, reel 2106/956310.

firmed the authenticity of what the noblewoman had written about Vyrubova and a number of other Russian courtiers.[86] Ballin felt unable to go to Norway and therefore asked Jäckh if he would go in his place. Bethmann's consent was obtained and Jäckh left on March 19th, provided by Ballin with a letter for the baroness encouraging her to treat him as a completely trustworthy agent. Jäckh talked to the baroness for three days and on March 23d returned to Hamburg to report to Ballin. On the 25th he went on to Berlin to give his impressions to under secretary Zimmermann at the Foreign Office and to Helfferich. Ballin as well as the two statesmen were all agreed that the German government should advance the baroness the necessary funds.[87] Bethmann concurred, provided that no attempt was made to murder the grand duke. Such a move, the chancellor declared, was the "*ultima ratio*."[88]

Jäckh set out again at the end of April, this time for Copenhagen, where he met the baroness, who by now had decided that the best means of arranging a Russian peace would be to bribe Grand Duke Nicholas and others in the war party. She claimed that 120,000,000 marks was the figure which would be necessary, half payable on the conclusion of an armistice, the other half on the signing of a peace treaty. When Jäckh communicated the baroness' plans to Bethmann and Zimmermann, he found that the two statesmen had changed their minds and now felt that the baroness should be handled dilatorily and that no decision should be made concerning the matter so long as Germany was negotiating in Rome for the maintenance of Italian neutrality.[89] When it appeared that the German government was not going to advance the sums necessary to

[86] Memo by Jäckh, March 28, 1915, *ibid.*, reel 2106/956298-306.
[87] *ibid.*
[88] *Holtzendorff-A*, III, report 136, April 7, 1915.
[89] *ibid.*, reports 142 and 144, April 24 and 27, 1915.

induce Grand Duke Nicholas to experience a change of heart, the baroness decided to set out for America to raise funds. Though Bethmann and Zimmermann were both opposed to such a move, the government apparently gave the baroness passage money. Under the code name of Fräulein X von Y, Baroness Seydlitz crossed the Atlantic in August 1915 and from America sent Jäckh vague telegrams and letters describing her purported conferences with secretary of state Lansing and other officials.[90] The last communication between Jäckh and X von Y was dated October 15, 1915. Thereafter there was only silence. The baroness had vanished without a trace, never again to be seen or heard from.

Though Ballin did what he could to assist the principals in these peace feelers, he himself remained pessimistic about their prospects. Neither Andersen nor the *Friedensjungfrau* were achieving much in the way of tangible results from their negotiations, possibly because—as Ballin had noted—it was not in Russia's interest to desert its allies considering its military and internal situation in 1915. Ballin was not persuaded that Germany could realistically hope to conquer Russia, for the land was simply too big and Austria too weak.[91] Even in the spring of 1915, when the Austro-Hungarian armies had completed their massive drive against the Russian lines in Galicia, Ballin could muster little enthusiasm for a peace overture to Russia, which now, presumably, would be more receptive to one. The reasoning behind his attitude was that Germany's real interests did not lie in an accommodation with Russia but in one with England. Peace with Russia was valuable only as a tool by which to force England to

[90] Ballin to Holtzendorff, Sept. 22, 1915, *ibid.*, v. See also *AA*, WK Nr. 2, geh., vol. 11, reel 2107/957725-26 and reel 2108/957899-902, vol. 13, reel 2109/958345-46.
[91] Ballin to Bülow, March 24, 1915, Bülow "Nachlass."

stop the war. Ballin feared, however, that a Russian peace might instead encourage Berlin to regard eastern Europe as Germany's primary area of interest. This, in his opinion, would be economic nonsense and political folly, for Germany's future, like its past, lay with the industrially advanced and politically enlightened nations of western Europe. But Jagow, Ballin complained, sat in the Wilhelmstrasse and dreamed of Russo-German friendship sworn on a peace treaty. "I can only explain this very unrealistic political speculation by a *complete ignorance* of Russia and Russian character," Ballin wrote to Rantzau, "which in Herr von Jagow reaches a particularly high degree."[92]

Ballin did not reject the idea of a separate peace with Russia, for it was one way in which pressure might be exerted on Great Britain to leave the war. After May 1915, however, he was less and less concerned with Germany's efforts to detach Russia from the Entente. His attention was now focused on the Atlantic, where a serious situation had arisen which threatened to bring the United States into the war against Germany.

[92] From internal evidence probably a letter by Ballin, dated July 6, 1915, in Brockdorff-Rantzau "Nachlass," reel 3439/232629-34.

CHAPTER IX

War with America

O N MAY 7, 1915, off the west coast of Ireland, a German submarine torpedoed and sank without warning the *Lusitania*, the flagship of Britain's Cunard Line, en route from New York to Liverpool with 1,257 passengers and a cargo consisting in part of ammunition and other contraband; 1,198 persons lost their lives, including 128 citizens of the United States. For one who, like Ballin, had advocated wider use of the U-boat, the news of the disaster, if regrettable as a human tragedy, was at least technically satisfying. On May 15th, he wrote to Harden that "there is at least one good thing about the *Lusitania*—up to now the hides of the English had not even been scratched and our U-boat campaign was beginning to become a little comical."[1] A month after the sinking, Ballin provided Holtzendorff with a detailed exposition of his views on the subject of submarine warfare and its effect on England.

> Whether it was right to torpedo a *Lusitania* with 1,600 [sic] passengers, most of them neutrals, is a question which I will leave aside for the moment. But every intelligent man must admit that our entire U-boat action has contributed to reducing the arrogance of the English and to complicating enormously the situation in England. It was certainly the only thing which we could undertake against England, and just as I considered the idea of sending zeppelins over Piccadilly so mistaken, so am I now as much as ever convinced of the correctness

[1] Harden "Nachlass."

of our U-boat action. If the English are not completely godforsaken, this action must show them how necessary it is for them in the future to engage in a sort of *Weltpolizei* together with Germany. If they do not perceive that now, then in the next war—which we will certainly not be spared—we will obtain with 200 submarines that which strange visionaries (*sonderbare Schwärmer*) already foresee: we will bring England to its knees and destroy its world power.[2]

The *Lusitania* disaster might have a very salutary effect on England, but what also concerned Ballin was the reaction which it produced in the United States.[3] On May 10th, secretary Jagow communicated the German government's "heartfelt sympathy for the loss of American life" to ambassador James W. Gerard, at the same time noting that Great Britain's attempt to starve Germany had necessitated retaliatory strikes against contraband-carrying British passenger vessels such as the *Lusitania*. It had not been possible to search the ship prior to torpedoing, or even to give notice, because of attempts made earlier in the war by British merchantmen to ram surfaced submarines.[4] On May 13th, in the first of its *Lusitania* notes, the United States declared its intention to impose a "strict

[2] Ballin to Holtzendorff, June 6, 1915, *Holtzendorff-A*, IV.

[3] On German-American relations during the *Lusitania* crisis, see especially United States, Department of State, *Papers Relating to the Foreign Relations of the United States, 1915 Supplement*, Washington, 1928 [hereafter cited as *FRUS* (1915S)]; Arthur S. Link, *Wilson: The Struggle for Neutrality 1914-1915*, Princeton, 1960, chaps. xii, xiii, xvi, and *Wilson: Confusions and Crises 1915-1916*, Princeton, 1964, chap. iii; Ernest R. May, *The World War and American Isolation 1914-1917*, Cambridge, Mass., 1959, chaps. vi, vii, x; A. von Tirpitz, *Politische Dokumente*, 2 vols., Stuttgart, etc., 1924-26, II, chap. ii, parts 2 and 3; Arno Spindler, *Der Handelskrieg mit U-Booten*, 3 vols., Berlin, 1932-34, II, chaps. vii, x, xi.

[4] Gerard to Bryan, May 10, 1915, *FRUS* (1915S), p. 389.

286

accountability" on any restriction of the right of American citizens to travel across the Atlantic on unarmed, belligerent steamers. Washington "expects," the note read, that such attacks would be disavowed, reparations paid, and steps taken by Germany to insure that there would be no repetition of the tragedy. Americans crossing the Atlantic on unarmed ships, whether of belligerent or neutral registry, were to be unconditionally secure.[5]

In Berlin, there was a sharp division of opinion as to how the American note should be answered. Chancellor Bethmann and Admiral Müller both feared that the outrage which the *Lusitania*'s sinking had provoked in the United States might lead it to join the Entente and enter the war. Admiral Tirpitz, as well as the chief of the Admiral Staff, Admiral Gustav Bachmann, refused to agree to any reduction in Germany's undersea campaign.[6] Even Jagow, who usually sided with Bethmann, argued that now that Italy had deserted the Central Powers it was necessary for Germany to take a strong line or the other neutral powers would follow Rome's example.[7]

Ballin came to Berlin a few days after the American note had been received. In his opinion, the United States was potentially a very dangerous enemy, one which had therefore to be treated with great solicitude. He criticized those who, like the Conservatives and Pan-Germans, made light of America's ability to wage a transatlantic war. Even if it sent neither men nor arms, the United States would supply the Entente with goods and money and would induce the neutral South and Latin American re-

[5] The American note is printed in *ibid.*, pp. 393-96.

[6] Walter Görlitz, ed., *Regierte der Kaiser?: Kriegstagebücher, Aufzeichnungen und Briefe des Chefs des Marine-Kabinetts Admiral Georg Alexander von Müller 1914-1918*, 2d edn., Göttingen, etc., 1959, p. 101.

[7] *Holtzendorff-A*, III, report 165, May 22, 1915.

publics to do the same.[8] On the other hand, Germany's honor and prestige would not allow it to give up the submarine attacks altogether merely because Washington protested. Ballin outlined a compromise whereby Germany would guarantee not to torpedo British merchantmen without prior search, provided that the United States in turn gave guarantees that there was no contraband on board and that the ships would neither bear arms nor ram submarines.[9] It seems certain that Ballin's proposal originated with ambassador Gerard, who had expressed similar views to Holtzendorff and also to secretary of state William Jennings Bryan.[10] While Ballin did not directly participate in the composition of the German answer to the American note, he described his compromise plan in writing to both Bethmann and Jagow.[11]

Tirpitz' adamant resistance to any compromise prevailed over the chancellor's conciliatory inclinations, however, and Ballin's advice was disregarded. The German answer, dated May 29th, dwelt merely on the accuracy of the facts alleged in the American note, although it did invite continued discussion of the incident. At the same time, William II, at Bethmann's behest, privately ordered that submarine attacks on neutral ships be avoided for the moment because of the delicacy of German-American relations, and that, furthermore, no large passenger ships, enemy or neutral, be attacked by U-boats.[12] A second American note—this one composed by the new secretary of state, Robert Lansing—followed on June 9th, again protesting the sinking of the *Lusitania* and repeating

[8] Ballin to Holtzendorff, June 11, 1915, *ibid.*, IV.
[9] *ibid.*, III, report 163, May 20, 1915.
[10] *ibid.*; Gerard to Bryan, May 19, 1915, *FRUS* (1915S), p. 402.
[11] *Holtzendorff-A*, III, notes for May 17 and 19, 1915; Ballin to Warburg, May 17, Warburg "Nachlass," 3737/265/803.
[12] Tirpitz, *Politische Dokumente*, II, 333-34, 349-50.

the demands made on Germany in the original note in somewhat stronger language.[13] Ballin had expected such an answer, for, he observed, England's influence had become predominant in America, while German-American citizens were politically naïve and hopelessly incapable of promoting a pro-German policy in Washington.[14]

In mid-June, Ballin again left Hamburg to go to Berlin, and he was called into conference by Bethmann, Jagow, and Tirpitz as they debated what the form of the reply to the second American note should be. Ballin reiterated his and Gerard's proposal that German U-boats permit belligerent passenger ships, which Washington was willing to guarantee carried no contraband, to cross the Atlantic without interference. On being informed of the Ballin-Gerard plan, Lansing tersely dismissed it as one which could not "advantageously be brought up for discussion at present time."[15] Gerard, however, did not abandon hope that the proposed compromise might eventually be accepted by his government, while in Berlin it continued to be given considerable attention.

At a conference held in the capital on July 1st, at which Tirpitz, Jagow, and Müller were also present, Ballin proposed that two British and two German ships be put at the United States' disposal for the transport of passengers under guarantees from Washington that the ships would carry neither arms nor contraband.[16] In the discussion which followed, a few changes were made in the text of Ballin's suggestion but its substance was preserved. Im-

[13] The German answer and the second American note are printed in *FRUS* (1915S), pp. 419-21, 436-38.

[14] Ballin to Holtzendorff, June 4, 1915, *Holtzendorff-A*, IV; same to same, Sept. 23, 1915, *Ballin-Holtzendorff*, *Private*.

[15] Gerard to Bryan, May 19, 1915; same to same, June 4; Lansing to Gerard, June 12, Gerard to Lansing, June 11, all in *FRUS* (1915S), pp. 402, 432-33, 439.

[16] Theodor Wolff, *Der Marsch durch zwei Jahrzehnte*, Amsterdam, 1936, p. 267; Tirpitz, *Politische Dokumente*, II, 375.

mediately after the meeting adjourned, however, Bernhard Dernburg, the former colonial secretary—who had just returned from New York, where he had served as a financial and public relations agent for the German government—declared that Washington would not allow German ships to be used for such purposes.[17] Ballin insisted, however, that he could not consider allowing the British to supply all four ships.[18] He was supported by Tirpitz and Müller, while Bethmann and Jagow, largely under Dernburg's influence, believed that the demand that German ships participate must be abandoned.[19] At Walther Rathenau's suggestion, Ballin consulted Karl von Wiegand, the chief of the United Press in Berlin, to determine whether Dernburg's assessment of American opinion was correct. Wiegand apparently advised him that some concession was necessary, for Ballin's next proposal, presented on the morning of July 3d, suggested that Germany indicate its willingness to negotiate the transfer to American registry of whatever ships "which bear the flags of belligerent powers" the United States might decide to use. The demand that equal numbers of British and German ships be used was thus dropped.[20] On the same evening, Ballin and Dernburg had dinner and Dernburg declared that Ballin's new plan was also unsatisfactory since it did not absolutely rule out the possibility of using German vessels. Ballin gave up and consented to still another draft answer to the American note in which the German government agreed to negotiate conditions under which *Entente* ships transporting American passengers might be guaranteed

[17] Tirpitz, *Politische Dokumente*, II, 375; Görlitz, ed., *Regierte der Kaiser?*, pp. 112-13.

[18] Wolff, *Marsch*, p. 267.

[19] *ibid.*; Tirpitz, *Politische Dokumente*, II, 376; Görlitz, ed., *Regierte der Kaiser?*, pp. 112-13.

[20] Tirpitz, *Politische Dokumente*, II, 375; *Holtzendorff-A*, IV, notes for July 3, 1915, reports 198 and 200, July 4 and 6.

against attack without warning by German submarines.[21]

The final German answer to the second *Lusitania* note, which was delivered to Gerard on July 8th, declared that Germany would consent to four British ships being used expressly for the purpose of transporting American citizens across the Atlantic, provided such ships were placed under American flags and, in less precise terms, provided that the United States would guarantee that they carried no contraband. They would then be treated as neutral ships. "Details of the arrangements for the unhampered passage of these vessels" were to be reserved for future conversations between American and German naval personnel.[22] The German answer greatly displeased Ballin, and he condemned the Foreign Office, and particularly Jagow, for having been responsible for giving up the demand that German as well as British ships be used.[23]

The German answer was also entirely unsatisfactory to Woodrow Wilson since it by no means admitted the principle expressed in the original *Lusitania* protest that United States citizens traveling on belligerent ships had a right to unconditional and uninterrupted passage across the Atlantic. Lansing therefore addressed a third and still sharper note to Germany on July 21st. Ballin did not participate in the deliberations which ensued as Bethmann formulated the German government's reply to Washington's third note. On August 19th, as the chancellor was still trying to draft an answer, German-American relations became further complicated when a German

[21] *Holtzendorff-A*, IV, notes for July 3, 1915.

[22] The note is printed in *FRUS* (1915S), pp. 463-66.

[23] Ballin was piqued at Jagow because he felt, not entirely without justification, that the secretary had been rude to him. See Ballin to Jagow, July 3 and 19, 1915, in *AA*, WK Nr. 18, geh., vols. 2 and 3, reel SA 5; notes for July 3 and report 200, July 6, 1915, in *Holtzendorff-A*, IV; Ballin to Harden, July 15, 1915, Harden "Nachlass."

submarine, believing that it was about to be rammed, torpedoed and sank a British liner, the *Arabic*. Forty-four lives were lost, two of them American. The German ambassador in Washington, Count Bernstorff, reported that the United States was on the verge of breaking off relations, and this warning increased Bethmann's desire to find a formula which would satisfy Wilson without undermining Germany's war effort. The *Lusitania* issue was finally settled on September 1st, when Germany gave the United States formal assurance that its submarines would not sink belligerent passenger ships sighted in the war zone "without warning and without safety of the lives of non-combatants, provided that the liners do not try to escape or offer resistance."[24] It was not the unconditional disavowal of U-boat attacks on passenger liners with American citizens on board which Wilson had demanded, but he did not press the point.

On the same day that the *Lusitania* crisis was disposed of, Admiral Bachmann, who had been opposed to Bethmann's conciliatory move, was dismissed as chief of the Admiral Staff and was replaced by Admiral Henning von Holtzendorff, who was less attached to Tirpitz. Tirpitz, already enraged by the September 1st decision, submitted his resignation to the Kaiser. Ballin wrote at once to the admiral to urge him, out of loyalty to the crown and to the nation, not to give up his office.[25] The effect of such an act on Germany's morale would be incalculably disastrous. "In my opinion," Ballin wrote to Max Warburg, "Tirpitz enjoys such a following among the people that to throw him out now would be just about as bad as dismissing Hindenburg."[26] Ballin continued to hold Tirpitz

[24] Bernstorff to Lansing, Sept. 1, *FRUS* (1915S), pp. 530-31.
[25] Letter of Sept. 5, 1915, in Tirpitz, *Politische Dokumente*, II, 421-22.
[26] Letter of Sept. 10, 1915, Warburg "Nachlass," -/25a/Privat.

personally accountable for the failure of Germany and England to have reached a naval agreement prior to the war, and he found the admiral guilty along with the Wilhelmstrasse, though to a lesser degree, for the outbreak of hostilities.[27] Moreover, Germany's inability to defeat England was attributable to a large extent to Tirpitz' failure to have recognized that U-boats, and not dreadnoughts, would be the weapon of the future, though Ballin blamed the admiral's miscalculation on bad advice rather than defective judgment.[28] But what Tirpitz had, and what Ballin admired in the man, were qualities which he found totally lacking elsewhere in Berlin: initiative and ability.

Two letters written by Ballin to Holtzendorff in the summer of 1915 indicate the nature of his regard for Tirpitz. In the first, written on June 6th, Ballin declared that "Tirpitz is and remains the strongest personality in our government and is undoubtedly the best organizer and also a man of great merit. It is unavoidable that such people encounter strong opposition. I just want to remind you of Bismarck."[29] The hostility which the admiral engendered was due, Ballin realized, to his imperious behavior and his tendency to involve himself in matters both strategic and political lying beyond his jurisdiction as secretary of the Imperial Naval Office. Ballin applauded the admiral's invasions of others' preserves, however. "I consider it a blessing," he wrote again to Holtzendorff on June 16th,

---

See also similar expressions by Ballin in Ballin to Harden, Sept. 9, 1915, Harden "Nachlass"; same to Rantzau, Sept. 22, Brockdorff-Rantzau "Nachlass," reel 3438/231214-15; same to Schinckel, Sept. 7, *Ballin-Schinckel*. See also *Holtzendorff-A*, v, reports 240 and 244, Sept. 5 and 9.

[27] *Holtzendorff-A*, v, notes for Sept. 26 and 27, 1915; Bernhard Guttmann, *Schattenriss einer Generation 1888-1919*, Stuttgart, 1950, p. 246.

[28] Ballin to Metternich, July 10, 1916, Bülow "Nachlass."

[29] *Holtzendorff-A*, iv.

"and a new evidence of the strength of his personality that Tirpitz does not suffer from bureaucratic anxiety and does not shrink from moving beyond the boundaries of his department when he believes that matters are being badly handled in the next room. It is certainly a pity that in the Foreign Office everyone feathers his own nest and that in spite of the great danger of the times jealousy is just as bad, or even worse, than before. I wish that there were also a Tirpitz in the Foreign Office so that Erzberger would not have to do all the work by himself."[30]

After some grumbling, Tirpitz withdrew his resignation and consented to remain at his post, a decision Admiral Müller attributed to the entreaties made by Ballin and Captain Löhlein of the Imperial Naval Office.[31]

For Tirpitz to have resigned would only have worsened a situation which, as far as Ballin was concerned, was already perilous enough. The defection of Italy, which joined the Entente and declared war on Austria on May 23, 1915, was particularly distressing to Ballin, for he had worked energetically to prevent a break between the two powers. From the beginning of the war, he had argued that Italy's continuing neutrality could be secured only if Vienna could be persuaded, or forced, to surrender the Trentino.[32] Swift action along such lines was imperative, for with its troops along the Italian frontier released, Austria could turn against Serbia and, by defeating it, force Russia to a separate peace.[33] Holtzendorff kept Zimmer-

[30] In *ibid.*

[31] Görlitz, ed., *Regierte der Kaiser?*, p. 127; *Holtzendorff-A*, v, report 247, Sept. 14, 1915, report 253, Sept. 20.

[32] Ballin to Bülow, Dec. 9, 1914, Bülow "Nachlass," partially printed without date in Bülow, *Denkwürdigkeiten*, 4 vols., Berlin, 1930-31, III, 198-99.

[33] Same to same, Jan. 13, 1915, Bülow "Nachlass," Nr. 39.

mann informed of these views and Ballin himself went to Berlin at the end of January to urge the government to exert pressure on Austria. Early in March, apparently at Jagow's request, Ballin traveled to Vienna to put what he referred to as his "not unmeaningful connections" to work on hammering out an Austro-Italian agreement.[34] Whether Ballin's influence was decisive is unclear, but on March 9th, while he was still in the Austrian capital, the foreign minister, Count Burián, agreed to discuss the cession of the Trentino to Italy. In conjunction with Prince Bülow, who was in Rome on a special mission to secure Italian neutrality, Ballin assisted in the organization of a conference which would negotiate the transfer. The meeting proved abortive, however, and at the end of May, Italy declared war on Austria because of Austria's refusal to meet its demand not only for the Trentino but for the south Tyrol and a number of strategic points in the Adriatic as well, claims which Ballin also believed to be insupportable. Italy's military contribution to the war was not likely to be significant, but its psychological effect in London, Paris, and Petrograd could not be underrated. The Entente powers would now be more than ever resolved to press on with the war.

Germany's unenviable position was made still more difficult by the fact that no one in either camp seemed to realize that the war, if not soon concluded, would prove the suicide of Europe. "I am very much for peace," Ballin wrote in October 1915 to Johannes Merck, a HAPAG colleague serving with the army in Posen, "but unfortunately I must say that presently neither in the west nor in the east are there any signs for a satisfactory end to this *wahnsin-*

[34] Same to same, March 11, 1915, Bülow "Nachlass." See also Josef Redlich, *Schicksalsjahre Österreichs 1900-1919: das politische Tagebuch Josef Redlichs*, 2 vols., Graz and Cologne, 1953-54, II, 23, 30.

nige war. It is as though we are living in a mad house when one reflects that the Great Powers of Europe are involved in converting Europe into a heap of ruins, all to the advantage of America and Japan."[35] The war had become a struggle for existence, the peoples of Europe poisoned by hatred, their governments reluctant to proffer an olive branch for fear that such a move would be interpreted as a sign of exhaustion.[36] By the summer of 1915, Ballin had decided that Germany should take the initiative in putting out peace feelers, provided that this could be done in a suitable manner. He proposed to Bethmann that the government determine what the minimal war aims of the German people were. Such a survey would furnish a clear idea of what it had to negotiate for, and if more could be wrested at the peace conference, then so much the better.[37] The next step, Ballin advised, would be for Bethmann, after consultation with party leaders, to publish a statement in the semi-official *Norddeutsche Allgemeine Zeitung* in which Germany, after noting that it had adequately demonstrated its prowess and had successfully resisted the attack made against the Fatherland in 1914, would offer to negotiate a peace. With German soil cleared of enemy troops and German soldiers firmly planted on Entente territory no one could regard Bethmann's overture as one proceeding from weakness.[38] If

[35] Letter of Oct. 11, 1915, in Merck "Nachlass," II 8 Konv. 5. See also Quadt (Prussian minister to the Hanseatic cities and the Mecklenburgs) to Bethmann, Nov. 12, 1915, in *AA*, WK Nr. 15, vol. 11, reel 401/00549-50.

[36] Memorandum by Gerard of a conversation with Ballin on Aug. 9, 1915, in Gerard, *My Four Years in Germany*, New York, 1917, pp. 413-14.

[37] *Holtzendorff-A*, IV, notes for July 8, 1915.

[38] *ibid.*, notes for July 3 and Aug. 10, 1915. See also Huldermann, pp. 334-35, in which Ballin's proposal to Bethmann that Pope Benedict XV or Wilson be used as peace mediators is mentioned.

296

Germany's leaders were wise, their peace terms would be moderate, though it would be impossible to formulate a definitive catalogue of German war aims until after the Entente had signified its willingness to enter into negotiations.[39]

Ballin recognized, however, that in the summer of 1915 there was little chance that any of Germany's enemies would respond positively to a German offer to negotiate. Russia could be ruled out. Private attempts by Andersen and others to encourage peace sentiment in Russia had come to nothing; the failure of Austria's Serbian campaign in addition to Germany's expansionist war aims in Poland had eliminated whatever inclination to peace there was in Petrograd. The situation with regard to England was equally dismal. A policy of force toward the British seemed the only course likely to produce success, for Ballin had given up almost all hope that a conciliatory attitude would persuade them of their community of interest with Germany. They had become steadily more embittered and there was no longer a will to peace among the island's politicians.[40] The war was now regarded by the British not as an economic or political battle with their greatest rival but as a moral crusade which had to be pursued to a victorious conclusion. The defection of Italy had given London an added measure of resolve to resist compromise and push on with the war. As long as Grey and Asquith had been the dominant voices in the cabinet there was hope for accommodation. But when, in the

[39] Ballin to Holtzendorff, Oct. 13, 1915, *Holtzendorff-A*, v.

[40] Ballin to Holtzendorff, Aug. 16, 1915, in *Ballin-Holtzendorff, Private*. See Gerda Richards Crosby, *Disarmament and Peace in British Politics 1914-1919*, Cambridge, Mass., 1957, pp. 20-23, and Kent Forster, *The Failures of Peace: The Search for a Negotiated Peace during the First World War*, Washington, 1941, pp. 17-19, for the hostility of most of the British government and of the public to negotiation at this time.

297

summer of 1915, David Lloyd George began to gain an increasingly powerful role in the cabinet the prospect vanished.[41]

If the chances that a peace offer would have positive results were slim, it could nevertheless do no harm for Bethmann to propose negotiations. Such a step would, besides, increase Germany's moral stature in the neutral camp. On August 1, 1915, William II, on Bethmann's advice, did in fact issue a proclamation published in the *Norddeutsche Allgemeine* calling for "a peace which provides the necessary military, political, and economic securities for our future, and which fulfills the conditions for the unhindered development of our creative forces at home and on the free seas." The bid evoked no response abroad, however, and only stirred up suspicion in annexationist circles in Germany.[42] There was, Ballin declared, therefore nothing left to do but to intensify the war and hope that defeats on land and sea would force the Entente to the negotiation table.[43]

The obvious means for sharpening the war was to unleash Germany's submarines. Tirpitz constantly reiterated

[41] Ballin to Wilhelm Cuno, Dec. 15, 1915, in "Corr[espondence] Ballin: Boden #7, Kiste #2, Politik 1915/1918 . . . ," HAPAG archive.

[42] See Hans W. Gatzke, *Germany's Drive to the West (Drang nach Westen): A Study of Germany's Western War Aims during the First World War*, Baltimore, 1950, pp. 69-70.

[43] Ballin to Cuno, Dec. 15, 1915, in "Corr. Ballin . . . ," HAPAG archive. See also same to Brockdorff, Feb. 11, 1916, in Brockdorff-Rantzau "Nachlass," reel 3439/232703-05. Ballin's pessimism at this juncture regarding the possibilities of peace with England was confirmed by the findings of Friedrich Baron von der Ropp, a German holding Russian citizenship who was active in Berlin political circles. At Ballin's request, Ropp had gone to England in Nov. 1915 to encourage Anglo-German peace feelers but had returned in Jan. 1916 convinced that England was interested only in total victory. See Ropp's account of his mission in his *Zwischen Gestern und Morgen: Erfahrungen und Erkenntnisse*, Stuttgart, 1961, pp. 95-100.

his claim that only a ruthless U-boat offensive could produce victory. Diplomacy and land warfare had been given
adequate opportunity to bring the conflict to a successful
conclusion, but neither had produced encouraging results. The war had become a miserable stalemate and
there was therefore no alternative save the last resort, unrestricted submarine warfare. By January 1916, Tirpitz had
gathered an impressive assembly of supporters, including
the chief of staff, General Erich von Falkenhayn, whose
opposition to unrestricted submarine warfare in the spring
of 1915 had been decisive in its being rejected. Falkenhayn
was convinced that the war could not be won on land unless England, the financial and military heart of the
Entente, was defeated.[44] The Tirpitz-Falkenhayn faction
was opposed, as it had been in the 1915 debate on U-boat
warfare, by a counter clique headed by Bethmann, Jagow,
and Admiral Müller.

Ballin's endorsement of unrestricted submarine warfare in the spring of 1915 had been notable for its buoy-
ant optimism and fierce language. But it was only with
the greatest difficulty and only after considerable hesitation that he could bring himself to support the demand
for such a campaign which Tirpitz made early in 1916.
Ballin was now overcome by doubts and reservations.
Would an intensified U-boat war effectively blockade
England as Tirpitz claimed? The admiral, after all, had
committed an egregious error on this point in 1915. Germany now had more submarines, but were they sufficient
to make his promises come true? If Tirpitz had his way,
would war with the United States result? Ballin was in a

[44] *Holtzendorff-A*, report 324, Jan. 4, 1916; May, *World War
and American Isolation*, pp. 229-31, for Falkenhayn's change of
heart. See also Falkenhayn's *Die oberste Heeresleitung 1914-
1916 in ihren wichtigsten Entschliessungen*, Berlin, 1920, pp. 184-
87.

299

somewhat delicate position, for if he joined Bethmann and advocated forbearance toward America he would only be accused of trying to save his ships at anchor in New York and other ports.[45] As Ballin mulled over all the factors involved, two things gradually became clear. First, Germany did not possess enough U-boats to establish an effective blockade, and, secondly, a policy of unrestricted submarine warfare would mean the rupture of relations with the United States and subsequently a declaration of war by Washington. Only if the naval experts, who had more detailed knowledge of the situation, believed that Germany commanded enough vessels to be able to guarantee a "huge limitation" of England's food imports could he support a policy of ruthless underwater warfare, regardless of America's intervention.[46] There is no question, however, that Ballin himself was convinced that the number of German submarines was not sufficient. Early in January 1916, he went to Berlin and told Holtzendorff that Germany had too few U-boats, that unrestricted submarine warfare would lead eventually to the intervention of the United States and other neutral powers. Besides, Ballin argued, England could always keep the Calais-Dover route open and if necessary provision itself from France. Therefore an intensified U-boat action should not, for the moment at least, be begun.[47]

Ballin had instead another plan. It was one which presumably he communicated to the Kaiser, Bethmann,

[45] Ballin to Holtzendorff, July 17, 1916, *Ballin-Holtzendorff, Private*. See also a copy of an article entitled "Ballin and the War Aims" written by Stresemann for the *Leipziger Neueste Nachrichten* (Jan. 2, 1917), noting that such charges were widespread and denying them. Stresemann "Nachlass," Politische Akten, vol. 193, reel 3077/135519-22. See also *ibid.*, 3077/135513.

[46] Ballin to Holtzendorff, Jan. 7, 1916, *Ballin-Holtzendorff, Private*; same to same, Jan. 6, and report 328, Jan. 8, 1916, in *Holtzendorff-A*, VII.

[47] *Holtzendorff-A*, notes for Jan. 12 and 13, 1916.

Tirpitz, and Falkenhayn, all of whom he saw while in the capital. Ballin proposed that the chancellor publicly declare that if by March 1, 1916, the Entente did not indicate its willingness to come to terms, Germany would treat occupied areas as spoils of war and would sell all private property therein to interested purchasers, using the proceeds to pay for the costs of war. Such a plan, he admitted, was an extreme measure, but it was preferable to the other equally stringent alternative, unrestricted submarine warfare, since it would not lead to American intervention in the war.[48] Ballin's notion was not seriously entertained by anyone in Berlin and he soon dropped it.

Throughout January 1916, Ballin continued to oppose Tirpitz and his confederates. He accused Falkenhayn, whom he did not like, of having gone over to Tirpitz only to shift the responsibility for the war's outcome from the army to the navy.[49] He addressed a memorandum to the Kaiser, declaring that Tirpitz had given him the figures on Germany's U-boat strength and that on the basis of that information he believed the empire's submarine power to be insufficient to blockade England. Ballin therefore recommended that the navy continue to build up its submarine fleet and use its U-boats against passenger ships with great caution until such time as there were enough submarines on hand to be absolutely certain of cutting off England's food and munitions imports.[50] Ballin himself became something of an authority on the subject,

[48] *ibid.*, notes for Jan. 12, 1916.

[49] *ibid.*, notes for Jan. 14, 1916; *ibid.*, VIII, Ballin to Holtzendorff, May 4, 1916. See also complaints by Falkenhayn at Ballin's meddling in the matter in *ibid.*, report 329, Jan. 15, and in Wolff, *Marsch*, p. 273.

[50] Huldermann, pp. 337-38; *Holtzendorff-A*, VII, notes for Jan. 14, report 329, Jan. 15, and Ballin to Holtzendorff, Jan. 31, 1916; Wolff, *Marsch*, p. 273. Cf. Franz von Papen, *Memoirs*, trans. Brian Connell, London, 1952, pp. 63-64.

supplying Bethmann with tonnage figures for the Entente's merchant marine which challenged the lower estimates submitted by Tirpitz, who wished to make the possibility of his submarines' starving England appear as plausible as possible. The cautious policy urged by Ballin and others was swamped, however, by the rising din throughout Germany in favor of a ruthless application of U-boat warfare. "Here everything is submarine war," he wrote from Berlin on February 17, 1916. "Whether with or against America is all the same to the people. It is asserting a certain anarchism in politics which I fear will finally wash away the leading statesmen."[51] Tirpitz once again succeeded in winning the Kaiser's support, and on February 11, 1916, an order was issued allowing the submarine flotillas to indulge in "sharpened" (*verschärfte*) submarine warfare after February 29th. Armed enemy merchantmen were to be sunk on sight provided that their arms could be clearly identified, while neutral ships were to be exempt from attack.[52]

On February 16th, Ballin came to Berlin and consulted with Bethmann, Zimmermann, Helfferich, Müller, and a number of other officials. While in Berlin, he reconsidered his opposition to unrestricted submarine warfare, and by the time he returned to Hamburg on the 20th he had concluded, with extreme reluctance, that such a policy should be introduced without delay. A number of factors prompted this abrupt shift in Ballin's opinion. He had become convinced, in the first place, that the German people were growing restless and were dissatisfied because the government was not employing every means at its disposal to win the war.[53] Ballin, moreover, was influ-

---

[51] Letter to Max von Schinckel, *Ballin-Schinckel*.
[52] The order is printed in Spindler, *Handelskrieg*, III, 86-87.
[53] *Holtzendorff-A*, VII, notes for Feb. 17 and 18, 1916.

enced by Falkenhayn's declaration that the success of the campaign in France depended on shutting off English troop transports, by the unreliable condition of Germany's allies, and by the empire's own desperate financial position.[54] At the same time, Ballin openly admitted that unrestricted submarine warfare at this time was not likely to succeed, for he believed that Germany had too few U-boats to impose an effective blockade of England.[55] The only result would probably be the intervention of the United States. Tirpitz, however, claimed that he could force England to its knees, and since Germany's situation was fast becoming critical, the admiral's prophesy was a hope which, however threadbare, had to be grasped. The consideration which probably led Ballin to cross over to Tirpitz' camp was the fact that he believed that the United States would not break off relations or declare war for at least six weeks following the introduction of unrestricted warfare. During that interval, Germany could observe the U-boats' progress. If the results measured up to what Tirpitz had predicted, then it did not matter what Washington did. If not, the campaign could be called off and relations with America hopefully smoothed over.[56] If Tirpitz, however, was going to be given a second chance to prove the effectiveness of his U-boats, Ballin felt that the admiral should be made chancellor so that he would have the diplomatic as well as the military responsibility for introducing unrestricted submarine warfare. Let Tirpitz wrestle not only with the task of sinking enough merchantmen to attain his goal but with that of keeping the United States and other neutrals out of the war as well. The result, according to Arndt von Holtzendorff: "It is Herr Ballin's firm con-

[54] *ibid.*, report 354, Feb. 19, 1916.
[55] *ibid.*, notes for Feb. 17 and 18, 1916.
[56] *ibid.*, report 354, Feb. 19, 1916; Papen, *Memoirs*, pp. 63-64.

viction that within a few weeks he would make so great a fool of himself (*sich blamieren*) that this matter would be settled once and for all."[57]

The authorization for the new U-boat campaign had no sooner been given than William II, like Bethmann alarmed that Wilson was ready to take the United States into the war, ruled that the regulations governing submarine warfare adopted on February 11th and put into effect on March 1st were to be suspended until the first day of April. A few days later, in a deliberate attempt to force Tirpitz' hand, Bethmann removed the naval press bureau from the admiral's jurisdiction. Tirpitz resigned.

Ballin was disturbed by the course which the rivalry between Bethmann and Tirpitz had taken. Tirpitz had advocated a policy which was sharply opposed to that defended by the chancellor, but he was nonetheless a distinguished man and a great idol among the people. His dismissal was therefore a decided mistake.[58] Some of Tirpitz' partisans, though not the admiral himself, blamed Ballin for having first secured the suppression of the submarine campaign and then engineered the secretary's fall from office. There was no truth in the charge, but rumors to that effect found wide acceptance, and public opinion, in Berlin at least, grew very heated against Ballin in the spring of 1916. One schoolteacher reported that he would be torn to pieces if he set foot in the capital, while the *Polizeipräsident* declared that Ballin was universally regarded as the "evil spirit" in the matter.[59] Even as late as

[57] *Holtzendorff-A*, VII, notes for Feb. 18, 1916.

[58] Ballin to Holtzendorff, March 10, 1916, *Ballin-Holtzendorff, Private*; same to Metternich, July 10, 1916, Bülow "Nachlass"; same to Heineken, March 16, 1916, *Ballin-Heineken*, II; same to Francke, March 21, 1916, Stubmann, p. 219.

[59] Ulrich Zeller, ed., *Schlaglichter: Reichstagsbriefe und Aufzeichnungen von Conrad Haussmann*, Frankfurt, 1924, pp. 58-59; *Holtzendorff-A*, VIII, report 374, March 21, 1916; Germany, Na-

September 1916, Stresemann reported to Ballin that there were threats current in Berlin that he would be defenestrated if he appeared in the capital.[60]

Tirpitz' defeat at Bethmann's hands in March 1916 proved a hollow victory for those who hoped his fall would keep the United States out of the war. U-boat commanders interpreted William II's injunction of March 4th as broadly as possible, and after April 1st unrestricted warfare was begun. Within a few weeks, a number of neutral and British steamers were sunk, and among the victims, much to Woodrow Wilson's indignation, were several American citizens. Tirpitz' claims that his submarines would bring England to its knees proved once again to be false. His raiders sent many an Entente merchantman to the bottom, but for every ship that went down, dozens of others scurried across the Atlantic laden with food and war goods. By the end of April, there was again alarm in Berlin that the United States was on the verge of entering the war. On the 24th, Bethmann succeeded in forcing the navy to retire its submarines from the war zone and then assured Wilson that in the future no German U-boats would attack merchantmen without giving notice and would render aid to survivors.[61]

Bethmann's surrender on the submarine warfare issue eliminated for the moment the danger of war with America, but it did nothing to ameliorate any of the difficulties which Ballin had catalogued during the struggle between Bethmann and the admirals during the winter of 1915-16. Germany's finances were still weak, inflation and

tionalversammlung, *Das Werk des Untersuchungsausschusses*, 4. Reihe, "Die Ursachen des deutschen Zusammenbruchs im Jahre 1918," 12 vols., Berlin, 1925-29, v, 98.

[60] Stresemann to Ballin, Sept. 24, 1916, Stresemann "Nachlass," Politische Akten, vol. 173, reel 3065/130738-40.

[61] See May, *World War and American Isolation*, pp. 249-52.

shortage crippled the consumer market, its allies continued to be undependable. The brief period in April during
which unrestricted submarine warfare had been in effect had
not brought England any closer to defeat and the prospect
for peace in the near future therefore remained virtually
nil. The U-boats had only excited Wilson. On the other
hand, the government's half-hearted endorsement of a
ruthless submarine campaign and its quick disavowal of
such a policy when confronted by stern warnings from
Washington was exposing the chancellor to charges of
pusillanimity and was causing murmurings of discontent
among the people. By the summer of 1916, Ballin for the
first time began to have premonitions about the future of
the dynasty if Germany did not score some sort of military
or diplomatic success. The Kaiser, he declared, should sack
Falkenhayn in favor of General Hindenburg so that—
as in the case of employing the last resort on the seas,
unrestricted submarine warfare—even if Hindenburg lost
the war, the German people could not reproach the crown
for having neglected to use everything in its power to
obtain victory.[62]

With Falkenhayn stalled at Verdun, the navy's submarine offensive greatly limited, the German economy beset with problems, the United States and Rumania
dangerously close to going over to the Entente, the prospects of a satisfactory outcome of the war appeared to be
very negligible in the summer of 1916. Given this unfortunate situation, Ballin reasoned that Germany could
do nothing but try to detach Russia while bargaining for
time to delay what he believed would be the inevitable
entry of the United States into the war. It was for such an
end that Ballin worked steadily from mid-1916 to the declaration of war by America in April 1917.

[62] Ballin to Holtzendorff, notes of June 1 and report 417, June
3, 1916, in *Holtzendorff-A*, IX. See also Huldermann, pp. 251-53.

If only Russia could be removed from the war, the Entente's ability to keep on fighting would be greatly diminished, and Germany could then put all its resources into a renewed attack by land and sea against England and France. Ballin expressed such a view in a letter to Holtzendorff in mid-August. "Today England can no longer be obtained for an agreement on the basis 'that there be neither victor nor vanquished.' Today England wants to emerge from the war as victor, and therefore there is no question of a peace with England. The shifting of the chief stress to Russia becomes ever more pressingly necessary. . . . In my opinion, separate peace with Russia is the only way to bring this war to the sort of conclusion we want. With Russia pacified, we would be able to carry on the war against England for a long time."[63]

To accomplish this aim, Ballin supported various private attempts at mediation, none of which met with any success.[64] He continued to advise using Hans Andersen as an agent, though he had less to do with Andersen's incessant travels and seems to have become disenchanted with the Dane's continuing lack of success in persuading the Russians to negotiate. Ballin pointed out to his friends in Berlin that there were a number of serious impediments, many of them the fault of the Central Powers, which stood in the way of arriving at a separate peace with Russia. First there was Falkenhayn, whose unsuccessful campaign to take Verdun had diverted troops from

[63] Letter of Aug. 16, 1916, *Holtzendorff-A*, IX. See also Huldermann, pp. 251-53; Ballin to Bassermann, March 21, 1917, Stresemann "Nachlass," Politische Akten, vol. 189, reel 3076/134880-86, and same to Stresemann, March 31, 3076/134907-13; same to Metternich, July 10, 1916, Bülow "Nachlass"; same to Lucius (minister to Sweden), Jan. 10, 1917, *AA*, WK Nr. 2, geh., vol. 28, reel 2122/962067-69.

[64] See *AA*, WK Nr. 2, geh., vol. 18, reel 2115/959430-44, for Ballin's involvement in peace feelers to Russia to be conducted through John D. Rockefeller's son-in-law, Harold F. McCormick.

the eastern front which might otherwise have been able to overrun Kiev and thus compel Nicholas II to conclude an armistice.[65] A victory at Verdun was essential, for Ballin believed that if the beleaguered citadel could be taken the neutral powers, impressed by Germany's strength, would be more willing to loosen their ties to the Entente and cooperate with the Central Powers. Prestige was at stake, and thus far no one had any reason to be awed by Falkenhayn's conspicuous lack of accomplishment. When Hindenburg finally succeeded Falkenhayn at the end of August, Ballin commented only that the change in command was six months overdue.[66] Secondly, there was Austria, that contemptible parasite. The German government should order Vienna to give Russia part of Galicia to induce Nicholas to make a separate peace. "We think we are the rider, but we are only the horse!," Ballin complained.[67] Once Rumania entered the war late in August, Austria was no longer in a position to talk back to Germany, and Ballin was insistent that Germany use its advantage to wring concessions from Vienna.[68] A third barrier which made negotiation with Russia difficult in 1916 was the agitation in both Germany and Austria for the annexation of Poland or for its creation as a quasi-independent kingdom. Either course, both unfortunately given vague support in Bethmann's speeches, would only create a Polish *irredenta* and lead to ceaseless friction between Russia and Germany.[69]

[65] Ballin to Metternich, July 10, 1916, Bülow "Nachlass"; same to Holtzendorff, June 14, 1916, *Holtzendorff-A*, IX.

[66] *Holtzendorff-A*, IX, notes for Aug. 30, 1916.

[67] Ballin to Metternich, July 10, 1916, Bülow "Nachlass."

[68] *ibid.*; Ballin to Holtzendorff, Aug. 16, 1916, notes for Aug. 31, in *Holtzendorff-A*, IX.

[69] Ballin to Warburg, April 15, 1916, Warburg "Nachlass," 3737/265/803; same to Holtzendorff, Nov. 2 and 15, 1916, in *Ballin-Holtzendorff, Private*; same to same, Oct. 26, 1916, and notes for

If Falkenhayn's troops at Verdun could be released, Austria made amenable to the concession of Galicia, and Bethmann's Polish plans set aside, there would remain only the task of convincing Russia that its withdrawal from the war was imperative. Ballin had favored encouraging such a detachment through negotiation, but the attempts by Andersen and others to such an end had failed. The tsar's government, in his opinion, lacked the necessary "courage" to disassociate itself from the Entente. The only alternative way to create enthusiasm for peace was to launch an attack on Petrograd rather than to press on with the campaign then under way in the Ukraine. But an assault against the capital would be very laborious—and probably altogether impossible—because of the lack of adequate railroad facilities in East Prussia and Courland and because of the insufficiency of labor with which to lay the necessary track.[70] Russia, it seemed, simply could not be conquered. It was not until the March 1917 revolution broke out that Ballin began to be optimistic that Russia might be detached from the Entente, for, as he observed, revolutions were sometimes made to begin wars but never to lengthen their duration.[71]

The failure of German arms to win a decisive victory on either front in the summer of 1916 reactivated the argument made by Tirpitz and his supporters, one now shared by more and more Germans, that only the reintroduction of unrestricted submarine warfare offered any hope of overcoming the stalemate. In August 1916, Ballin decided that the U-boat campaign to blockade England should quietly be resumed, but he declined to represent such a

Nov. 26, in *Holtzendorff-A*, x; same to Francke, Sept. 13, 1915, in Stubmann, p. 216.

[70] Ballin to Lucius, Jan. 10, 1917, *AA*, WK Nr. 2, geh., vol. 28, reel 2122/962067-69.

[71] *Holtzendorff-A*, xii, notes for March 17, 1917.

viewpoint in Berlin because he lacked detailed information on the navy's submarine strength.[72] No sooner, however, had Ballin come to this decision than he changed his mind because of the German declaration of war on Rumania on August 28th. It was now more than ever essential to do nothing which would cause America to become involved in the conflict. Quickly reversing himself, Ballin declared that unrestricted submarine warfare should not be introduced but rather that the submarines should be kept safely in port until such time as negotiations for a general peace got under way. By then, he argued, Germany would have still more U-boats, and its ability to threaten to use them in order to obtain satisfactory peace terms would be a very valuable diplomatic lever.[73] The final decision about the use of submarines must, however, lie with Hindenburg, who alone had sufficient information to pass judgment on so momentous an issue.[74]

In Ballin's opinion, the most feasible way, in conjunction with restraining Germany's submarines, in which to keep the United States out of the war, would be for Bethmann Hollweg to enlist Woodrow Wilson's aid in mediating a peace. Since, in the spring of 1916, the military situation, if stationary, was not unfavorable, Germany could risk assuming the initiative for such a move without exposing itself to charges of weakness. It would admittedly be difficult to arrive at a formula for negotiation which would be simultaneously acceptable both to Wilson and to Germany, but Count Bernstorff, the German ambassador, could at least sound out the president on the subject.[75] By

[72] Ballin to Holtzendorff, Aug. 16, 1916, notes for Aug. 4, in *ibid.*, IX; same to same, Oct. 6, 1916, *Ballin-Holtzendorff, Private.*
[73] *Holtzendorff-A*, X, notes for Aug. 28 and 30, Sept. 1, 1916.
[74] *ibid.*, notes for Sept. 13, 1916.
[75] Ballin to Warburg, April 25, 1916, Warburg "Nachlass," 3737/265/803; *Holtzendorff-A*, VIII, report 399, April 26, 1916, and notes for April 29. See also Johann Heinrich Graf Bernstorff,

the fall of 1916, the military situation had improved because of Germany's success against Rumania. Early in November, Ballin, responding to a suggestion originally made to him by his friend, Count Metternich, who recently had resigned as German ambassador in Constantinople, proposed to Bethmann that the chancellor declare Germany's willingness not only to enter a league of nations (*Völkerbund*) to preserve peace but also to agree to submit the war aims issue to a court of arbitration.[76] Like Ballin, Bethmann also believed that it was essential that Germany openly declare its desire for peace. The chancellor was particularly worried that the new Habsburg emperor, Karl I, who had succeeded Francis Joseph on November 21st, might independently sue for peace because of the Dual Monarchy's debilitated condition. Bethmann felt, moreover, that in making such an announcement he would have German public opinion on his side. Consequently, on December 12th, in a speech before the Reichstag, the chancellor affirmed Germany's readiness to negotiate with the Entente, and formal notes embodying this proposal were dispatched to Washington and other neutral capitals.[77] Less than a week later, on December 18th, Wilson called on the belligerents to state their peace terms.

Ballin applauded Bethmann's move but noted that it should have been made a few weeks earlier while Grey was still foreign minister and Asquith still prime minister. On December 4th, Lloyd George had formed a government, and with him in charge the chances of England's

---

Memoirs of Count Bernstorff, trans. Eric Sutton, New York, 1936, p. 101.

[76] Ballin to Holtzendorff, Nov. 1, 3, and 13, 1916, report 522, Nov. 12, notes for Nov. 11, in *Holtzendorff-A*, x.

[77] On Bethmann's attitude at this juncture, see May, *World War and American Isolation*, pp. 400-02.

responding positively to Bethmann's offer became negligible. But, at least, the offer would strengthen Germany's moral position in the neutral countries and place the British in a difficult position. Bethmann should be prepared for the British to reject his offer, and, Ballin concluded, such a rejection would probably be the signal for a resumption of unrestricted submarine warfare.[78]

As Ballin had predicted, the British spurned Bethmann's advances on December 30th, and on January 10, 1917, Lloyd George replied to Wilson's appeal by declaring that only a peace which restored the *status quo ante bellum* in western Europe, provided the payment of reparations to the Entente, and reorganized central Europe at the expense of the Habsburg and Ottoman empires could be entertained. In the face of such enormous demands, Bethmann agreed reluctantly that unrestricted submarine warfare was the only means left to Germany. On January 8th, William II consented, and on the 31st Germany informed Washington in a firmly written note that its navy would introduce such a policy on the next day. Ballin was appalled by this note, finding it both premature and unnecessarily harsh, sure to destroy Wilson's clearly demonstrated desire to arrange a peace between the belligerents. The tone and contents of the German message, he declared with exaggeration, were as provocative to America as the Austrian ultimatum to Serbia in July 1914. If the United States could remain neutral in the face of such effrontry it would be miraculous.[79] Two days after the new U-boat policy went into effect, Washington broke off diplomatic relations with Germany.

[78] Ballin to Holtzendorff, Dec. 12, 1916, *Holtzendorff-A*, x.
[79] Same to same, Feb. 3, 1917, *Ballin-Holtzendorff, Private*. The German note is published in United States, Department of State, *Papers Relating to the Foreign Relations of the United States, 1917 Supplement 1*, Washington, 1931, pp. 100-01. See also Bülow, *Denkwürdigkeiten*, III, 264.

During the next two months, as Woodrow Wilson deliberated on the awesome choice between peace and war which had been forced on him, Ballin watched apprehensively, but like the German government he was unwilling to offer any concessions on the U-boat question.[80] The decision had been taken and there could be no retreat with honor. Conflict with America had become inevitable. On April 6th, the Congress, responding to Wilson's call, declared war on Germany.

[80] Ballin to Bassermann, March 21, 1917, Stresemann "Nachlass," Politische Akten, vol. 189, reel 3076/134880-86; *Holtzendorff-A*, XII, report 616, March 30, 1917.

CHAPTER X

"An End with Dread"

T HE ENTRY of the United States in the war against Germany in April 1917 followed by a month the outbreak of the Russian revolution. At first, Ballin was pessimistic that the tempestuous events in Petrograd and Moscow would prove to be to Germany's advantage.[1] Once the initial chaos had subsided, however, the prospects of a separate peace with Russia would become considerably brighter. "Wars have been started to avoid revolution," he wrote to Ernst Bassermann a week after Nicholas II abdicated, "and wars have been ended under pressure of revolution, but to persist, in the face of famine . . . in a war which has been going on without real success for three years is a plan which the Russians soon will reject."[2]

Before peace with Russia could be negotiated, however, one of the quarreling factions in the country would have to consolidate its power so that it could speak for the nation. Ballin favored Lenin's Bolsheviks, since they, unlike the other parties, insisted that Russia retire from the war at once.[3] To encourage peace sentiment wherever it might exist, Germany should not take advantage of the revolutionary unrest to force a costly and humiliating peace on

---

[1] Ballin to Warburg, March 15, 1917, Warburg "Nachlass," 3988/-/39.

[2] Same to Bassermann, March 21, 1917, Stresemann "Nachlass," Politische Akten, vol. 189, reel 3076/134880-86; *Holtzendorff-A*, XII, notes for March 17, 1917.

[3] Ballin to Stresemann, March 31, 1917, Stresemann "Nachlass," Politische Akten, vol. 189, reel 3076/134907-13.

Russia. Ballin's willingness to offer attractive terms was based on several considerations. First of all, the prospects of a favorable settlement would weaken Russia's will to continue fighting. And peace with Russia would greatly improve Germany's position. Strategically, the tens of thousands of men on the eastern front could be put into action in the west, thereby reducing the demands made on Germany's logistic resources. This added measure of strength hopefully would enable the army to force the Entente armies drawn up in north eastern France to fall back on Paris. A Russo-German peace treaty, moreover, would have the psychological effect of undermining the resistance and determination of the remaining Entente powers.[4]

Ballin therefore argued that Berlin should demand no fiscal indemnities from Russia and agree to open the Dardanelles to Russian merchantmen. The two nations would form a close economic partnership, while Russia would free itself of its former dependence on English and French finance simply by declaring bankruptcy. Germany would retain Courland, but Austria would cede eastern Galicia to Russia, in return for which it would be allowed to attach Serbia as a vassal state and find additional compensation in Wallachia.[5] Ballin urged that the Social Democrat leader, Philipp Scheidemann, should be sent to Petrograd to put out feelers along these lines to the Russian socialists. But the German government, he complained, would have nothing to do with Scheidemann, and Russian affairs were being left to drift, while every bureaucrat fought to have his views adopted. "Any corner cigar store," Ballin lamented, "is better run than the German government."[6] A few weeks later, he outlined an even more conciliatory peace with Russia. He now proposed that Beth-

[4] ibid.   [5] ibid.
[6] Ballin to Holtzendorff, April 20, 1917, *Ballin-Holtzendorff, Private; Holtzendorff-A*, XII, report 616, March 30, 1917.

mann declare that Germany was prepared to sign a peace with Russia on a *status quo ante bellum* basis, except that Russia was to award Courland to Germany in return for German support of Russia's claims to Constantinople. Germany would also extend Russia financial help to enable it to overcome the ravages of war.[7] Separatist nationalist movements by Ukrainians, Finns, and Cossacks challenging the Petrograd government should be given no encouragement by Berlin. "The world," Ballin asserted, "will certainly have no rest if a new Balkans is created in Russia."[8] In return, Russia would be expected to enter into a tightly integrated economic and political bloc with Germany. The two powers acting together would be strong enough to keep England, France, and the United States "in respect" (*in Respekt zu halten*).[9]

The economic implications of such a Russo-German partnership were extremely distasteful to Ballin, however, for an eastern orientation of Germany's economy would mean the substitution of a foreign and colonial trade by ship by one with neighboring countries which would be serviced by rail, rivers, and canals. The Entente would rule the oceans, Germany would be left with the backwash. There would be no place in such a world for the Hamburg-American Line. Nor would there be anything for many Germans to do if the visionary Danubian schemes of Friedrich Naumann—that "comedian and preacher"— were translated into reality. Ballin estimated that the per-

[7] Ballin to Holtzendorff, May 10, 1917, *Ballin-Holtzendorff, Private*. The Polish question is discussed in same to Stresemann, June 27, 1917, Stresemann "Nachlass," Politische Akten, vol. 172, reel 3075/132017-19, and in same to Holtzendorff, Oct. 29, 1917, *Holtzendorff-A*, XIII.

[8] Ballin to Holtzendorff, Dec. 4, 1917, *Holtzendorff-A*, XIV; same to Harden, Dec. 13, 1917, Harden "Nachlass."

[9] Same to Hugo Stinnes, Sept. 6, 1917, so identified in letter of same to Wilhelm Cuno, Sept. 8, both in *Ballin, Misc. Corr*. Ballin's letter to Stinnes is printed in Huldermann, pp. 364-70.

centage of the German population involved in foreign trade would drop from a prewar figure of 22 per cent to a mere 3 per cent. "The prospectus you sent me bearing the title '*Mitteleuropa* and the Question of our Future' is frightful," Ballin wrote to Holtzendorff on July 2, 1917. "This word throws a prophetic light on our future. If *Mitteleuropa* should be our future, then we will have to force half our population to emigrate."[10] It was one thing to favor a close political and economic connection with Russia, but quite another to argue that Germany's entire outlook, both economic and diplomatic, should be directed toward the east. The public propagation of *Mitteleuropa* ideas was also dangerous in that it was provoking the Entente to countermeasures. The most important of these was the Paris Economic Conference of June 1916, at which resolutions endorsing stronger post-war ties between France, Great Britain, and the United States —with Germany excluded—were adopted. The notion of a division of the world into hostile and mutually exclusive economic constellations was, to Ballin, monstrous. He was insistent that even if Germany was forced by necessity to join with Russia in a peace treaty tying the two nations together, it must regard a *Mitteleuropa* economy not as a desideratum, but as a last resort. German dependence on such an economy would hopefully be only a temporary phenomenon to tide Germany over during the immediate postwar period, in which Germany's relations with the western powers would undoubtedly be very difficult. It was therefore only in this negative sense that a "*Dreibund* of discontent," which would combine German leader-

[10] Letter in *Ballin-Holtzendorff, Private*; same to Stresemann, April 24, 1917, Stresemann "Nachlass," Politische Akten, vol. 192, reel 3076/135420-21; same to Cuno, April 24, 1917, *Ballin, Misc. Corr.* See also Henry Cord Meyer, *Mitteleuropa in German Thought and Action 1815-1945*, The Hague, 1955, pp. 240-42.

ship, Russian resources, and Japanese "adaptability and bold enterprise" was to be accepted.[11] The *permanent* basis of Germany's postwar economy must be world trade, and Ballin held that one of the prerequisites of a general peace must be the restoration of prewar economic relations and the abandonment of the localized economies visualized by the Paris Economic Conference and by the proponents of *Mitteleuropa*.[12]

Ballin's optimism concerning the effects of the revolution on Russia's war effort proved incorrect. The Bolsheviks did not emerge as the dominant force in the March provisional government. Instead, affairs of state fell more and more into the hands of Alexander Kerensky, a moderate socialist, who was determined to press on with the war with utmost vigor, hoping thereby to galvanize the nation into patriotic support of his government. Instead of negotiating, the Kerensky regime launched a new campaign against the German front, but it soon collapsed, again plunging Russia into an internal struggle from which Lenin and the Bolsheviks emerged victorious in November 1917.

Peace with Russia was, as Ballin put it, a *Friedensersatz*. While an end to the war in the east was desirable in itself, to Ballin the primary importance of an accommodation with Russia was that by mid-1917 it alone seemed to offer any hope of forcing England to retire from the war. Unrestricted submarine warfare, which in February 1917 had been the means by which Germany had expected to

[11] See Herbert Bayard Swope, *Inside the German Empire in the Third Year of the War*, New York, 1917, pp. 12-13. Ballin was confused as to Japan's postwar role, for he also placed it in an Anglo-American economic coalition. See page 329.

[12] Ballin to Stinnes, Sept. 6, 1917, *Ballin, Misc. Corr.* See also same to Stresemann, April 24, 1917, Stresemann "Nachlass," Politische Akten, vol. 192, reel 3076/135420-21, and an interview by Ballin in the *Neue Hamburg Zeitung* (Aug. 20, 1918).

vanquish the British, had failed—after a brief initial period of striking success—because the Entente had devised an effective convoy system. At the rate the German raiders were sinking ships and the Entente building new ones, the U-boat war could, if ever, succeed only after four or five years, and certainly not in the six-month term predicted by the navy before the campaign had been begun.[13] Ballin forgot that in the spring of 1917 he, too, had approved the introduction of submarine warfare *à outrance*, and he now railed against all those who had argued that England would soon be brought to its knees, begging for peace. He singled out Karl Helfferich and Admiral Holtzendorff as the two principal villains, charging them with having falsely represented both Germany's submarine strength and the Entente's merchant tonnage.[14] The entire U-boat action, Ballin declared, was truly a "fiasco without comparison."[15] The submarines had been the last resort in dealing with England and they had failed. The British knew now that Germany could not starve them into surrender; it was becoming clear to all Englishmen that determination and endurance would eventually bring the war to a successful conclusion. The people, not the government in London, were in command, and they were resolved to wage a war of total victory.[16] The only chance that existed to compel Great Britain to accept something less than that would be for Germany to confront it with a Russo-German peace which would enable the Kaiser to throw all his resources

[13] Ballin to Holtzendorff, Aug. 25, 1917, *Holtzendorff-A*, XIII.

[14] Ballin to Cuno, May 21, 1917, in *Ballin, Misc. Corr.*; memo by Ballin for Baron von Reischach, June 6, *ibid.*, also printed with many alterations in Stubmann, pp. 246-49. See also Ballin's letters to Holtzendorff of May 10, June 11 and 29, July 17, in *Ballin-Holtzendorff, Private*.

[15] Ballin to Holtzendorff, Jan. 22, 1918, *Holtzendorff-A*, XIV.

[16] Same to same, July 2, 1917, *Ballin-Holtzendorff, Private*. See also *Holtzendorff-A*, XIII, notes for July 8, 1917.

against the trenches in France. The British would then be faced with the prospect of an endless war of attrition. On March 17, 1917, just after Nicholas II abdicated, Ballin went so far as to rhapsodize that if Germany was able to settle things in the east, England, "in order to make a virtue out of necessity," would offer Germany sizeable concessions outside of Europe and browbeat France into paying Berlin a war indemnity, while Italy would be forced to surrender some of its territory to Austria.[17]

Before all this could happen, however, several changes in personnel were necessary. Kerensky would have to make way for Lenin.[18] Lloyd George would have to be replaced as prime minister by a more conciliatory figure.[19] At the same time, some alterations in the German government were imperative. Bethmann, for one, would have to go, for the Entente would never agree to negotiate with a man whose government had been in office when the war began. Ballin therefore rejected a proposal by Stresemann that a coalition ministry which could command wide parliamentary support be established under Bethmann for the purpose of negotiating a peace.[20] Dismissing Bethmann was an unpleasant decision for Ballin, for he was hard pressed to find a man suitable to take over the chancellorship. Whoever replaced Bethmann could not be identified

[17] Ballin to Stresemann, March 17, 1917, Stresemann "Nachlass," Politische Akten, vol. 189, reel 3076/134907-13; same to Bassermann, March 21, 3076/134880-86.

[18] Same to Stresemann, March 17, 1917, Stresemann "Nachlass," Politische Akten, vol. 189, reel 3076/134907-13.

[19] *Holtzendorff-A*, XIII, notes for July 8, 1917; Ballin to Bassermann, March 21, 1917, Stresemann "Nachlass," Politische Akten, vol. 189, reel 3076/134880-86.

[20] Stresemann to Ballin, April 21, 1917, Stresemann "Nachlass," Politische Akten, vol. 192, reel 3076/135418-19; Ballin to Stresemann, April 24, 3076/135420-21; *Holtzendorff-A*, XIII, notes for July 12, 1917. See also *ibid.*, XII, notes for May 2, 1917, from which it appears that Ballin did momentarily favor a coalition under Bethmann.

with conservative interests, since the appointment of such a man would stir up the German working class and provoke suspicion abroad that the new head of the government was only another representative of the Junker oligarchy. Ballin considered a number of officials as likely candidates: Count Rödern, the secretary of the Imperial Treasury; Richard von Kühlmann of the Foreign Office; Count Brockdorff-Rantzau, minister to Denmark; Count Monts, ambassador in Rome prior to the war; Count Hertling, the minister-president of Bavaria; and Count Bernstorff, the ambassador in Washington. All were good men and none were noted for their conservatism, but all, for one reason or another, were unacceptable. Brockdorff's nerves, for example, were notoriously excitable, while Kühlmann, though an excellent choice for a secretaryship, lacked sufficient stature to be chancellor.[21] Of all the men available, Ballin preferred Prince Bülow, whose suavity and experience would be valuable in peace negotiations, but here again there were difficulties because the former chancellor was closely linked to the traditional governing elite. What was needed in the office was a firm hand which could stand up to the army and to the court and "defy a revolution from above." Although Bülow's appointment would raise problems, he had enough guile and resolve to make his will prevail. He was therefore the best man for the position.[22]

The question of a successor for Bethmann remained in the realm of speculation until July 12, 1917, when Hindenburg and Ludendorff announced to the Kaiser that they could no longer support the chancellor because of differences of policy and that either they or Bethmann must be

[21] Ballin to Holtzendorff, May 10, 1917, *Ballin-Holtzendorff, Private.*
[22] Same to same, June 29 and July 2, 1917, *ibid.; Holtzendorff-A,* XII, notes for July 8.

321

dismissed. Captain von Voss, a confidant of Ludendorff's, at once telephoned Ballin, who was in Berlin, to inform him of this development.[23] Ballin instructed Arndt Holtzendorff to ask his friend, Major Deutelmoser at the Supreme Command, to keep the news out of the press until the possibility of replacing Bethmann—the alternative Ballin much preferred—could be investigated. On July 13th, Ballin called on the chief of the Civil Cabinet, Rudolf von Valentini. Valentini agreed with Ballin that Bethmann would have to be sacrificed but could not name a suitable successor. Ballin communicated the results of this conversation to Voss so that Ludendorff could be advised. On Voss' recommendation, he next wrote to Hugo Baron von Reischach, the Kaiser's *Oberhof- und Hausmarschall*, to say that he was in Berlin and was at William II's disposal should he desire to see him. Ballin was not anxious to have an audience but was resolved that if the call came he would tell the Kaiser that Bethmann's dismissal was essential.[24] By the evening of the 13th, however, he had become convinced that the chancellor's position was so untenable that he would fall without any intercession with the Kaiser on his part. He therefore asked Holtzendorff to telephone Reischach and ask him to disregard the letter.[25]

Prince Lichnowsky, the former ambassador in London, had written earlier to Ballin to suggest that Ballin himself should be appointed. Such a choice, Ballin declared, was "naturally impossible," and, besides, he was too old

[23] *Holtzendorff-A*, XIII, notes for July 12, 1917.

[24] *ibid.*, notes for July 13, 1917; A. von Tirpitz, *Politische Dokumente*, 2 vols., Stuttgart, etc., 1924-26, II, 609; Walter Görlitz, ed., *Regierte der Kaiser?: Kriegstagebücher, Aufzeichnungen und Briefe des Chefs des Marine-Kabinetts Admiral Georg Alexander von Müller 1914-1918*, Göttingen, 1959, p. 302.

[25] *Holtzendorff-A*, XIII, notes for July 13, 1917.

and worn out.[26] Ballin meanwhile had decided that the colonial secretary, Wilhelm Solf, might qualify as chancellor since he was a middle class man and a moderate liberal in politics. Ballin did not think that there was much chance of Solf's obtaining the post, but on July 14th he instructed Holtzendorff to advise Admiral Müller of his consideration of the secretary, doubtless in the expectation that the admiral would pass the word on to the Kaiser.[27] It was already too late, however, for on the same day Bethmann resigned in favor of Georg Michaelis, the hitherto little known under secretary of the Prussian Ministry of Food, who was Ludendorff's candidate for the position.

In Ballin's judgment, the choice could hardly have been worse. Michaelis' appointment was an "experiment," a "leap in the dark," the man was an "embarrassment candidate," the mere "discovery" of Helfferich. Either a "man of vision or a Bismarck" was needed to bring the war to an honorable conclusion, but instead the German people were given Michaelis. Within a few days, Ballin declared that the situation was impossible. The new chancellor's first blunder, according to Ballin, was his inaugural speech to the Reichstag on July 19th, the day on which the chamber officially presented its Peace Resolution. The resolution renounced all annexations and indemnities, condemned postwar economic reprisals, and called for a "peace of understanding and the permanent reconciliation of peoples."[28] In his address, Michaelis misleadingly de-

[26] *ibid.* For a similar opinion, see Hetta Gräfin Treuberg, *Zwischen Politik und Diplomatie: Memoiren*, Strassburg, 1921, p. 157.

[27] *Holtzendorff-A*, XIII, report 678, July 14, 1917.

[28] On the Peace Resolution and the reaction it produced, see Klaus Epstein, *Matthias Erzberger and the Dilemma of German Democracy*, Princeton, 1959, chap. viii; Fritz Fischer, *Griff nach der Weltmacht: die Kriegszielpolitik des kaiserlichen Deutschland*

clared that the resolution, "as I understand it," incorporated his own war aims. Ballin was aghast that such a novice had had the audacity to open his mouth at all. He should have held his tongue and deferred expressing his opinion until such time as he had learned something about foreign affairs.[29] As far as Ballin was concerned, Michaelis' deportment as chancellor did not improve with time. He was soon revealed as a national disaster, incapable of being taken seriously by any one in the Reichstag. Once again, however, Ballin could think of no one who, as chancellor, could consolidate the nation behind him and also be acceptable to the Entente as a peace partner, though he now preferred Kühlmann or Bülow to the other candidates.[30]

Ballin was particularly disturbed by Michaelis' intention to establish a government body which would supervise the German economy in the crucial phase immediately following the end of the war. No one doubted that this period of transition from a war to a peace economy—the *Übergangswirtschaft*, as it was termed—would be a difficult one, but from the beginning of the war there had been little agreement between the government and the leaders of business and industry as to how actively the state should participate in this readjustment. Bethmann had proposed a mixed economy system which would permit the state to exercise extensive control over economic affairs, a position subsequently endorsed by

---

1914/18, Düsseldorf, 1961, pp. 516-23; Hans W. Gatzke, *Germany's Drive to the West (Drang nach Westen): A Study of Germany's Western War Aims during the First World War*, Baltimore, 1950, pp. 197-205.

[29] Ballin to Holtzendorff, Aug. 1, 1917, *Holtzendorff-A*, XIII.

[30] Same to same, Aug. 25, 1917, *ibid.*; also report 678, July 14, and notes for Sept. 24, *ibid.*, as well as Bülow "Nachlass," Notizen 1919 (I), p. 108.

Michaelis. Germany's business interests were intent on keeping the government's role in the *Übergangswirtschaft* to a minimum. No one was more explicit on this point than Ballin, who was alarmed that the shipping industry would be among the first to be converted into a mixed enterprise.

On September 6, 1917, Ballin wrote to Hugo Stinnes that the whole idea of state intervention was "unnatural" and that businessmen should do everything in their power to preserve their "full freedom" in the postwar economy.[31] Free enterprise, after all, had proved eminently profitable in the prewar empire. To substitute a mixed economy would only invite disaster. The personal, entrepreneurial touch, which Ballin believed essential for any business success, would be severely undermined.[32] Furthermore, to devise programs for the postwar economy was entirely unrealistic until such time as Germany knew precisely with what sort of peace hostilities would be concluded.[33] Germany's former enemies would find it distasteful to do business with firms which were closely bound to the government against which the war had been fought.[34] And, finally, if the government succeeded in imposing control over the economy it would serve only to increase the undesirable tendency to subordinate the German economy to Berlin's undivided authority. It was therefore incumbent on Hamburg to lead the resistance against this attempt at encroachment.[35]

What distressed Ballin even more than Michaelis' inept

[31] Letter in *Ballin, Misc. Corr.*

[32] *ibid.*

[33] Ballin to Harden, July 7, 1918, Harden "Nachlass"; Ballin's article entitled "Übergangswirtschaft" on the front page of the *Tägliche Rundschau* (Jan. 15, 1917).

[34] Ballin to Stinnes, Sept. 6, 1917, *Ballin, Misc. Corr.*

[35] Same to Warburg, May 8, 1918, Warburg "Nachlass," 3988/-/39.

diplomacy and his disturbing views on the postwar economy was the fact that the Kaiser was apparently oblivious to Germany's deteriorating condition. William II, he declared, dwelled in "cloud cuckoo land," removed both from men who might tell him the real state of affairs and from the German people, who were gradually losing their devotion and loyalty to the crown because of the monarch's seclusion.[36] It was essential that headquarters be moved to Berlin and that William appear before his subjects. Ballin himself had an opportunity to see the Kaiser and Hindenburg in the spring of 1917, but he complained after the meeting that he had been warned by the entourage not to say anything that would alarm William.[37] Ballin's letters to men whom he knew at court, which he hoped would reach the Kaiser's attention, similarly failed to attain their objective.[38] Ballin advised Holtzendorff to invite men close to William, particularly Baron Reischach and *Hofmarschall* Count Platen, to his parties in the Viktoriastrasse in order that "the men around the Kaiser might for once hear something of the voice of the nation."[39]

In October 1917, Michaelis' incompetence forced his replacement as chancellor by Count Hertling. Ballin was not convinced that it was a significant change for the better, for he found the seventy-four year old former Minister-

[36] Görlitz, ed., *Regiere der Kaiser?*, pp. 176-77, 295, 302.

[37] Ballin to Warburg, May 10, 1917, Warburg "Nachlass," 3988/-/39; same to Harden, April 7, 1917, Harden "Nachlass"; Johann Heinrich Graf Bernstorff, *Deutschland und Amerika: Erinnerungen aus dem fünfjährigen Kriege*, Berlin, 1920, p. 409.

[38] For one such letter, addressed to Baron Reischach in June 1917, see Theodore Wolff, *Der Marsch durch zwei Jahrzehnte*, Amsterdam, 1936, p. 277. The letter is filed in *Ballin, Misc. Corr.*, and is printed with some alterations in Stubmann, pp. 246-49.

[39] Ballin to Holtzendorff, Oct. 27, 1917, *Ballin-Holtzendorff, Private.*

President of Bavaria a "completely decrepit old man."[40] Ballin had again supported Bülow as Michaelis' successor and this time personally appealed to the Kaiser to appoint the former chancellor to his old office. According to Bülow, William II seemed momentarily to agree but was apparently in the end unable to overcome his lingering aversion to Bülow because of his role in the *Daily Telegraph* incident.[41] In the fall of 1917, peace appeared to be utterly out of the question, and every sign indicated that the war could not be won by arms and that it might go on indecisively until the masses rose and ended the conflict themselves. In late November, however, the Marquess of Lansdowne's letter to the *Daily Telegraph* gave Ballin a brief moment of hope. Lansdowne, foreign secretary under Salisbury and Balfour and a member without portfolio in Asquith's cabinet in 1915-16, declared that Belgium was the principal issue outstanding, called for an end to the war, the arbitration of disputes between nations, a renunciation of commercial hostilities after the war, and assured Germany that the Entente had no wish to annihilate it.[42] Ballin hailed the letter as an "extraordinarily happy sign," for he believed that Lansdowne's message represented the appearance of a strong peace party opposed to the Lloyd George government. He admitted, however, that the prime minister was not a man likely to be moved by Lansdowne's pronouncements. It was therefore improbable that the letter would have any effect on Eng-

[40] Same to same, Nov. 19, 1917, *ibid*. It should be recalled that Ballin had mentioned Hertling as a possible chancellor only three months earlier. See p. 321.

[41] Bülow "Nachlass," Notizen 1917 (II), notes for Sept. 30, 1917, p. 14a; *ibid.*, Notizen 1919 (I), p. 108.

[42] For a sympathetic treatment of the Lansdowne letter, see Lord Newton, *Lord Lansdowne: A Biography*, London, 1929, pp. 463-83.

land's conduct of the war against Germany.[43] Ballin was quite correct, and the only result of the venerable nobleman's statement was to expose him to an outburst of denunciation in the British press. By the end of the year, in looking back on 1917, Ballin could only write plaintively to Harden that "it's all over with me; what I have had to go through was enough to kill anybody. . . ."[44] Even the Bolshevik victory in November and Lenin's immediate call for peace failed to cheer him.

The new year began dismally, with Ballin ailing and depressed at Hamfelde. He wrote to Harden again on January 4, 1918, that there was "nothing to be done against the forces which are at work. One can only be resigned to watch the development of this frightful experience. I am seized by a deep melancholy from which I cannot deliver myself."[45] To another friend he wrote a few weeks later that "You would not find things pleasant in Berlin. Men not measures! Of the first we have a devastating collection, of the latter only in military affairs. Germany will perish from this tragic onesidedness."[46] Yet even the military, Ballin felt, had failed. It was a grave mistake, he warned, to think that the German army could pursue the war to a victorious conclusion, and Hindenburg's impressive gains in the west early in the spring did nothing to alter this gloomy view.[47] Even if German troops poured into Paris and Calais, the result would only be that the French government would move to Bordeaux and the English would retire across the Channel. The French would not stop fighting and Germany would never succeed

[43] Ballin to Harden, Dec. 4, 1917, Harden "Nachlass."
[44] Letter of Dec. 27, 1917, *ibid.*
[45] Letter in *ibid.*
[46] Letter to Eduard Arnhold, Jan. 20, 1918, in Arnhold, *Ein Gedenkbuch*, Berlin, 1928, p. 173.
[47] Ballin to Holtzendorff, Jan. 22 and March 23, 1918, *Holtzendorff-A*, XIV.

328

in crushing the Gallic will to resist. Hostilities would slow down and in their place an economic battle would begin in which an American-English-Japanese coalition would force Germany back on *Mitteleuropa*.[48] But this miserable situation would not last long, for the people, sick of war, would take over the governments of Europe. Even a German conquest on land in the west would not satisfy the people, and at the conclusion of the war, whether it ended successfully or not, the masses were going to demand a new order. The revolt from below would not come at once, but it was inevitable. A friend who saw Ballin in Hamburg sometime in 1917 recalled a conversation on this point with him. "When I asked him if he expected that any serious social upheavals . . . would take place in Germany he shook his head. 'No,' he said, 'not yet; there will be no revolution until the war is at an end, or virtually at an end. If our soldiers bring home victory, the revolution may take the form of a peaceful penetration of moderate socialistic ideas, but, if we lose, a bloody revolution will crown our misery."[49]

At the end of March 1918, as Hindenburg's armies were sweeping the Entente back toward Paris in the last great offensive of the war, Ballin wrote a long letter to Holtzendorff detailing the state of affairs which would prevail when Europe was inundated by revolution.

> The course of these great, splendid events unfortunately strengthens me in my fear that this greatest war in world history will be ended not by governments and armies but by revolution. If it comes to us first, we will lose. For revolution here means military debilitation,

[48] Same to same, Jan. 22, *ibid*. See also Hans Peter Hanssen, *Diary of a Dying Empire*, trans. Oscar G. Winther, Bloomington, Ind., 1955, p. 293, and Stubmann, pp. 184-85.

[49] Bjarne Aagaard, "The Life of Albert Ballin," *Fairplay* (Jan. 26, 1922), 398.

and our enemies will not let this fact go by unused before they settle their differences with our revolution. Alsace-Lorraine, our Polish possessions, and northern Schleswig will then be lost. Revolution in Germany will immediately occasion revolution in Austria-Hungary, if it will not already have broken out there. Revolution as a result of this war, revolution born out of the war, means the elimination of the monarchy. Then all the German tribes, with the exception of the Swiss, will come together, so that Germany will not necessarily emerge from the revolution reduced in size. In England an evolution is in progress which will lead to the supremacy of the workers' party if the war lasts longer. A powerful convulsion which will lead to exhaustion is at the least to be expected there. A worker government in England will lead the socialists to power in France and make bourgeois government impossible without revolutionary upheavals, which would suffice to weaken the country enormously. The French will not have to throw anyone out, for they are all republicans and democrats—only one president in place of another. All will want to find allies, but a socialist government [in France] will try to come to an understanding with socialist Germany under a formula of free suffrage in Alsace-Lorraine. . . . Italy will certainly be democratically governed, but the revolution there will nonetheless take a powerful form because the lower classes are oppressed by incompetent administration and their hunger has been increased. . . . Austria and Italy appear ripest for revolution. The Austro-German Social Democrats were once the most docile of all. Since the revolution in Russia they can hardly be checked and press for peace in a most unruly fashion. The nationality principle, recently strengthened through the right of self-determination, will become the battle of all against all.

Until it has sown its wild oats, a league of nations is but a chimera. For the Central Powers will not voluntarily dismember themselves. But if power comes from below, political boundaries will dissolve . . . and Slav and German may make their peace with the French. It will no longer be a pleasure to live in this new world.[50]

If the situation in the west looked bleak in spite of Hindenburg's victories, the east offered no more hope. As German diplomats and Soviet commissars began their protracted peace negotiations at Brest-Litovsk in December 1917, Ballin dropped his insistence that Germany retain Courland, and he wrote to Ludendorff appealing for a peace with Russia along anti-annexationist lines.[51] He continued to voice his opposition to the separation from Russia of various revolting nationalities. The treaty which was finally arrived at in March 1918 was exactly the opposite of what Ballin wanted, for Poland, Lithuania, the Ukraine, Finland, and other areas were detached from Russia and established as independent republics or as tributaries of Germany. This was a mistake, Ballin argued, for by involving itself in these eastern principalities Germany not only would alienate Russia but would diminish its maneuverability in negotiating peace with the remaining belligerents. Like Alsace-Lorraine and Belgium, Germany's eastern gains were not only prizes of war but valuable material with which to enter into eventual peace talks with England, France, and the United States. Besides, Ballin declared, no wise man could possibly believe that

[50] Letter of March 27, 1918, *Ballin-Holtzendorff, Private.*
[51] Ballin to Harden, Dec. 13, 1917, Harden "Nachlass"; *Holtzendorff-A*, XIV, report 776, Dec. 14, 1917.

the provisions adopted at Brest-Litovsk could long be kept in force.[52]

By early 1918, Ballin had become more than ever convinced that only Woodrow Wilson could save Europe from being plunged into revolutionary disaster. This was so because the United States had replaced Great Britain as the leading member of the Entente. Any peace which was to be made with Germany's enemies would have to be conducted through Washington.[53] Besides, in Ballin's opinion, the president was an idealist who would prefer to end the war "ideologically" rather than watch Europe be consumed in a bloody apocalypse.[54] It was high time that Berlin took advantage of Wilson's good offices, for the specter of revolution was steadily drawing closer at hand.[55] Unfortunately, Germany's will to peace did not equal Wilson's, and the opportunities for negotiation which the president had advanced earlier in the war had been left unacted upon by Berlin. The military now ran Germany, and peace could be made only when and if Hindenburg and Ludendorff wanted it.[56] The generals hoped, however, that the summer's western offensive might prove by fall to be Germany's deliverance from the stalemate war.

For such a view Ballin had only contempt. He wrote to Holtzendorff on August 1st: "I consider our situation to be more than questionable and find it laughable that one still

[52] Ballin to Holtzendorff, March 5, 1918, *Ballin-Holtzendorff, Private*; same to Francke, March 12, in Stubmann, pp. 224-25; memo by Ballin, March 13, 1918, *BAB*.

[53] *Holtzendorff-A*, XIV, notes for Jan. 7, 1918.

[54] Gorlitz, ed., *Regierte der Kaiser?*, p. 408.

[55] Ballin to Harden, Jan. 4 and March 6, 1918, Harden "Nachlass"; *Holtzendorff-A*, XV, notes for April 4 and 15, 1918, and Ballin to Holtzendorff, March 1; Bülow "Nachlass," Notizen 1918 (I), p. 64.

[56] *Holtzendorff-A*, XV, notes for April 4, 1918.

is waiting for a wonder which is supposed to happen by the first of October. There are no longer any wonders, and every day that we delay worsens our position. Time goes against us and for Wilson, and peace can be made only through Wilson. Today we could save much which must be held in the interest of the Fatherland. Tomorrow, everything will go topsy-turvy (*kopfüber*)."[57] Negotiation with Wilson would not be easy, for Ballin knew that the president was being subjected to much pressure from his countrymen and from his allies not to stop short of total victory. "You should realize," Ballin cautioned Holtzendorff, "that the Americans are in the springtime of their enthusiasm for war while we find ourselves in the late fall of our optimism."[58] Still, Wilson was the last, the only hope. If Germany did not act soon, Wilson might declare that he would negotiate not with the Kaiser but only with a German republic.[59]

On August 8th—which Hindenburg later described as the "darkest day" of the war—the allied armies at last stemmed the German advance and began to force the enemy back. Hindenburg and Ludendorff now reluctantly agreed that Germany had no alternative but to sue for peace. But before negotiations could begin, the Kaiser would have to be informed of the gravity of the situation and Hertling would have to be disposed of. On August 20th, Colonel Bauer, one of Ludendorff's aides who presumably was acting on the orders of his chief, called on Hugo Stinnes and asked him to request Ballin, his friend and business associate, to come to Berlin. Stinnes telephoned Hamburg, but Ballin declined, saying that he

[57] Letter in *ibid.*, XVI.

[58] Ballin to Holtzendorff, Aug. 8, 1918, *ibid.*

[59] Bülow "Nachlass," Notizen 1918 (I), pp. 135-36, entry of Aug. 20, 1918.

foresaw that "the duty which one intended to push off on me would be of a very unpleasant nature."[60] He did agree to see Stinnes in Hamburg on Friday, August 23d. At their meeting, which lasted almost three hours, Stinnes declared that Germany was on the point of collapse and that this fact had to be made clear to the Kaiser. Ballin replied that he would be willing to undertake this "painful mission" only if he and Ludendorff previously could agree on a successor for Hertling. Stinnes said that he believed that the general was in favor of Bülow, but Ballin rejected this choice as one which would be unacceptable to the German people, and particularly to the Socialists. Stinnes and Ballin were unable to agree on any candidate, and Stinnes left Berlin to consult with Bauer.

Ballin went to Berlin on September 2d, and on arrival conferred with Stinnes and another of Ludendorff's assistants, Major Christian von Harbou. The three could not decide on a new chancellor, but Ballin agreed to see William II anyway. On the 4th, he telephoned Wilhelmshöhe, the royal palace high above Kassel, where the court was in residence, to request an audience with the Kaiser. Several hours later, an adjutant called to say that William would receive him at one o'clock on the following afternoon. At a luncheon on the same day attended by Arndt von Holtzendorff, Helfferich, Rödern, and others, Ballin declared that the Kaiser had bluntly to be told that Germany must conclude the war within two weeks.[61]

Later in the afternoon of September 4th, Ballin called on Admiral Müller and told him that he was going to Wilhelmshöhe that evening to tell William that the choice was peace at once or revolution. He gave Müller a memorandum containing his ideas on Germany's negotiating

---

[60] The account of Stinnes' intercession with Ballin is taken from Ballin's memo of Aug. 25-26th, in Huldermann, pp. 372-74.

[61] *Holtzendorff-A*, xv, notes for Sept. 3, 1918.

position.[62] The gist of the document was as follows. The U-boat war had not measured up to the claims of its proponents and therefore Germany had failed to attain a military victory before the United States could render the Entente substantial assistance. The situation was not lost, however, if Germany acted wisely. The empire still possessed two "trumps" with which to appease its enemies and make peace possible. First, it could offer to give up the lands it had occupied during the war and thereby spare the Entente a long and costly battle to liberate these areas. Secondly, Germany could agree to a "rapid and sensible modernization" of the internal structure of the empire. Such a move would not only secure the dynasty by placating demands for reform within Germany, but Germany's foes would see in such an act the abolition of the old militaristic, Prussian system which they believed had been responsible for the disruption of peace. To Germany's advantage, moreover, was the fact that Wilson wanted a diplomatic, not a military, conclusion to the war; the fact that England was adverse to increasing the United States' prestige by owing an eventual victory solely to America's intervention; the fact that the working classes of all the western nations wanted peace; and, finally, the interest commonly shared by all the European nations to salvage their financial interests in Russia and to protect the west against Bolshevism. Ballin then listed what Germany could expect to receive from, and what it would have to contribute to, the settlement. There must be provision made for "fairplay" in the division of the world's raw materials and food supplies. A guarantee of Germany's prewar boundaries must be made and its acquisition of "lucrative" colonial areas secured. Germany, however, would have to be internally reformed before any negotiations were begun so

---

[62] The memo is printed in Görlitz, ed., *Regierte der Kaiser?*, pp. 408-09, and in Stubmann, pp. 226-27.

that it would appear that such constitutional renovations were due to conviction and not to pressure exerted by the Entente.

On the evening of the 4th, Ballin departed for Kassel by train. His friend, Count Hutten-Czapski, a Silesian aristocrat also bound for Wilhelmshöhe, was aboard the train. The two men spotted one another and sat up until early morning discussing Ballin's forthcoming task. Ballin told Hutten that within the last few days he had received reports from the United States which "made a direct change of policy and an end of the war unconditionally necessary."[63] On his arrival in Kassel, Ballin was met by a royal motorcar and driven at once to the castle. At Wilhelmshöhe, matters were in a serious state. Three days previously, the Kaiser had taken to his bed in a condition of "complete apathy" similar to his nervous collapse ten years earlier which had followed the outraged reaction to his *Daily Telegraph* interview.[64] William's entourage was very concerned and called the chief of the Civil Cabinet, Friedrich Wilhelm von Berg, who was in Berlin, to come to Wilhelmshöhe at once. Meanwhile the Kaiserin, herself seriously ill, succeeded in coaxing her consort from his catatonic state, and by the time Berg arrived the Kaiser was able to go walking with him in the majestic palace gardens.[65]

On his arrival at the huge red stone palace, Ballin saw Berg. Berg was a rigid Prussian, sharply censorious of anyone who did not share his east Elbian lineage, suspicious, given to airs, and fanatically devoted to the Kaiser.[66] Toward Ballin, he was polite but firm, and he

[63] Bogdan Graf von Hutten-Czapski, *Sechzig Jahre Politik und Gesellschaft*, 2 vols., Berlin, 1936, ii, 502.
[64] Berg "Nachlass," p. 50.
[65] *ibid.*
[66] For Ballin's opinion of Berg, see Ballin to Harden, Sept. 7, 1918, Harden "Nachlass"; Görlitz, ed., *Regierte der Kaiser?*, p.

asked him not to say anything to depress William now that he was safely revived from his stupor. Ballin next saw the ailing Kaiserin, who pleaded with him not to discourage her husband for fear that he might suffer a relapse.[67]

Ballin was then ushered into the Kaiser's audience chamber. It was the last time the two men would meet. Their encounter was not, as Ballin had hoped it might be, a private one, for Berg never left the Kaiser's side. The three men left the building and walked—with Berg in the middle—outside for several hours. Hutten observed the trio from a window. "The Kaiser," he wrote, "made a very lively impression, Ballin a very dejected one. Herr von Berg talked constantly between the two—so it went on for a long time."[68] Ballin found the Kaiser horribly misinformed about the military situation and, as a result, quite optimistic. He did manage to tell William of his "great misgivings" and declared that in his opinion negotiations should not be begun with England but that contact must be made with Wilson without delay. The Kaiser agreed that Wilson was the figure to be approached—but not until fall, by which time the German armies in the west would be securely entrenched behind the Hindenburg line. Then, William declared, he would take advantage of an offer to mediate extended by Queen Wilhelmina of Holland. Both Berg and the Kaiser were of the opinion that England must make the first move, while Ballin urged

---

428; Bülow, *Denkwürdigkeiten*, 4 vols., Berlin, 1930-31, III, 283; Stubmann, p. 228; Huldermann, p. 376.

[67] Bülow "Nachlass," Notizen 1921, pp. 160-61. According to a very unlikely story told to Gustav Mayer by General Groener, it was the Kaiserin who asked that Ballin be called in to remove the Kaiser's rose-colored glasses. Ballin would come, sit on the side of William's bed, and, clasping the monarch's hand, gently tell him the truth. Mayer, *Vom Journalisten zum Historiker der deutschen Arbeiterbewegung: Erinnerungen*, Vienna, 1949, pp. 151-52.

[68] Hutten-Czapski, *Sechzig Jahre*, II, 503.

that Germany should take the initiative. Ballin apparently attempted to bring up the matter of a successor for Hertling, but this topic of conversation was brushed aside either by Berg or by the Kaiser.[69] As soon as the interview was terminated, Ballin returned to his hotel in Kassel, where Hutten had arranged to meet him. The count described the scene. "When I entered I met an utterly broken man. He told me that he had wished to inform the Kaiser openly of the situation in the enemy capitals and in Germany, but Herr von Berg had continuously interrupted him so that he would in no way be in a position to say anything to the Kaiser that he had in his heart. . . . He, Ballin, had now given up hope, because he saw that in political affairs the Kaiser was completely under the influence of the extreme parties and particularly of Berg."[70] It is possible, however, that Berg's interference was only one reason for Ballin's having failed to speak frankly to the Kaiser. Earlier in the war, Ballin himself had admitted that when William was in an optimistic mood he lacked the courage to deflate him by telling him the plain truth. "His Majesty," Ballin had confessed on that occasion, "was in such a sunny disposition that it seemed to me quite impossible to spell out, or even to intimate, the seriousness and the frightful danger in which Germany found itself. My determination collapsed."[71]

[69] For Ballin's account of his talk with the Kaiser and Berg, see his memo in Huldermann, pp. 375-77; Hutten-Czapski, *Sechzig Jahre*, II, 503; Wolff, *Marsch*, pp. 277-79; *Die Zukunft*, XXX, no. 53 (Sept. 30, 1922), 238-39; Ballin to Holtzendorff, Sept. 7, 1918, *Holtzendorff-A*, XVI; same to Harden, Sept. 7, Harden "Nachlass"; same to Bülow, Sept. 16, and Notizen 1918 (I), pp. 223-24, 230, in Bülow "Nachlass." For Berg's version of the conversation, see his "Nachlass," p. 50. See also Max Nordau's fanciful account in his *Die Tragödie der Assimilation*, Vienna, 1920, pp. 10-11.

[70] Hutten-Czapski, *Sechzig Jahre*, II, 503.

[71] Wilhelm Herzog, *Menschen denen ich begegnete*, Bonn and Munich, 1959, pp. 19-21, describing a dinner given in Berlin by

From Kassel, Ballin went to Bad Eilsen, where he joined his wife for a brief vacation. Ballin greatly needed rest, for his health was failing and he seems to have had premonitions that he would not live much longer.[72] In spite of the negative reaction at Wilhelmshöhe to his entreaties, he did not give up his efforts to persuade the government to negotiate with Wilson, either directly through a Reichstag deputation or indirectly through the good offices of Swiss diplomats in Washington, who had been entrusted with attending to German interests in the United States after April 1917.[73] On September 30th, Ballin returned to Berlin and was in and out of the capital until the middle of October, conferring repeatedly with the chancellor and other officials. Hugo Stinnes now struck Ballin as the wisest replacement for Hertling, for he believed that the industrialist would be acceptable both to the Supreme Command and to the Reichstag parties, while his own business interests and his desire to preserve his war profits would make him insist on an immediate peace.[74] On October 4th, the Kaiser replaced Hertling not with Stinnes but with Maximilian, Prince of Baden, a man whom Ballin did not know, but of whom he had heard much good. Still, as he had remarked a few weeks earlier in opposing Count Monts as a candidate for the chancellorship, the era of aristocratic heads of state was over.[75]

Rathenau in the summer of 1916. See also the quotation on p. 212.

[72] Ballin to Holtzendorff, Sept. 9, 1918, *Ballin-Holtzendorff, Private.*

[73] Same to Harden, Sept. 11, 1918, Harden "Nachlass"; same to Francke, Sept. 10, Stubmann, pp. 227-28.

[74] Same to Harden, Sept. 16, 1918, Harden, "Nachlass," in which Ballin rejected Harden's proposal that he should become chancellor, for he was, he said, too opposed in Germany, too suspected abroad, and too tired. See also same to same, Sept. 19, in *ibid.*, and Huldermann, p. 375.

[75] Same to Harden, Sept. 19, 1918, Harden "Nachlass." For an

On the same day Prince Max was appointed chancellor, Germany and Austria made a joint appeal to Wilson for a peace based on the Fourteen Points which the president had outlined to the Congress early in January 1918. Ballin commented on this move by the new government in a letter written to Wilhelm Solf.

> I do not want to force my advice on you, but I would nevertheless like to say that if the declaration of the new government does not separate itself from the entire past with a broad stroke, if it does not boldly stress a strong will to atone for all injustices, including those committed by former German governments, and if it does not mobilize all the pacifistic powers of the world by the moral elevation of its thought, then it is worthless and can be answered by a demand for simple capitulation, thereby pulling the empire into the greatest catastrophe in world history. . . ."[76]

Ballin continued to believe that Wilson could arrange a peace if only Germany would be cooperative and reasonable and if the president could prevail over the war parties in the Entente.[77] When, after the Austro-German declaration of October 4th, Wilson demanded that German forces evacuate all occupied lands, Ballin held that the Kaiser should comply and join the United States in the establishment of a court of arbitration composed of neutral powers. This court would in turn protect the empire from any penetration by Entente forces.[78]

---

appraisal of Max by Ballin, see same to Holtzendorff, Oct. 23, 1917, in *Ballin-Holtzendorff, Private*. See also Eberhard von Vietsch, *Wilhelm Solf: Botschafter zwischen den Zeiten*, Tübingen, 1961, p. 197.

[76] Solf "Nachlass"; see also same to same, Oct. 11, in *ibid*.

[77] Ballin to Harden, Oct. 8, 1918, Harden "Nachlass."

[78] Same to Holtzendorff, Oct. 9, 1918, *Holtzendorff-A*, xvi.

At the same time, Ballin repeated his opinion that constitutional reforms were a necessary prelude to peace negotiations. This was a painful decision for him and one which he probably would never have come to had there been no external impetus. Ballin did so now only to save the dynasty. The alterations he proposed were moderate, not radical; what he spoke of was a "modernizing" of the constitution, a word he found preferable to "democratization." The Prussian franchise should be liberalized, and to offset the great number of socialists who would thereby win seats in the lower house, more representatives of trade and industry should be introduced into the appointive upper chamber, the *Herrenhaus*.[79] As far as the crown was concerned, its power—especially that of declaring war—would have to be greatly limited. "We would like to preserve the dynasty in a modified form," Ballin wrote to Count Bernstorff, "but it imperils its own existence by attempting to keep everything unchanged."[80] The best plan would be to keep William II on the throne as a constitutional monarch patterned on the British model, although Ballin believed that the Kaiser really wanted to abdicate and spend his last years cruising on the *Hohenzollern*.[81] By the middle of October, Ballin realized that William's abdication, whether voluntary or not, was the price of preserving the monarchy. But again, the question, as in the case of the appointment of a chancellor, was that of who

[79] Same to same, Feb. 6, 1918, *ibid.*, xiv; Ballin's notes of circa Sept. 5, 1918, in Huldermann, p. 376.

[80] Johann Heinrich Graf Bernstorff, *Memoirs*, trans. Eric Sutton, New York, 1936, p. 100. See also Ballin to Harden, Oct. 25, 1918, Harden "Nachlass," and Harry F. Young, *Maximilian Harden, Censor Germaniae: The Critic in Opposition from Bismarck to the Rise of Nazism*, The Hague, 1959, p. 217.

[81] Bülow "Nachlass," Notizen 1918 (I), notes of Oct. 14, 1918, p. 265. See also Ernst Jäckh, *Der goldene Pflug: Lebensernte eines Weltbürgers*, Stuttgart, 1954, p. 438, and Görlitz, ed., *Regierte der Kaiser?*, p. 428.

341

should succeed. Certainly not the crown prince, who was "even more impossible" than his father, nor a south German prince such as Max von Baden or Crown Prince Rupprecht of Bavaria. Ballin concluded that a regency for the eldest son of the Prussian crown prince, a boy of twelve, should be established under one of the Kaiser's younger sons or under Prince Henry of Prussia, the Kaiser's brother.[82]

On October 12, 1918, Ballin left Berlin for the last time and returned to Hamburg. He continued to write to Holtzendorff and to Professor Francke, letters full of bitterness and despair. He feared now that Berlin had spoiled all hopes of making peace with Wilson, and Germany would have only a "Clemenceau peace" to look forward to, one which would be far worse.[83] Even a peace negotiated by Paris, however, would be nothing compared to the revolution which Ballin saw looming once German troops returned home. His last letter went to Holtzendorff on November 1st.

The Kaiser is not guilty of the war, but what the crown prince, your brother, Helfferich, and the leading Pan-Germans have accomplished with Ludendorff will not go unavenged. . . . When the revolution comes, those who have done wrong will, of course, be hung. I am very clear on that point.

The solution of the housing, lighting, employment, and particularly the food problems outweighs almost all

[82] Bülow "Nachlass," Notizen 1918 (I), notes of Oct. 14, 1918, pp. 261-62. See also *Holtzendorff-A*, xvi, reports 946 and 947, Oct. 14 and 17, 1918, and Ulrich Zeller, ed., *Schlaglichter: Reichstagsbriefe und Aufzeichnungen von Conrad Haussmann*, Frankfurt, 1924, p. 250.

[83] Ballin to Holtzendorff, Oct. 18, 1918, *Ballin-Holtzendorff, Private*; same to Francke, March 12 and Oct. 18, 1918, Stubmann, pp. 224-25, 229-30; Bülow "Nachlass," Notizen 1918 (II), notes of Oct. 20, p. 5.

others. A retreating army, for which no housing is available, to which one cannot guarantee food, and which must get by without artificial light, which is forced to go out into the streets at four on a winter's afternoon, naturally constitutes an extraordinary danger. You must also not believe that the officers have such control over their men that the soldiers will fire on their own brothers—they have not done that for some time now. Today it is even likely that they will go over to them. If the Social Democrats of Scheidemann's faction think that they have their people under control just as the unions believe that they have theirs, it is something to be believed only with the greatest caution. Come the revolution, they will surge over the unions, the Social Democrats, and even the Independent Socialists. Haase and Ledebour will not be the leaders, but new men, perhaps with Liebknecht at the top. But even he could be outdone by others.[84]

Even if revolution within Germany could miraculously be averted, there was still the danger of the Bolsheviks importing their own revolution into the empire. This was a threat which not only Germany, but every other European nation, faced. Ballin therefore appealed to Prince Max to press for the formation of an international army which would march into Russia and destroy the Soviet peril before it could menace the west.[85]

Ballin's premonitions of revolution, of course, proved correct in many details. On November 3d, the seamen at Kiel mutinied aboard their ships and then quickly won support among the working class and with army enlisted men on land. The insurrection was not long making its way

[84] In *Ballin-Holtzendorff, Private*, printed with numerous alterations and exclusions in Stubmann, pp. 259-61. See also Bülow "Nachlass," Notizen 1918 (II), notes of Oct. 20, p. 5.
[85] *Holtzendorff-A*, XVI, notes for Oct. 10-12, 1918.

to Hamburg.[86] On November 5th, a Soldier and Workers' Council was established, and by the afternoon of the same day the city was completely in its hands. The Hamburg-American Line held a board meeting at noon on the 6th at which Ballin presided. Holtzendorff, who had returned from Berlin, was present and reported that Ballin had described the situation with "particularly comforting calm," as compared to the nervous state of other HAPAG officials.[87] Two days later, on November 8th, the Council occupied part of the HAPAG building and for the next few days used its directors' room as its meeting place. Even in the face of such events, Ballin's friend Eduard Rosenbaum found him quite collected early in the afternoon of the 8th, although his manner was somewhat resigned. Ballin and Rosenbaum discussed the problems which the postwar shipping industry would have to face, and as Rosenbaum left Ballin assured him that they would meet frequently in the future to solve these matters.[88]

[86] The best portrayals of the revolution in Hamburg from the perspective of the city's mercantile artistocracy are in Carl August Schröder, *Aus Hamburgs Blütezeit*, Hamburg, 1921, pp. 325-60, and in Max Warburg, *Aus meinen Aufzeichnungen*, n.p., 1952, pp. 85-93. There is also much interesting material in "Allgemeine Korrespondenz von Holtzendorff 1918/1919, A23," HAPAG archive, especially Holtzendorff's notes for Nov. 19, 1918. For a considerably more sympathetic view of the proceedings, see Institut für Marxismus-Leninismus beim ZK der SED, Berlin, *Vorwärts und nicht vergessen: Erlebnisberichte aktiver Teilnehmer der Novemberrevolution 1918/1919*, Berlin, 1958, pp. 101-38, 233-61; Hermann Müller-Franken, *Die Novemberrevolution: Erinnerungen*, Berlin, 1928, pp. 29-36; Fred S. Baumann, *Um den Staat: ein Beitrag zur Geschichte der Revolution in Hamburg 1918/19*, Hamburg, 1924, pp. 27-32. The best secondary study is Richard A. Comfort, *Revolutionary Hamburg: Communism and Labor Politics in the Early Weimar Republic*, Stanford, 1965.
[87] "Allgemeine Korrespondenz von Holtzendorff," XVIII, HAPAG archive, notes for Nov. 19, 1918.
[88] Rosenbaum, "Albert Ballin: A Note on the Style of His Economic and Political Activities," Leo Baeck Institute for Jews from Germany, *Year Book*, III, London, 1958, 298. On the same

Apparently after Rosenbaum left Ballin's office, the revolutionaries in the building threatened Ballin with arrest and bodily harm.[89] As soon as the crowd had cleared out, Ballin walked to his house in the Feldbrunnenstrasse on the other side of the Alster. Frau Ballin was waiting at the gate to tell her husband that during the afternoon she had received anonymous telephone calls advising her that her husband would soon be behind bars.[90] Ballin's nerves, which up to now had been remarkably steady, gave way, and he swallowed a large number of sleeping tablets which he always kept on hand for his insomnia. Shortly thereafter he collapsed. His personal physician, Professor Schottmüller, was called at once, and he and a servant carried the unconscious man to a nearby clinic. Ballin's stomach was pumped out, but to no avail. An ulcer in the digestive tract, apparently aggravated by the drugs, hemorrhaged and Ballin's heart failed. At one o'clock on the afternoon of November 9th, he died.[91]

Whether, in taking the sleeping pills, Ballin intended to end his life remains a mystery. His friends were divided as to whether it was a natural death or a suicide.[92] The

day, Ballin wrote a long letter to Bülow outlining his plans for the rebuilding of the shipping industry. See Bülow, *Denkwürdigkeiten*, III, 284.

[89] Bülow, *Denkwürdigkeiten*, III, 284; Hans Fürstenberg, *Carl Fürstenberg: die Lebensgeschichte einer deutschen Bankiers*, Wiesbaden, n.d., p. 555.

[90] Die Zukunft, XXX, no. 53 (Sept. 30, 1922), 72-73; Merck "Nachlass," II 8 Konv. 4, vol. 2, "Nachtrag zu meinen Erinnerungen."

[91] The accounts of Ballin's death differ in their details. The most accurate is probably in Stubmann, pp. 262-64, which prints a facsimile of the death certificate. See also Bülow, *Denkwürdigkeiten*, III, 284; Wolff, *Marsch*, p. 280; Eric M. Warburg, "Das Ende Ballins," *Die Zeit*, no. 52 (Dec. 27, 1956); and Stubmann's "Albert Ballins letzte Studen," *Welt am Sontag* (Nov. 9, 1958).

[92] Ernst Jäckh, Theodor Wolff, and Max von Schinckel believed that it was suicide. See Jäckh, *Goldene Pflug*, pp. 459-60;

345

evidence which is available indicates that in consuming the tablets Ballin merely wanted temporarily to quiet his excited nerves. There was nothing in his behavior in the last few days of his life to show that he had such an end in mind. To the contrary, he had continued until his last conscious hour to lay plans for the rebirth of the HAPAG once the war was ended. But his body, worn out by the nervous depression of four long years of war and then burdened by an overdose of drugs, was at last simply unable to carry on any longer.

It was, in any case, a fit moment for his departure, for Ballin himself had said that he had no desire to survive to live in a new and frighteningly different world. His own lifework was at an end, the HAPAG destroyed, and Germany vanquished. The new order seemed likely to be a socialist, workers' state, dedicated to the abolition of free enterprise and of a society of orders, ranks, and classes. Death, under such circumstances, must to Ballin have seemed preferable to life. If he did not will to die, it was fortunate that his body deserted him in the hour of imperial Germany's collapse. He did not live to see the disgrace of William II's flight into Holland, the establishment of the socialist republic, the armistice, the humiliating peace, the occupation, and the dismemberment of the Hamburg-American Line as a prize of war. And finally, as a Jew, he was spared that which Warburg and Wolff and other of his

---

Wolff, *Marsch*, pp. 280-82; and Schinckel, *Lebenserinnerungen*, Hamburg, n.d., p. 269. For the view that Ballin's was a natural death, see Warburg, *Aus meinen Aufzeichnungen*, p. 69; Bülow, *Denkwürdigkeiten*, III, 284. Rosenbaum admits that there is circumstantial evidence pointing to suicide, but holds that in taking the tablets Ballin was "undecided whether he wanted a long or an eternal sleep." Rosenbaum, "A Note," 298-99, and letter to author, Sept. 4, 1964. Among Ballin's biographers, Stubmann (pp. 263-64) indicates that he rejects the suicide theory, while Huldermann (p. 378) avoids the issue altogether.

friends would later have to suffer. "Better," he had often said, "an end with dread, than dread without end." (*Lieber ein Ende mit Schrecken als Schrecken ohne Ende.*)

The funeral was held on November 13th at Ohlsdorf, a suburb of Hamburg. In the midst of revolution, the city paused to pay tribute to its most distinguished citizen, and from Amerongen the ex-Kaiser telegraphed his condolences to Frau Ballin.[93] Hundreds of mourners followed the coffin, draped by the blue and white HAPAG ensign, as it was borne to the grave. In Hamburg fashion, Max Warburg delivered an oration praising not Ballin the man, but Ballin the great entrepreneur, the visionary and pioneer, the businessman without peer. Some months later, a rustic boulder was placed at the site. No inscription was cut into this stone, but only the name of the uncommon and tragic man whose resting place it was to guard.

[93] In later years, William II continued to remember his friend. On the occasion of Frau Ballin's 80th birthday in 1934, the Kaiser sent her a photograph and the following wire. "Along with you, I think today of your husband, who left us and his work all too soon. I will always retain an esteemed memory of this true and loyal man. I owe much stimulation to his creative spirit. His name will live on in the history of German shipping." Frau Ballin died in 1937, while the couple's only child, Irmgard, succumbed to influenza only six months after her father's death. The wire to Frau Ballin is framed and hung in the Hamburg office of Eric M. Warburg, who kindly allowed me to copy it.

CHAPTER XI

Conclusion

T HE EMERGENCE in Germany in the second half of the nineteenth century of men such as Albert Ballin, Hugo Stinnes, the Rathenaus, and the Siemens, together with their banker associates, meant that a force had evolved which would give to Prussia and to the German empire over which it presided after 1871 a radically new character. It was these men at the top of the middle class who raised Germany to a commercial and industrial preeminence which it had never before known and to a wealth which was the envy of many another nation.

The growth of a successful and vastly wealthy upper middle class in Germany raised two problems, one external, the other internal. First, what was to be the relation of this new industrial Germany which these men had created to the long established Great Powers of Europe, and especially to England? Secondly, how could this new plutocracy be fitted into the traditional social and political structure of Prussia and of the empire?

The rapid economic development of Germany after 1850 was profoundly disturbing to the British, who regarded it as a threat to the commercial and industrial hegemony which they had secured in almost every area of the world. They soon came to regard the bustling activity in Hamburg, Essen, and Düsseldorf as equally pernicious a manifestation of the new Germany as the eccentric diplomacy of William II and the mammoth fleet being constructed by Admiral Tirpitz. There was, of course, good reason for concern, for not only Germany, but also the United States and Japan, were gradually insinuating themselves into markets or industries which had traditionally been the preserve of the British.

As a man of commerce, Ballin was well aware of the necessity of keeping the world at peace and the seas free of interference so that Germany's trade could flourish. Without the cooperation of the British this would not be possible, for Great Britain was the pivot of the world economy, the diplomatic arbiter of Europe, and possessed as well a navy which could at will drive the ships of other powers from the seas. Ballin therefore never ceased to preach that the preservation and deepening of Anglo-German harmony should be the keystone of German policy. He knew that he himself was a thorn to the British, for the principal victims of the HAPAG's rise had been those English shipping lines which had theretofore enjoyed a leading position in the moving of goods and passengers to and from Europe. Ballin was ruthless and enormously ambitious, to be sure, but he believed that the HAPAG had constantly to move forward if it was to maintain its commanding position in world shipping. He did everything he could, given the dictates of competition and the legitimate expectations of his stockholders, to mollify the rivalry between the HAPAG and its British rivals. On a broader front, Ballin tried to convince the British that the world was large enough and undeveloped enough for the trade of both nations, and that there was therefore no reason why the two kindred peoples could not forever enjoy a peaceful and profitable coexistence.

Unfortunately, commercial rivalry was only one item of friction between Germany and England. After 1880, Germany's imperial ventures in Africa and in the Pacific enlarged the area in which conflict between the two empires was possible. There was, moreover, the antic behavior of

349

William II, who elevated an unerring sense for tactlessness to the level of virtuosity. The Kaiser did much to undermine the work of men like Ballin who were sincerely interested in building better relations between Englishmen and Germans. More alarming to the British than the Kaiser was Admiral Tirpitz and the navy which he began to construct after 1898, one which they could not help but believe was being directed against England. Although the naval race between the two powers was quickly recognized as a leading cause of ill-feeling, which, if stupidly handled, could lead to war and the dissolution of oceanic commerce, some of Tirpitz' chief supporters were those very men of business, including Ballin, whose first concern was peace with England. It was not until Tirpitz had been in office for over a decade that Ballin realized the dangerous consequences of the admiral's ambitions. But by then irreparable damage had been done to Anglo-German relations, and so powerful had Tirpitz' grasp on the German people and their ruler become that attempts to fashion a compromise on the naval question proved impossible.

The second question occasioned by the emergence of the German plutocracy was that of its relation to the German state ruled by the Prussian aristocracy and William II. The examination made here of Ballin's association with the Junkers indicates that he, and his colleagues in the business world, were not absorbed into this aristocracy, but rather that they were allowed to coexist in a socially inferior and politically officeless position, one which—whatever its irritations and humiliations—did not prevent their continuing amassment of still greater wealth. The leaders of the German middle class accepted the role assigned them without protest, and it was not until the end of a catastrophic war that Ballin realized that the Junker regime had been responsible for Germany's ruin. Only then did he call for a "modernizing" of the constitution.

In England, the first nation in which a wealthy middle class appeared, the effect of such a development had been a liberalization of political institutions through a broadening of the parliamentary base of the government. Much the same sequence had also occurred in France and elsewhere in Europe. In Germany, however, where the pulse of industrialization was more intense and its spead as, if not more, extensive, a liberal state failed to materialize. The vital question in any discussion of imperial Germany's history is why this was so.

Part of the explanation lies in the obdurate refusal of the Prussian aristocracy to embrace any program of liberal political reform. There were few nineteenth century Junkers who were ideologically related to the second Earl Grey, or Shaftesbury, or to the other great aristocratic pillars of English liberalism. The German *haute bourgeoisie* would therefore have been forced to assume the leadership of any movement in favor of political reform. It could expect only hostility from above; it was suspicious of associating with those who occupied inferior positions in society for fear that reform might all too easily slip into revolution.

The upper reaches of the German middle class declined, however, to lead the struggle for a liberal empire. There were three reasons for their failure to do so. The first was the fact that for many years they had no fundamental objection to the way in which affairs of state were being conducted. What they desired from the government was that their economic interests be favored, and this, more often than not, the government was willing to do. In Ballin's case, it was only in 1908 that Tirpitz' naval mania caused him to begin to protest actively against a political program endorsed by the government because he believed that it was endangering the continuation of peace between Germany and England.

Secondly, although liberal constitutional reform would give the upper middle class a more regular form of political power, Ballin regarded such reform as dangerous because, once introduced, its subsequent progress could not be controlled. A parliamentary regime similar to that in England might be desirable inasmuch as it would give the moneyed interest an official position in the government. Had Ballin felt that it would have been possible to call a halt to reform at this point he might have approved alterations in the constitution which would have effected such a change. But parliamentary liberalism, to him, would be only a way station on the rapid descent into a socialistic Germany, a prospect so chilling that any inclination to tamper with the political structure vanished. Ballin's horror of socialism, one should remember, was not imaginary. Hamburg was, next to Berlin, the great center of Social Democrat strength, much of which resulted from the party's hold on the seamen who were employed by the HAPAG and other lines. The Social Democrats commanded more votes and more Reichstag seats than any other party, and they were growing. If most of the rank and file of the party was revisionist in outlook, its leadership was noted for its impassioned and incendiary avowal of orthodox Marxism.

The third cause for the failure of important businessmen such as Ballin to aid the liberal movement was their confidence that reform really was not necessary. Although the upper middle class might be socially and politically excluded from the Junker establishment, its members were nonetheless frequently able to influence policy along lines which would serve their interests. This influence they felt they wielded in many ways: through pressure groups which they organized or to which they belonged; through newspapers which they owned and edited; through banks which handled the financial affairs of countless politically important aristocrats and many of the corporations in which they had investments; by using their vast wealth to entertain and render favors to government dignitaries; and especially by making their wants known to those in power, from the lowliest *Ministerialrat* to the crown itself. There were numerous occasions on which no amount of cajolery or pressure by Ballin and other businessmen could budge William II or his government, but there were also many others—in Ballin's case, for example, the Morgan Trust agreement of 1902, the Bagdad railroad affair, and the shipping indemnity bill during the war— in which their efforts bore fruit. Success bred satisfaction with the established order.

There were, unfortunately, a number of inaccuracies in Ballin's estimation of his political position in Wilhelmine Germany. The sort of government in which he and his friends acquiesced was only a perpetuation of the old semi-autocratic and aristocratic regime, one which now deigned to admit to its deliberations—on an unofficial, consultative basis—a small circle of economic leaders. Ballin's first error was his belief that a government based on such foundations would be stable and effective. In taking his place in such a system, he failed to perceive that while he could now with some justification feel that he was an influence in Berlin, the government was still an infirm anachronism. It did nothing to include the great majority of the middle class in the political structure, it excluded the working class entirely, it relegated the Reichstag to a decorative appendage in which much could be said but little accomplished. As Germany became increasingly industrialized, such a government became more and more outmoded and the people increasingly insistent on being given a voice in the government. But Ballin was oblivious to such stirrings at the heart of the nation. Like the Junkers, he was elitist and paternalistic. If the economy continued to prosper and peace was preserved, the people had neither cause nor right to complain at the sort of government which controlled the state. It was like running the HAPAG: a comfortable annual balance sheet discouraged stockholders from modifying the administrative mechanism or from questioning the wisdom of the long-range goals of the concern. Ballin and the upper middle class were conspicuous for their inability to understand that the success of the HAPAG and thousands of other German firms had created a Germany in which an intelligent, ambitious, and quickly growing working population would naturally protest against a social and political structure based on feudal, agricultural relationships. To Ballin, these were not legitimate complaints, and he therefore rejected them, as did the governing aristocracy, sometimes with force, sometimes with calculating benevolence.

Secondly, Ballin erred in believing that his influence —or anyone else's—could ever be thoroughly effective with the ultimate source of power in imperial Germany— William II. With the Kaiser, the determination or alteration of policy through the application of influence would always be unsatisfactory, for there could never be any guarantee that William would follow the advice tendered to him, no matter how reasonable or logical it might be. In spite of his fraudulent bonhomie, the Kaiser was an autocrat with pretensions, and it was almost impossible to talk to him man to man. The ruler could not be corrected or rebuked, and indeed his excitable nerves necessitated his being mollycoddled. The attention which men of wealth showered on William—in which he took a delight as vulgar as the obsequious deference paid him—did nothing to attenuate his tendencies toward megalomania. When one of the Kaiser's oral forays resulted in a diplomatic embarrassment, as in the case of the *Daily Telegraph* incident, Ballin might lament the *gaffe* in private but he did not feel that he could speak boldly to William. In Ballin's defense, one should remember that it is not easy to wax pedagogic with emperors, especially not with one such as William II. Besides, the Kaiser was very persuasive, and he could make others believe that he had actually been the hapless victim of a mistake committed by someone else. Like many other men of sharp vision in the world of business, when he came to court Ballin developed cataracts which greatly reduced his effectiveness. He was aware of William's unfortunate characteristics, and it was doubtful wisdom to acquiesce in the concentration of immense power in the hands of an emotionally disturbed man who was not likely to be amenable to good counsel. Only constitutional reform of the crown's prerogatives could protect the empire from the caprice of its sovereign, but Ballin could not bring himself to such a step until the end of the war.

There was one last error in Ballin's estimation of his position. He knew that there were powerful voices in Berlin which were strongly opposed to what he stood for, but he persisted, at least until the collapse of the Haldane Mission in 1912, in believing that the counsels of peace which he represented would prevail over those which spoke ominously of the inexorable, and even welcome, approach of a war with England. He overlooked the fact that it was essentially only in *economic* affairs that the specialized opinion of businessmen was heeded by the government. In *political* questions, the advice given by Ballin was often reviewed but seldom followed, and sometimes his intervention in affairs of state was regarded as gratuitous and offensive. Ballin failed to understand that for every man like himself or Warburg or Fürstenberg, occasionally present at court or in the Wilhelmstrasse to further some political or economic end, there were ten Junkers permanently at work there; that for every plea for friendship with England, there were ten warnings by Tirpitz and his followers that compromise would only invite disaster. Although the upper middle class had succeeded in gaining entrée in Berlin for themselves as advisers to the leaders of the government, their numbers were insufficient and their presence too spasmodic. They could not prevail against the bellicose inclinations of the admirals and the reactionary counsels of the Junkers surrounding a ruler who was inclined at times to act without consulting anyone and who was constitutionally empowered to indulge in such reckless independence.

Because of their success in resolving economic problems and the ease with which they had access to the centers of political power, the German *haute bourgeoisie* was misled into believing that it was also influential in politics. Ballin's tragedy was that he did not realize in time that he had exaggerated his ability to affect political as well as economic policy. When he at last became aware of his error, it was too late. In the struggle for influence, Ballin lost and the Anglophobes won. The result was an ever larger navy, an unaccommodating diplomacy, an increasingly fixed committal to Vienna's Balkan ambitions, and, in the end, war with England.

Bibliographical Essay

I am indebted to the following publishers for permission to quote excerpts from works which they have brought out: Charles Scribner's Sons, Winston S. Churchill, *The World Crisis*; Hermann Böhlaus Nachf., Josef Redlich, *Schicksalsjahre Österreichs 1908-1919*; Hans Christians Druckerei und Verlag, Peter Franz Stubmann, *Mein Feld ist die Welt: Albert Ballin, sein Leben*; Deutsche Verlags-Anstalt, Ernst Jäckh, *Der goldene Pflug*; C. A. Starke Verlag, Magnus von Braun, *Von Ostpreussen bis Texas*; H. M. Stationery Office, G. P. Gooch and H. W. V. Temperley, eds., *British Documents on the Origins of the War 1898-1914*; Musterschmidt-Verlag, Walter Görlitz ed., *Der Kaiser . . . : Aufzeichnungen des Chefs des Marinekabinetts Admiral Georg Alexander v. Müller*; F. J. Steinkopf, Friedrich von der Ropp, *Zwischen Gestern und Morgen*.

I. Unpublished Sources

Berlin-Dahlem, Hauptarchiv

The collection of Holtzendorff-Ballin papers (*Holtzendorff-A*) deposited here is the most extensive source dealing with Ballin which has survived, and is, besides, a very valuable commentary on German politics during the Great War. These papers have never before been used by scholars. The 16 volumes of material are assembled in fifteen bulky cartons, amounting to a total of approximately 6,000 pages, and consists of the correspondence between Ballin and Arndt von Holtzendorff from August 1914 to November 1918. The collection is not complete, for one volume has been lost and there are documents missing from most of the others. The reports (*Berichte*) are numbered chronologically and run from 1 to 25 pages in length. In them, Holtzendorff describes his activities day by day

for Ballin, often repeating Ballin's directions and record-
ing the gist of calls or letters. Of Holtzendorff's 968
Berichte, the Hauptarchiv has 875. When Ballin was in
Berlin, Holtzendorff composed *Notizen*, or notes, also
from 1 to 25 pages long, so that Ballin would have a record
of what he had said and done while in the capital. Since
the *Notizen* are almost completely concerned with what
Ballin did and not with Holtzendorff's activities, they are
generally more valuable than the reports. Finally, there are
a number of letters between the two men.

Hamburg, HAPAG archive

The Hamburg-American Line possesses an immense
collection of company records covering the period during
which Ballin served as managing director, as well as a large
store of newspaper clippings and photographs, and an
excellent library of monographs dealing with the shipping
industry. Those records which were made available to me
—notably the Haller "Nachlass," HAPAG, "Privat-Post,"
and the line's secret "Contract Buch"—were most informative. The HAPAG's house organ, *Zeitschrift der Hamburg-
Amerika Linie*, is very valuable, especially until the end
of 1907, when its size was drastically reduced. The *Zeitschrift*, published for private circulation among certain of
the company's office and ship personnel, in 1915 became
the *Kriegs-Zeitschrift der Hamburg-Amerika Linie*, a
somewhat polemical bulletin which was no longer considered confidential. Personal material on Ballin in the
line's files is very thin, especially for the prewar years, for
which there is only the Landau "Nachlass," which
contributes little of interest, and a guest register, "Zu
Gast bei Albert Ballin," kept in Ballin's fine hand from
1902 to 1918. For the war years, the HAPAG's holdings are
more extensive, containing Ballin's letters to his rival,
Philipp Heineken of the North German Lloyd, and to his

Hamburg banker friend, Max von Schinckel. Both files, cited as *Ballin-Heineken* and *Ballin-Schinckel*, stick narrowly to business matters. There is also a file (*Ballin-Holtzendorff, Private*) of Ballin's letters to his Berlin agent, Arndt von Holtzendorff, letters which deal more with political affairs and tell much. The HAPAG archive also contains extracts of a small part of Holtzendorff's business correspondence with Ballin, cited in the text as *Holtzendorff-B*. This collection contains some material which is missing from, or not included in, the originals of this correspondence, cited as *Holtzendorff-A*, which is discussed above under Berlin-Dahlem, Hauptarchiv. Additional material of some importance is located in three miscellaneous files: HAPAG-V, BAB, and *Ballin, Misc. Corr.*

Hamburg, Staatsarchiv

The "Nachlass" of Johannes Merck, a director of the HAPAG from 1910 to 1915, is an unusual source, for it is one of the few accounts which provides insight into Ballin's relations with his colleagues within the Hamburg-American Line. Much that Merck says, however, has to be discounted because of the violent antipathy he felt toward Ballin. His account is nonetheless of the greatest value, as is the accompanying collection of newspaper clippings and other memorabilia which is assembled in the appendices to the "Erinnerungen." There are also 5 letters and 2 telegrams by Ballin to Merck, all dating from the war years, as well as many more between Merck and other associates in the HAPAG.

Koblenz, Bundesarchiv

Of particular importance for Ballin are folders 4 through 7 of the Maximilian Harden "Nachlass," containing some 160 letters from Ballin to Harden, dating from 1909 to 1918. In addition to these letters, there is also a smaller file of "Fragmente," which contains correspondence by Harden which is related to Ballin. Some of the material in the letters between Ballin and Harden has been printed in Helmuth Rogge, *Holstein und Harden: politisch-publizistisches Zusammenspiel zweier Aussenseiter des Wilhelminischen Reichs*, Munich, 1959, and by Harden himself in "Nach dreissig Jahren," *Die Zukunft*, xxx, no. 53 (Sept. 30, 1922), 229-52. A recent study by Harry F. Young, *Maximilian Harden, Censor Germaniae: the Critic in Opposition from Bismarck to the Rise of Nazism*, The Hague, 1959, is of some help in using this collection. Included in the Harden "Nachlass" are over a hundred letters by Carl Fürstenberg and his wife to Harden, both friends of Ballin. These letters are closed to scholars, but I am advised by Dr. Wolfgang Mommsen of the Bundesarchiv that, surprisingly, they contain nothing of importance on Ballin.

The immense collection of papers left by Prince Bülow includes many items of interest, but it must be used with discretion because of the chancellor's tendency to indulge in exaggeration, if not prevarication. The Bülow "Nachlass" contains 21 letters by Ballin to the prince and a copy of one very important communication by him to Count Metternich. There is a small amount of additional material on Ballin in folders 32 and 131, referred to in the Key to Abbreviations on page xvi, and considerably more in the diary (*Notizen*) which Bülow kept, as well as in his *Merkblätter*, notebooks in which the prince scribbled miscellaneous observations and reflections. An exhaustive survey of the "Nachlass" is Friedrich Freiherr Hiller von Gaertringen, *Fürst Bülows Denkwürdigkeiten: Untersuchungen zu ihrer Entstehungsgeschichte und ihrer Kritik*, Tübingen, 1956.

The Freyer "Nachlass" is a sprawling collection, alternately tiresome and revealing, of use in exposing the hostility to Ballin in Hamburg maritime circles.

The "Nachlass" of Wilhelm Solf, successively colonial secretary and foreign secretary under William II, contains 7 items by Ballin to Solf from the years 1913-18, one letter by Solf to Ballin, and one by Wilhelm Cuno to Solf.

Two other collections, both very important for the period but of only marginal interest for Ballin, are the "Nachlass" of Friedrich von Berg and that of Wilhelm Widenmann. The Berg papers give details of Ballin's last audience with the Kaiser in September 1918, while Widenmann's account contributes to an understanding of Tirpitz' relationship to Ballin.

London, Public Record Office

The Public Record Office has on deposit a hoard of documents dealing with the imperial German navy. Of particular interest for Ballin were the records of the *Marine-Kabinets* cited on page xiv. For a guide to these papers, see F. H. Hinsley and H. M. Ehrmann, *A Catalog of Selected Files of the German Naval Archives Microfilmed at the Admiralty, London . . .* , London, 1959.

London, Warburg Institute

The correspondence between Max Warburg and Ballin filed here contains scores of letters, the first written in 1909, the last in 1918. Though the two men were very close friends, the "Nachlass" is disappointing, for the letters are short and often restricted to business affairs. The reason for their brevity is undoubtedly the fact that Ballin and Warburg saw one another almost daily when both were in Hamburg and besides had a private telephone line between their offices. As a result, what confidential exchanges they had were not made on paper. Often obscure references are made in the letters to conversations in

361

which important matters were discussed. A small part of the material has been published by Eduard Rosenbaum in two articles, "Albert Ballin: A Note on the Style of His Economic and Political Activities," Leo Baeck Institute of Jews from Germany, *Year Book*, III, London, 1958, 257-99, and "A Postscript to the Essay on Albert Ballin," *Year Book*, IV, 1959, 267-70.

Washington, The National Archives

The National Archives possess a vast collection of microfilms of German Foreign Office records, the originals of which are located in the Politisches Archiv des Auswärtigen Amtes in Bonn. These films include, in addition to the regular diplomatic files, the Stresemann "Nachlass," which is rich in material on Ballin. Most of the letters date from the war period, but there is some correspondence to and from Ballin prior to August 1914. For an introduction to the microfilms of the "Nachlass," see Hans W. Gatzke, "The Stresemann Papers," *Journal of Modern History*, XXVI, no. 1 (March 1954), 49-59. Less valuable than the Stresemann papers is the Ulrich von Brockdorff-Rantzau "Nachlass," for Ballin's correspondence with the diplomat deals mainly with peace overtures to Russia and not with broad questions of German policy. The material runs from 1913 to 1917, except for a few items from the early 1900's, when Rantzau was consul general in Budapest and, as such, was involved in the HAPAG's emigration business. Admiral Paul von Hintze, briefly state secretary of the Foreign Office in 1918, corresponded with Ballin in the winter of 1916 on the subject of a separate peace with Russia. These letters, which are not of great importance, are filed in the Hintze "Nachlass," 2/6i, xxxii., "Friedensmöglichkeiten des Jahres 1916...," AHA II, reel 6/00464, 00481-83, 00564-65.

It proved impossible to obtain access to several privately held manuscript collections which would doubtless tell much about Ballin. I particularly regret that Paul Joseph Count Wolff Metternich, of Heppingen an der Ahr, Rheinland-Westfalen, could not make available for my inspection the letters between his kinsman, Paul Count Wolff Metternich zur Gracht, and Ballin. An intimation of their importance can be discerned in Eberhard von Vietsch, ed., *Gegen die Vernunft: der Briefwechsel zwischen Paul Graf Wolff Metternich and Wilhelm Solf, 1915-1918, mit zwei Briefen Albert Ballins*, Bremen, 1964. Bethmann Hollweg's private secretary, Kurt Riezler, has left a presumably revealing "Nachlass," but his heirs have not elected to open these papers for research. Finally, the "Nachlass" of Ballin's friend, Admiral Georg von Müller, chief of the Naval Cabinet from 1906 to 1918, deposited in the Bundesarchiv, is closed to scholars until 1971.

II. Printed Documents

Johannes Lepsius, *et al.*, eds. *Die grosse Politik der europäischen Kabinette 1871-1914 . . . ,* 40 vols., Berlin, 1923-27, contains a few items which have subsequently been lost and which therefore are missing from the microfilm copies of the German Foreign Office records. The official British edition of prewar documents, G. P. Gooch and H. W. V. Temperley, eds., *British Documents on the Origins of the War, 1898-1914*, 11 vols., London, 1925-38, contains much information on Ballin, while the more extensive France, Ministère des Affaires Etrangères, *Documents diplomatiques français (1871-1914) . . . ,* Paris, 40 vols., 1929-36, makes only fleeting reference to him. Germany, Nationalversammlung, *Das Werk des Untersuchungsausschusses*, 4. Reihe, "Die Ursachen des deutschen Zusammenbruchs im Jahre 1918," 12 vols.,

Berlin, 1925-29, includes some information on Ballin for the war years. A vital source for his involvement in naval matters is A. von Tirpitz, *Politische Dokumente*, 2 vols., Stuttgart, etc., 1924-26, which contains many letters between Tirpitz and Ballin and much additional documentation in which Ballin figures. Of great importance for the HAPAG's role in the Russo-Japanese War are the two collections of correspondence between William II and Nicholas II: Herman Bernstein, ed., *The Willy-Nicky Correspondence: Being the Secret and Intimate Telegrams Exchanged between the Kaiser and the Tsar*, New York, 1918, and Walter Goetz, ed., *Briefe Wilhelms II. an den Zaren 1894-1914*, Berlin, n.d.

III. MEMOIRS

I list here only those memoirs which are essential for an investigation of Ballin. Those of less importance are cited in the footnotes when they have something to contribute.

A search through the memoir sources for imperial Germany yields surprising results. Often, where one might expect to find a detailed treatment of Ballin, almost nothing is said about him. William II's *Ereignisse und Gestalten aus den Jahren 1878-1918*, Berlin 1922, for example, makes reference to him only in passing. Bethmann Hollweg, with whom Ballin had many dealings, does not indicate that he knew the man in his *Betrachtungen zum Weltkriege*, 2 vols., Berlin, 1919-21. Other friends and associates, however, turned back to dwell on Ballin, his personality, character, and accomplishments in considerable detail. The most revealing portrait is in Theodor Wolff's *Der Marsch durch zwei Jahrzehnte*, Amsterdam, 1936, pp. 238-82. Bernhard Guttmann, an editor of the *Frankfurter Zeitung*, contributed a shorter but also very perceptive appraisal in his *Schattenriss einer Generation 1888-1919*, Stuttgart, 1950, pp. 240-47. Of interest are the reminiscences of Ballin's friend, Eduard Rosenbaum, in the publication of the Leo Baeck Institute, cited above, as well as his review of Huldermann's biography in *Der neue Merkur*, VI, no. 2 (May 1922), 111-16.

A number of business friends or associates recorded their impressions of Ballin. Bjarne Aagaard, a Norwegian shipping figure long intimate with Ballin, recalled him in "The Life of Albert Ballin," *Fairplay* (Jan. 5, 12, 19, and 26, 1922). Of great importance are the memoirs of Carl Fürstenberg, in Hans Fürstenberg, *Carl Fürstenberg: die Lebensgeschichte eines deutschen Bankiers*, Wiesbaden, n.d. [1961], originally published in 1932, as well as Arnold Petzet, *Heinrich Wiegand: ein Lebensbild*, Bremen, 1932. Equally significant are the privately printed recollections of Max Warburg, *Aus meinen Aufzeichnungen*, n.p., 1952. Among HAPAG personnel, there are the critical descriptions by Max von Schinckel in his *Lebenserinnerungen*, Hamburg, n.d., and by Johannes Merck in his "Erinnerungen" in the Merck "Nachlass," as well as the more flattering portrayal by Ferdinand Haller in his "30 Jahre im Dienste der Hamburg-Amerika Linie," cited above.

A number of figures active in politics before the war described Ballin's role in government affairs. The most extensive source, though it must be handled with caution, is the *Denkwürdigkeiten*, 4 vols., Berlin, 1930-31, of Bernhard von Bülow, which are supplemented by Hermann Baron von Eckardstein, *Die Entlassung des Fürsten Bülow*, Berlin, 1931. Alfred von Tirpitz, *Erinnerungen*, Leipzig, 1919, and the first volume of his *Politische Dokumente* are rich both in polemics and information. Walter Görlitz, ed., *Der Kaiser. . .: Aufzeichnungen des Chefs des Marinekabinetts Admiral Georg Alexander v.*

Müller über die Ära Wilhelms II., Berlin, 1965, is very important. The memoirs of the press chief of the Foreign Office, Otto Hammann, *Um den Kaiser*, Berlin, 1919, should be noted, while Hammann's later *Bilder aus der letzten Kaiserzeit*, Berlin, 1922, which contains a sketch of Ballin, is almost exclusively derived from other printed sources. Richard von Kühlmann offers an interesting picture of the German diplomatic community in London prior to the war and also provides information on his friend Ballin in his *Erinnerungen*, Heidelberg, 1948. Rudolf Vierhaus, ed., *Das Tagebuch der Baronin Spitzemberg: Aufzeichnungen aus der Hofgesellschaft des Hohenzollernreiches*, 2d edn. Göttingen, 1960, adds details concerning Ballin's relations with the governing aristocracy.

Memoirs concentrating on the war period are more numerous and many are most informative about Ballin's considerable political activity from 1914 to 1918. Of the greatest significance is the second volume of Tirpitz' *Politische Dokumente*, as well as the admiral's *Erinnerungen*. Almost equally important is the valuable diary printed in Walter Görlitz, ed., *Regierte der Kaiser? Kriegstagebücher, Aufzeichnungen und Briefe des Chefs des Marine-Kabinetts Admiral Georg Alexander von Müller 1914-1918*, Göttingen, 1959. *Der goldene Pflug: Lebensernte eines Weltbürgers*, Stuttgart, 1954, is the curious record of an unusual man, Ernst Jäckh, who had considerable traffic with Ballin.

A few memoirs by English figures are important, especially Lord Haldane's *Before the War*, London, etc., 1920, and *An Autobiography,* London, 1929; the first volume of Winston Churchill's *The World Crisis*, 5 vols., New York, 1923-29; and the recollections of Henry Wickham Steed, *Through Thirty Years 1892-1922: A Personal Narrative*, 2 vols., Garden City, 1924.

IV. WORKS ON BALLIN

Of the six biographies of Ballin which preceded this one, only the first appeared in his lifetime. F. Goetz, *Ballin: ein königlicher Kaufmann*, Berlin, 1907, was doubtless inspired by the 60th anniversary celebration of the HAPAG's founding as well as Ballin's 50th birthday, both of which occurred in 1907, and deals entirely with the line rather than with Ballin. The next study to appear was Bernhard Huldermann's *Albert Ballin*, Oldenburg i.O. and Berlin, 1922, a long and judicious work written by one of Ballin's most intimate co-workers at the HAPAG. Huldermann was given access to Ballin's personal papers, some of which are printed here. After Huldermann's death in the late 1920's, his widow sold these papers at auction. My efforts to trace the present ownership of these documents proved vain; many of them, I fear, were destroyed between 1933 and 1945. Huldermann's work is stronger on Ballin's business life than it is on his political activities, although there are three chapters devoted to the latter. This biography is also important as a personal memoir, for Huldermann often confides to us his own relationship to Ballin and repeats what Ballin said to him on various occasions. The tone, as might be expected, is laudatory, and no attempt is made to use any sources other than the private papers. There is a rather inadequate translation by W. J. Eggers, *Albert Ballin*, London, etc., 1922, and a better one in French, *La vie de Albert Ballin d'auprès ses notes et sa correspondance*, Paris, 1923, with a long introduction by Félix Roussel, president of the *Messageries Maritimes*.

Huldermann's biography was followed in 1926 by Peter Franz Stubmann's *Ballin: Leben und Werk eines deutschen Reeders*, Berlin, 1926, a work which also concentrates on Ballin's development of the HAPAG. Stubmann

knew Ballin well and he occasionally adds his personal recollections to the material he presents. The text of this
biography is less informative than Huldermann's, but Stubmann has included a number of letters by Ballin to his
friend, the journalist Ernst Francke, which are of great
interest, as well as some miscellaneous papers, none of
which are included in Huldermann's biography.

The Nazi regime confiscated the biographies by Huldermann and Stubmann, thereby making way for the authorized exposé of the Jewish capitalist by Kaspar Pinette. This
brief work, a Göttingen dissertation, appeared in 1938 as
*Albert Ballin und die deutsche Politik: ein Beitrag zur
Geschichte von Staat und Wirtschaft 1900-1918*, Hamburg, 1938. The contents are not as promising as the title,
and the book's only value lies in its references to the anti-
Semite literature on Ballin, which occasionally yields an
interesting fact. The thesis shakily advanced is that Ballin's
influence on politics was dangerous, for he did not understand that war with England was inevitable, that an alliance
with London was therefore impossible, and that the powerful fleet demanded by Tirpitz was absolutely necessary.

Whatever its defects, Pinette's biography is better than
the next work on Ballin to appear. Hans Leip, a prolific
writer of popular commodities, made Ballin the subject of
a fantastic "biography," *Des Kaisers Reeder: eine Albert
Ballin-Biographie*, Munich, 1956. As history the book is
absurd, and as fiction it is tedious and dull. It will not de-
tain anyone in search of either information or pleasure.

In 1957, Hamburg celebrated the 100th anniversary of
Ballin's birth, and to mark the occasion the Hamburg-
American Line commissioned Stubmann to turn out a
handsome brochure, "Albert Ballin: ein deutscher Reeder
auf internationalem Feld. . .," which, however, contains
almost no information not included in Stubmann's 1926
biography or Huldermann's study of 1922. In 1960, Stub-

368

mann published a new biography of Ballin. By this time, he had accumulated additional letters, and they are included in somewhat mutilated form in this volume, *Mein Feld ist die Welt: Albert Ballin, sein Leben,* Hamburg, 1960. The text itself is a virtually unaltered copy of his 1926 work, with the new letters added and an occasional observation appended based on the memoirs of Müller, Bernstorff, Fürstenberg, and others published since the original life appeared.

V. MISCELLANEOUS

There are a number of shorter sketches of Ballin, in particular Rudolf Martin, *Deutsche Machthaber,* Berlin and Leipzig, 1910, pp. 52-60; Frederic William Wile, *Men around the Kaiser: The Makers of Modern Germany,* London, 1913, pp. 10-18; Georg Bernhard, *Meister und Dilettanten am Kapitalismus im Reiche der Hohenzollern,* Amsterdam, 1936, pp. 213-18; and M. G. de Boer, "Het Leven un het Werk van Albert Ballin," *Tijdschrift voor Geschichte,* no. 18 (1922), 168-89.

Index

INDEX

Bernstorff, Johann Heinrich Count von, 110, 258, 292, 310; Ballin's estimation of, 125, 321

Bethmann Hollweg, Theobald von, German statesman, 135, 167, 203, 210, 212, 224, 236, 242, 253, 258, 260, 273, 299-302, 306, 308-10, 316; Ballin considers suitable as chancellor, 120; Ballin's relation with, 121-23, 126; authorizes Ballin to open discussions with Cassel (1909), 172-73; Moroccan crisis of 1911, 176-79; Haldane Mission, 183-86, 188-90, 192, 194, 196; uses Ballin as unofficial emissary, 199; and *Berliner Tageblatt* letter, 203, 209; proposes no annexations in return for British neutrality, 209-10; and submarine warfare, 272-74, 304, 312; peace negotiations with Russia, 277-79, 282-83; *Lusitania* crisis, 287-92; Ballin proposes peace feelers to, 296-97; invites Entente to state peace terms, 311; Ballin wants replaced by Bülow, 320-21; removal demanded by Hindenburg and Ludendorff, 321-22; resignation of, 323

Bismarck, HAPAG liner, 61, 114, 200, 293, 323

Bismarck, Otto Prince von, German statesman, 35, 198

Bolsheviks, 318, 328, 335; Ballin favors over other factions, 314; Ballin proposes international army against, 343

Boulogne, 268; Ballin calls for annexation of, 267

Braun, Magnus Baron von, German official, and Holtzendorff circle, 256

Bremen, maritime competition with Hamburg, 7-9; emigration from, 8-10

Brest-Litovsk, Russo-German negotiations at, 331-32

Britain, *see* Great Britain

British-India Steamship Co., 21

Brockdorff-Rantzau, Ulrich Count von, German diplomat, 110, 252, 258, 284; Ballin's estimation of, 125, 321; and Ballin in negotiations with Russia, 276-79

Brown, Thomas, agent of Wönckhaus & Co. in Persian Gulf, 85 n42

Bryan, William Jennings, American statesman, 288

Bucknall Bros., British shipping firm in Persian Gulf, 76

Bülow, Bernhard von (subsequently Count and Prince), 51, 75, 100, 106, 122, 135, 161, 167, 169, 172, 198, 258, 295, 327; approves extension of HAPAG to Persian Gulf, 79, 81; Ballin's relationship with, 114-22; and *Daily Telegraph* interview, 117-20; fall from office, 120-21; Ballin favors his return as chancellor, 126; sees Ballin on outbreak of war, 210; preferred by Ballin as Bethmann's successor, 321, 324, 327; rejected by Ballin as candidate for chancellorship, 334

Bund der Industriellen, 130, 133

Bund der Landwirte, 54; Ballin opposes, 113

Bund Neues Vaterland, 255

Burián von Rajecz, Stephan Count von, Austro-Hungarian statesman, 195

Cambon, Jules, French diplomat, 176, 179

375

286-92; HAPAG ships in, 300; war with Germany, 312-13

Valentini, Rudolf von, Prussian official, 195; and Ballin on successor for Bethmann, 322
Vaterland, HAPAG liner, 61, 200, 219, 232
Verdun, siege of, 306-08
Verein der Kapitäne und Offiziere der Handelsmarine in Hamburg, 34-35
Verein Hamburger Reeder, 33, 35, 267
Victoria, queen of England, 99-100
Virgin Islands, HAPAG in, 152-53
Voss, Capt. von, German army officer, 322
Vyrubova, Mme., Russian courtier, 281-82

Wahnschaffe, Arnold, German official, and Holtzendorff circle, 253, 256
Waldersee, Alfred Count von, German general (later field marshal), 68, 107, 114
Walter, John, British newspaper owner, 211
Wangenheim, Hans Baron von, German diplomat, 124
war aims, Ballin and: 264-65; in Belgium, 264-65; Boulogne and Canaries, 267; in Ottoman empire, 268-69; in Africa, 269; in China, 269; in *Mitteleuropa*, 269; in Courland and Lithuania, 276, 315-16, 331; restoration of prewar economic relations, 318; Ballin on Lansdowne proposal, 327-28; economic "fairplay" and annexations, 335-36
Warburg, Aby, German scholar, 36

Warburg, M. M. & Co., Hamburg bank, 177
Warburg, Max, German banker, 36, 98, 118, 141, 162, 168, 179, 213, 258, 292, 346, 355; Ballin's friendship with, 136; opposition to constitutional reform, 140; introduces Ballin to Cassel, 101; interests in Morocco, 176-78; and Belgian relief, 224; and Ballin's funeral, 347
Westarp, Kuno Count von, German politician, 254
"Wet Triangle, The," article by Ballin, 264-65
White Star Line, 48-50, 55
Widenmann, Wilhelm Capt., German naval officer, attacks Holtzendorff circle, 255
Wiegand, Heinrich, managing director of North German Lloyd, 46, 51-53; and Tirpitz, 158
Wiegand, Karl von, American journalist, 290
Wilhelmina, queen of the Netherlands, 337
Wilhelmstrasse, see Foreign Office
William II, King of Prussia and German Emperor: 69, 98-99, 111, 121, 124, 126, 128, 135, 151, 153-54, 167-69, 172, 183, 185, 199-200, 205, 247, 319, 323, 327, 333-35, 340, 346, 348, 350, 353; reaction to Morgan Trust, 51-52; and J. P. Morgan, 55; decorates Ballin, 55, 60; intervenes in shipping quarrel, 52, 61; intervenes in Russo-Japanese war, 74-75; intervenes in Basra-Bagdad railroad negotiations, 90-93; and Jews, 100-01; relationship with Ballin, 102-08, 353-56; uses